Continuing the Journey to Reposition Culture and Cultural Context in Evaluation Theory and Practice

A volume in
Evaluation and Society
Jennifer C. Greene and Stewart Donaldson, *Series Editors*

Continuing the Journey to Reposition Culture and Cultural Context in Evaluation Theory and Practice

edited by

Stafford Hood
University of Illinois–Urbana Champaign

Rodney Hopson
George Mason University

Henry Frierson
University of Florida

INFORMATION AGE PUBLISHING, INC.
Charlotte, NC • www.infoagepub.com

Library of Congress Cataloging-in-Publication Data

A CIP record for this book is available from the Library of Congress
http://www.loc.gov

ISBN: 978-1-62396-935-6 (Paperback)
      978-1-62396-936-3 (Hardcover)
      978-1-62396-937-0 (ebook)

CONTENTS

SECTION III

APPLICATIONS OF CRE IN GLOBAL
AND INDIGENOUS SCHOOL CONTEXTS

SECTION IV

CLAIMING NEW TERRITORIES OF CRE: CULTURALLY SPECIFIC
METHODS, APPROACHES, AND ECOLOGIES

INTRODUCTION

THIS IS WHERE WE CONTINUE TO STAND

Stafford Hood
University of Illinois, Urbana Champaign

Rodney Hopson
George Mason University

Henry Frierson
University of Florida

In 2005, three of the editors for this volume and a group of chapter authors produced an edited volume on the role of culture and cultural context in evaluation to proclaim then (as well as now) that we had been compelled to "loudly" take an unequivocal stand as members of our evaluation community on a core principle yet unarticulated. We coalesced around a core principle that "without the nuanced consideration of cultural context in evaluations conducted within diverse ethnic, linguistic, economic and racial communities of color, there can be no good evaluation." We started with culture because that is where our social science and applied training, research, disciplines, and lived experiences had left us wondering about its role as well as place in evaluation. Other practice disciplines like edu-

Continuing the Journey to Reposition Culture and Cultural Context in Evaluation Theory and Practice, pages ix–xviii
Copyright © 2015 by Information Age Publishing

cation, psychology, social work, and anthropology had embraced culture and cultural context long before 2005, and our evaluation community was considerably behind as far we editors were concerned. Our first book, *The Role of Culture and Cultural Context: A Mandate for Inclusion, the Discovery of Truth, and Understanding in Evaluative Theory and Practice* (Hood, Hopson, & Frierson, 2005), featured a smorgasbord of chapters aimed to plant our flag of culture and cultural context stake on evaluation's territory, as has been done by others in the way that empowerment, collaborative, utilization-focused, and other approaches had been "discovered." The book's contents featured how and why evaluation plays a role in evaluation theory and practice in multiple contexts and settings. The cumulative and collective impact of the 2005 book was to serve as an introduction to the topic.

Nearly a decade later, that group of editors (plus one: Obeidat) remains firm in our conviction on the core principle and intends for this volume to continue (and deepen) the conversation around the role of culture and cultural context in evaluation. We would like to believe that our 2005 book has laid the foundation for further study and scholarship on the topic. A recent search of scholar.google.com of the terms "culturally responsive evaluation" (CRE) and "culturally competent evaluation" (CCE) anywhere in an article or chapter or title between 1990 and 2013 indicates the major increase in this discourse over a little more than a decade is illustrated in Table I.1 below. At the same time it can be noted that Hood et al. (2005) has been cited 19 times with its respective chapters also being cited 41 times.

In this volume, we are joined by a majority of the authors who previously contributed chapters in the initial edited volume while also including a considerably expanded group of new authors who can help us answer these questions and stretch our thinking on the topic of culture and cultural context in evaluation. Those authors who contributed chapters previously in the first volume and are contributing chapters in this current volume have not provided edited versions of their previous chapters but new chapters, with new ideas and orientations about culture as well as cultural context in evaluation. Ultimately, this volume represents new voices from seasoned and emerging colleagues in evaluation, many of which are collaborative,

TABLE I.1 Usage of Terms *Culturally Responsive Evaluation* and *Culturally Competent Evaluation* in the Literature 1990–2013

	CRE term anywhere in article/chapter	CCE term anywhere in article/chapter	CRE in title of article/chapter	CCE in title of article/chapter
1990–2000	7	99	0	3
2001–2005	43	37	8	6
2006–2013	113	147	10	7

multi-authored manuscripts. The book's 17 chapters are authored by over 50 contributors, representing decades of evaluation knowledge, experiences, and committed action in multi-ethnic, multicultural, transcultural, and indigenous settings. We do not all agree about the most applicable ways to situate CRE theoretically or practically, but we do not disagree about the core principle that binds us as we move forward as socially responsible members of this community.

Our 2005 edited volume, *The Role of Culture and Cultural Context: A Mandate for Inclusion, the Discovery of Truth, and Understanding in Evaluative Theory and Practice* (Hood et al., 2005), reflected the rapidly emerging and frequently contentious discourse on this topic during the early years of this new millennium. The series editors at that time (Katherine Ryan and Thomas Schwandt) challenged us to prepare an edited volume that would contribute to as well as push the dialogue around the role of culture and cultural context in evaluation. That initial volume sought to address select questions drawn from the set of complex issues related to CRE. We asked, What is culturally responsive evaluation? What makes an evaluation culturally responsive? Should evaluation be culturally responsive? Is the field heading in the right direction in its attempt to become more culturally responsive in a practical sense? Additionally, we asked, What were the roots of CRE? How did CRE roots contribute to the evolution and development of the field of evaluation? What was the state of CRE then and what might it become tomorrow? We believe that the 2005 volume partially provided answers to some of these questions but raised many more questions than we had answered.

The current series editors, Jennifer Greene and Stewart Donaldson, once again challenged us by asking for an "update" to the 2005 edited volume. The current state of affairs, in our global discourse on the role of culture and cultural context in evaluation, suggests that encouraging signs have emerged since the publication of the 2005 volume. For example, there is a recognizable growth in what some may now call our culturally responsive evaluation community, particularly in the presence of a younger and more diverse cadre of evaluators. We feature some of these younger and emerging, more diverse cadre of evaluators in this volume. At the same time, there has been an increase in the number and breadth of scholarly contributions to the evaluation literature addressing both CRE theory and practice. This work has been enlightening, provided refinements in our discourse on this topic, and has challenged us to explore more as well as different types of questions beyond what we had initially anticipated. Therefore, it seemed reasonable for the initial focus of this volume to be a refined and expanded discussion of what had transpired in evaluation regarding the role of culture and cultural context since the 2005 volume. However, as we began to contact those who contributed chapters to the 2005 book and others we believed could make important contributions, it became clear that this new project would be far more than a mere update.

Our current volume on *Continuing the Journey to Reposition Culture and Cultural Context in Evaluation Theory and Practice* does indeed provide an expansion and refinement of our 2005 conversation about culturally responsive evaluation theory as well as what it looks like in practice across multiple settings within the United States and internationally. Yet it also provides a rare introspective look from "aspiring" culturally responsive evaluators who are at different points on this lifelong journey. One particularly significant contribution of this volume is that we believe it provides one of the largest collections of chapters focusing on evaluation in indigenous contexts and settings to be found in a single edited volume. The indigenous members of our community from North America and Aotearoa New Zealand have broadened the focus as well as nature of our theoretical and practice-oriented inquiry about what culturally responsive evaluation can or should look like in those spaces. Further, our increasing international footprint of this discourse is further evident in the inclusion of the experiences of "new immigrants" in Irish schools and juxtaposed with those of Roma children in Greece (as well as in Ireland, known as "Travellers").

At the same time, this collection of chapters continues the exploration of the foundational questions raised in the 2005 volume but in most cases raise more questions, even though more refined, while still in search of answers. Such as

- How can we be sure that the evaluation is culturally responsive?
- How do we evaluate CRE?
- How should evaluators who work in communities of color be required to exhibit an acceptable level of cultural competence beyond their technical knowledge?

These are but a few of the questions that were pursued by the chapters and in an assortment of ways, with there being more questions needing to be addressed as well.

Why Is the Time for Culturally Responsive Evaluation Overdue?

Cultural, racial, and ethnic diversity has become of global importance in places where many of us would never have imagined. The racial and ethnic diversity currently being found in places in the United States, Europe, Africa, New Zealand, and Asia, where we would have never imagined, strongly suggests that a homogeneity-based focus is rapidly becoming an artifact of what is becoming history. Therefore, CRE should no longer be viewed as a luxury or an option in our work as evaluators. The continued acceleration in the acknowledgment of racial, ethnic, language, and cultural diversity within the U.S. population and those of other Western nations demands social science researchers and evaluators who inextricably link culturally responsive approaches in their work. It is unacceptable for most mainstream university evaluation programs, philanthropic agencies, federal agency-sponsored training institutes, professional associations, or any other entity promoting professional evaluation practices not to substantively address CRE or how evaluation generally addresses culture and diversity contexts. This continues to be an opportune time to shift from merely "simple" linear cause-effect models and reductionist thinking to include more holistic and culturally responsive approaches.

The development of policy and policy decision making that is meaningfully responsive to the needs of traditionally disenfranchised stakeholders and also optimizes the use of limited resources (human, natural, and financial) is an extremely complex process. Fortunately, we are presently witnessing developments in methods, instruments, and statistical techniques that are mixed methods in their paradigm/designs and likely to be more effective in informing policymaking and decision making. Culturally responsive evaluation is one such phenomenon that positions itself to be relevant in the context of dynamic international and national settings where policy and program decisions take place.

The recent establishment of the Center for Culturally Responsive Evaluation and Assessment (CREA) in the College of Education at the University of Illinois at Urbana-Champaign in 2011, with its sibling CREA-Dublin (School of Education Studies, Dublin City University, Dublin, Ireland), represents an important benchmark in our evolution as a community since the first volume. CREA is an outgrowth of the collective work and commitments by numerous scholars and practitioners who have and have not contributed chapters to this particular edited volume. It is an international and interdisciplinary evaluation center that is grounded in the need for designing and conducting evaluations and assessments that embody cognitive, cultural, and interdisciplinary diversity that are actively responsive to culturally diverse communities and their academic performance goals. The Center's purpose is to address questions, issues, theories, and practice related to CRE and culturally responsive assessment. Therefore, the CREA will also serve as a vehicle for our CREA community's continuing discourse on culture and cultural context in evaluation and also a point of dissemination for not only the work that is included in this edited volume but also the subsequent work it will encourage.

Organization of the Volume

The volume is organized into five sections: (a) CRE Theoretical and Historical Legacies and Extensions; (b) Evaluators' Journeys of Introspection and Self-Exploration; (c) Applications of CRE in Global and Indigenous School Contexts; (d) Claiming New Territories of CRE: Culturally Specific Methods and Approaches; and (e) Epilogue: Reflections on this volume and a look forward.

Section I: CRE Theoretical and Historical Legacies and Extensions

This section explores theoretical and historical legacies of Culturally Responsive Evaluation by asking probing and challenging questions in evaluation theory and practice. In particular, the chapters in the first section, beginning with Katrina Bledsoe and Stewart Donaldson's "Culturally Responsive Theory-Driven Evaluation," builds off earlier foundational work and TDE's application in underserved communities, as they argue how cultural responsiveness can be embedded within the TDE approach. Their chapter relies on the CRE framework (Frierson, Hood, Hughes, & Thomas, 2010) to illustrate new TDE understandings of culturally responsive, cultural competence, and cultural humility in evaluation. The next chapter by Wanda Casillas and Bill Trochim, "A Systems Approach to Culturally Responsive Evaluation Practice: Culturally Responsive Uses of the *Systems Evaluation Protocol* (SEP)" draws further conceptual parallels between specific systems heuristics and specifically culturally responsive principles to reposition a future discussion on the adaption of systems evaluation protocol (SEP) to operationalize culturally responsive practices.

The chapter by Joan Lafrance, Karen Kirkhart, and Richard Nichols, "Cultural Views of Validity: A Conversation," captures the critically important consideration about the role of validity and whether it can or should be situated within indigenous evaluation frameworks (IEF). In a timely and valuable dialogue among key thinkers in the field of multicultural validity and indigenous evaluation, the authors raise questions about the role of culture in conversations about validity, whether "validity" is a relevant concept for indigenous inquiry, and the role of "validity" in IEF. This chapter also has special meaning for our community, as it includes a final contributive voice of a recently departed warrior and friend, Richard Nichols. The final chapter in this section by Pamela Frazier Anderson and Tamara Bertrand Jones, "An Analysis of *Love My Children*: Rose Butler Browne's Contributions to Culturally Responsive Evaluation," provides another historical installment to the early foundations of CRE by focusing on the life and work of Rose Butler Browne, the first African American woman to receive a doctorate in education from Harvard University with her dissertation titled as an "evaluation." In placing Browne in the historical discourse beside Reid E. Jackson (Hopson & Hood, 2005) and other explorations of early CRE scholars and activists (Hood, 2001), the chapter reviews Browne's autobiography to discover the alignment of ideas that made CRE theory and practice palatable.

Section II: Evaluators' Journeys of Introspection and Self-Exploration

This section is intentionally reflective and introspective, illustrating how the CRE journey is deliberate and self-exploring. The cumulative content of these chapters indicate, through rich examples and dialogues, why and how CRE requires new thinking and practices. Jennifer Greene's chapter, "Culture and Evaluation: From a Transcultural Belvedere," reflects on the role of the culturally responsive and responsible evaluator based on valuable insights and experiences during travel study leave in Aoteaora New Zealand in 2012. Hazel Symonette's chapter, "Culturally Responsive Evaluation as a Resource for Helpful-Help," calls for embracing a stance on culturally and contextually responsive action research. Like her own seminal work, Symonette's chapter offers a holistic framework for evaluators who care to sensitize themselves and their practice with concepts and questions for understanding the complex contexts of evaluation and toward the development of a comprehensive self-assessment framework for evaluators who are committed to the work of CRE.

Rae Torrie and her colleagues from Aotearoa New Zealand describe the journey of five Pākehā ("White" New Zealanders of Anglo or other European ancestry) evaluators who work in culturally responsive ways. Like other authors in the volume, but especially and uniquely within their work, they argue that working in the "cultural" space is inherent in all evaluation practice in Aotearoa New Zealand and is often insufficiently addressed. By using their personal vignettes and storying, throughout their reflective dialogue processes, the authors focus on their own stories to illustrate how their articulation of what it means to be Pākehā evaluators requires a reterritorializing of evaluation practice.

Similarly, in the chapter "Beginning a Conversation About Spirituality in *Māori* and *Pasifika* Evaluation," Vivienne Kennedy and her colleagues from Aoteoarea New Zealand, the Pacific Islands, and Polynesia raise key questions about the spiritual dimensions of practice for evaluators in their experiences as Māori and Pasifika peoples. Their chapter raises new questions about ways in which evaluation protocols integrate not just ethical and moral practices but spiritual aspects as well. Dominica McBridge's chapter, "Cultural Reactivity vs Cultural Responsiveness: Addressing Macro Issues Starting with Micro Changes in Evaluation," closes this section. Her chapter introduces and explains the notion of cultural reactivity by building on how the brain works to signal a potentially needed shift in the way that readings and applications of emotional and social intelligence build on notions of cultural responsiveness for the evaluation practitioner.

Section III: Applications of CRE in Global and Indigenous School Contexts

The chapters in this section describe the comparative depth of CRE in schools globally and one indigenous context to identify some of the integral and critically important issues relevant to culture and evaluation in schools. By focusing on subgroup issues in Ireland, education of Roma children in Macedonia, and among Navajo children in Arizona, the authors build a case for the application of CRE in international and indigenous educational settings. The chapter by Joe O'Hara and his colleagues in Ireland, "Culture Changes, Irish Evaluation, and Assessment Traditions Stay the Same?" undertakes the conversation of culturally responsive evaluation in Irish education and especially education among a particular ethnically diverse subgroup who are contributing to a curricular change due to rapidly changing student demographics. Their chapter seeks to answer questions posed by the editors of what CRE looks like in Irish education and in the development of an Irish evaluation culture.

The second chapter in this section, "Implementing Culturally Sensitive Assessment Tools for the Inclusion of Roma Children in Mainstream Schools" by Soula Mitakidou and her colleagues in northern Greece, also reflects on the education of a subgroup of ethnic children and communities, in this case Roma. They extend their CRE work to assessment in schools and the distinct issues that affect the school going, attendance, and completion issues faced by Roma children. Carolyn White and Guy Senese's chapter, "Evaluating Alch'i'ni Ba/For the Children: The Troubled Cultural Work of an Indigenous Teacher Education Project," provides an account of a federal project which set out to create an opportunity for Native American (Dine'/Navajo) students to enter the field of elementary and secondary school teaching and to serve children in schools on the Navajo reservation. They describe their evaluation as a critical cultural education project and offer insights into ways that this work is both cultural and political, reminding those of us who practice CRE about the inherent challenges that underlie doing culturally responsive evaluation work amidst conflicting program realities and milieus.

Section IV: Claiming New Territories of CRE: Culturally Specific Methods, Approaches, and Ecologies

The chapters in this final section call upon CRE scholars, practitioners, and activists to apply more culturally specific methods and approaches in the settings in which they work and practice. The call for new territories and culturally specific methods and approaches are driven by evaluators who work in increasingly diverse communities where language, politics, and development play a role in how CRE continues to play equitable and transformative roles in dynamic and complex evaluation ecologies. The opening chapter in this section, "A Transformative Framework for Culturally Responsive Evaluation" by Donna Mertens and Heather Zimmerman provide an overview and explanation of the basic assumptions associated with the transformative paradigm, specifically the axiological, ontological, epistemological, and methodological concepts. The authors apply this transformative paradigm to evaluations in the deaf community and international development contexts to provide another, more nuanced understanding of CRE.

Fiona Cram and her Māori colleagues in the second chapter of the final section, "Being Culturally Responsive Through Kaupapa Māori Evaluation" ground their evaluations in "Kaupapa Māori" (i.e., a Māori way). Their work gives value to their language and culture while building upon evaluation methodology based on their Māori worldview. In doing so, they both reposition evaluation and reaffirm how and why culture and cultural context matters in indigenous contexts. The application of CRE in the Maori context is reflected in the following chapter by Kirimatao Paipa and her colleagues, in the chapter "Culturally Responsive Methods for Family Centered Evaluation," continuing a variation on a similar theme found in this section. In their consideration of evaluation methods used in Māori contexts, the authors argue for evaluation methods used for Māori whanau (family). A principled approach to the selection of methods is then explored, with examples provided of the use of these methods within cultural responsive evaluations with Māori. Nicole R. Bowman and her colleagues in the following chapter, "Responsive Indigenous Evaluation: A Cultural and Contextual Framework for Indian Country" describe the unique political/legal and cultural/traditional contexts that should be considered for a culturally responsive Indigenous evaluation design. Much like the Kaupapa Māori chapters that precedes, Bowman and her colleagues suggest a repositioning and reiteration of best strategies, lessons learned, and future considerations for designing and conducting culturally responsive Indigenous evaluations, especially those conducted in the United States or North America. Joan LaFrance and her colleagues complete the section of the book within their chapter, "Spanning the Pacific: Decolonizing Education and Evaluation in Polynesia and

Micronesia." The chapter describes the promises and the challenges faced by a small group of external evaluators as they study the work of the projects while shaping their evaluation processes in ways that are respectful of Pacific indigenous contexts, protocols and practices.

Epilogue

An epilogue chapter provides a summary of the book sections and urges the continued discussion of CRE in contemporary and comparative evaluation theory and practice.

REFERENCES

Frierson, H., Hood, S., Hughes, G., & Thomas, V. (2010). A guide to conducting culturally responsive evaluation. In National Science Foundation, *The 2010 user-friendly handbook for project evaluation* (pp. 75–96). National Science Foundation, Directorate for Education and Human Resources, Division of Research, Evaluation, and Communication. REC 99-12175.

Hood, S. (2001). Nobody knows my name: In praise of African American evaluators who were responsive. *New Directions for Evaluation, 92*, 31–43.

Hood, S., Hopson, R., & Frierson, H. (Eds.). (2005). *The role of culture and cultural context: A mandate for inclusion, the discovery of truth, and understanding in evaluative theory and practice*. Greenwich, CT: Information Age.

Hopson, R., & Hood, S. (2005). An untold story in evaluation roots: Reid E. Jackson and his contributions toward culturally responsive evaluation at three quarters of a century. In S. Hood, R. Hopson, & H. Frierson (Eds.), *The role of culture and cultural context in evaluation: A mandate for inclusion, the discovery of truth, and understanding in evaluative theory and practice* (pp. 85–104). Greenwich, CT: Information Age.

SECTION I

CRE THEORETICAL AND HISTORICAL LEGACIES
AND EXTENSIONS

CHAPTER 1

CULTURALLY RESPONSIVE THEORY-DRIVEN EVALUATION

Katrina L. Bledsoe
DeBruce Foundation

Stewart I. Donaldson
Claremont Graduate University

PREFACE AND OVERVIEW

Evaluators often aspire to achieving maximum "objectivity" in an evaluation. But perhaps one of the greatest foundations of evaluation is the evaluator's ability to acknowledge his or her personal and professional philosophies and beliefs, and to engage in thoughtful self-reflection about how those philosophies and beliefs can impact an evaluation's design and implementation. Thus, it would seem that the key to conducting a good evaluation starts *within* the evaluator. Indeed, the *American Evaluation Association's Statement on Cultural Competence in Evaluation* (2011) stresses that self-reflection and admittance of privilege and positioning are important to conducting ethically and culturally competent evaluation.

When Bledsoe (2005) wrote about using theory-drive evaluation (TDE) in underserved communities in the first volume of *Culture and Evaluation*, she tacitly referred to cultural responsiveness. At that time, Donaldson had

Continuing the Journey to Reposition Culture and Cultural Context
in Evaluation Theory and Practice, pages 3–27
Copyright © 2015 by Information Age Publishing

only initially begun to focus on TDE's ability to understand and respond to context. Over the past several years, our views have evolved. Our self-reflection has included understanding that *competence* is an ever-changing state of being, is only momentarily present, and is not a finite skill level or expertise that can be fully obtained (e.g., AEA, 2011). We have come to understand that we must be vigilant in addressing our own issues, such as unearned privilege due to background and positioning, and our own stereotypes and biases (e.g., Pon, 2003). We also realize that we must consistently be willing to expose oppression and institutional discrimination, and to address issues of social justice (e.g., Mertens, 2009; Mertens & Wilson, 2012).

In short, our self-reflective process has brought changes to our practice of evaluation. Bledsoe's self-reflection deepened with her participation in the development task force and advisory board for AEA's *Statement on Cultural Competence* (2011). And Donaldson observed that his own perspective on cultural responsiveness and social justice began evolving when he realized that responding to and incorporating culture could and should be accomplished within some traditional evaluation approaches and designs. When the first annual Center for Culturally Responsive Evaluation and Assessment's inaugural conference, themed "Repositioning Culture in Evaluation and Assessment," was hosted in 2013, we realized the call for cultural responsiveness was timely and relevant to us.

Cultural responsiveness, cultural competence, cultural humility, and cultural responsibility are becoming integrated into program development, implementation, and evaluation. While there is debate over whether these terms are synonymous, separate, or are extensions of one another, they all emphasize the need to address the desires and requirements of diverse communities. Societies demand attention to culture and cultural context due to the changing fabric of the communities, programs, schools, governments and agencies. But this is not a new phenomenon in programming or in evaluation practice and theory. Theorists such as Yvonna Lincoln and Egon Guba, and more recently, Rodney Hopson, Veronica Thomas, Karen Kirkhart, and others (e.g., Donna Mertens, Fiona Cram, Joan LaFrance) have discussed the importance of culture and by extension competence and responsiveness in evaluation. For instance, Kirkhart (2010, 2013) has consistently underscored that culture must be considered in design, measurement, data and data collection, and dissemination to insure an evaluation's validity.

AEA's *Statement on Cultural Competence in Evaluation* (2011) is a public mandate on the critical importance of cultural responsiveness in the field. Noting that, "effective and ethical use of evaluation requires... respecting different worldviews" (para. 21), the statement encourages evaluators to recognize that the world in which we live, and develop and evaluate programs, is experiencing a time of intense and unstoppable cultural expansion and change. And although the statement has arguably become one of the guiding principles evaluators should consider in the conduct of good and ethical evaluation, it is often up to the discretion of the evaluator to make use of its tenets in his or her own work. Thus, practitioners are often in need of guidance on how evaluation approaches that are seemingly (but deceptively) culture-free can be practiced in a culturally responsive manner.

It is not lightly stated that evaluation is, more than ever, a mechanism that can respond to dynamic times by helping to articulate the strategies and programs that serve a full variety of individuals, communities, organizations, and governments. Given the contemporary currency, even urgency regarding cultural diversity around the globe, approaches to conducting evaluation must be adapted to the complex cultural fabric of the communities in which they are located. In this way, evaluation can contribute to how best to understand diverse contexts and which programs are best suited to meet community- and organizational-level needs. The purpose of this chapter then is to discuss how one evaluation approach, theory-driven evaluation (TDE), can become more culturally responsive and thereby be included in the growing family of culturally competent evaluation. But first let us situate the terms of cultural competence and responsiveness as a backdrop for the discussion of TDE.

WHAT ARE CULTURAL COMPETENCE AND CULTURAL RESPONSIVENESS?

Although there are many definitions of cultural competence (and by extension, cultural responsiveness) in evaluation, some have described it as the development of program standards and criteria, programs and interventions, and measures, so that they are relevant, specifically tailored, credible, and valid for the unique groups and communities of focus (Hopson, 2009). SenGupta, Hopson, and Thompson-Robinson (2004) have broadly defined culturally competent evaluation as a systematic and responsive inquiry that is cognizant of, understands, and addresses the cultural context in which evaluation takes place. This understanding includes the articulation of appropriate methodology; the position and inclusion of stakeholder perspectives in not only articulating the program, but also in measurement development; and interpretation of data, subsequent results, and dissemination. AEA's *Statement* (2011) broadens these perspectives to evaluators themselves noting that, "cultural competence [in evaluation] is a stance take toward culture, not a discrete status or simple mastery of particular knowledge and skills" (para. 4).

Although theorist Sandra Mathison (2004) has not overtly termed it cultural competence and/or cultural responsiveness, she noted that evaluation could be enhanced by an empathetic view and consideration of context. Specifically, she advocates that an empathetic view alters an evaluator's preconceptualizations and stereotypes and thereby helps the evaluator provide a contextual understanding of the program's process and stakeholders' perspectives and experiences. For Mathison, empathy in evaluation helps to broaden the evaluator's understanding of a program and promotes reflexivity toward the program and the evaluation. Being able to understand the feelings and attitudes of those who are recipients of a program's benefits can allow the evaluator to develop the methods that can accurately assess the program. The ability to empathize with a community provides an opportunity to acknowledge and respect the unique context and situations in which the program resides.

Other authors and theorists are similarly aligned. For instance, Mertens (2008) has discussed cultural competence and cultural responsiveness in reference to inclusion of marginalized others in the process of evaluation design, measurement, and interpretation. Mertens' transformative evaluation approach encourages the use of stakeholder cultural perspectives in the design of the evaluation, and emphasizes using multiple methods and approaches to ascertain credible and accurate measurements (Mertens, Bledsoe, Sullivan & Wilson, 2010). Mertens et al., (2010) theorize that without cultural competence and cultural responsiveness, the risks of the evaluation "otherizing" underserved communities and perpetuating inequality become great.

Still others, notably Kirkhart (2013), contend that valid measurements of an evaluand can only be accomplished by the consideration of culture within every part of the evaluation framework and via an intentional *commitment* to conducting a culturally responsive evaluation. Kirkhart's work in multicultural validity posits that validity is framed by culture and context and is affected by what she refers to as justifications and threats. She discusses five areas in which justifications and threats need to be considered: (a) the life and situational experiences of the community and key stakeholders, (b) the relationship between participants and environment, (c) the type of method used to assess their truth, (d) the theoretical foundation (including stakeholder theory) upon which that "truth" is based, and (e) the consequences of the information gathered to support the claims. In conceptualizing culture and context as the foundation, validity is accomplished though the development of more responsive and precise measurement development and thereby increased accuracy in representation of the environment, program, and participants.

However, Gordon Pon (2003), in his article "Cultural Competence as the New Racism: An Ontology of Forgetting," warns that the focus on "competence" runs the risk of further perpetuating biases, stereotypes, and discrimination. His rationale is that competence both denotatively and connotatively insinuates that a finite level of skill and knowledge can be attained, transferrable to any context. Pon is concerned that researchers and practitioners will look for signs and cues that seem to be universal across groups and ignore the unique context and situations of the communities as well as individual differences. His concern is valid; admittedly, many evaluators look for a specific "toolkit" or "toolbox" of strategies that can be used to work in diverse communities and contexts without the necessary regard for the uniqueness of the context. However, responsiveness is much more of a human and *vulnerable* perspective. In being responsive, evaluators begin with the very human and vulnerable process of being self-reflective and addressing internal characteristics that can ultimately influence the manner in which the evaluation is conducted. Ultimately, the difference between competence and responsiveness is the focus on the internal process of understanding the self.

CULTURAL RESPONSIVENESS AND CULTURAL COMPETENCE IN EVALUATION

As we have discussed in the previous section, the call for cultural responsiveness and cultural competence in the field of evaluation has reached a deafening crescendo. Noted theorists and practitioners such as, but not limited to, Kirkhart (2005), Hopson (2009), Mertens (2011), Symouette (2004), Cram (2009), and Bledsoe and Hopson (2009) have discussed the need to consider culture in evaluation and have asked evaluators to address cultural awareness, conduct culturally responsive evaluation, and embrace its omnipresence in all areas of the evaluative process. Specifically, they contend that culture and cultural responsiveness must be present beginning with the inception and conceptualization of the evaluation team, evaluation questions, and evaluation approach and continuing through the collection of data and subsequent dissemination of results (e.g., Frierson, Hood, & Hughes, 2010; Hood, Hopson, & Frierson, 2005). These theorists contend that accurate measurement and understanding of programs cannot be accomplished without consideration of the cultural contexts in which they were developed and now operate. Indeed, AEA has strongly endorsed the consideration of culture in its *Guiding Principles for Evaluators* (2004) and further in the most recent revision of the *Program Evaluation Standards for Evaluators* (Yarbrough, Shulha, Hopson, & Caruthers, 2010), Cultural responsiveness has been woven throughout the standards and posited as central to ethical and responsive evaluation practice. For example, the standard of feasibility asks evaluators to consider contextual viability, defined as the ability of the evaluator to consider, monitor, and balance both the cultural and the political interests of the communities of focus.

AEA's *Statement on Cultural Competence in Evaluation* (2011) underscores the Association's commitment and stance to conducting culturally competent and responsive evaluation, and to ensuring that evaluator training includes attention to culture and context. This call has been especially urgent; evaluators such as Botcheva, Shih, and Huffman (2009) have found that cultural competence and responsiveness have become standard criteria for conducting sound evaluation in areas such as HIV/AIDS education in international and developing countries. Additionally, Cram (2009) and LaFrance and Crazy Bull (2009) stress that understanding cultural competence and being culturally responsive is integral to enabling social justice, and to the amelioration of inequalities among indigenous populations such as Maori and North American Tribal communities.

THE CULTURALLY RESPONSIVE EVALUATION (CRE) FRAMEWORK

According to Frierson, Hood, and Hughes (2010), an evaluation is culturally responsive if it fully takes into account the culture of the program. In other words, the evaluation is based on an examination of impacts through lenses in which the culture of the participants is considered an important factor, thus rejecting the notion that assessments must be objective and culture free if they are to be unbiased. Moreover, a culturally responsive evaluation attempts to fully describe and explain the context of the program or project being evaluated. Culturally responsive evaluators honor the cultural context in which an evaluation takes place by bringing needed, shared life-experience understandings to the evaluation tasks at hand (NSF, 2010).

Theorists Frierson, Hood, and Hughes (2010; as well as Hopson, 2009) have articulated a framework in which to conduct culturally responsive evaluation. Specifically, Hopson (2009) posits that there are several steps to conducting a Cultural Responsive Evaluation (CRE). These include (a) prepare for the evaluation (e.g., understand the context, seek out constituents in the community); (b) engage stakeholders (e.g., include stakeholders of multiple perspectives, understand power issues); (c) identify the purpose of the evaluation (e.g., understand the distribution of resources); (d) frame the right questions (e.g., include stakeholders in the decisions behind questions); (e) design the evaluation (e.g., build a design that is appropriate for both the questions and the context); (f) select and adapt instrumentation; (e.g., adapt instruments as needed to the context); (g) collect data (e.g., procedures of both qualitative and quantitative data must be sensitive to the context); (h) analyze data (e.g., consider cultural context in the interpretation of data analyzing outliers, particularly those that indicate resiliency); and (i) disseminate and use the results (e.g., consider broad dissemination of results). See Figure 1.1 for the CRE model.

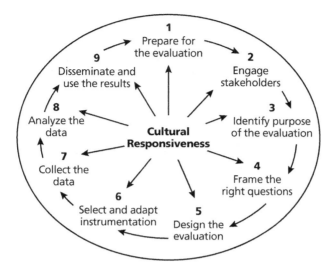

Figure 1.1 Culturally Responsive Evaluation framework.

Using the framework illustrated in Figure 1.1, Hopson (2009) seek to acknowledge that culture is imbued within and throughout the evaluation process. Its circular nature indicates that the process is iterative. The framework corroborates Greene's (2011) perspective on democracy in evaluation: that discussing issues such as culture, context, historical perspective, power, oppression, and privilege (or lack thereof) calibrates the evaluation, and provides equity in perspectives. This further affirms Kirkhart's (2013) position on multicultural validity to accomplish greater precision and validity in evaluation's ability to provide results that are truly representative of the community and the context. Thus evaluation approaches must evolve to address the issue of cultural context, responsiveness, etc. We begin by exploring the theory-driven evaluation framework.

THE THEORY-DRIVEN EVALUATION FRAMEWORK

Theory-Driven Evaluation

The theory-driven evaluation approach has often been described as an integration of social science, evaluation theory, and small theories of change of how programs work and how participants in those programs change (or not) (Chen, 1990; Donaldson, 2007; Rossi & Freeman, 1979; Weiss, 1997). Ultimately, TDE is concerned with the *quality* of the questions and indicators it measures. A TDE evaluation focuses on assessing goals, perspectives, and policies that have a qualitative and contextual impact on the way people live. Questions that address quality and context are What outcome is most valuable to the community? In what manner is change expected to occur? Who is most affected by the proposed change and goals, and in what ways? What is most meaningful to stakeholders? What values and what context are driving the goals? Ultimately, the emphasis of the TDE is upon what is considered most credible to those who would be impacted by the program or programmatic change.

Furthermore, TDE (Donaldson, 2007) can not only be considered a participatory approach, but also one that considers a wide variety of theories, including, but not limited to, contingency theory and integrative evaluation theory (e.g., Shaddish, Cook, & Leviton, 1991). As mentioned earlier in this chapter, it is arguable that TDE might be at odds with a culturally responsive approach, primarily due to its *perceived* inflexibility. As well, the use of the term "theory" can distance communities (Donaldson, as cited in Fitzpatrick, Christie, & Mark, 2009) as it often carries loaded connotative meanings that seem exclude the life experiences of poorly and underserved populations. However, we contend that TDE naturally dovetails with Frierson et al.s' (2010) CRE specifically because it is participatory, considers validity and community-designated credible evidence, and in essence, is culturally responsive.

Although Huey Chen's (1990) work served to establish the theory-driven framework, that early work generally focused on a typology of conducting evaluation rather than a specific actionable perspective. While it is arguable that Chen's TDE supports the conduct of culturally responsive evaluation, this assertion was not explicitly stated in his early work. However, His more recent work (2005, 2012) on *viable validity* is much more to congruent with Kirkhart's work on multicultural validity, advocating a more bottom up, participatory, contextually and community-defined validity, rather than a top down positivistically defined one. In addressing validity in this manner, Chen (2012) contends that programs and by extension, evaluations will provide credible evidence, and be responsive to the context.

Donaldson's Three-Step Process to TDE

Donaldson's (2007) work in program theory-driven evaluation science has articulated practical, actionable steps of the approach that are malleable enough to be used in any context, in coordination with any other approach. The three-step TDE process—(a) developing program impact theory, (b) formulating and prioritizing evaluation questions, and (c) answering said evaluation questions—specifically considers contextual, situational, and cultural perspectives. It also parallels the evaluation model of the Centers for Disease Control and Prevention (1999), which articulates continuous and dynamic steps for evaluation (see Figure 1.2).

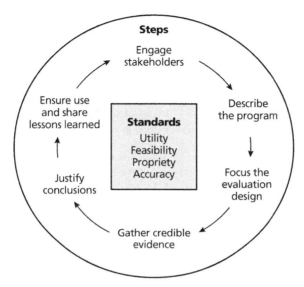

Figure 1.2 Centers for Disease Control and Prevention Evaluation Framework (CDC, 1999).

The first step in the TDE model describes the development of program theory in consideration of the content, the program's desired effects, and its processes. Specifically, the inner workings of the program are essential to understanding its effectiveness on program participants and the context in which it operates. At the second step, formulating and prioritizing questions, identified stakeholders are asked to discern and articulate the questions that are most valuable to them, including those that address program fidelity, intended consumers, as well as short-term and long-term outcomes (to name a few). Prioritizing these questions demands consideration of stakeholders' needs, the context, and the ability of the program and evaluation to support the answering of the questions. In answering questions, the third step in the process, the TDE model ecumenically welcomes the most appropriate, useful, and valid methodologies for answering the identified evaluation questions. Additionally, consideration of what type of evidence would be considered most credible and persuasive to the community at-large is paramount. It is during this final step that stakeholders collaborate, provide feedback, and consult on the best empirical design to answer the questions (Donaldson, as cited in Fitzpatrick et al., 2009). See Table 1.1 for the three-step process.

Donaldson's and Gooler's (2007 as cited in cited in Fitzpatrick et al., 2009) evaluation of the *Work and Health Initiative,* specifically, their work with the *Winning New Jobs Program,* is an excellent example of how using a TDE perspective rather than one that focused on efficaciousness was, in essence, culturally responsive. This evaluation began with the evaluators' recognition

TABLE 1.1   Program Theory and Theory-Driven Evaluation Science Three-Step Model

Step	Example Considerations
(1) Develop program impact theory	• Engagement of stakeholders • Discussion of values • Consideration of contextual factors
(2) Formulate and prioritize evaluation questions	• Identify questions that have the most value • Address issues that affect the program and how it responds to the needs of the community
(3) Answer evaluation questions	• Design questions representative of the context and community • Design appropriate methodology to answer questions • Consider various data collection, analytic, and dissemination strategies

that job search skills strategies that were taught and used within working class White communities in the Midwest would likely be ill-fitting in diverse Latino populations confronting language barriers in Southern California. Donaldson and Gooler then designed the evaluation to respond to the unique issues facing that specific community such as immigration, migrant population culture, and job skills needed for work in an agrarian work environment. They used the three-step process to develop an impact theory that was more representative of the diverse Southern California community landscape; questions that addressed the contextual environment; and data-collection strategies to effectively recruit hard-to-reach and linguistically diverse populations.

The Challenges of Conducting TDE

We realize that in entitling the chapter *Culturally Responsive Theory-Driven Evaluation*, we run the risk of unintentionally indicating that there are two ways to do TDE: a nonculturally responsive way and/or a culturally responsive way. Although this may be true in general, the point we want to make is that TDE should *always* be culturally and contextually responsive, because such attention to culture and context is naturally inherent within the approach. This of course flies in the face of the TDE purists who may or may not believe that considering context is violating the ethos of the scientific method. Yet, with society firmly entrenched within the 21st century and with changing demographics all over the globe, our ways of conceptualizing good, credible evaluation must be responsive, dynamic, and inclusive of varying contexts. Indeed, the evaluator who is called to perform an evaluation without understanding the context and culture of the environment is becoming a rarity (e.g., Rog, Fitzpatrick, & Conner, 2012). Quite the contrary, evaluators are often chosen based upon their ability to understand the culture, context, and environmental influences, and to discern the unique factors of the community, policy, or product (Dahler-Larsen & Schwandt, 2012; LaFrance, Nichols, & Kirkhart, 2012).

Over the years, the reputation of theory-driven as well as associated evaluation approaches (such as theory-based or program stakeholder evaluation) has endured varying degrees and kinds of attention. Yet these criticisms, while certainly worthy of consideration, are limited and perpetuate a one-dimensional perspective and understanding of TDE. These variations range from the belief in the need for understanding the theoretical perspectives (both lay and scholarly) that guide program development and functioning (e.g., Donaldson, 2007; Donaldson & Crano, 2011) to an unwise and misguided use of evaluator time and effort (Scriven, 1998; Stufflebeam, 2001) to the presupposition that the approach is, in its most elitist form, based upon a prescript of power and privilege in its association with a positivist/postpositivist paradigm, often ignoring variables such as culture and context (e.g., Mertens & Wilson, 2010).

Because of the criticism of TDE (Donaldson [2007] himself notes that the approach is considered by many to be "ivory tower"), we want to address what seem to be the standout issues. Specifically, critics and purists of TDE alike often focus on the perceived static nature of the approach and its simplistic linear aspects such as logic modeling (rather than, for example, those models that are overtly described as inclusive and/or complex models) or on the perceived need of the approach to model specific internal workings at all (Coryn, Noakes, Westine, & Schröter, 2010) or, in some instances, on the concern that defining these internal workings may lead to possible categorization of groups, situations, and circumstances (e.g., Coryn et al., 2010). These limited perspectives ignore TDE's ability to be used as a valid evaluation approach in ascertaining credible evidence that can articulate the situations, contexts, and circumstances of communities—in short, all of the considerations needed to conduct culturally responsive evaluation.

CONDUCTING CULTURALLY RESPONSIVE PROGRAM THEORY-DRIVEN EVALUATION SCIENCE

AEA's *Statement on Cultural Competence in Evaluation* (2011) states that, "Evaluations cannot be culture free" (para. 14). In understanding that evaluations reflect culture, we are able to produce more accurate designs that are, in a best-case scenario, relatively unencumbered by the values of the evaluator and more representative of the community in which the evaluation is being conducted. Below, we articulate how the TDE three-step process can be conducted in a culturally responsive manner. Specifically, we use the CRE framework to illustrate how the approach is inherently culturally responsive and reflective of cultural competence in evaluation.

Developing a Program-Impact Theory

In the first step of the TDE framework, developing a program theory, engagement with stakeholders such as program staff, clients, administration, and other invested constituents such as community members-at-large is essential. Continued iterations of an agreed-upon (but living) model are important (Donaldson, 2007). At this stage, theoretical perspectives would be incorporated into the program theory of the model, especially those that are (a) community generated (e.g., theories based on the context and demographics of the community and might be considered generated because of ongoing practice or practiced-based evidence) or (b) appropriate well-known theories about culture and cultural perspectives (e.g., theories that are specifically designed for a particular group such as African Americans; Bledsoe, 2005). For example, strands or principles from the following kinds of theory might be included in the program model and adapted to represent the context of the identified population within the particular community and program: critical race theory (Thomas, 2009), feminist theory (Brabeck & Brabeck, 2009), LGBT studies (lesbian, gay, bisexual, transgendered; e.g., Halperin, 2003), theories of indigenous peoples (Cram 2009; LaFrance & Crazy Bull, 2009), disabilities theory (e.g., Mertens et al., 2010; Sullivan, 2009). When this step is mapped onto step one of CRE, and the evaluator engages with stakeholders, issues of power, wealth distribution, and historical context would also be discussed (Hopson, 2009). For instance, historical contexts such as a continued long-term structure of institutional racism would be discussed and accounted for in the model (Bledsoe, 2009). Thus, there would be a heavy reliance on the community's understanding of the theory of change. Articulating what a community considers most important and culturally relevant can help in developing a responsive theory. In making this step culturally responsive, the evaluator might make use of a variety of local or contextual theoretical perspectives that are relevant to the program. These might include "theories" of and by the community and/or those who are the focus of the evaluation. To this end, the evaluation team might also recruit community members to be part of the evaluation team at the decision-making stage (Bledsoe, 2010).

Although the mere mention of theoretical processes can evoke negative connotations and images of stagnation and imperialism, as Donaldson (as cited in Fitzpatrick et al., 2009) has found, we contend that the development of a program theory allows both lay and scholarly theoretical perspectives about communities, communities of color, and other historically stigmatized groups to be used as the grounding framework of the theory. Thus, theories that are rooted in resilience (rather than pathology; Trueba, 2002) can be used to develop impact theory. Additionally, these theories can be used to consider mediating or moderating factors as to how certain cultural norms, mores, and behaviors can impact the strength, dosage, and perceptions of a program. Such factors would include, but not be limited to, community experiences that are most relevant to the community and by extension to the program and participants (Bledsoe & Hopson, 2009).

For instance, an evaluator might work with community members of all levels, including possible program participants, by holding a discussion group to gather information to develop a culturally responsive impact theory. The proposed impact might consider nontraditional and cultural theories, as well as how that impact might be valued. Issues to consider and to model might include the historical perspective concerning the proposed outcomes and/or institutional discriminations or possible successes that might affect that perspective. Other aspects such as cultural norms or a community's value of collectivism might be considered in what is believed to be program success.

Logic modeling.

Although logic modeling has been primarily presented as a linear activity, (e.g., Chen, 1990; Coryn et al., 2011), this perspective is not necessarily prescribed. A culturally responsive TDE would work to develop the model in tandem with stakeholders in a way that is most responsive to the community. Rather than approaching logic modeling in what might be considered a traditional linear process, participants could be engaged using innovative strategies such as visual facilitation to help them identify possible mediators (absolute must-haves for the program to work) and moderators (facilitators and/or barriers to program success such as values of family involvement or poverty). To this end, recent program theory models have become more interactive (e.g., Donaldson & Azzam, in press) to reflect the complexity of the community and its respective cultural context (see Figure 1.3).

In Figure 1.3, the model reflects a larger overarching environment, one that addresses issues such as sustainability, but one that also recognizes the community's capacity for development. It is here that the evaluator might consider concerns such as institutional racism, and this might be reflected in the larger overarching environment. Additionally, models can be designed to reflect more complex macrolevel to microlevel perspectives and situations.

Leslie Goodyear and her colleagues at Education Development Center (Goodyear, Bledsoe, Rodriguez, & Cox, 2013) have worked with communities to develop multiple theories and logic models to represent the

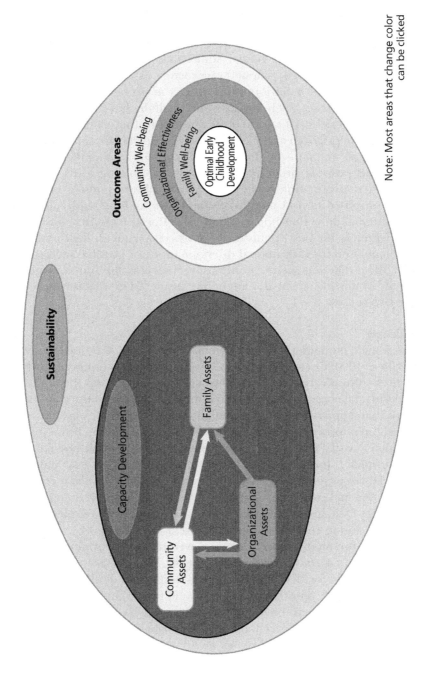

Figure 1.3 Interactive model of diverse stakeholder perspectives. Reprinted with permission from Donaldson and Azzam (in press).

viewpoints of five main groups of community stakeholders (students, families, teachers/professionals, programs, and supporting organizations) for a statewide evaluation of the 21st Century Community Learning Centers in the state of Illinois. Although each group seeks to achieve similar outcomes (e.g., to increase student and education system success), the theories, mechanisms, and inputs of how to achieve change vary from stakeholder to stakeholder. For instance, it is expected that teachers would have a different logic and process, as well as theoretical underpinning (that professional development can contribute to student achievement; Costa, 2003), than the logic and process of parents (e.g., that parent participation in after-school activities can contribute to student achievement; Henderson, Mapp, Johnson, & Davies, 2007).

Formulating and Prioritizing Questions

In formulating and prioritizing questions as per TDE, the next two steps of the CRE are also mapped: (b) framing the evaluation and (c) framing the questions. These two phases of CRE focus on activities such as understanding the sociocultural context of the evaluation (including relevant history) and assembling an evaluation team whose collective lived experience is appropriate to the context of the evaluand. During the second step of TDE, the focus is on identifying the questions that have the most value to the stakeholders and community members, and acknowledging issues that might affect in what ways the program may or may not meet the needs of the consumers. In prioritizing questions, we might ask in what manner is the program being distributed and to whom? In what ways are various groups affected? Would more (or less) dosage of the program work for certain groups but not others? What has been the history of discrimination for the population of interest? What resources are already available to the community that could encourage program success? We would also discuss the agenda of the program (e.g., exactly why was the program funded and under what auspice does it operate?), and (a) determine what would be considered credible evidence that stakeholders (e.g., funders, program staff, consumers, indirect recipients, and disenfranchised groups) would accept, and in a best case scenario, use; and (b) decide how best to obtain the evidence, using methods and strategies appropriate for the situation, program, culture, and context.

Bledsoe's (2010) work with an inner-city high school obesity-prevention program in central New Jersey allowed for reprioritization and revision of top-down developed questions for the evaluation and stakeholders. Working closely with students through "listening sessions" and "discussion groups," Bledsoe concentrated on survey questions that focused on self-esteem (or lack thereof) and individual deficit-model thinking, and revised them to address contextual issues such as cultural traditions and outlook, socioeconomic status, and the privilege gap between low- and high-income communities and groups with regard to equal access to food and economic resources. Ultimately, rather than answering questions relevant to the top-level stakeholders (administrators and teachers), the questions were reprioritized to answer questions of the consumers and downstream recipients (students, parents, community organizations).

Answering Evaluation Questions

The final step of TDE can be broadly mapped onto the final five processes of CRE: (e) design the evaluation approach; (f) select and adapt instrumentation; (g) collect the data; (h) analyze the data; and (i) disseminate and use the results. Greene (2011) notes that what is considered credible evidence from particular methods, designs, program theories, and the like is context driven. The CRE model considers culture at each step and tries to appropriately design the evaluation to be responsive by including key stakeholder groups in the process; being sensitive to language and dialect for instrumentation; considering alternative ways to collect data including picking up on nonverbal communication; considering outliers, especially those that foster positive perspectives rather than those that articulate and confirm a deficit model of the community; and considering the various audiences and stakeholders to whom the results of the evaluation would be disseminated.

Design the evaluation methodology.

Similar to the CRE model, the third step in the TDE model seeks to design methods that are inclusive and representative of the context. Although TDE has a reputation for being associated with randomized control trials and comparison groups, theorists such as Donaldson (2007) and Funnell and Rogers (2011) advocate for the use of multiple methods as well as mixed methodology. To illustrate, let's return once again to Bledsoe's (2010) work with the obesity program. Multiple methods were used to collect information about the participants and community, including site maps of the community to indicate all food-accessible establishments, geographical information systems, and electronic diaries that documented students' eating habits. These multiple methods sought to provide a multi-level-model perspective at the individual and community level.

Select and adapt instrumentation.

At this step of the CRE model, the focus is on paying attention to the selection, development, and adaptation of credible, reliable, and above all, valid instrumentation. In a culturally responsive TDE, evaluators work closely with stakeholders to discuss and refine instrumentation so that it is representative of the theoretical framework and model established by the community. For example, Donaldson (2007) illustrated this process with stakeholders from 14 community computing centers in 11 low-income California communities with the evaluation of the *Computers in Our Future Program.* Each community was intentionally chosen by the funder because of its diversity. Donaldson (2007) and his colleagues worked closely with each center to design instruments that addressed both the overarching initiative questions of the funder and those of the unique and diverse communities.

Finally, the CRE model advocates bringing the voices of all stakeholders to the table in whatever manner those voices can be heard. In conducting a culturally responsive TDE, Bledsoe (2010) used listening sessions and discussion groups with students to gather input and direction for the development of surveys and instruments that included attention to ethnic culture and to the varying regional and historical context of the city.

Collect the data.

Parallel to the CRE model, a culturally responsive TDE would consider alternative ways the data could be collected, including, but not limited to, what understandings or shared experiences would enhance and increase accuracy in data collection. For instance, Donaldson and Gooler (2007, as cited in Fitzpatrick et al., 2009) found in their work with the *Work and Health Initiative* funded by the California Wellness Foundation that understanding of the experiences and cultural contexts of Latino immigrant populations including, but not limited to, language barriers and job skills needed to work in an agriculture context helped to inform the instrumentation and data collection procedures used for the *Winning New Jobs Program.* Specifically, they considered issues such as translation of instrumentation (primarily into Spanish, since many of the participants were Spanish speaking) and data collection context (during the program activities).

Analyze the data.

Theory-driven evaluation has long since discussed various strategies by which to analyze and interpret data (Chen, 1990, 2005). The CRE method suggests considering outliers as well as disaggregating groups to further understand the unique perspectives of cultural groups and stakeholders. Let us return to Donaldson and Gooler's (2007) work with the *Winning New Jobs Program* (as cited in Donaldson, 2007). They note that when the original program that was designed in Michigan was implemented in California, it operated very differently in the diverse populations of both Northern and Southern California, arguably one of the most diverse states in the country. For example, Latino immigrants had very different job-skills training needs than recently laid-off technology workers who were casualties of the 1990s dot com bust. In disaggregating this information, Donaldson and Gooler were able to pinpoint strategies needed to address the various contexts of each unique stakeholder. Immigrant Latino workers needed to be taught skills that focused on enhancing manual-labor skills and an understanding of the issues that face migrant farmworkers.

Disseminate and use the results.

The CRE model emphasizes that dissemination of results must inform a wide range of stakeholders and that communications must be responsive to stakeholder needs. In his interview with Jody Fitzpatrick about the *Work and Health Initiative*, Donaldson (cited in Fitzpatrick et al., 2009) said that the evaluation team, "killed a lot of trees with our reports" in trying to keep open communications with stakeholders. Since trust and reciprocity had been established between the evaluators and stakeholders, the team encouraged feedback and input from the Foundation and shared results in a variety of settings to multiple communities. These included briefing reports to funders and presentations to both lay and practice communities as well as media service announcements.

THE VALUE OF CONDUCTING CULTURALLY RESPONSIVE THEORY-DRIVEN EVALUATION

Earlier, we discussed some of the concerns of those who advocate for a culturally responsive approach to evaluation in relation to theory-driven evaluation. Issues mentioned include narrow definitions and perspectives of theory and the concern that the approach can be insensitive to the cultural context. Yet we argue that TDE is focused on working to best understand the program in the context and increase the accuracy, precision, and contextual relevance of the evaluation design and methods. And thus, we further argue that the ability of the approach to be conducted in a culturally responsive manner, and to provide credible evidence, is great. Bledsoe's (2005) work with historically disadvantaged communities discerning the inner workings of the program as well as considering the history, socioeconomic status, and cultural milieu demonstrates that such attention contributes to greater precision to measurement and inches the evaluator closer to achieving multicultural validity (Kirkhart, 2005). For example, Bledsoe found in her work in understanding the lack of success of a program focused on providing prenatal services to young African American mothers that understanding the historical perspectives of medical programming in the community (always dismantled), socioeconomic status (women in a city with a median income of $36,000), and demographic make-up (highly segregated area) allowed for the development of instruments that could more accurately address the reasons behind the program's failure in outreach (Bledsoe, 2005). In this case, TDE was instrumental in identifying those aspects (which in essence were moderators) that can determine in what manner the program will function. In the aforementioned case, the identification of moderators (e.g., cultural context, economic history) was helpful in discerning how the program would work and under what circumstances and how potential participants would resonate with the program efforts.

Other Considerations for Insuring Cultural Responsiveness in TDE

Participatory approaches and participation in the evaluative process.
Although Chen's (1990) early work alludes to the ability of the approach to work with more participatory approaches, his later work (2005, 2012) as well as that of Donaldson (e.g., cited in Fitzpatrick et al., 2009) has been more forthcoming about TDE's ability to work collaboratively with approaches that are traditionally participatory. Bledsoe and Graham's (2005) work with a family literacy program in central New Jersey has been especially illustrative of this: They found that the theory-driven approach was flexible enough to use with multiple approaches, including transformative and empowerment evaluation. David Fetterman's (Program Theory and Theory-Driven Evaluation TIG Business Meeting, 2010) AEA presentation made the case for the integration of empowerment and program theory-driven evaluation; and Mertens and Wilson (2012) have discussed the ability of TDE to work in tandem with approaches that are more social-justice oriented such as transformative mixed methods.

The National Institutes of Health (2011) adapted a framework from the International Association for Participation that specifically frames the community involvement perspective on a continuum and outlines a typology of engagement. At the *outreach stage*, there is some community involvement, with communication flowing in an informational manner. At the *consult stage*, there is more community involvement, and the communication is feedback seeking and some sharing of information. The *involvement stage* is improved community involvement, and communication is much more participatory, with greater participation from the community, and there is shared information. At the *collaborative stage*, which is where many evaluations strive to be, there is community involvement, members may be a part of the team, and the communication is bidirectional. Partnerships are pursued. Finally, at the *shared leadership stage* of participation, there is a strong bidirectional relationship, and decision making, rather than relying on the evaluation team, is at the community level (see Figure 1.4). In a culturally responsive TDE, the community would determine the impact model.

Increasing Level of Community Involvement, Impact, Trust, and Communication Flow

Outreach	Consult	Involve	Collaborate	Shared Leadership
Some Community Involvement	*More Community Involvement*	*Better Community Involvement*	*Community Involvement*	*Strong Bidirectional Relationship*
Communication flows from one to the other, to inform	*Communication flows to the community and then back, answer seeking*	*Communication flows both ways, participatory form of communication*	*Communication flow is bidirectional*	Final decision making is at community level.
Provides community with information	Gets information or feedback from the community	Involves more participation with community on issues.	Forms partnership with community on each aspect of project from development to solution.	Entities have formed strong partnership structures.
Entities coexist.	Entities share information.	Entities cooperate with each other.	Entities form bidirectional communication channels.	Outcomes: Broader health outcomes affecting broader community. Strong bidirectional trust built.
Outcomes: Optimally establishes communication channels and channels for outreach	Outcomes: Develops connections.	Outcomes: Visibility of partnership established with increased cooperation.	Outcomes: Partnership building, trust building.	

Reference: Modified by the authors from the International Association for Public Participation.

Figure 1.4   Community Engagement Continuum (NIH, 2011, p. 8).

Consideration of ethical treatment.

Bledsoe and Hopson (2009) note that taking into account ethical treatment of underserved communities and fostering cultural responsiveness allows for the consideration of nontraditional data analytic methods as well as the reconceptualization of what is considered to be a significant outcome within the community. In conducting culturally responsive TDE, evaluators must be willing to explore diverse and nontraditional methods such as visual facilitation (Ukeyi, 2010), which captures data pictorially. They also must reconceptualize what is considered to be significant and a "gold standard." Bledsoe posits in her 2005 chapter that consideration of what is sanctioned to be an effect must be decided in conjunction with communities and stakeholders. For example, a less than .05 p-value is often considered to indicate statistical significance of a program's effect or in the achievement of its outcomes. However, many programs simply don't meet that standard. Consideration of what is considered an effect or a meeting of the outcome has to be determined by the community and/or stakeholders. In short, what is considered by communities to be credible evidence must be at the core of the discussion of program effectiveness (Donaldson, 2009).

CONCLUSION

At the beginning of this chapter, we stated that AEA's (2011) *Statement on Cultural Competence in Evaluation* demonstrates the Association's and, one could argue by extension, the field's understanding and acceptance of the dynamic and changing nature of societies, organizations, and communities as related to culture. In acknowledging the salience of culture and the importance of evaluating in a culturally responsive manner, we also seek to evaluate in an ethical manner (AEA, 2004). Given this, what are the implications for evaluators of conducting culturally responsive TDE? For one, it means consideration of multiple perspectives, theoretical and otherwise. The contention is that focusing on the interplay of multiple perspectives such as those related to culture and context rather than simply focusing on, for instance, program theory, allows for a broader, more responsive, and more far-reaching "theory" of how and in what manner the program can and should work. Although evaluators are stepping forward to explore what culturally responsive evaluation means in all facets and types of evaluation ranging from program to policy, they are further encouraged to think about how *all* evaluation approaches are imbued with culture.

The move to conducting TDE in a culturally responsive manner is long overdue. And we realize in our own practice that acknowledging the profound influence of culture in the evaluation work we do does not diminish the credibility of the approach—instead it enhances it. In understanding our self-reflective process in conducting an evaluation and our own issues with culture (e.g., what is the culture that drives our own evaluation perspective? What are biases of other cultures and how does that affect the work we do?), we enable truly responsive and more accurate evaluations. That is, in conducting culturally responsive theory-driven evaluation, we conduct *better* evaluations that more accurately represent the evaluands, communities, and world in which we live. It is our hope that more theory-driven evaluations in the future will consciously examine culture and used culturally responsive evaluation concepts at every step of the TDE process.

AUTHORS' NOTE

The authors would like to thank the editors of the series and this volume for their invaluable comments. All comments and inquires can be sent to the first author, Katrina L. Bledsoe, of the DeBruce Foundation at 1050 30th Street, NW, Washington, DC. 20007, kbledsoe@accelresearch.org; 202-748-8944.

REFERENCES

American Evaluation Association (AEA). (2004). *Guiding principles for evaluators.* Washington, DC: American Evaluation Association.

American Evaluation Association (AEA). (2011, April 22). *American Evaluation Association statement on cultural competence in evaluation.* Washington, DC: American Evaluation Association. Retrieved from http://www.eval.org/p/cm/ld/fid=92

Bledsoe, K. L. (2005). Using theory-driven evaluation with underserved communities: Promoting program development and program sustainability. In S. Hood, R. H. Hopson, & H. T. Frierson (Eds.), *The role of culture and cultural context: A mandate for inclusion, the discovery of truth and understanding in evaluative theory and practice* (pp. 175–196). Greenwich, CT: Information Age.

Bledsoe, K. L. (2009). Evaluation of the Fun with Books Program: An interview with Katrina Bledsoe. In J. Fitzpatrick, T. Christie, & M. Mark (Eds.), *Evaluation in action: Interviews with the experts* (pp. 299–323). Thousand Oaks, CA: Sage.

Bledsoe, K. L. (2010). Presto it's gone! When research ceases to exist right before your eyes. In D. Streiner & S. Sidani (Eds.), *When research studies go off the rails: Solutions and prevention strategies* (pp. 344–352). New York, NY: Guilford.

Bledsoe, K. L., & Graham, J. A. (2005). Using multiple evaluation approaches in program evaluation. *American Journal of Evaluation, 26,* 302–319.

Bledsoe, K. L., & Hopson, R. H. (2009). Conducting ethical research in underserved communities. In D. M. Mertens & P. Ginsberg (Eds.), *Handbook of ethics for research in the social sciences* (pp. 391–406). Thousand Oaks, CA: Sage.

Botcheva, L., Shih, J., & Huffman, L. C. (2009). Emphasizing culture in evaluation: A process-oriented approach. *American Journal of Evaluation, 30,* 176–188.

Brabeck, M. M., & Brabeck, K. M. (2009). Feminist perspectives on research ethics. In D. M. Mertens & P. Ginsberg (Eds.), *Handbook of ethics for research in the social sciences* (pp. 23–38). Thousand Oaks, CA: Sage.

Centers for Disease Control (CDC). (1999). *Centers for Disease Control Program Evaluation Framework MMWR 48,* (No. RR-11), 1–40. Retrieved from http://www.atsdr.cdc.gov/communityengagement/pdf/PCE_Report_508_FINAL.pdf

Chen, H. T. (1990). Theory-driven evaluations. Thousand Oaks, CA: Sage.

Chen, H. T. (2005). Practical program evaluation: Assessing and improving planning, implementation, and effectiveness. Thousand Oaks, CA: Sage.

Chen, H. T. (2012). The roots and growth of theory-driven evaluation: Assessing viability, effectuality, and transferability. In M. Alkin (Ed.) *Evaluation roots* (pp. 113–129). Thousand Oaks, CA: Sage.

Coryn, C., Noakes, L., Westine, C., & Schröter, D. (2011). A systematic review of theory-driven evaluation practice from 1990 to 2009. *American Journal of Evaluation, 32*(3), 199–226.

Costa, A. L. (Ed.). (2003). *Developing minds: A resource for teaching thinking* (3rd ed.). Alexandria, VA: Association for Supervision and Curriculum Development.

Cram, F. (2009). Maintaining indigenous voices. In D. M. Mertens & P. I. Ginsberg (Eds.), *Handbook of social research ethics* (pp. 308–322). Thousand Oaks, CA: Sage.

Dahler-Larsen, P., & Schwandt, T. A. (2012). Political culture as context for evaluation. In D. Rog, J. Fitzpatrick, & R. Conner (Eds.), *Context: A framework for its influence on evaluation practice* (pp. 59–74). San Francisco, CA: Jossey-Bass/American Evaluation Association.

Donaldson, S. I. (2007). *Program theory-driven science: Strategies and applications.* Mahwah, NJ: Erlbaum.

Donaldson, S. I. (2009). A practitioner's guide for gathering credible evidence in the evidence-based global society. In S. I. Donaldson, C. A. Christie, & M. M. Mark (Eds.), *What counts as credible evidence in applied research and evaluation practice?* (pp. 239–251). Los Angeles, CA: Sage.

Donaldson, S. I., & Azzam, T. A. (2014). Tending the garden of evaluation theory: Flourishing trees and PhDs. In A. Vo & C. A. Christie (Eds.), *Evaluation use and decision making.* Greenwich, CT: Information Age.

Donaldson, S. I., & Crano, W. C. (2011). Theory-driven evaluation science and applied social psychology: Exploring the intersection. In M. M. Mark, S. I. Donaldson, & B. Campbell (Eds.), *Social psychology and evaluation.* New York, NY: Guilford.

Frierson, H. T., Hood, S., & Hughes, G. B. (2010). A guide to conducting culturally-responsive evaluations. In J. Frechtling (Ed.), *The 2010 user-friendly handbook for project evaluation* (pp. 75–96). Washington, DC: National Science Foundation.

Funnell, S., & Rogers, P. (2011). *Purposeful program theory: Effective use of theories of change and logic models.* San Francisco, CA: Jossey-Bass.

Goodyear, L., Bledsoe, K., Rodriguez, S., & Cox, J. (2013). *Evaluation of the Illinois State Board of Education's 21st Century Community Learning Centers.* Education Development Center.

Greene, J. (2011). The construct(ion) of validity as argument. In H.T. Chen, S. I. Donaldson, & M. M. Mark (Eds.), *Advancing validity in outcome evaluation: Theory and practice* (pp. 81–130). San Francisco, CA: Wiley

Halperin, D. (2003). The normalizing of Queer Theory. *Journal of Homosexuality, 45,* pp. 339–343.

Henderson, A., Mapp, K., Johnson, V., & Davies, D. (2007). *Beyond the bake sale: The essential guide to family-school partnerships.* New York, NY: New Press.

Hood, S., Hopson, R., & Frierson (2005). This is where we stand. In S. Hood, R. H. Hopson, & H. T. Frierson (Eds.). *The role of culture and cultural context: A mandate for inclusion, the discovery of truth and understanding in evaluative theory and practice* (pp. 1–5). Greenwich, CT: Information Age.

Hopson, R. K. (2009). Reclaiming knowledge at the margins: Culturally responsive evaluation in the current evaluation moment. In K. Ryan & B. Cousins (Eds.), *International handbook on evaluation* (pp. 431–448). Thousand Oaks, CA: Sage.

Kirkhart, K. (2010). Eyes on the prize: Multicultural validity and evaluation theory. *American Journal of Evaluation 31,* 400–413.

Kirkhart, K. E. (2005). Through a cultural lens: Reflection on validity and theory in evaluation. In S. Hood, R. H. Hopson, & H. T. Frierson (Eds.), *The role of culture and cultural context: A mandate for inclusion, the discovery of truth and understanding in evaluative theory and practice.* (pp. 175–196). Greenwich, CT: Information Age.

Kirkhart, K. E. (2013). Advancing considerations of culture and validity: Honoring the Key Evaluation Checklist. In S. I. Donaldson (Ed.), *The future of evaluation in society: A tribute to Michael Scriven* (pp. 129–160). Charlotte, NC: Information Age.

LaFrance, J., & Crazy Bull, C. (2009). Researching ourselves back to life: Taking control of the research agenda in Indian country. In D. M. Mertens & P. Ginsberg (Eds.), *Handbook of ethics for research in the social sciences* (pp. 135–149). Thousand Oaks, CA: Sage.

LaFrance, J. Nichols, R., & Kirkhart, K. E. (2012). Culture writes the script: On the centrality of context in indigenous evaluation. In D. Rog, J. Fitzpatrick, & R. Conner (Eds.), *Context: A framework for its influence on evaluation practice* (pp. 59–74) San Francisco, CA: Jossey-Bass/American Evaluation Association.

Mathison, S. (Ed.) (2004). *Encyclopedia of evaluation.* Thousand Oaks, CA: Sage Publications.

Mertens, D. M (2008). *Transformative research and evaluation.* New York, NY: Guilford.

Mertens, D. M., Bledsoe, K. L., Sullivan, M., & Wilson, A. (2010). Utilization of mixed methods for transformative purposes. In C. Teddlie & A. Tashakkori (Eds.), *Handbook of mixed methods research* (2nd ed., pp. 193–214). Thousand Oaks, CA: Sage.

Mertens, D. M., & Wilson, A. (2012). *Program evaluation theory and practices: A comprehensive guide.* New York, NY: Guilford.

Myers, D. G. (2009). *Introduction to psychology* (9th ed.). San Francisco, CA: McGraw-Hill.

National Institutes of Health (NIH). (2011, June). Principles of community engagement (2nd ed.). NIH Publication No. 11-7782. Retrieved from http://www.atsdr.cdc.gov/communityengagement/pdf/PCE_Report_508_FINAL.pdf

National Science Foundation (NSF). (2010). *The 2010 user-friendly handbook for project evaluation.* Washington, DC: National Science Foundation.

Pon, G. (2003). Cultural competence as the new racism: An ontology of forgetting. *Journal of Progressive Human Services, 20,* 59–71.

Program Theory and Theory-Driven Evaluation TIG Business Meeting and Panel. (2010). *Improving evaluation quality by improving program quality: A theory-based/theory-driven perspective.* American Evaluation Association annual conference, San Antonio, TX.

Rog, D. J., Fitzpatrick, J. L., & Conner, R. F. (2012). Context: A framework for its influence on evaluation practice. New Directions for Evaluation. In D. J. Rog, J. L . Fitzpatrick, & R. F. Conner (Eds.), *When background becomes foreground: Towards context-sensitive evaluation practice* (pp. 25–40). San Francisco, CA: Jossey-Bass/American Evaluation Association

Rossi, P. H., & Freeman, H. E. (1979). *Evaluation: A systematic approach.* Thousand Oaks, CA: Sage.

Scriven, M. (1998). Minimalist theory: The least theory that practice requires. *American Journal of Evaluation, 19,* 57–70.

SenGupta, S., Hopson, R., & Thompson-Robinson, M. (2004). Cultural competence in evaluation: An overview. In M. Thompson-Robinson, R. Hopson & S. SenGupta (Eds.), *In search of cultural competence in evaluation: Toward principles and practices* (pp. 5–19). (New Directions for Evaluation, 102). San Francisco, CA: Jossey-Bass.

Shaddish, W., Cook, T., & Leviton, L. (1991). *Foundations of program evaluation.* Thousand Oaks, CA: Sage.

Stufflebeam, D. L. (2001). Evaluation models. San Francisco, CA: Jossey-Bass.

Sullivan, M. (2009). Philosophy, ethics, and the disability community. In D. M. Mertens & P. Ginsberg (Eds.), *Handbook of ethics for research in the social sciences* (pp. 391–406). Thousand Oaks, CA: Sage.

Symonette, H. (2004). Walking pathways toward becoming a culturally competent evaluator: Boundaries, borderlands, and border crossings. *New Directions for Evaluation, 102,* 95–109.

Thomas, V. G. (2009). Critical race theory: Ethics and dimensions of diversity in research. In D. M. Mertens & P. Ginsberg (Eds.), *Handbook of ethics for research in the social sciences.* (pp. 54–68). Thousand Oaks, CA: Sage.

Trueba, H. T. (2002). Multiple ethnic, racial, and cultural identities in action: From marginality to a new cultural capital in modern society. *Journal of Latinos and Education, 1,* 7–28.

Ukeyi, T. (2010, November). *Visual facilitation of the American Evaluation Association's Public Statement on Cultural Competence in Evaluation.* American Evaluation Association annual conference, San Antonio, Texas.

Weiss, C. H. (1997). How can theory-based evaluation make greater headway? *Evaluation Review, 21,* 501–524.

Yarbrough, D., Shulha, L. M., Hopson, R., & Caruthers, F. (2010). The program evaluation standards: A guide for evaluators and evaluation users (3rd ed.) Thousand Oaks, CA: Sage.

CHAPTER 2

A SYSTEMS APPROACH TO CULTURALLY RESPONSIVE EVALUATION PRACTICE

Culturally Responsive Uses of the Systems Evaluation Protocol (SEP)

Wanda D. Casillas
University of Michigan

William M. Trochim
Cornell University

Over the last few years, the field of evaluation has witnessed increasing discourse related to culturally responsive evaluation or *CRE* (Madison, 1992; Manswell-Butty, Reid, & LaPoint, 2004; Mertens, 2009; SenGupta, Hopson, & Thompson-Robinson, 2004; etc.). However, as a relatively new area of evaluation, many professionals still struggle with basic definitional questions such as, "What is culturally responsive evaluation?" and with practical questions such as, "How can I be culturally responsive in my own work?"

Continuing the Journey to Reposition Culture and Cultural Context in Evaluation Theory and Practice, pages 29–48
Copyright © 2015 by Information Age Publishing
29

To date, responses to these questions as presented in evaluation literature are varied, and for the individual professional, this variation can be overwhelming. Professionals wanting to learn more about how to be culturally responsive in their practice are in need of an organized way to conceptualize CRE and clear protocols for practicing CRE. Though it is undoubtedly counterintuitive to suggest that we address cultural context through guiding practice protocols, this is precisely the argument that needs to be engaged. This chapter suggests that systems approaches to evaluation, like the *Guide to the Systems Evaluation Protocol or SEP* (Trochim et al., 2012), provide a much-needed framework for thinking about and implementing culturally responsive evaluation. Aligning CRE principles, including considerations of cultural context, with systems evaluation activities in the SEP will advance the systematization of CRE practice.

An obvious question is How are systems approaches to evaluation and culturally responsive evaluation related to one another? Or perhaps, Why would approaches like the SEP be a logical choice for operationalizing CRE practice? There are two potential responses to these questions: The first is that systems approaches to evaluation recognize and attempt to address the complex nature of evaluation environments. However, though these approaches emphasize complexity in evaluation contexts, they do not necessarily focus on *cultural* context (e.g., Fredericks, Deegan, & Carman, 2008; Williams & Hummelbrunner, 2010). On the other hand, CRE focuses specifically on the complex nature of *cultural* factors in the environment.

The second is that research regarding a systems approach to evaluation and research regarding CRE practice (Casillas & Trochim, in preparation), though existing in isolation from each other, have followed a similar strategy for attending to the complexity of contextual factors in evaluation work (Casillas & Trochim, in preparation). For example, within the SEP, a systems approach to evaluation has been presented as a set of *systems heuristics*, which provide a framework for thinking about evaluation planning from a systems perspective. These heuristics are used to create a protocol which is partially systematized but exceedingly flexible in application across evaluation contexts. Similarly, proponents of culturally responsive evaluation have referred to CRE as a "stance taken" (AEA, 2011) or as a *way of thinking* about evaluation, that is, as a framework for thinking about evaluation from a perspective of cultural respect. Granted, the SEP has provided a more cohesive set of heuristics representing decades of conceptualization by scholars of systems theory from multiple disciplines. However, in recent work by Casillas and Trochim (in preparation), a concept-mapping study revealed a set of CRE principles representing an initial step toward organizing concepts around evaluators' "way(s) of thinking" in CRE. Though these are not *heuristics* as in systems theory, these CRE *principles* can serve a similar purpose.

But there is more to be said regarding the notion of systems perspectives from a developmental orientation. Bronfenbrenner's (1994) ecological model of human development adapts a similar *systems* approach to positioning a person's development in his/her environmental context and provides additional logical evidence for the link between systems approaches to evaluation and CRE. In the current discussion, the perspective offered by Ecological Systems Theory is relevant for multiple reasons: First, programs are often created to affect the developmental trajectory of their participants on some specific dimension (e.g., increase participant interest and affinity for the sciences). Second, programs themselves, especially as presented in the SEP, are undergoing developmental processes. Third, cultural context would be considered a macrolevel system with varying influences on individuals as participants in a program and on the program itself. Thus, treating *culture* and context as systems variables is not new, and treating them as systems variables from an evaluation perspective is consistent with theories of human development (e.g., Lewis, 2000; Thelen, Smith, Karmiloff-Smith, & Johnson, 1994).

Additionally, unpublished evidence from the Cornell Office for Research on Evaluation that produced the SEP suggests that approaches to the complex nature of organizational and, possibly social systems, *can* be successfully addressed with a protocol in order to conduct evaluations that properly contextualize programs and program stakeholders. If it is possible to systemize an approach to complex systems, and the SEP successfully does so, it would be prudent to extend its reach to the complexity of cultural influences on an evaluation and its participants for all of the reasons discussed thus far. In the following section, we draw a conceptual parallel between specific systems heuristics and specific culturally responsive principles, positioning a future discussion on the adaptation of activities in the SEP to aid in the field-wide struggle to operationalize culturally responsive practices. We argue that because there is overlap between the systems heuristics and CRE principles, examples of activities provided in the SEP will be well suited for making CRE principles actionable.

Systems Heuristics and Culturally Responsive Principles: Review and Overlap

The Systems Evaluation Protocol is an evaluation approach framed by systems thinking and is articulated in *The Guide to the Systems Evaluation Protocol* (CORE, 2012). The SEP represents the most clearly outlined attempt to identify and apply systems-thinking heuristics to evaluation. Eleven systems heuristics and their potential for framing evaluation work are summarized and then operationalized through steps and activities in the SEP. These heuristics are outlined below.

- *Part-whole relationships.* Systems are "wholes" composed of "parts," and part-whole relationships are central to systems thinking. In dynamic systems, systems are often thought to be more than the sum of their parts. Additionally, there should be emphasis on the relationships among the components within the system and the resulting system with each of its components. In terms of evaluation work, this conceptualization draws focus to where a program "fits" in relation to the organizational system to which it belongs.
- *Local and global.* Thinking of local and global levels of scale is a way of conceptualizing relationships in a system hierarchy. When applied to evaluation, this heuristic most often refers to the position of the program being evaluated. Positioning the program as local or global entails considering things such as is this program operating at the county level (local), state level, national level (global), and so forth.
- *Boundaries.* Systems are bounded. Sometimes the boundaries are clearly identifiable, and sometimes the boundaries are less distinguishable. In terms of evaluation work, systems theory urges us to define what activities and outcomes fall within the scope of a program or within the boundaries of a program.
- *Complexity and simple rules.* Complex systems or phenomena result from individual agents operating by simple rules and receiving feedback from the environment. In terms of evaluation practice, this heuristic has a primary driver for the creation of the SEP. The SEP is, after all, a set of simple rules that can be flexibly used to evaluate complex systems.
- *Static and dynamic processes.* Static and dynamic processes have to do with the predictability of an object or subject. This is often exemplified as the difference between throwing a bird and throwing a rock. As a static object, the trajectory of the rock is predictable to various degrees. However, the trajectory of a complex system, such as a bird, is influenced by many things and is less predictable. An evaluation may fall anywhere on a continuum between static and dynamic processes, requiring your evaluation approach to be adaptive, reflexive, and iterative.
- *Ontogeny and phylogeny.* Ontogeny concerns the evolution of an organism through its lifespan. Likewise, an evolutionary systems perspective suggests that we consider the developmental phases of a program and of an evaluation and their life cycles. The SEP goes further in promoting alignment of a program and its evaluation regarding their respective life cycles.

- *Symbiosis and co-evolution.* This is the idea that certain organisms evolve together and assist in one another's survival and development. For evaluation work, this heuristic helps us to focus on the relationship between evaluation and programs as one in which both are necessary for the other's survival.
- *Causal pathways.* This describes the ideas that causal chains exist within a system and that causes have effects, and feedback may exist on the chain of events. This has direct relevance to the underlying logic of a program in which certain activities are expected to result in certain outcomes. This is typically captured in a logic model, although the SEP goes beyond this to utilize causal pathway models. Evaluations are often a process of feedback for a program's cause-and-effect logic.
- *Feedback.* Feedback is the idea that a process or system requires information about whether process components are working. Evaluations are feedback mechanisms for programs.
- *Evolution and fitness.* In evolutionary theory, organisms (thought of as complex systems) persist relative to the extent that they are adaptive. The point is that not all organisms survive. This could also be true of programs. Evaluations can help programs to adapt and survive to their contexts, but not all programs will or should persist.
- *Multiple perspectives.* A system can be perceived as many things depending on whose point of view you take, and it cannot be fully understood unless you view it from all perspectives. This is directly applicable to an evaluation in which gathering as many perspectives as possible will provide the most accurate view of the program being evaluated.

The list of culturally responsive evaluation principles compiled by Casillas and Trochim (in preparation) is somewhat shorter. These principles were systematically compiled using a concept-mapping procedure in which evaluators and program staff were asked to complete a statement about practices that they engage in in order to be culturally responsive. Participants were recruited online through the American Evaluation Association and represented a national sample of evaluators and program staff. At least half of the sample worked in educational evaluation settings and half worked in health care and other sectors. The participants also varied greatly in their experience. The number of participants varied in each of the three phases of the study from 19 to 47. The study resulted in 7 overarching principles and 12 subprinciples, whose organization was informed by both the concept-mapping study and by the extant literature on CRE. The resulting list of principles represents a preliminary attempt to organize how CRE is being conceptualized by practicing professionals. This provisional and still-evolving list of CRE principles is summarized below.

- *Understand and recognize the larger context for programs or projects.* This principle refers largely to the community within which a program is embedded. Within this principle, three other subprinciples were identified that further emphasize cultural factors and clarify ways to understand the community context: Research and learn about the cultural group, be aware of cultural labels and historical context, and identify potential historical inaccuracies.
- *Design evaluation with participants in mind.* The idea that an evaluation should hold participants at the center of planning and decision making has some overlap with principles below pertaining to stakeholder involvement. However, it recommends that participants specifically, and not stakeholders in general, be emphasized. Specifically, there are three subprinciples that further characterize this idea: be culturally specific in design, use a multifaceted approach and appropriate methods, and collect data in culturally responsive ways.
- *Allow for self-determination by stakeholders and program participants.* This principle includes engaging directly with a wide range of participants through discussion and in other culturally appropriate ways and engaging diverse stakeholders in general planning and in theory development.
- *Build trust and facilitate communication.* Although one could argue that communication and trust are essential in any evaluator-program relationship, the subprinciples identified for this overarching principle make clear that the CRE emphasis is on diversity: Allow for representativeness, build the diversity of the organization/evaluation team, access diversity from external sources, and be inclusive of diversity. These subprinciples suggest that trust and communication will only occur if the evaluator/evaluation team is representative of the members that constitute the program context.
- *Understand the evaluation audience and help the audience to understand the evaluation purpose and process.* This principle focuses on the needs of the evaluation audience as a way to frame dissemination of evaluation information. This includes information that introduces evaluation work to the community, encourages input and communication, and shares evaluation results.
- *Make the evaluation accessible to a variety of stakeholders.* Accessibility of the evaluation is central to this principle and includes using the majority language in a community, being present at culturally appropriate community venues, and using appropriate technologies for differently-abled community members when possible.

- *Understand evaluator attributes that may affect professional practice.* Another important emphasis regards the interpersonal attributes and qualities of the evaluator. This principle encourages an evaluator to reflect on his or her own position of authority and the dynamics of power relevant to his or her own cultural position when entering a new evaluation context.

At first glance, some major differences exist between the two theoretical approaches, systems thinking, and culturally responsive evaluation. For example, systems thinking, as applied in the SEP, emphasizes structural and institutional dynamics. In contrast, CRE is highly interpersonal, reflective, and reflexive at the level of individual professionals. Additionally, systems heuristics are clearly influenced by technical and computational fields (Midgley, 2003), whereas CRE is influenced by conceptions and representations of race, indigenous frameworks, and social agenda/advocacy models in evaluation (Hopson, 2009). Despite these differences, the utility for adapting a systems perspective in CRE is explored in the following section.

The Intersection of CRE and Systems Theory

There is considerable conceptual overlap between the ideas represented by systems heuristics and those represented by culturally responsive evaluation principles, and an initial point of convergence resides in how a systems perspective is implicit to a view of "culture." From a cultural psychologist's perspective, it is necessary to have an understanding or a definition of culture if you are to work at the intersection of culture and research (Matsumoto & Juang, 2013) or at the intersection of culture and evaluation, as the case may be. This concern opens an initial discussion on the connection between systems and CRE.

Defining culture.

One impactful issue an evaluator faces is that of how to define culture and position in a way that is relevant to one's work. The endeavor to construct a definition of *culture* is by no means a new one and has been tackled in many social science and service delivery domains (e.g., Gay, 2002; Kreuter & McClure, 2004; Lee, 2001; Thomas, Fine, & Ibrahim, 2004; etc.). Culturally responsive evaluators have looked to these efforts for guidance. The result is a plethora of possible definitions from which any given evaluator can choose to frame his/her work, and this decision is relevant for how he/she comes to implement CRE. For example, Heine (2008) defines culture as "any idea, belief, technology, habit, or practice that is acquired from others" and "a particular group of individuals...who are existing within some kind of shared context" (p. 3). Another definition suggested in the literature is that culture is "an [*sic*] historically created system of meaning and significance" (Parekh, 2006, p. 143). Both of these examples present a vague and neutral construal with little indication of the implications for how culture might be a meaningful construct to practicing evaluators. Kirkhart (2010), on the other hand, espouses that culture "refers to a set of beliefs, values, knowledge, and skills that collectively creates identity. Cultural understandings and commitments may be shared across cohorts or generations, often passed on as assumptions about 'what is' or 'how things operate'" (p. 401). Conceptualizations of culture vary greatly in the extent to which they are elaborated to include many complex dimensions or remain simple and "quantifiable" indicators of a social address.

At present, the term *culture* within the evaluation field, as in related social science fields, functions as a placeholder in discourse about social differences onto which professionals project a definition or perception of their choosing. On the one hand, having an amorphous understanding of *culture* allows evaluators to adapt a personalized framework for understanding and working with cultural sensitivity. However, another way to think about having a "placeholder" for *culture* is that the field has not reached a consensus on how our profession should treat the concept, leading to insufficient guidance for what *culture* as a factor means to our evaluation work. Another possible implication is that evaluators can choose to practice without adopting a definition of *culture* at all, a choice which was observed in a recent literature review of 52 empirical studies on culturally responsive evaluation (Chouinard & Cousins, 2009).

Not only is it necessary to develop a definition of *culture* to guide professional practice, it must be done in a way that creates relevance between the often esoteric dimensions of culture as an academic construct and the practical implications of cultural characteristics for everyday evaluation practice. Systems theory can be used to inform the theoretical framework in which an evaluator positions his/her understanding of *culture* for application in evaluation settings and is well suited for this purpose. The many definitions of culture available converge on the notion of culture as a dynamic, ever-changing set of concepts and activities that surround individual and group development (Kroeber & Kluckhohn, 1952). Systems theory appropriately addresses this dynamism and helps professionals to think of culture as a complex system akin to an organism. From this perspective, an evaluator may gain sufficient appreciation for the complexity of cultural factors, which can help a professional to understand why, for instance, it is important to use mixed-methods approaches and choose appropriate research designs. Without a properly situated understanding of cultural factors and how they may potentially influence evaluation results, an evaluator may find it difficult to accept CRE theory and approaches. Thus, rather than simply prescribe steps and activities, a systems perspective provides a framework for thinking about and defining culture as a factor of relevance in evaluation work.

Overlapping principles and heuristics.

In addition to the overlap between systems theory and cultural theory, there are specific points of intersection between culturally responsive evaluation principles and systems heuristics. For instance, understanding the context in which a program is embedded, as proposed in the list of CRE principles, resonates with the systems heuristics of *local-global scale* and *boundaries*. Cultural psychologists have long struggled with issues of the boundaries between individual characteristics and group characteristics and between subgroup and group characteristics (Cole, 1996). For evaluators, a similar struggle can be described using the language of the systems approach in the SEP. The global scale characteristics of a cultural group may be those general descriptors associated with, for example, Mexican American groups in general. Some of these characteristics might be based on a statistic that Mexican Americans have a higher incidence of diabetes in the United States or participate more actively in the religious traditions of Catholicism, which emphasize family values. However, the extent to which these descriptions are accurate for and relevant to any particular local Hispanic community in which a program is embedded is a different concern. Thus, while one CRE principle, *understand and recognize the larger context for programs and projects*, reminds us to understand the context of an evaluation, the systems *local-global scale* heuristic encourages us to differentiate between the local and the broader contexts.

Another conceptual overlap resides in the idea that the reality of how a program operates and what outcomes are achieved is based on the perceptions of numerous stakeholders with various expectations, or in *multiple perspectives*, as the systems heuristic holds. This heuristic emphasizes the mutually constituting perspectives of individuals and holds that a program cannot be fully understood without understanding these *multiple perspectives*. Additionally, a CRE principle, *allow for self-determination by stakeholders and program participants*, encourages professionals to empower stakeholders, and participants specifically, with the idea that they are best positioned to understand the program and thereby should tell professionals how they perceive it, what they hope to gain by participating, and whether it meets their expectations. A related principle encourages professionals to *make the evaluation accessible to a variety of stakeholders*. This expands on the systems idea that *multiple perspectives* hold value for defining the program and evaluation scope and aid in evaluation planning. However, these perspectives are also affected by the information that is redistributed as a result of an evaluation.

The complex nature of programs and evaluations in context is further characterized by systems theory, which draws attention to the differences between *static* and *dynamic processes,* as well as by a conceptualization of changing individuals in changing contexts through a discussion of *ontogeny* and *phylogeny.* These two heuristics overlap with the CRE principles that focus on interpersonal skills like *build trust and facilitate communication* and *understand evaluator attributes that may affect professional practice.* Firstly, the idea that programs and evaluations are *dynamic processes* stems not only from the nature of a program embedded in a system with other programs, but from the fact that programs are constituted by humans. It is a human who designs programs and evaluations, humans who interact to implement and receive services, and humans who constitute nearly all other aspects and actions of program development and evaluation. These humans and their relationships to one another in a program context are continually changing and, hopefully, developing. Whereas the systems heuristics remind us to attend to the complex relationships between programs and among levels of a system, CRE principles focus on the relationships between individuals and the systems in which they are embedded. Using these two theoretical orientations of CRE and systems allows a professional to navigate the complexity of relationships within a system along various levels of a hierarchy, as presented in Figure 2.1.

In general, the conceptual overlap between CRE principles and systems heuristics can be characterized by a question of scope, where systems theory in evaluation focuses on the structural characteristics of a system and

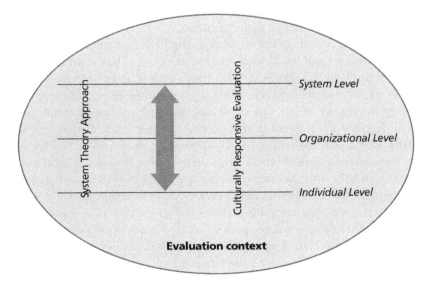

Figure 2.1 Navigating system hierarchy levels in program evaluation.

culturally responsive evaluation approaches focus on interpersonal aspects of individuals embedded within an organizational system. It is through the application of interpersonal skills and relationships that structural components are addressed in CRE. Additionally, because CRE emphasizes interpersonal relationships in an evaluation and/or program context, it extends discussion of context to include social systems which may affect these interpersonal relationships. However, by using systems and CRE approaches together, there is more potential to move freely through the levels and components of a system, to include both structural and social system components.

ADAPTING SEP ACTIVITIES FOR CRE PRACTICE

The conceptual overlap between systems heuristics and culturally responsive evaluation principles is theoretically interesting and important for understanding why the application of the SEP makes sense for CRE practice. However, the most important facet of the integration of these ideas is that of operationalizing CRE practices by using selected steps and activities in the SEP. Armed with a practice-relevant definition of culture and an understanding of the relationship between systems heuristics and CRE principles, we review selected SEP steps and activities which lend themselves to CRE practice. For a comprehensive review of the SEP, please refer to *The Guide to the Systems Evaluation Protocol: Phase I Planning* (CORE, 2012) in its entirety.

The Preparation Stage

The SEP begins with the preparation stage of an evaluation (see Table 2.1). In this initial step, an evaluator enters the evaluation or program system, creates a Memorandum of Understanding describing the scope of the work and an agreement on expectations, and makes general assessments regarding history and capacity for evaluation within an organization.

The preparation stage is of particular importance to culturally responsive evaluators. This is evident in the most comprehensive articulation on how to implement a culturally responsive evaluation approach to date, "A Guide to Conducting Culturally Responsive Evaluations" (Frierson, Hood, Hughes, & Thomas, 2010). Table 2.2 provides a compilation of typical evaluation activities as may be present in any basic evaluation approach and enriched further by suggested activities in the Frierson et al. (2010) chapter. It is apparent that in preparation for an evaluation, culturally responsive evaluators engage in many activities to learn about and attend to cultural and contextual factors of an evaluation. How this is achieved, though, varies substantially among professionals, and for some professionals, remains

TABLE 2.1 Summary of SEP Stages, Steps, and Activities

Preparation Stage		Modeling Stage		Evaluation Development Stage	
Steps	**Activities**	**Steps**	**Activities**	**Steps**	**Activities**
Create a shared understanding of expectations	Introductory presentation	Stakeholder analysis	Launch Meeting (includes a variety of activities related to each of these steps)	Introduce evaluation plan	Question-Claim Match-Up, Stakeholder Review
Assess capacity	Complete Evaluation Capacity checklist	Program review	Stakeholder affinity diagram	Develop evaluation questions	Peer evaluation plan brainstorm
		Program boundary analysis	Program history	Develop sampling plan	Finalize evaluation plan
		Lifecycle analysis	Evaluation history	Identify or develop measures	
		Initial logic model draft	Lifecycle alignment review	Develop evaluation design	
		Pathway model	Logic and pathway model peer review	Develop analysis plan	
		Program system links	Mining the model: Parts 1 & 2	Develop evaluation reporting plan	
		Evaluation scope	Stakeholder interview	Develop evaluation Schedule/ implementation plan	
		Program/Logic model synthesis		Finalize evaluation plan	

Note: Adapted from Trochim et al. (2012), *The Guide to the System Evaluation Protocol.*

TABLE 2.2   Basic and Culturally Specific Activities in Evaluation Planning

Typical Evaluation Activities	Culturally Responsive Activities
Prepare for evaluation	Analyze context
	Explore communication styles
	Consensus on evaluation purpose
	Assemble evaluation team
	Acquire foundational knowledge
Identify purpose of the evaluation	Process evaluation
	Progress evaluation
	Summative evaluation
Frame the right questions	Determine appropriate type of evidenc
	Critically question evaluation questions
Design evaluation	Identify appropriate design
Select/Adapt instruments	Decide to identify, develop, and/or adapt existing measures
	Pilot test for appropriateness to population
	Translate when necessary

a mystery. We offer an interpretation of how these CRE behaviors may be realized as an evaluator progresses through steps of the Preparation stage in the SEP.

Enter the system.

Every evaluation begins with the introduction of an evaluator to the program he/she will evaluate. In the SEP, entering the evaluation system is about the interpersonal introductions that must take place between evaluator(s) and program representatives. For the culturally responsive evaluator, entering the evaluation system also requires becoming acquainted with the social and cultural context of an evaluation, especially if the context is an unfamiliar one. Since a culturally situated program is embedded in socially relevant systems and not just in an organizational system, entering the social system requires researching and learning about the cultural group and community that the program targets. It also requires a certain amount of reflexivity on behalf of a professional negotiating a relationship and program context. Guidance on how to enter the system is limited within the SEP, but well informed by the extant literature on CRE. Whereas the SEP may describe simple introductions among colleagues, other CRE practices encourage identifying and then learning about the cultural group with whom an evaluator will be working, for example, through a key informant. When using the SEP, activities that CRE professionals engage in early on are appropriate at later stages of the evaluation.

For example, an important activity upon entering the evaluation system involves an assessment for capacity within the organization and the program. The Organization Evaluation Capacity Checklist in the SEP can be used to assess an organization's capacity to enact CRE principles by including relevant items on the checklist. For example, a resources question such as, Do you currently have staff who are versed in the cultural characteristics of the target population or who have shared lived experiences with the target population? could be included. An important training question would be, Do you have regular cultural competency trainings? or What methods does your organization utilize to access cultural knowledge relevant to the target population? Relevant to evaluation policies, one might ask, Does your organization implement any specific policies for working with diverse populations? When integrating such questions, the facilitating evaluator should provide guidance and explanations of what each question is intending to elicit for the context of the program in question.

Responses to the Organization Evaluation Capacity Checklist not only demonstrate an organization's capacity to conduct an evaluation, but by including additional suggested questions can also determine an organization's capacity to conduct a *culturally responsive* evaluation. By knowing what resources, training, and policies are available to a program, an evaluator can make decisions about how to include diversity in the evaluation process moving forward, how to engage stakeholders who have a cultural stake in planning, how to learn further about the cultural context of the program, and more. For example, *building trust* and *facilitating communication through inclusion of diversity* can be achieved through the use of a cultural informant or by hiring multicultural staff. The capacity assessment may reveal that the option to hire multicultural staff is feasible and desirable as compared to communicating with a cultural informant.

Create MOU.

The second major step identified in the SEP involves creation of a Memorandum of Understanding (MOU). Each component of the MOU should be considered from a culturally responsive perspective insofar as it is possible to do so. For instance, in outlining evaluation project goals, evaluators and program representatives that inform the MOU process should go out of their way to identify perspectives that may be traditionally overlooked and consider what the goals of the evaluation may be from those perspectives as well. Additionally, the composition of the evaluation partnership working group needs to be representative of multiple perspectives. To date, the typical working group in implementation of the SEP has been composed of program staff and administrators. From a CRE perspective, important members of the community with a stake in the program should also be invited to participate. When considering the costs and budget within the MOU, evaluators and program representatives should also factor in a budget for cultural-competence training or other culturally responsive activities. For instance, if the evaluator will engage with community members through a cultural event, budget should be planned accordingly.

The Modeling Stage

The Modeling Stage within the SEP represents the bulk of collaborative activity among evaluator(s) and program staff, administrators, and/or stakeholders and therefore holds the most potential for realizing CRE practice. This stage consists of several steps and activities that culminate in a draft-logic model and pathway model for a given program. Traditionally, most activities presented in this stage (see Table 2.1) are included in a 2–3 day workshop or planning meeting referred to as the Launch Meeting. Though there is flexibility in how the launch meeting is implemented, it is not necessary to complete all suggested activities during this one meeting. In this chapter, each step is addressed individually and whether steps and activities are grouped into a Launch Meeting is left to individual practitioners. However, they are often discussed in the context of group work that would take place as such a meeting.

Evaluation Cafe.

The Evaluation Cafe is an activity designed to develop a definition of evaluation. It is also a good opportunity for the working group to voice concerns or apprehensions regarding evaluation. In the SEP, this activity is suggested through the use of prompts which group members answer in small groups and then share out to the workshop at-large. From a culturally responsive perspective, we suggest using a prompt to encourage thinking about the cultural context of the evaluation. Some social groups may have less than positive perspectives and experiences with evaluation in their communities, so this activity provides opportunity to surface what those apprehensions may be and how they are positioned in stakeholders' culture. The SEP, as most evaluation methodologies, includes an assessment of evaluation capacity in the preparation stage. In the SEP, this assessment is conducted with a formal checklist of resources, training, information technology resources, and evaluation policy components (CORE, 2012). As part of the CRE principle related to building trust and communication, practitioners suggest building diversity of the evaluation team and accessing diversity from external sources.

Boundary analysis.

Another activity in the systems-evaluation protocol is a boundary analysis, which is related to the system concept of identifying boundaries of system components and the system itself. This is a facilitated discussion in which program staff make decisions about what activities or components define the program in question and which are "outside" of program boundaries. In this way, the SEP facilitates a "birds-eye view" perspective of the program in context while clarifying the defining components of a system. However, this activity does not explicitly focus on the cultural system(s) in which a program may be embedded. This exercise can be expanded to address CRE principles related to understanding the cultural context of a program and its participants. From Casillas and Trochim (in preparation.), the principle of *understand(ing) cultural context* is expanded to include being aware of cultural labels and histories, understanding possible inaccuracies of those labels, and learning about the participant group. A boundary analysis activity, guided by these principles, can facilitate an exploration of program staff knowledge and attitudes related to the program target population. It can also lead evaluators and program staff through a decision-making process about which cultural characteristics are relevant to the evaluation.

Evaluators would begin, simply, by drawing a large circle on a whiteboard or chalkboard. Much like in the original SEP methodology, this circle will represent the program and its boundaries. Then the staff and evaluators would work together to create a list of all the characteristics of this participant population, such as age, gender, socioeconomic position, racial/ethnic identification, and anything else that may be relevant to the group. Additionally, discussion about what is believed to be true about these characteristics would be added to the list, for example, *our population is an immigrant Asian population and may speak a language other than English or is bilingual.* Ideally, a multicultural evaluation staff will facilitate discussion about which cultural characteristics are accurate or inaccurate while also making decisions about which of these characteristics belong inside the circle and which belong outside. Characteristics placed inside the program circle, or the program boundary, are those that the group decides are likely to have the most impact on the program and its evaluation. Other items of potential impact but less importance for the current evaluation scope could be listed outside of the circle and marked with an asterisk for future discussion or consideration. Such an exercise allows for the systematic exploration the groups' assumptions about the cultural context of the evaluation and brings individuals into agreement about what considerations are important.

Stakeholder affinity diagram.

In a systems approach to evaluation, multiple stakeholders at varying levels of a system represent multiple perspectives from different positions in the system hierarchy, which can translate into various program goals, diverse ideas about program implementation, and disagreements or misunderstandings in general (Trochim et al., 2012). Thus, an important step in a systems evaluation is identifying various stakeholders and locating their position in the system relative to the program. The CRE principle *engage stakeholders in general* resonates with this SEP goal in that stakeholders must first be identified before they can be engaged. In the SEP, identifying and locating stakeholders is achieved by constructing a *stakeholder map*. In order to bring this CRE principle into alignment with SEP methodologies, the stakeholder-analysis activity needs to be expanded to identify stakeholders who represent the intersection of stake in the program and stake in the cultural context of the program.

In a stakeholder map, a program is represented as the center in a diagram surrounded by other increasingly larger circles, appearing similar to a target. Program staff and evaluators work together to generate a list of possible stakeholders and place them at various levels of the map. Stakeholders central to the evaluation or program are placed proximal to the program center and stakeholders with less stake are placed distal to the program center. Culturally responsive evaluators must encourage participants to decide which stakeholders are culturally relevant to a program and place them on the map as well. For instance, perhaps a given program is targeted to middle school students and is a single-site program. Students are placed central to the program on the stakeholder map. The program may not be targeted to the family of students, though they generally influence how a student performs in a program, so family is placed on the periphery of the stakeholder map. However, perhaps family is a particularly prevalent value in the surrounding community, which leads mothers to regularly be present at program activities even if they do not participate in any particular way. The presence of mothers at program activities could affect program outcomes, and neglecting to consider the cultural value of *family* would result in placing "family" further away from the program center on the map. At a later stage in the evaluation, having identified mothers as central to the program could lead to a valuable data collection opportunity. Thus, when facilitating a stakeholder analysis, evaluators must challenge program staff to think about the roles stakeholders may play from a culturally accurate perspective and not just from a program perspective.

Each of these Preparation and Modeling Stage steps, when properly examined from a culturally responsive perspective, is key to informing the products of these stages: the Logic and Pathway Models. Most logic models, which portray the underlying logic of a program, contain some space for "context" or contextual factors drawn as an arrow that follows across the entirety of the model. The approach described herein, by in-depth discussion and guided consideration and diagramming of cultural issues, can better inform this space in a logic model. Creating an increased focus on culture with these activities may dimensionalize *culture* and *context* in the minds or professionals beyond the limited representation of an arrow under a logic model diagram.

The Guide to the SEP was used as an illustrative example of how a professional may take existing methodologies and protocols, apply a philosophical understanding of CRE principles, and create a relevant and pragmatic CRE practice. This text, however, is not a comprehensive guide for all the ways in which steps in the SEP can be made actionable, as that is beyond the scope of the current goal. Instead, this chapter offers an example of how theoretically grounded approaches, like systems approaches, that have an existing guide or protocol for practice, like the SEP, can be used to operationalize the sometimes vague principles of CRE practice.

CONCLUSIONS

Noteworthy efforts of evaluators arguing for culturally responsive approaches have successfully led professionals and researchers to seek innovative and appropriate ways of practicing CRE. The work of evaluators such as Frierson et al. (2010) represents a much needed step toward organizing a cohesive vision of CRE practice and provides an important foundation on which to anchor other approaches. However, there is a great deal of flexibility in how evaluators may choose to implement CRE and little guidance on how to access and best use the inherent flexibility of culturally responsive approaches. As such, we reviewed another malleable approach, systems thinking in evaluation, which fits well with CRE theory, and expanded upon the potentiated utility of both frameworks when used in conjunction. Though this is an imperfect marriage, it illustrates the potential for developing methodological approaches with pragmatic suggestions for implementing CRE practice moving forward.

REFERENCES

American Evaluation Association. (2011). *American Evaluation Association public statement on cultural competence in evaluation.* Fairhaven, MA: Author. Retrieved from www.eval.org.

Bronfenbrenner, U. (1994). Ecological models of human development. In M. Gauvain, & M. Cole, (Eds.), *Readings on the development of children* (2nd ed., pp. 37–43). New York, NY: Freeman.

Casillas, W., & Trochim, W. M. (in preparation). *Addressing diversity in STEM program planning, immplementation, and evaluation.*

Chouinard, J. A., & Cousins, J. B. (2009). A review and synthesis of current research on cross-cultural evaluation. *American Journal of Evaluation, 30*(4), 457–494.

Cole, M. (1996). *Cultural psychology: A once and future discipline*. Cambridge, MA: Belknap Press of Harvard University Press.

Cornell Office for Research on Evaluation. (2012). *The guide to the systems evaluation protocol* (V2.2.). Ithaca, NY.

Fredericks, K. A., Deegan, M., & Carman, J. G. (2008). Using system dynamics as an evaluation tool: Experience from a demonstration program. *American Journal of Evaluation, 29*(3), 251–267.

Frierson, H., Hood, S., Hughes, G., & Thomas, V. (2010). A guide to conducting culturally responsive evaluation. National Science Foundation. *The 2010 user-friendly handbook for project evaluation*. National Science Foundation, Director-ate for Education and Human Resources.

Frierson, H., Hood, S., Hughes, G., & Thomas, V. (2010). *A guide to conducting cultur-ally responsive evaluations*. In J. Frechtling (Ed.), *The 2002 user-friendly handbook for project evaluation*. Arlington, VA: NSF.

Gay, G. (2002). Preparing for culturally responsive teaching. *Journal of Teacher Edu-cation, 53*(2), 106–116.

Heine, S. J. (2008). *Cultural psychology*. New York, NY: Norton.

Hopson, R. K. (2009). Reclaiming knowledge at the margins: Culturally respon-sive evaluation in the current evaluation moment. In K. Ryan & J. B. Cousins (Eds.), *The Sage international handbook of educational evaluation* (pp. 431–448). Thousand Oaks, CA: Sage.

Kirkhart, K. E. (2010). Eyes on the prize: Multicultural validity and evaluation theo-ry. *American Journal of Evaluation, 31*(3), 400–413.

Kreuter, M. W., & McClure, S. M. (2004). The role of culture in health communica-tion. *Annual Review of Public Health, 25,* 439–455.

Kroeber, A. L., & Kluckhohn, C. (1952). *Culture: A critical review of concepts and definitions*. Papers. Peabody Museum of Archaeology & Ethnology, Harvard University,

Lee, C. C. (2001). Culturally responsive school counselors and programs: Address-ing the needs of all students. *Professional School Counseling, 4*(4), 257–261.

Lewis, M. D. (2000). The promise of dynamic systems approaches for an integrated account of human development. *Child Development, 71*(1), 36–43.

Madison, A. (1992). Primary inclusion of culturally diverse minority program par-ticipants in the evaluation process. *New Directions for Program Evaluation, 1992*(53), 35–43.

Manswell-Butty, J. L., Reid, M. D., & LaPoint, V. (2004). A culturally responsive eval-uation approach applied to the talent development school-to-career interven-tion program. *New Directions for Evaluation, 2004*(101), 37–47.

Matsumoto, D. R., & Juang, L. P. (2013). *Culture and psychology*. Belmont, CA: Wad-sworth Cengage Learning.

Mertens, D. M. (2009). *Research and evaluation in education and psychology: Integrating diversity with quantitative, qualitative, and mixed methods*. Thousand Oaks, CA: Sage.

Midgley, G. (2003). Systemic intervention: Philosophy, methodology, and practice. *Journal of Community and Applied Psychology, 13*(4), 330–333.

Parekh, B. C. (2006). *Rethinking multiculturalism: Cultural diversity and political theory* (2nd ed.). Basingstoke, UK: Palgrave Macmillan.

SenGupta, S., Hopson, R., & Thompson-Robinson, M. (2004). Cultural competence in evaluation: An overview. *New Directions for Evaluation, 2004*(102), 5–19.

Thelen, E., Smith, L. B., Karmiloff-Smith, A., & Johnson, M. H. (1994). *A dynamic systems approach to the development of cognition and action.* Cambridge, MA: MIT Press.

Thomas, S. B., Fine, M. J., & Ibrahim, S. A. (2004). Health disparities: The importance of culture and health communication. *American Journal of Public Health, 94*(12), 2050.

Trochim, W. M., Urban, J. B., Hargraves, M., Hebbard, C., Buckley, J., Archibald, T., … Burgermaster, M. (2012). *The guide to the systems evaluation protocol* (Vol. 2). Ithaca, NY: Cornell Digital.

Williams, B., & Hummelbrunner, R. (2010). *Systems concepts in action: A practitioner's toolkit.* Stanford, CA: Stanford University Press.

CHAPTER 3

CULTURAL VIEWS OF VALIDITY

A Conversation

Joan LaFrance, Karen E. Kirkhart, and Richard Nichols

INTRODUCTION[1]

Collaboration among the coauthors of this chapter began in 2004 when Karen Kirkhart was invited to serve as a consultant to a National Science Foundation (NSF) grant to the American Indian Higher Education Consortium (AIHEC). The grant supported the development of an Indigenous Evaluation Framework (IEF) by Joan LaFrance and Richard Nichols.[2] At the beginning of the project to develop the IEF, the NSF recommended that AIHEC engage an evaluation theorist with the suggestion that it would be useful to the evaluation profession to understand how an Indigenous perspective contributes to Western evaluation theory. Over the years, the authors have engaged in conversations about ways in which culture itself, and an Indigenous cultural lens in particular, influences views on evaluation theory.

In this chapter, we share our exploration of culture and Western evaluation notions of validity. Our conversation was spurred by Karen's question to Richard and Joan regarding the role or placement of validity within the

Continuing the Journey to Reposition Culture and Cultural Context in Evaluation Theory and Practice, pages 49–72
Copyright © 2015 by Information Age Publishing

IEF. Given her work in proposing a theory of multicultural validity, she was especially interested in how the creators of the IEF viewed validity. Since the IEF does not address validity directly, the question generated our exploration of ways in which validity is addressed in the literature and how the notion of validity fits within an Indigenous cultural framework. This exploration was guided by the following questions: What is the role of culture in conversations about validity? and Is "validity" a relevant concept for Indigenous inquiry? What is the role of validity within the IEF? We also explored the ways in which our conversations and collaborations have influenced our own views of validity in evaluation practice, specifically the contributions to Karen's theory of multicultural validity and Joan and Richard's views on the relevance of validity to the IEF.

Our intent in this chapter is to expand the construct of validity by exploring how it is approached from within Indigenous epistemology through Joan and Richard's discussions with Elders who are members of their respective tribes. Our collaboration continues to mold and reshape appreciations of validity. Reflections on Indigenous epistemology and on IEF in particular have led to shifts in how the construct of multicultural validity (Kirkhart, 1995, 2005, 2013) is understood and portrayed. IEF both affirms and expands the construct of multicultural validity and its justifications; it also reveals limitations.

We conclude with a discussion of the value of positioning culture as central to our work as evaluators and the importance of probing further into the cultural expressions of how "trustworthiness" or "correctness" is expressed within different tribal languages. Our intent is not to press for a singular viewpoint but to open a conversation that engages the assumptions and values from multiple perspectives. With that in mind, we have indicated the conversations we have had by noting our names next to the sections in which we took a lead role in sharing information or views.

WHAT IS THE ROLE OF CULTURE IN CONVERSATIONS ABOUT VALIDITY? (KAREN)

Culture and Validity

Our conversation is grounded in the assumption that validity must be fundamentally understood as a cultural construction (Johnson, Kirkhart, Madison, Noley, & Solano-Flores, 2008; Kirkhart, 2005; Kvale, 1995). Citing Cronbach, Johnson et al. (2008) remind us that all constructs are cultural products. It follows that it is necessary to note both the location and boundaries of those constructions. Neither validity nor validation carries the same meaning across cultural contexts (Kirkhart, 2005). Kvale (1995) addresses linguistic boundaries of validity in noting that as a psychology student in Norway, "the very terms *validity* and *reliability* did not belong to the Norwegian vernacular, but were some foreign English-Latin terms" (p. 20; emphasis in the original).[3] Cultural location is not neutral with respect to the exercise of power. Historically, validity has been situated within the social history and culture of dominant groups, such that the legitimizing function of validity, discussed below, reflects and reinforces that social history and power, with negative consequences for persons in nondominant groups. (Scheurich & Young [1997] make this point eloquently with respect to race and racism.)

Validity has long been contested space. Efforts to redefine or reposition validity are not new. Conversations have been percolating over several decades. (See, for example, Argyris, 1968; Campbell, 1979, 1986; Chen, 2010; Cronbach, 1980, 1988; House, 1980; Kane, 1992, 2003; Lather, 1986, 1993, 2001; Lissitz, 2009; Messick, 1989, 1995; Moss, 1995, 2005a, 2005b; Scheurich, 1996; Shepard, 1993; Thomas, 2006.) However, culture has not always been part of these conversations nor has inclusion been their motivation. While assumptions of "culture-free" testing have long been abandoned by measurement specialists (Haertel, 2013), meaningful inclusion of culture in validation has not consistently followed. This concern notwithstanding, culture has been explicitly included in perspectives on validity emerging from critical race theory (e.g., Scheurich, 1996; Stanfield, 2011; Zuberi & Bonilla-Silva, 2008), feminist theory (e.g., Collins, 1991; Haraway, 1988; Lather, 1986, 1993, 2001), measurement theory (e.g., Moss, 1998; Shepard, 1997), and clinical assessment (Ridley, Tracy, Pruitt-Stephens, Wimsatt, & Beard, 2008).

Throughout validity discussions, differences emerge on its core definition: Is validity best understood as a single unified construct or as composed of different distinct subtypes? Scholars from different epistemological positions have defined validity by dividing it. Maxwell (1992) subdivides it by type of understanding (descriptive validity, interpretive validity, theoretical validity, generalizability, evaluative validity) as does Lather (1993; ironic validity, paralogical validity, rhizomatic validity, voluptuous validity). Shadish, Cook, and Campbell (2002) propose four types of validity: statistical conclusion validity, internal validity, construct validity, external validity. Brinberg and McGrath (1985) propose a Validity Network Schema (VNS), which maps the relations of different aspects of validity to different phases of the research process. VNS groups "validities" (p. 23) by stages: validity as value, validity as correspondence, and validity as robustness. Cronbach (1988) and Messick (1989, 1995) came to reject an emphasis on validity "types" in favor of a unified validity theory, seeing previously named "types" of validity as "strands within a cable of validity argument" (Cronbach, 1988, p. 4). Cronbach (1988) spoke instead of different perspectives from which validity can be argued, foreshadowing our attention to justifications of multicultural validity, discussed below.

Given that validity is culturally located, how useful is it in diverse contexts of evaluation? Or, expressed in the inverse, is validity so inextricably tied to majority perspectives that it is implicitly a privileged imposition, an appropriation, a "colonization" (Smith, 2012) of local understandings? To address this question first requires an understanding of how validity has been invested with power to recognize and legitimate.

Validation and Legitimation: Inclusion or Exclusion?

Validity is recognized as occupying a position of privilege as an affirmation of good inquiry. Intersecting culture, which itself is not neutral but infused with both privilege and discrimination, validity stands as a powerful gatekeeper of whose ideas, methods, and worldviews are recognized as legitimate. Validity carries cultural authority, owing to the power that we have invested in the construct. Validation is used to inform but also to legitimate, regulate, and control (House, 1993).

> Validity holds authority in systems of inquiry—both research and evaluation. It signifies power and control over the legitimation and representation of knowledge (Bishop, 1998), which is contested space in decolonization. Who determines what is valid and invalid, legitimate and illegitimate? What is given heavy consideration and what is discounted? (Hopson, Kirkhart, & Bledsoe, 2012, pp. 65–66)

Scheurich (1996) argues that the different types of validity discussed above are actually masks concealing an underlying sameness, which resides in the exercise of power to set a boundary line between acceptable and unacceptable research. He asserts that "validity boundaries are always ideological power alignments. They always create insiders and outsiders" (p. 53). Recognizing the capacity of validity to selectively delegitimize worldviews, ways of knowing, and methods of inquiry even as it affirms others, one must exert caution in setting definitional boundaries (Johnson et al., 2008). It is important to move across epistemologies to open conversations about validity to cultural perspectives appropriate to the context at hand. The capacity to include multiple worldviews may be seen as a criterion of the validity of validity itself (Kirkhart, 2005, Kvale, 1995). However, if validity is broadened to include everything, it becomes nothing—it is no longer a useful construct. Therefore, one must be clear, not sloppy, about definitions and rationale, avoiding "flabby pluralism" (Bernstein, 1992, as cited in Moss et al., 2009). This chapter pushes the boundaries of validity by examining its role in contexts of Indigenous inquiry and evaluation.

IS VALIDITY A RELEVANT CONCEPT FOR INDIGENOUS INQUIRY? (RICHARD AND JOAN)

The IEF grew out of an extensive consultation with American Indian evaluators, educators, and cultural experts. Although it does not reject Western evaluation practice, the framework places evaluation within Indigenous epistemology and core values. In developing the IEF, we were guided by an understanding that an Indigenous framing could incorporate broadly held values while remaining flexible and responsive to local traditions and cultures. The framework is illustrated in Figure 3.1.

Indigenous epistemology is founded on the traditions of a people, their creation stories, clan origins, and their oral record of encounters with the world. It also includes empirical knowledge and knowledge that is acquired through dreams, visions, and ceremonies. Core values acknowledge that Indigenous peoples are located in a specific place, that community and family are paramount, and there is a deep respect for the gifts of each member of the community. A value central to Indigenous peoples is sovereignty, which is expressed politically and through preservations of language and culture.

Figure 3.1 Indigenous Evaluation Model.

The IEF suggests a process by which tribal colleges and communities can use their own ways of knowing and core values to guide their evaluation practices. It does not discuss validity or the role of this concept within an Indigenous epistemology. From a Western perspective, validity is an aspiration that guides methodology. From an Indigenous perspective, it is difficult to separate out validity from methodology and, in fact, the Indigenous Evaluation Framework doesn't address validity as separate from process.

Indigenous Perceptions: Honoring the Talk

Although the IEF establishes a general framing of an Indigenous way of knowing or epistemology, it recommends that the ways of knowing be guided by specific tribal constructs expressed within a tribal language. We explored the concepts of "validity" within our own tribal contexts through a series of discussions with Tewa and Ojibwe Elders and native language speakers.[4] In so doing, our goal was to gain their sense of how one would describe the ideas of "correctness" or being able to trust the information one is learning. It is important to note that in both tribal languages, there is no literal translation for a Western term like validity. Truth or correctness is related to the discussion; it is through the action of speaking together that the truth is known.

In Tewa, the cultural protocol most appropriate when beginning the discussion is the offering of a traditional prayer to mark the seriousness of the conversation about to take place. As a Tewa language expert at Santa Clara Pueblo noted, "I've heard people say that they were discussing something so that the truth will come out: '*Heranho I' ta'ge na pii-iri*.'" This word, *ta'ge* (the truth) and its variants *ta'gendi* (true), *ta'gen dan*—the emphasizer "an" is used to say "that's true"—are the most equivalent Tewa terms to get at the sense of validity in the evaluation sense. Interestingly, another meaning for *ta'ge* is "straight," as in drawing a straight line, plowing a straight row, or a carpenter making a straight cut. This incidental meaning indicates the value put on getting something straight, which supports using *ta'ge* as the Tewa equivalent of validity.

In other discussions with the Tewa speakers at Santa Clara Pueblo, there was another word, *kori* (correct) and *korindi* (something is correct or right), that we considered as also getting at the concept of validity. However, put in the context of having discussions to come to a conclusion that something is valid—*Heranho I' kori na pii-iri*—it didn't "sound right," as the Tewa elder noted. Again, interestingly, *kori* used as a verb, also means "to fix" or "to make correct."

In the Ojibwe tradition, tobacco is used to honor the speaker and establish the importance of what is to be discussed. To understand how to approach the concept of validity, tobacco was offered in discussions with two

Ojibwe elders.[5] In an initial Elder discussion, the term *apaenimoowin* which means "to trust, count on or to put confidence in it" (Johnston, 2007, p. 57), was chosen as the best way to convey a notion of trusting that the information shared is correct. Another expression is *apaenimoondaugaewin*. This word expresses an engagement with the speaker and stresses the importance of listening. One Elder explained that *imoon* connotes paying attention to the sound of the voice; *daugaewin* is the sound of the voice which is coming to you. It is important to listen mindfully to hear the speaker who is giving information that you can have confidence or trust it. Listening mindfully is not a passive act; rather, the listener engages in discussion to fully understand the speaker. It is through a relational engagement that the listener can trust what the speaker is conveying. Johnston (2007) describes the Ojibwe word *gawakeinaendumoowin* as meaning truth, certitude, correctness, which he notes means literally "the right mind." However, in the Elder discussion, the preferred word to use for the construct was *apaenimoowin*.

The discussions with the Tewa and Ojibwe Elders reinforce the notion that "validity" emerges when attention is given to doing things in the correct way. It is an understanding that "truth will come out" through talking together. Kovach (2009), a Cree scholar, emphasizes the centrality of relationship within Indigenous research methodology, noting that Indigenous knowledges can never be standardized for "they are in relation to place and person" (p. 56). Relationship with the place or context informs the necessary protocols and ethics related to doing research or evaluation. This same notion of relationship is captured by Wilson's (2008) "relational accountability." He describes the essence of this accountability as research within a community context which is respectful, responsible, and has reciprocity. In his book, *Research is Ceremony*, Wilson (2008) uses a dialectic mode, a conversation, to illustrate the principles of his view of an Indigenous research paradigm. In one of the dialogues with fellow Indigenous scholars, he explains that

> Studies conducted by some researcher on an Indigenous topic may successfully meet the criteria by which dominant system research is judged, such as validity and reliability. . . . But if the researcher is separated from the research and it is taken away from its relationships, it will not be accepted within the Indigenous paradigm. . . . Rather than the goals of validity and reliability, research from an Indigenous paradigm should aim to be authentic or credible. . . . The research must accurately reflect and build upon the relationships between the ideas and participants. The analysis must be true to the voices of all the participants and reflect an understanding of the topic that is shared by research and participants alike. In other words, it has to hold to relational accountability. (pp. 101–102)

These notions of relational accountability, or what constitutes authenticity, are central to the IEF. The framework attempts to shift the focus of evaluation toward responsiveness to tribal values and community needs. The IEF suggests ways to choose methods and processes that create a credible relationship between evaluation (and the evaluators), the program implementers, those served by a program, and the contextual setting of the community. The evaluation and implementation of program are intertwined, interrelated. The truth emerges through a relationship between the evaluator, stakeholders, participants, and the utility of the evaluation to the community.

The suggestion of the elders that truth emerges through the talking fits within the Indigenous focus on storytelling. The IEF notes that Indigenous evaluation is a form of storytelling—creating the means through which a program can be understood in its own context through capturing the experience of those involved and analyzing the lessons learned. Kovach explains that "The privileging of story in knowledge-seeking systems means honouring 'the talk.' To provide openings for narrative, Indigenous researchers use a variety of methods, such as conversations, interviews, and research/sharing circles" (2009, p. 99). Regarding validity, Kovach notes,

> Inevitably, the personal nature of a story will bring to light questions about the legitimacy of knowledge. Does relationship imply subjectivity? Does subjectivity contaminate evidence of "real" knowledge? In Western research, this is about the validity of research. Knowledge then becomes that which can be proven true. (p. 102)

Kovach cites Stevenson's (2000, p. 249) work with Cree knowledge holders and the use of tobacco as a reciprocal gift ensuring "to speak from the heart, to speak their truth." And she cites how, in her own research practice, "the exchange of tobacco signified that what was spoken was truth as each person knew it." This mutual belief in another's integrity leads to maintaining relational balance. "If relational balance is not a high cultural value, such methods of 'validity' will fall flat" (p. 103).

In the Indigenous Evaluation Framework, we emphasize similar holistic, less structured discussions for data gathering as well as using cultural protocols to set the conversation "in a good place." Methodologically, then, it is also important in Santa Clara and Ojibwe traditions to gather oral information and to get as many perspectives as possible. When evaluators use discussion as a prime method for data collection, they must trust the content of the discussions to be valid. The use of cultural protocols is important to set the discussion in the right place. It is through this process that evaluators understand the truths as expressed by those with whom they are speaking. When things are done the "right way," the program's story as it develops during the evaluation process can be trusted. In this sense, validity is discovered along the way.

The Indigenous Evaluation Framework emphasizes the use of mixed methods for gaining useful information. Although quantitative measures are often necessary and not discouraged in the IEF, they need to be complemented by the relational act of conversation to fully understand the program's story. This relationship also necessitates communicating the analysis in multiple formats to ensure the lessons learned are of value to the community.

THE INFLUENCE OF OUR COLLABORATIONS (JOAN, RICHARD, AND KAREN)

Over the years, we have gained understandings and deepened our thinking through our collaborations and conversations. Karen has adapted her thinking about multicultural validity, and Richard and Joan have reflected on the influence of multicultural validity on their view of the IEF and evaluation in Indian communities. Our exploration of the questions posed in the conversations leading to this chapter have also had an influence on our perspectives of the roles and limitations of the Western notion of validity. We discuss these in this section with our voices noted in the subtitles.

Multicultural Validity: Origins and Evolutions (Karen)

Before I explain how my collaboration with Joan and Richard has molded my understanding of validity, I need to tell the story of how the idea of multicultural validity came to be and continued to grow. Multicultural validity emerged from my examination of validity and culture, specifically the variety of ways in which validity is argued or justified. I first proposed multicultural validity against a backdrop of societal relevance, historical tradition, and social justice, with particular emphasis on social justice (Kirkhart, 1995).

I introduced the term *multicultural validity* at the annual meeting of the American Evaluation Association in 1994. It was defined as the accuracy and trustworthiness of understandings and actions across multiple, intersecting dimensions of cultural difference (Kirkhart, 1995). From the outset, I favored a single unified validity theory (Messick, 1995), avoiding carving validity into categories by attaching modifiers. "Multicultural" is used not to subdivide validity but to explicitly acknowledge the diversity among and within cultural dimensions and the value of examining multiple means of argument and validation. It is a "situated" validity (Lather, 2001).

In my early work, I saw multicultural validity as drawing positive and necessary attention to culture by moving it to the center of validity arguments (Kirkhart, 1995). Today, I understand multicultural validity as centering validity arguments in culture (Kirkhart, 2013). Because culture infuses *all* understandings, the emphasis on differences becomes redundant (and potentially "othering"), though standpoint theories or "epistemologies of specificity" (Carter, 2003, p. 30) have been central to my development of the construct, as discussed below. This marks a significant shift in emphasis, though my original definition continues to anchor the construct.

Working within an inclusive definition of culture, theory development proceeded both by reflecting on the cultural location of traditional majority definitions of validity (in both measurement and design) and exploring understandings of validity embedded in standpoints or perspectives of specificity. Feminist theory, critical race theory, queer theory, disability studies, aging studies, and Indigenous epistemology all contribute nuances of meaning that challenge and expand majority definitions of validity.

My conceptualization of multicultural validity is grounded in the well-articulated arguments-based approach that has evolved over the past four decades (Cronbach, 1988; Greene, 2011; Kane, 2003; Shepard, 1993). Determinations of validity are arrived at through considerations of available evidence that pair justifications supporting confidence in the accuracy of understandings and actions with opposing arguments (threats) that undermine such confidence. Theory development itself mirrored this conceptualization, moving back and forth between threats and justifications.

Justifications were originally presented as "dimensions" of validity (Kirkhart, 1995), and the first three dimensions I proposed were methodological, interpersonal, and consequential. Methodological validity referred to "the soundness or trustworthiness of understandings warranted by our methods of inquiry" (Kirkhart, 1995, p. 4), inclusive of measurement validity and design logic validity. This dimension was rooted in conceptions of validity from psychometrics and experimental design. By contrast, interpersonal validity was grounded in qualitative methods and drew attention to "the soundness or trustworthiness of understandings emanating from personal interactions" (Kirkhart, 1995, p. 4). Consequential validity called attention to "the soundness of change exerted on systems by evaluation and the extent to which those changes are just" (Kirkhart, 1995, p. 4). Attention to consequences bridges quantitative and qualitative methods and is heavily influenced by critical theory's attention to how power is exercised in evaluation.

Over the next decade, language shifted to justifications rather than dimensions, to avoid fragmenting validity. I added two more justifications to the original three (Kirkhart, 2005). I understood experiential justifications as separate from interpersonal justifications following Stanfield's 1998 AEA plenary address (Stanfield, 1999). Stanfield used the term "relevance validity" to pose the question, "Even if the design and data meet the reliability and validity standards of Campbell and Stanley (1966) or of a particular social scientific or policy-making community, *do the data fit the realities of the people it supposedly represents?*" (1999, p. 419; emphasis added). Experiential justifications of validity focus on the extent to which interpretations are, in Stanfield's words, "isomorphic with the experiences of real people" (p. 418). In the context of evaluation, this refers to "congruence with the lived experience of participants in the program and in the evaluation process" (Kirkhart, 2005, p. 23).

Theory was the fifth justification addressed, inclusive of theory underlying the program, the evaluation, and assumptions of validity itself (Kirkhart, 2005). Theory came into clearer focus as I revisited Messick's (1989) core definition of validity as "an integrated evaluative judgment of the degree to which empirical evidence and theoretical rationales support the *adequacy* and *appropriateness* of *inferences* and *actions* based on test scores or other modes of assessment" (p. 13; emphasis in the original). Theory can work for or against validity (Kirkhart, 2005). Theories themselves are culturally located and can be sources of prejudice and/or used to support same (see Haertel's [2013] example of heriditarian theory supporting IQ testing). To support validity, theory must be congruent with cultural context (Kirkhart, 2010).

As the justifications expanded, I continued to watch for corresponding threats as well (Kirkhart, 2011). Each was sharpened by juxtaposition with the other. The five justificatory perspectives are not independent of one another. They are used in concert; none is sufficient on its own. The relative weight and attention given to each justification depends on the context of use.

When I began to collaborate with Joan and Richard, I read works by Indigenous scholars and observed Richard and Joan's interactions with tribal college and community members and with members of their Advisory Board. I had many questions. Our conversations expanded my thinking and challenged my previous understandings of culture and validity. Their influence is visible in the evolution of the justifications themselves, in how multicultural validity is visually represented, and in reflections on the location of the validation process.

First, my understanding of the five justifications and connections among them has continued to evolve. While evaluation has long been understood as a social practice (Abma & Widdershoven, 2008), social relations have often been viewed within the confines of *human* interactions. Indigenous literature suggested that my focusing interpersonal justifications on interactions among people was too narrow. Indigenous epistemology makes clear that the relationships that are central to meaning-making extend beyond relationships among people (Deloria, 1999c). *Interpersonal justifications* have therefore been recast and renamed *relational justifications* (Kirkhart, 2012), to address relationships among all forms of life in the natural world, inclusive of relations among people, the land, plants, birds, and animals.

Working within the IEF also led to a new appreciation of the centrality of epistemology. *Methodological justifications* feature a growing recognition of the primacy of epistemology (Hopson et al., 2012). Although the justifications are interrelated, the early placement of epistemology under theory was problematic, potentially contributing to a disconnection and undervaluing of its foundational role in methodology. When I read Kovach's (2009) work, her placement of epistemology alongside method, under methodology resonated with me. My initial conceptualizations approached methodology more narrowly in terms of design validity and measurement validity, but Indigenous perspectives revised and expanded this justification by inextricably linking method and worldview.

The IEF framework aligns evaluation theory with Indigenous contexts, and in so doing, it stretches previously defined parameters of evaluation theory, expanding *theoretical justifications* of validity. I've always appreciated the five components of evaluation theory laid out by Shadish, Cook, and Leviton (1991) for helping the profession think clearly within and across evaluation theory. While IEF speaks to these five components—social programming, knowledge use, valuing, knowledge construction, and evaluation practice—it does so in ways that expand the dimensions themselves. For example, the social programming component as described by Shadish et al. takes social problem-solving as the central issue. The focus on social problems may have the unintended consequence of drawing attention to deficits rather than strengths. An Indigenous worldview places value on living a good and ethical life rather than correcting deficits or remediating problems. Similarly, in considering knowledge use, social betterment replaces social problem-solving as the organizing issue. In the valuing component, IEF builds upon core values—people of a place, recognizing our gifts, centrality of community and family, and sovereignty—but it also engages values in ways that differ from the vision of Shadish and colleagues. Evaluation is seen as an opportunity for learning rather than as a judgment of merit or worth, the notion of judgment having a very toxic history among Indigenous peoples, associated with exploitation, oppression, and loss.

As I discussed above, *experiential justifications* originated in concerns about accurately representing the human condition, articulated in Stanfield's (1999) concept of relevance validity. My early understandings related to people's lived experience, particularly with oppression, discrimination, or colonization. Indigenous epistemology expands the parameters of experience in terms of both time and space. Time frames are lengthened; human life is marked in generations, not decades (Deloria, 1999b). Experience includes both outward and inward space, physical and metaphysical, objective and subjective (Ermine, 1999). Dreams, visions, and prophecies and any information received from birds, animals, or plants are understood as a natural part of the human experience, rather than separating fact and experience into artificial categories (Deloria, 1999a). This was new territory for me.

Consequential justifications appeared as one of the original elements in the multicultural validity framework (Kirkhart, 1995), recognized for its connection to social justice (House, 1980, 1993) as well as to the history of social consequences considered in measurement validation (Cronbach, 1980, 1988; Messick, 1989, 1994, 1995; Moss, 1998; Shepard, 1993, 1997). Consequences are viewed in terms of impacts resulting from participation in evaluation or from actions taken based on results. Typically, the impacts in question are traced to a specific person or group of persons. Under IEF, consequences are also viewed in terms of the good of the whole—the sovereignty and well-being of the tribe or community (LaFrance & Crazy Bull, 2009; LaFrance & Nichols, 2010). Preservation or restoration of tribal traditions, cultural practices, and language are paramount (Crazy Bull, 1997). As in relational justifications, the core values of IEF draw attention beyond human concerns to include impacts on the land and environment.

Beyond enriching the particular justifications of multicultural validity, Indigenous worldviews reinforce a healthy skepticism about categories and categorization. To avoid getting "stuck" in categorical thinking, the image used to represent multicultural validity as a construct has also evolved. The previously hard-edged pentagons (Kirkhart, 2005, 2012) have been replaced by a circular representation (see Figure 3.2).[6] Validity is now

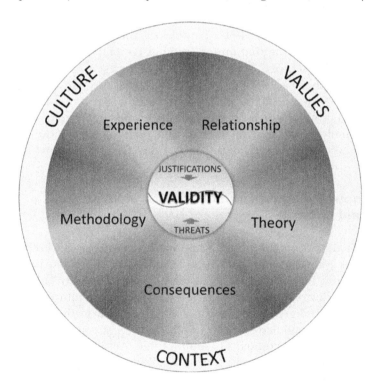

Figure 3.2 Validity, centered in culture, showing sources of justification and/or threat (Kirkhart, 2013).

centered in culture, grounded in values and context (LaFrance, Nichols, & Kirkhart, 2012). Borders among the five perspectives are intentionally softened or blurred, consistent with moving away from categorical thinking and acknowledging the interactions among the perspectives. The fluid, argument-based nature of validity is represented in the center symbol in which justifications and threats emanating from each perspective interact dynamically to support or challenge validity.

In addition to (re)shaping the conceptualization and representation of multicultural validity, Indigenous epistemology underscores attention to the location of the validation process and who is involved in it. Johnson et al. (2008) point to the cultural location of validation as a point of critique. *Where* tales are told is as important as *how* they are told (Carter, 2003). In discussing race-conscious research, Carter speaks to "the illegitimacy of the academy as the validation site" (2003, p. 34), cautioning that rules governing academic discourse may serve to protect dominant understandings and preserve traditional modes of inquiry. This is an important statement regarding how power acts through validation, but one must recognize that such critique comes from within the academy itself, thus avoiding a straw person positioning of academic scholarship in opposition to local knowledge. For example, Moss (1998) emphasizes the importance of meaning in local context, noting that understandings depend on "particular sociohistorical circumstances" (p. 7). Validation of Indigenous understandings occurs not in the academy but in the community, through community accountability (Kovach, 2009, p. 52) or relational accountability (Wilson, 2008, p. 99), both of which refer to the process through which understanding is gained—respectful, reciprocal, and relational—and the relevance and value of what is learned to the community.

Indigenous Evaluation and Multicultural Validity (Joan and Richard)

Karen's arguments for multicultural validity resonate with both of us, in our roles as evaluators and as authors of the IEF. We appreciate her groundbreaking work in creating a critical dimension for validity, one that that respects our diversity and recognizes the influence of culture. Indigenous as well as non-Indigenous evaluators need to reflect on the cultural competency of their practice and the implications of the cultural location of programs within the context of communities. We also appreciate her reconceptualization of the multicultural validity model. By grounding validity within culture and context, she mirrors our own conceptualization of an Indigenous framing where the epistemology specific to an Indigenous people and their values influences the validity of evaluation methodologies within their context. Although all of the justifications within her framework inform good practice when working in Indigenous communities, we would highlight two in particular: relational and consequential justifications.

Evaluation is at its heart a relational activity. As evaluators, we have clients and stakeholders for whom we establish relationships and contractual agreements regarding the focus of the evaluation, questions to be addressed, and the audiences for reporting. Both the Indigenous evaluation and Indigenous research frameworks are at their heart community-based, relational activities. Kovach's (2009) notion of relational balance and Wilson's (2008) relational accountability center their research work within respectful and meaningful relationship with the community The importance of respectful relationship is excellently described by Smith (2012) when she explains,

> From the indigenous perspective, ethical codes of conduct serve partly the same purpose as the protocols which govern our relationships with each other and with the environment. The term "respect" is consistently used by indigenous peoples to underscore the significance of our relationships and humanity. Through respect the place of everyone and everything in the universe is kept in balance and harmony. (p. 125)

We heard references to the importance of respectful relationships in our conversations with Tewa and Ojibwe Elders. As evaluators, attending to the dictates of the relational justification involves understanding how to "do things in the right way." Evaluators, whether Indigenous or non-Indigenous, will need to attend to the protocols important in establishing a good relationship. LaFrance (2004) suggested that those evaluators not from an Indigenous community include the time it takes to establish a proper relationship as an element of doing an evaluation. This can mean attending community dinners; or dropping in on the Elders lunch program to meet people and share food; attending feast days or other ceremonial activities; or participating in cultural activities such as powwows, canoe journeys, or rodeos. This allows the community to know the evaluator and to build relationships that are friendly and not solely based on being an evaluation expert. Indigenous evaluators follow protocols appropriate for the setting, such as the giving of tobacco or other practices that are the established customs.

Kovach (2009) outlines a framework for her research among the Cree. It involves preparations that include understanding the tribal epistemology and cultural protocols, gathering knowledge, making meaning, and giving back. We believe that to be respectful or to make meaning, at a minimum, qualitative methods have to be used. Relationship within an Indigenous evaluation context requires "listening mindfully" to a number of perspectives and allowing for multiple voices to be heard through conversation and storytelling. The "validity" of our evaluations is best described as striving to be *authentic and credible* in our retelling of the story (Wilson, 2008).

The "test" for the validity of the evaluation is best understood by the value placed on reciprocity or the giving back to the community, which brings us to the importance of Karen's consequential justification.

As noted in the IEF, Indigenous evaluation is grounded in a commitment to give back to the community This is especially important given the negative feelings of many communities who have experienced evaluations that focused only on funder priorities and failed to capture the relevancy of the local work within the context of tribal circumstances and histories. In our discussions with American Indian educators, we learned of the distrust that "evaluation" connotes when participants described their experience with evaluations that justified claims of program failures and rationales to divert resources away from tribes (LaFrance & Nichols, 2009).

Deloria (1999b) explains an Elder traditional view regarding use of knowledge. "The old Indians . . . were interested in finding the proper moral path upon which human beings should walk. All knowledge, if it is to be useful, was directed toward that goal" (pp. 43–44). Within the IEF, this belief suggests that the knowledge learned through an evaluation should be put to use and it should be celebrated, not feared or ignored. The IEF views evaluation as a reflective process that leads to learning—and learning should be acted on. The spiral of acting, reflecting, learning, moving to improved action, is continuous and positions evaluation as contributing to better or improved ways to support community well-being.

> As the story of the program unfolds, we must allow ourselves time to reflect on information we are gathering and analyzing, and to celebrate what we have learned. . . . Our reflections on what we are learning allow us to extend our knowledge and to move forward. The knowledge we have gained from our story is reason to celebrate and should be viewed as both an educational and celebratory event. (LaFrance & Nichols, 2009, p. 118)

COMING FULL CIRCLE AND CONTINUING THE CONVERSATION (KAREN, JOAN, AND RICHARD)

As Indigenous and non-Indigenous evaluators, we face a question: What have we gained from our conversation? Our reflections on this question are shared in this concluding section.

Joan and Richard: This conversation was prompted by Karen's question about the role of validity in the IEF. Since it is not directly addressed in the IEF, nor had we found any reason to address it, we needed to reflect on how to respond her query. We realized that validity was rooted in the Western traditions of research and, as graduate students, we had learned the traditional positivist classifications and the various threats to validity described by Cook and Campbell (1979). As we have become aware of different perspectives on the nature of validity through our discussions with Karen, we find some resonance with our views in the IEF. If the IEF were to embrace a position, it is perhaps in the constructivist or postmodern camp of Kvale (1995). Rejecting the notion of a universal truth, he recognizes "the possibility of specific local, personal and community forms of truth, with a focus on daily life and local narrative" (p. 21). In our experience, Indigenous evaluation is ultimately local and tribal. It is within the specific contextual circumstances of the community that the "truth" emerges.

Kvale (1995) suggests validity is found through the quality of craftsmanship, communication, and action. We would agree with these; however, within an Indigenous circle, they would take on cultural characteristics that differ somewhat from his descriptions. Craftsmanship involves the credibility of the inquirer in the eyes of the professional research and evaluation community. Such credibility is based on the quality of his or her past research and evaluations, and how well he/she maintains high standards. We would concur that the quality of the research or evaluation design, and the care taken in the questioning, interviewing, and interpretation processes are important in Indigenous evaluation. However, we would expand the craftsmanship to include the reputation of the evaluator in the Indigenous or tribal community. Professional reputation and position do not speak first; rather it is the care taken by the evaluator to respectfully establish the proper relationships and demonstrate the correct local protocols that establishes the credibility of the evaluator. It is from this base that the evaluator can participate in discussions and interviews that will lead to a credible representation of the findings in an evaluative investigation.

The notion of communicative validity also resonates (Kvale, 1995). However, in an Indigenous setting, it does not emerge from dialogue that is argumentative or continually questioning. Personal perceptions are respected and understood based on the personal experience of the speaker (Castellano, 2000). Indigenous communicative validity is a "social validity" (Castellano, 2000):

> In a council or talking circle of elders, you will not find arguments as to whose perception is more valid and therefore whose judgment should prevail. In other words, people do not contest one another to establish who is correct— who has the truth. Aboriginal societies make a distinction between perceptions, which are personal, and wisdom which has social validity and can serve as a basis for common action. Knowledge is validated through collective analysis and consensus building. (Castellano, 2000, p. 26)

The call to action, or to give back, as Kovach (2009) describes, is somewhat similar to the notion of pragmatic validity, which Kvale (1995) says goes beyond agreement reached through dialogue; it includes a commitment to act on the interpretations of the evaluation. Indigenous knowledge is focused on utility, and Indigenous evaluation places emphasis on learning and applying these lessons to enhance community health, healing, and well-being.

Although we learned how others from a Western tradition viewed validity in ways compatible to our own understandings of how it might look in the IEF, we also were compelled to explore the notions of validity within our own tribal cultures. Ultimately, the concepts and principles of Indigenous evaluation should emerge from conversations *within*, conversations that involve our own languages, which seek meanings and understandings that are molded by our own tribal worldviews. Validity is an English word, one that we learned is not easily translated into our own Native languages. Cavino (2013) argues that only when her Maori peoples have the capacity to meet their evaluation needs using their own people and through their own models, will they realize the ultimate expression of sovereignty. We would agree with this view; however, our conversations with Elders to fully understand the nature of evaluation from our own traditional cultural and linguistic experience are just beginning.

Karen: You've also introduced me to important unpublished dissertation work that is undertaking such conversations, such as that of kas aruskevich (2010), Lakota scholar Dawn Frank (2010), and Hawai'ian scholar Peter K. Hanohano, Jr. (2001). It's significant to see how this literature is building, complementing and supporting your own work.

Joan and Richard: As our capacity grows to take ownership of our own conversations within our cultural and linguistic settings, and to conduct and control our own evaluations, we will be exercising ownership and sovereignty. It is from this position that Indigenous evaluation will be fully realized. However, this is not to say that we do not benefit from conversations with our non-Indigenous colleagues nor that we would no longer need to converse. In fact, our conversations will grow richer and deeper as we understand evaluation from very different cultural worldviews—just as we are learning from Western thinkers, we can offer the field our own Native wisdom.

Karen: I look forward to our continued collaborations during the next phase of your work, *Indigenous Evaluation Framework, Research and Capacity Building.*[7] What are implications for continuing the conversation or "advancing sensible discussion" (Cronbach, 1980) within the evaluation community?

Since our collaboration has been and remains a learning experience for me, I'm perhaps most aware of what I, as a non-Indigenous evaluator, have gained from this conversation. I think my learning differs depending on whether the context of practice is Indigenous or non-Indigenous. As a non-Indigenous evaluator potentially practicing (as a member of a team) in Indigenous contexts, I have learned a greater respect for and appreciation of alternate epistemologies and a willingness to embrace a postmodern stance of not knowing. I have learned to watch and listen. Direct questioning and note-taking may be counterproductive and perceived as disrespectful, depending on the context of the conversation. I think it's also led me to slow down and not hurry to grasp at understanding. Experiences accumulate over the years, and some things will never be fully understood.

I increasingly notice and appreciate the significance of circles (Graveline, 1998) as our collaboration leads me into new Indigenous literature, then turns me around to revisit Western literature I had read quite some time ago and set aside. An example of the latter is Kvale's work, which has been central to our recent conversations, as indicated above. My early thinking on validity was also influenced by his work. This experience has made me more attentive to the value of circling back and being more patient with the process.

These lessons also carry over to my work as a non-Indigenous evaluator practicing in non-Indigenous contexts. It's led me to pay even closer attention to the cultural location of evaluation and to the dimensions of privilege that come from dominant positions. It's led me to be more aware of the edges of my competence and the limitations of my understanding. It's taught me to take the time to know the history of a place before evaluating it in the present moment.

Do these lessons ultimately speak to validity? I believe they do. They enhance the trustworthiness of our understandings and raise necessary challenges to reveal when validity is threatened.

Our conversations turn our attention reflexively back on the validity of validity, a question previously raised by Kvale (1995). In questioning the validity of the validity question itself, Kvale challenges us to "live so that we do not have to continually pose questions of validity" (p. 38). This seems congruent with "finding the proper moral and ethical road" on which to walk (Deloria, 1999b, p. 43). Ermine (1999) makes clear that this is an inward journey of connection to the Universe as well as an external one. It makes academic debates on validity seem very small in relation to the vastness of the topic.

NOTES

1. It is with great sorrow that we acknowledge Richard Nichols' passing early this year. His loss seems immense as we recall his thoughtful contributions to our writing and conversations. He is sorely missed. We dedicate this chapter to his memory.

2. National Science Foundation Grant No. REC-0438720, Carrie Billy, Principal Investigator.

3. As Thomas (2006) reminds us, the term *validity* has its origins in the Latin words *validus* (strong) and *valēre* (to be strong).

4. We want to acknowledge the tribal Elders who provided the words and helped in understanding their meanings. *Ku'daa wohaa* to Wanda Dozier, Santa Clara Pueblo Elder and Tewa Language Orthography Expert; *Chi miigwetch* to Ojibwe Elders Dr. Rosemary Christensen, who identified *apaenimoowin* as one word from the Ojibwe language that could be an approximation of the Western notion of validity and Ms. Jacqui LaValley, who further explained the meanings within the word. Another *miigwetch* to Ojibwe scholar Dr. Megan Bang, who shared her understanding of the interaction between speaker and listener to establish a truthful understanding.
5. Since the author lives a number of miles from the elders, the offering was made symbolically by voicing the offering and promising to send it with gifts via the mail.
6. Thanks to Kelly D. Lane, MSW, Syracuse, NY for creating this graphic.
7. National Science Foundation Grant No. NSF DRL 1337347, Carrie Billy, Principal Investigator.

REFERENCES

Abma, T. A., & Widdershoven, G. A. M. (2008). Evaluation and/as social relation. *Evaluation, 14*(2), 209–225. doi:10.1177/1356389007087540

Argyris, C. (1968). Some unintended consequences of rigorous research. *Psychological Bulletin, 70*(3), 185–197.

aruskevich, k. (2010). *Telling a story about Indigenous evaluation: Insights of practitioners from Australia, Canada, New Zealand, and the United States* (Unpublished doctoral dissertation). University of Hawai'i, Manoa, HI.

Brinberg, D., & McGrath, J. E. (1985). *Validity and the research process.* Newbury Park, CA: Sage.

Campbell, D. T. (1979). A tribal model of the social system vehicle carrying scientific knowledge. *Knowledge: Creation, Diffusion, Utilization, 1*(2), 181–199.

Campbell, D. T. (1986). Science's social system of validity-enhancing collective belief change and the problems of the social sciences. In D. W. Fiske & R. A. Shweder (Eds.), *Metatheory in social science: Pluralisms and subjectivities* (pp. 108–135). Chicago, IL: University of Chicago Press.

Campbell, D. T., & Stanley, J. C. (1966). *Experimental and quasi-experimental designs for research.* Chicago, IL: Rand McNally.

Carter, M. (2003). Telling tales out of school: "What's the fate of a Black story in a White world of White stories?" In G. R. López & L. Parker (Eds.), *Interrogating racism in qualitative research methodology* (pp. 29–48). New York, NY: Lang.

Castellano, M. B. (2000). Updating Aboriginal traditions of knowledge. In G. J. Sefa Dei, B. Hall, & D. G. Rosenberg (Eds.), *Indigenous knowledges in global context: Multiple readings of our world* (pp. 21–36). Toronto, ON, Canada: University of Toronto Press.

Cavino, H. M. (2013). Across the colonial divide: Conversations about evaluation in Indigenous contexts. *American Journal of Evaluation, 34*(3), 339–355.

Chen, H. T. (2010). The bottom-up approach to integrative validity: A new perspective for program evaluation. *Evaluation and Program Planning, 33*, 205–214.

Collins, P. H. (1991). *Black feminist thought: Knowledge, consciousness, and the politics of empowerment.* New York, NY: Routledge.

Cook, T. D., & Campbell, D. T. (1979). *Quasi-experimentation: Design and analysis issues for field settings.* Boston, MA: Houghton Mifflin.

Crazy Bull, C. (1997). A native conversation about research and scholarship. *Tribal College Journal of American Indian Higher Education, 9,* 17–23.

Cronbach, L. J. (1980). Validity on parole: How can we go straight? In W. B. Shrader (Ed.), *Measuring achievement: Progress over a decade. New Directions for Testing and Measurement, 5,* 99–108.

Cronbach, L. J. (1988). Five perspectives on validity argument. In H. Wainer & H. I. Braun (Eds.), *Test validity* (pp. 3–17). Hillsdale, NJ: Erlbaum.

Deloria, V., Jr. (1999a). Ethnoscience and Indian realities. In B. Deloria, K. Foehner, & S. Scinta (Eds.), *Spirit and reason: The Vine Deloria, Jr. reader* (pp. 64–71). Golden, CO: Fulcrum.

Deloria, V., Jr. (1999b). If you think about it, you will see that it is true. In B. Deloria, K. Foehner, & S. Scinta (Eds.), *Spirit and reason: The Vine Deloria, Jr. reader* (pp. 40–60). Golden, CO: Fulcrum.

Deloria, V., Jr. (1999c). Relativity, relatedness and reality. In B. Deloria, K. Foehner, & S. Scinta (Eds.), *Spirit and reason: The Vine Deloria, Jr. reader* (pp. 32–39). Golden, CO: Fulcrum.

Ermine, W. (1999). Aboriginal epistemology. In M. Battiste (Ed.), *First Nations education in Canada: The circle unfolds* (pp. 101–12). Vancouver, BC, Canada: University of British Columbia Press.

Frank, D. T. (2010). *Integrating Lakota culture and biological science into a holistic research methodology: Lakol Wico Un na Wico Han Wopasi* (Unpublished doctoral dissertation). South Dakota State University, Brookings, SD.

Graveline, F. J. (1998). *Circle works: Transforming Eurocentric consciousness.* Halifax, Nova Scotia, Canada: Fernwood.

Greene, J. (2011).The construct(ion) of validity as argument. In H. T. Chen, S. I. Donaldson, & M. M. Mark (Eds.), *Advancing validity in outcome evaluation: Theory and practice. New Directions for Evaluation, 130,* 81–91.

Haertel, E. (2013). How is testing supposed to improve schooling? *Measurement, 11,* 1–18. doi:10.1080/15366367.2013.78352

Hanohano, P. K., Jr. (2001). *Restoring the sacred circle: Education for culturally responsive Native families* (Unpublished doctoral dissertation). University of Alberta, Edmonton, Alberta, Canada.

Haraway, D. (1988). Situated knowledges: The science question in feminism and the privilege of partial perspectives. *Feminist Studies, 14*(3), 575–599.

Hopson, R. K., Kirkhart, K. E., & Bledsoe, K. B. (2012). Decolonizing evaluation in a developing world: Implications and cautions for equity-focused evaluations (EFE). In M. Segone (Ed.), *Evaluation for equitable development results* (pp. 59–82). New York, NY: UNICEF.

House, E. R. (1980). *Evaluating with validity.* Beverly Hills, CA: Sage.

House, E. R. (1993). *Professional evaluation: Social impact and political consequences.* Newbury Park, CA: Sage.

Johnson, E. C., Kirkhart, K. E., Madison, A. M., Noley, G. B., & Solano-Flores, G. (2008). The impact of narrow views of scientific rigor on evaluation practices for underrepresented groups. In N. L. Smith & P. R. Brandon (Eds.), *Fundamental issues in evaluation* (pp. 197–218). New York, NY: Guilford.

Johnston, B. H. (2007). *Anishinaubae thesaurus.* East Lansing: Michigan State University Press.

Kane, M. T. (1992). An argument-based approach to validity. *Psychological Bulletin, 112,* 527–535.

Kane, M. T. (2003). Validation. In R. L. Brennan (Ed.), *Educational measurement* (4th ed., pp. 17–64). Westport, CT: American Council on Education/Praeger.

Kirkhart, K. E. (1995). Seeking multicultural validity: A postcard from the road. *Evaluation Practice, 16*(1), 1–12.

Kirkhart, K. E. (2005). Through a cultural lens: Reflections on validity and theory in evaluation. In S. Hood, R. Hopson, & H. Frierson (Eds.), *The role of culture and cultural context: A mandate for inclusion, the discovery of truth, and understanding in evaluative theory and practice* (pp. 21–39). Greenwich, CT: Information Age.

Kirkhart, K. E. (2010). Eyes on the prize: Multicultural validity and evaluation theory. *American Journal of Evaluation, 31*(3), 400–413.

Kirkhart, K. E. (2011, May). *Missing the mark: Rethinking validity threats in evaluation practice.* Paper presented at the 34th annual conference of the Eastern Evaluation Research Society, Absecon, NJ.

Kirkhart, K. E. (2012, October). Cultural responsiveness in evaluation practice: Validity and validation. In T. B. Jones (Chair), *Conversations with senior evaluators: Wisdom about practicing in complex ecologies.* Roundtable conducted at the 26th annual conference of the American Evaluation Association, Minneapolis, MN.

Kirkhart, K. E. (2013, April). *Repositioning validity.* Plenary panel presented at the inaugural conference of the Center for Culturally Responsive Evaluation and Assessment (CREA), Chicago, IL.

Kovach, M. (2009). *Indigenous methodologies: Characteristics, conversations, and contexts.* Toronto, ON, Canada: University of Toronto Press.

Kvale, S. (1995). The social construction of validity. *Qualitative Inquiry, 1*(1), 19–40. doi:10.1177/107780049500100103

LaFrance, J. (2004). Culturally competent evaluation in Indian Country. In M. Thompson-Robinson, R. Hopson, & SenGupta (Eds.), *In search of cultural competence in evaluation: Toward principles and practices. New Directions in Evaluation, 102,* 39–50.

LaFrance, J., & Crazy Bull, C. (2009). Researching ourselves back to life: Taking control of the research agenda in Indian Country. In D. M. Mertens & P. E. Ginsberg (Eds.), *The handbook of social research ethics* (pp. 135–149). Thousand Oaks, CA: Sage.

LaFrance, J., & Nichols, R. (2009). *Indigenous Evaluation Framework: Telling our story in our place and time.* Alexandria, VA: American Indian Higher Education Consortium (AIHEC).

LaFrance, J., & Nichols, R. (2010). Reframing evaluation: Defining an Indigenous Evaluation Framework. *The Canadian Journal of Program Evaluation, 23*(2), 12–31.

LaFrance, J., Nichols, R., & Kirkhart, K. E. (2012). Culture writes the script: On the centrality of context in Indigenous evaluation. In D. J. Rog, J. L. Fitzpatrick,

& R. F. Conner (Eds.), Context: A framework for its influence on evaluation practice, *New Directions for Evaluation, 135*, 59–74.

Lather, P. (1986). Issues of validity in openly ideological research: Between a rock and a soft place. *Interchange, 17*(4), 63–84.

Lather, P. (1993). Fertile obsession: Validity after poststructuralism. *Sociological Quarterly, 34*(4), 673–693.

Lather, P. (2001). Validity as incitement to discourse: Qualitative research and the crisis of legitimation. In V. Richardson (Ed.), *Handbook of research on teaching* (4th ed., pp. 241–250). Washington, DC: American Educational Research Association.

Lissitz, R. W. (Ed.). (2009). *The concept of validity: Revisions, new direction, and applications.* Charlotte, NC: Information Age.

Maxwell, J. A. (1992). Understanding and validity in qualitative research. *Harvard Educational Review, 62*(3), 279–300.

Messick, S. (1989). Validity. In. R. L. Linn (Ed.), *Educational measurement* (3rd ed., pp. 13–103). New York, NY: Macmillan.

Messick, S. (1994). The interplay of evidence and consequences in the validation of performance assessments. *Educational Researcher, 23*, 13–24.

Messick, S. (1995). Validity of psychological assessment: Validation of inferences from persons' responses and performances as scientific inquiry into score meaning. *American Psychologist, 50*(9), 741–749.

Moss, P. A. (1995). Themes and variations in validity theory. *Educational Measurement: Issues and Practice, 14*(2), 5–13.

Moss, P. A. (1998). The role of consequences in validity theory. *Educational Measurement: Issues and Practice, 17*(2), 6–12.

Moss, P. A. (2005a). Toward "epistemic reflexivity" in educational research: A response to scientific research in education. *Teachers College Record, 107*(1), 19–29.

Moss, P. A. (2005b). Understanding the other/understanding ourselves: Toward a constructive dialogue about "principles" in educational research. *Educational Theory, 55*(3), 263–283.

Moss, P. A., Phillips, D. C., Erickson, F. D., Floden, R. E., Lather, P. A., & Schneider, B. L. (2009). Learning from our differences: A dialogue across perspectives on quality in education research. *Educational Researcher, 38*(7), 501–517.

Ridley, C. R., Tracy, M. L., Pruitt-Stephens, L., Wimsatt, M. K., & Beard, J. (2008). Multicultural assessment validity. In L. A. Suzuki & J. G. Ponterotto (Eds.), *Handbook of multicultural assessment: Clinical, psychological and educational applications* (3rd ed., pp. 22–33). New York, NY: Wiley.

Scheurich, J. J. (1996). The masks of validity: A deconstructive investigation. *Qualitative Studies in Education, 9*(1), 49–60.

Scheurich, J. J., & Young, M. D. (1997). Coloring epistemologies: Are our research epistemologies racially biased? *Educational Researcher, 26*(4), 4–16.

Shadish, W. R., Cook, T. D., & Campbell, D. C. (2002). *Experimental and quasi-experimental designs for generalized causal inference.* Boston, MA: Houghton Mifflin.

Shadish, W. R., Jr., Cook, T. D., & Leviton, L. C. (1991). *Foundations of program evaluation: Theories of practice.* Newbury Park, CA: Sage.

Shepard, L. A. (1993). Evaluating test validity. *Review of Research in Education, 19,* 405–450.

Shepard, L. A. (1997). The centrality of test use and consequences for test validity. *Educational Measurement: Issues and Practice, 16*(2), 5–8, 13, 24.

Smith, L. T. (2012). *Decolonizing methodologies: Research and indigenous peoples* (2nd ed.) New York, NY: Zed.

Stanfield, J. H., II (1999). Slipping through the front door: Relevant social science evaluation in the people of color century. *American Journal of Evaluation, 20*(3), 415–431.

Stanfield, J. H., II (Ed.). (2011). *Rethinking race and ethnicity in research methods.* Walnut Creek, CA: Left Coast.

Stevenson, W. L. (2000). *Decolonizing tribal histories* (Unpublished doctoral dissertation). University of California, Berkeley.

Thomas, A. B. (2006). Validity and management studies. In A. B. Thomas (Ed.), *Research concepts for management studies* (pp. 118–149). New York, NY: Routledge.

Wilson, S. (2008). *Research is ceremony: Indigenous research methods.* Halifax & Winnipeg, Canada: Fernwood.

Zuberi, T., & Bonilla-Silva, E. (Eds.) (2008). *White logic, White methods; Racism and methodology.* New York, NY: Rowman & Littlefield.

CHAPTER 4

AN ANALYSIS OF *LOVE MY CHILDREN*

Rose Butler Browne's Contributions to Culturally Responsive Evaluation

Pamela Frazier-Anderson
Frazier-Anderson Research & Evaluation, LLC

Tamara Bertrand Jones
Florida State University

As with any practice, there are associated theories, methods, and historical contexts. Culturally responsive evaluation (CRE) exists as a unique practice within the larger field of program evaluation. Unfortunately, missing from the historical annals of CRE are the voices of early culturally responsive evaluators whose contributions were instrumental in shaping the field. Rodney Hopson (Hopson & Hood, 2005) and Stafford Hood (2001) have made an extensive effort to identify African American men and women engaged in culturally responsive practices when undertaking educational research and evaluation prior to and since the landmark Supreme Court case of

Continuing the Journey to Reposition Culture and Cultural Context
in Evaluation Theory and Practice, pages 73–87
Copyright © 2015 by Information Age Publishing

Brown v. Board of Education (1954). Providing current and aspiring evaluators with knowledge of CRE's historical foundation further explicates and defines this emerging practice by addressing such questions as What is the history of CRE? Who are the individuals and communities who helped to define it? How did culture influence their evaluation or research practice? What are the practical and theoretical contributions of their work?

Documenting the historical foundations of CRE provides an opportunity to define an emerging model of program evaluation in which individuals from traditionally marginalized groups are recognized as the principal pioneers. In this chapter, the authors have selected to highlight the work and life of Rose Butler Browne (1897–1986). Butler Browne is acknowledged as the first African American woman in education whose dissertation title included the word "evaluation" (Hood, 2001). Among her many accomplishments, Butler Browne was the first African American woman to earn both a Bachelor's of Education degree and a Master's of Education degree from the University of Rhode Island (formerly known as Rhode Island College). She was also the first African American woman to earn a PhD in education from Harvard University in 1937 (Tsering, 2010). In this chapter, we will use a CRE theoretical framework (Frazier-Anderson, Hood, & Hopson, 2012) to discuss Butler Browne's life and work, starting with her autobiography, *Love My Children: The Education of a Teacher* (Browne & English, 1969). We also examine how Butler Browne's work embraces the theory and practices of CRE and provide evidence for why she deserves recognition as a pioneer in the evaluation field.

THE LIFE OF ROSE BUTLER BROWNE: A CULTURALLY RESPONSIVE EVALUATOR IN THE MAKING

The events recounted in her book, *Love My Children* (Browne & English, 1969), provide us with insight into Butler Browne's lived experiences that ultimately shaped her views as an educator, researcher, and evaluator. Her maternal great-grandmother, Charlotte Ann Elizabeth Lindsey, also known as High Priestess, was most influential in Butler Browne's life. High Priestess, as Butler Browne and her siblings called her, was the daughter of a Native American chief and therefore not a slave. With permission from his master, she married Reuben Lindsey, a Virginia house slave, and birthed Butler Browne's grandfather (William) and his siblings, who were considered free because of High Priestess' free status. Given her husband's precarious situation, High Priestess went on to work for 6 years to secure his freedom. Despite his freedom, her husband was unable to find work, nor could he denounce a "lifetime of servitude." With the hope of improving her younger three children's lives, High Priestess migrated north to Boston, while her husband stayed behind in Virginia, returning to the plantation to work.

Butler Browne acknowledges that her grandfather recalled little of their early years in Boston, only narrating the story of a woman's generosity by welcoming them into her home upon their arrival in the city. William Lindsey later married Rose (for whom Butler Browne was named), and Frances, Butler Browne's mother, was born. Frances, a housekeeper, married John Butler, who by trade as a bricklayer. Butler Browne identified her mother as the family's primary breadwinner and noted her likeness to High Priestess in her desires for a better life for her children. Likewise, she describes her father as a self-righteous dreamer, noting that he dropped out of Hampton Institute and joined the Navy. Her paternal grandfather, a Baptist preacher in Virginia, died before she was born. Her paternal grandmother had remarried and lived close to the family in Boston.

Butler Browne's formative years in Boston and later Newport, Rhode Island, shaped her initial understandings of culture and education. She (the third of seven children and the oldest female child) was born in Boston in 1897. The Butler family lived in Boston's South End, a multicultural neighborhood in Boston. Growing up in this neighborhood provided Butler Browne with access to Jewish, Italian, Irish, and other immigrant families, which included a diverse mix of cultures and races/ethnicities. Despite access to such diversity, maybe even because of it, her early views on race and racism, class, and education were fairly rigid. Butler Browne did not consider her family like other low-income families in the South End. For example, her mother "used her brains" to creatively provide for her family; and her mother read the "Housekeepers' Column" in the *Boston Globe* to get ideas for local educational and cultural activities and events she and her children could attend. The description provided of her mother's ingenuity in comparison to other economically disadvantaged families helps readers comprehend Butler Browne's early belief that individuals' circumstances stem from an inherent lack of fortitude. Consequently, sociopolitical influences were not considered as contributing factors for those who lived outside of her neighborhood and therefore did not share her lived experiences.

In hopes of securing additional work for her father and improving their economic status, the Butler family moved to Newport, Rhode Island, while Butler Browne was in the fifth grade. Her great-grandmother, widowed after the death of her husband, followed the family to Rhode Island. The events that occurred within these two locales contributed greatly in shaping Butler Browne's perceptions of race, culture, and the importance of education, and later caused her to rethink her positions.

Throughout Butler Browne's schooling, her academic achievements earned her recognition and accolades, further cementing her belief in personal achievement. Given her own focus and intellectual abilities, Butler

Browne developed similar expectations for her peers and later her own students. Throughout her educational career, she found an advocate—a teacher, counselor, or community member—who supported and encouraged her, as well as provided the connections she needed to advance. Accordingly, after she graduated from high school, her school principal helped her to get accepted into the Rhode Island State College, where she later enrolled to pursue teacher education. While working as a domestic, like her mother, she became the first African American woman to earn bachelor's and master's degrees at Rhode Island College, now the University of Rhode Island. As an example of Butler Browne's tenaciousness, during her graduate studies, she had two choices for her major: the School of Home Economics or the College of Engineering. Butler Browne chose engineering to demonstrate her ability to excel in complex mathematics and science subjects.

After completing her master's degree, Butler Browne left Rhode Island to pursue a teaching position in Virginia. In preparation for her move to the South, Butler Browne's father gave her parting advice that she recognized as valuable—valuable enough to pass on to her students later in her career. He told her,

> Rose, find a task no one wants, and do it so thoroughly that you become the unquestioned expert. You must be able to stand up to criticism, just and unjust. You don't know the South and you are fresh and headstrong. Listen and look. Don't be a crusader. Find a point of entry where you can fight segregation. Never give up principle, but don't be too proud to act with compassion toward those who treat you unjustly. (Browne & English, 1969, pp. 115–116)

While conducting multiple 6-week summer school institutes in rural Virginia, she developed relationships with rural teachers, students, and their families. As a result of one of these summer institutes, she met her future husband, a Baptist preacher and principal of a small school affiliated with his Church. They were married a year later. It was during these summer school sessions that Butler Browne first encountered the separate-but-equal way of life in the South. She began to experience students not being prepared because of a lack of resources available in their schools. This marked a shift in Butler Browne's belief in self-reliance to an understanding of the role race and racism were contributing to educational disparities.

From 1930 to 1936, she attended summer school sessions at Harvard University. In 1936, she began to pursue her doctorate in education at Harvard. She later won a prestigious scholarship from the General Board of Education of the Rockefeller Foundation to continue her studies. When the time came to propose her dissertation topic to the committee, she met with much resistance.

Butler Browne proposed to do what would now be considered a quasi-experimental study of three reading programs for African American children. During the oral defense of her dissertation prospectus, the committee placed many unrealistic stipulations on her research and erected roadblocks before granting their approval for her work. As recounted in her book, Butler Browne acknowledged that the committee's remarks had racial and gendered undertones throughout the entire process. The committee's concerns included the strength of her methods (although she met and garnered the approval of her methodologist prior to defense). They suggested that Butler Browne would have to conduct her study "in a test situation where [she] had complete and isolated control over the total school curriculum" (Browne & English, 1969, p. 17). In earlier discussions, Butler Browne and her advisor had ruled this option as "desirable, but impractical and quite unattainable" (Browne & English, 1969, p. 17).

Throughout the committee defense, her advisor did not advocate for Butler Browne. As a result, she felt alone and did not pass the qualifying examination. This delay might have caused problems with her fellowship from the Rockefeller Foundation. However, Butler Browne shrewdly reminded the committee of the implications, not only for her but for the institution if the roadblocks and delays caused her not to complete her research. In an account shared in her book, Butler Browne tells the story of how her connections with men from the Rockefeller Foundation and conversations with them in a meeting one week later helped to ensure that her committee no longer caused delays in her research.

A professional position in a school district in Petersburg, Virginia, allowed Butler Browne access to the school district and paved the way for her "uncontaminated" data collection as provided in the stipulations from her dissertation committee. She went on to collect her data and successfully defend her dissertation in 1937. Butler Browne's dissertation would later be titled *A Critical Evaluation of Experimental Studies of Remedial Reading* (Browne, 1939). Her dissertation examined the outcomes of three different remedial reading programs for African American students with reading difficulties. The results concluded that there were no significant gains made across any group. However, the results did suggest that teachers, when trained on specific methods of reading instruction and when receiving close supervision, can improve reading outcomes for African American children. The premise of this dissertation was influenced by her teaching experiences in the South, her interest in the "high percentage of reading failure in the Negro students of Virginia," as well as a lack of resources available to address reading deficiencies with this group (Browne, 1939, p. 144).

In 1939, Butler Browne's husband accepted a pastorate in West Virginia. While there, the Brownes built a home, no small feat for an African American couple during that time, and established roots in the community. She had secured a teaching position at Bluefield State College, a historically Black college, before moving to West Virginia. Since she was not scheduled to start until the next semester, a friend and colleague asked her to temporarily serve in his faculty position while he finished his doctorate. Butler Browne agreed, and she taught for one semester at West Virginia State College. After her colleague completed his doctorate, Butler Browne returned to Bluefield State College and gave birth to her son soon after her arrival. Once she returned to Bluefield, Butler Browne went on to help Bluefield State College earn accreditation while she became involved in the community and church. While at Bluefield, Butler Browne found a point where she could "fight segregation," as instructed by her father. Her position as a preacher's wife and faculty member at the local college afforded her the requisite degree of respectability in many circles. This positioning later allowed Butler Browne to engage with the community as she was thought to be one of them.

In 1948, she and her family moved to Durham, North Carolina, after her husband accepted a position at a new church. While in Durham, Butler Browne further established herself in education. Her life in North Carolina until her death will be described in the next sections as evidence of her development as a culturally responsive evaluator. In 1950, she received an honorary degree from Rhode Island College and in 1969, a 7-story Rhode Island College residence hall was named in her honor. Browne died in 1986 at the age of 89.

Rose Butler Browne as a Historical Figure in Culturally Responsive Evaluation (CRE)

Identifying historians of color in the field of evaluation who meet the criteria as CRE evaluators remains an engaging task. One reason is that although publications exist referencing the abilities and competencies of current CRE evaluators, mutual agreement on a definitive skillset necessary to effectively conduct CRE has yet to be achieved (Frazier-Anderson et al., 2012). Not having this mutual agreement makes it difficult to hold to a standard not only for those evaluators currently working in the field, it also makes it difficult to contend that the work of historical figures is representative of CRE. We do contend that a historical review can assist with documenting the work of those whose beliefs and practices helped to pave the way for our current and future culturally responsive evaluators, further validating CRE as having its own unique evaluation paradigm.

For this chapter, the authors believe that the African American Culturally Responsive Evaluation System for Academic Settings (ACESAS) is a defensible framework for delineating Butler Browne's work as historically culturally responsive. The ACESAS is a comprehensive theoretical logic model created as a guide for conducting culturally responsive evaluations in academic settings. As such, it contains what are believed to be many of the core components of CRE. (See Frazier-Anderson et al. (2012) for a more detailed explanation of the model.) The ACESAS model outlines a series of steps that evaluators can use to ensure incorporation of culturally responsive practices into their evaluation. The model and the steps encourage evaluators to conduct evaluations emphasizing culture and context in evaluation. The steps of the ACESAS include

- identify the cultural and sociopolitical factors at work in the upcoming evaluation (this is most efficient and authentic when evaluators have had shared lived experiences with the group being evaluated);
- understand the historical and current context of the evaluation setting;
- identify fiscal, material, and human resources necessary to conduct the evaluation;
- plan and implement an evaluation that truthfully represents and respects all stakeholders groups (most importantly program participants);
- have the evaluation outcomes reviewed by a panel of individuals who are knowledgeable about participants and the program;
- ensure that the results of the evaluation are delivered to and reviewed with stakeholders and program participants in a manner that is relevant and meaningful;
- aspire that the evaluation results will be useful for the all stakeholder groups and used to equip programs with making positive changes in the lives of program participants. (Frazier-Anderson et al., 2012; Frierson, Hood, & Hughes, 2002).

Remarkably, given the evidence provided in Butler Browne's personal and professional accomplishments, her practices and mindset are similar to those of modern culturally responsive evaluators as presented in the ACESAS model and by others in the field. These practices include (a) recognizing worldview differences and understanding the value of having shared lived experiences with another group; (b) understanding the roles of social capital and civic capacity in evaluation and program planning; (c) including a thorough analysis of the context in which evaluation/research is performed; and (d) incorporating social justice into her work (and life). In the next sections, we will discuss each of these practices and identify how they are each reflected in Butler Browne's work.

Recognizing Worldview Differences Through Shared Lived Experiences

One of the qualities of an effective CRE evaluator is the ability to gauge the extent to which cultural differences exist and may influence evaluation outcomes. Culture influences not only how we as evaluators think and behave, but how we react to and interpret the actions of others. Therefore, the more skilled an evaluator is in understanding her own culture and worldview (how she sees and experiences the world) and/or the more shared lived experiences she has with the group(s) being evaluated, the higher the potential of the evaluation being culturally responsive (Frazier-Anderson et al., 2012).

As an outsider from the metropolitan Northeast, Rose Butler Browne's shared lived experiences in the rural South were influential in creating significant changes in her worldview. Immersion in Southern culture helped shift her view of the students, parents, and teachers she encountered from "them" to "us." Each direct encounter and experience as she lived and worked daily in the South transitioned her from out-group membership (Northern African American visitor) to in-group membership (Southern African American resident). As she became an active participant in Southern living, she was able to directly observe and modify her assumptions concerning the resourcefulness of *and* the resources available to support African Americans in achieving their educational goals. In her autobiography, Butler Browne stated,

> I was attempting to draw on the experiences that I assumed my students had had. I based my assumptions on their chronological ages and years of school. Until I began my work with the rural teachers and lived in their homes and became one of them, I did not know how different were their environmental resources from what I knew. I was to learn that their environment had more in it than had ever been utilized. (Browne & English, 1969, pp. 156–157)

Evaluators who do not share similar cultural backgrounds with the group being evaluated and/or who are not familiar with the communities and other contextual factors present within the evaluand may be at a disadvantage in some communities and with some stakeholder groups.

One benefit of an evaluator having shared lived experiences with the stakeholder group(s) is that the evaluator is better able to interpret events from an in-group perspective. Shared lived experiences also enable the evaluator to be mindful of the plight of others. Finally, this understanding aids in the acceptance that the evaluator's knowledge or way of doing things may not be useful or relevant in all situations. In reflecting on her own acceptance of this notion, Butler Browne stated, "One important lesson learned in the seven years that I traveled over Virginia was that there are many different kinds of knowing. In some kinds of knowledge I was adept, in others abysmally ignorant" (Browne & English, 1969, p. 130).

One area in which Butler Browne altered her beliefs was in understanding the plight of African Americans in the United States. Prior to her experiences in the South, Butler Browne believed a person's failure to achieve in life was largely due to a lack of education. She stated, "Although I had heard about the rural ghettos of the South, it was my belief that all my people really needed to improve their lot in life was education, education as I knew it" (Browne & English, 1969, p. 115).

However, not long after her arrival in Virginia, as she taught and lived with students and their families in rural areas, she was able to observe that African Americans required equal educational instruction (and resources) as well as equal opportunities in order to succeed in life. These were key elements missing for most African Americans in the rural South during that time. Butler Browne stated,

> I don't know what I had expected to find at that college in Virginia, but what I found was a half-baked form of so-called education. In comparison to both Rhode Island schools, miseducation would be a more appropriate term, although they were trying to do with what they had. (Browne & English, 1969, p. 116)

Butler Browne observed external factors at work that maintained the status quo and prevented educational advancement for African Americans in the South. For example, African American schools were only open 5 to 6 months out of the school year, a curtailed schooling schedule which was exacerbated by the White land owners of farming communities who encouraged parents to keep their children working in the fields rather than in schools. There was also limited funding available to support the segregated schools for African American students (Browne & English, 1969). As Butler Browne observed, "Virginia is unable to support adequately two good school systems, and since there is no legal requirement that the separate schools be equal, the Negro schools throughout the state are generally inferior to those maintained for whites" (Browne, 1939, p.151). Additionally, teachers were not as well trained as their White counterparts and lacked incentives to attain additional training and degrees. Butler Browne noted, "Many a rural county educational superintendent let it be known that the county had no funds to pay an increase to anyone who upgraded himself, but he would promise to see that every teacher's temporary certificate was renewed" (Browne & English, 1969, p. 123).

Butler Browne's experiences are demonstrative of the importance of CRE evaluators having an "insider's" view into the lives of the groups they are evaluating (Frazier-Anderson et al., 2012; Frierson et al., 2002). Not only was Butler Browne able to directly observe day-to-day life, she experienced life herself as an African American in the South. These shared lived experiences slowly changed her worldview as she strove to interpret her observations of and interactions with the people around her. Without these direct experiences, Butler Browne may not have changed some of her original beliefs, softened her stance in other areas, or otherwise made as significant an impact on the lives of many African American students, families, educators, and communities through her research, professional work, and community involvement.

Understanding the Roles of Social Capital and Civic Capacity

The resources necessary to conduct culturally responsive evaluations include more than fiscal and material considerations. Evaluators who use CRE must be equally observant in their ability to gauge social capital and civic capacity, since both deal directly with culture and cultural influences. These two ideas are integral for achieving an evaluation that accurately reflects the voices of those represented.

One definition of social capital is "the network of social connections that exist between people, and their shared values and norms of behaviour, which enable and encourage mutually advantageous social cooperation" (Collins English Dictionary, n.d.). Social capital is maintained and reproduced through information channels (i.e., knowledge, skills, and resources) within social networks (Smith, 2007). In evaluation, understanding the dynamics of how social connections unfold and exist within the program's micro and macro systems can aid a culturally responsive evaluator with recognizing factors that promote and disallow inclusion. Butler Browne's experiences in the South provided her with the ability to more accurately discern the cultural dynamics present on multiple levels in the communities she engaged. She stated,

> One summer I supervised four six-week summer schools and did full time teaching in one of them. Out of these experiences came an awareness of the day to day needs of the teachers, the needs of the college staff for more information and understanding of the community and also for the patterns of co-existence between the races. (Browne & English, 1969, p. 130)

These experiences allowed Butler Browne to better navigate systems due in part to her personal knowledge about the needs of teachers, college staff, and the community. As a result she was able to plan and implement programs that were most representative of and beneficial to those she served.

When conducting evaluations, civic capacity allows the evaluator to understand what human resources are available to effectively solve the problem or answer the question (Frazier-Anderson et al., 2012) and creates a starting point for fostering stakeholder group(s) participation in the evaluation. Civic capacity is defined as "various sectors of the community coming together in an effort to solve a major problem" (Stone, Henig, Jones, & Pierannunzi, 2001, p. 4). Once evaluators understand the knowledge, abilities, and resources stakeholders possess, evaluators are able to recruit stakeholders to participate as members of the evaluation team or as panel members who provide feedback on the interpretation of evaluation results.

When her husband assumed leadership of Mount Calvary Baptist Church in Durham, North Carolina, Butler Browne became adept at understanding civic capacity as a resource for achieving church goals. As first lady, she was able to directly observe the needs of those around her as she engaged with the church community. Shortly after her arrival, Butler Browne learned that one of the salient issues presented by parents was concern for their children's educational attainment and success. She also recognized the level of effort necessary to address the difficult task of advancing educational opportunities for Mount Calvary's youth. This knowledge prompted a desire in Butler Browne to make a difference. She stated, "Once I felt the depth of the people's feeling I did not want the church to wait" (Browne & English, 1969, p. 190–191).

Butler Browne met each week as part of the church's planning committee. At these meetings, they were able to "set objectives and choose ways of training children which gave greatest promise of success within our limitations of available funds and presently available trained volunteer services" (Browne & English, 1969, p. 191). Butler Browne was once again able to assist with an informal assessment of the community's needs and then use the church and community resources to address these concerns.

One of the human resources used to address concerns and create solutions was the church's Adult Council. This council became the policymaking body for the church's youth program and the educational committee. Eventually the council was used as a resource for promoting a "stay-in-school-and-go-to-college emphasis" (Browne & English, 1969, p. 193). Butler Browne stated,

> I watched these people work. I marveled at what they accomplished. This is why I know that with proper organization, participating and working through established channels, my people can promote effective educational goals even in such places described by the white press as the culturally deprived inner city. (Browne & English, 1969, p. 193)

Butler Browne became adept at identifying social patterns and networks within the church and educational communities. She organized individuals in order to accomplish tasks and achieve evaluation and/or program goals. Her ability to organize was instrumental in engaging program leaders (civic capacity) as well as participants in needs analysis, program planning, and implementation. This leadership led to many successful program outcomes.

Including a Thorough Contextual Analysis

In preparation for entry into any environment where program evaluation is to occur, the evaluator must conduct a contextual analysis. The contextual analysis allows the evaluator to "obtain a thorough description of the environment" (Frazier-Anderson et al., 2012, p. 365). When conducting a contextual analysis, information is gathered on the history and current state of the community as well as the program. As culturally responsive evaluators, it is important to gather information from a variety of sources, including, but not limited to, a review of relevant records, interviews with insiders, and observations (Frazier-Anderson et al., 2012). For example, community members living in a community for an extended period of time (decades) provide rich insight into not only current conditions but contributing factors leading to that community's existing state. Spending time at the program site as well as walking or driving through the community multiple times and at different periods of the day helps to better capture the unique characteristics of that environment. Additionally, the more data the culturally responsive evaluator is able to gather about the cultural and sociopolitical institutions at work, the better equipped she will be to understand how factors influence or possibly limit evaluation results. These issues can either be addressed or regarded as limitations of the evaluation.

As suggested in the ACESAS model, a thorough analysis of the history of the region would be necessary by modern CRE evaluators when conducting an evaluation. When placed in a historical context, Butler Browne's analysis of the environment in which her evaluation/ research of educational programs was to take place was thorough. At the community, level she included a detailed description of her study's locale as well as a comparison of surrounding ones. Her analysis also included comparisons of the cities by population, ethnic distributions, socioeconomic status, and the influence of industrial organizations (such as the railroad and naval yard) on employment opportunities. Conducting a contextual analysis is one of the ways that culturally responsive evaluators ensure understanding of the context in which the evaluation occurs. By providing this information, Butler Browne was able to paint a clear picture of the social and environmental conditions present in her dissertation work. As Butler Browne demonstrated, it is important for CRE evaluators to thoroughly understand the environment in which the evaluation is to occur. This understanding provides evaluators with a foundation for understanding relevant factors within the macro and micro systems of the evaluand.

Incorporating Social Justice

Traditional evaluators will most likely argue that the role of the evaluator is to be as impartial as possible when conducting evaluations. For culturally responsive evaluators, this is a complicated task. If one is to truly be culturally responsive, then one goal of the evaluation is to ensure that the results have a lasting and positive impact on program participants by ensuring that all viewpoints are accurately represented in the results. It is also important for culturally responsive evaluators to consider how their results will be used, particularly with historically subjugated groups, and how their work can ultimately create positive changes for these populations (Frazier-Anderson et al., 2012).

Butler Browne's goal was to improve the education (and economic) conditions of African Americans. As such, her work extends into the area of social justice. Each experience in the South moved her closer to understanding the impediments preventing successful educational outcomes for those with whom she was most concerned. Out of these observations and experiences grew a belief that reading achievement was paramount in changing the existing state of affairs for African Americans. This was so important to her that it became the focus of her dissertation research:

> The most pressing problem of the Negro in the fourteen southern states grows out of his lack of a common school education. It is directly a causal factor to almost every other social ill of the group, including poor housing conditions, short-life expectancy, high delinquency rate and economic inferiority. Although the education of the common school is not the only approach to the solution of the manifold of problems of the Negro, it certainly is a basic one. Wilkerson (1931) has shown that the Virginia Negroes are, as a group, dropped out of the school at the end of the fourth grade. It is obvious that a race of fourth-graders cannot find a worthy place in American civilization. (Browne, 1939, p. 144)

Butler Browne's life resonates with elements of social justice. She worked tirelessly with administrators to establish and maintain educational programs and then with educators to ensure that they received necessary training and certification. Reportedly, she refused to send African American educators to fill teaching jobs in West Virginia due to unequal pay for African Americans (Associated Press, 1986). While first lady at Mount Calvary Baptist Church, Butler Browne helped to establish a credit union for church members. The funds were used by families to help pay for the cost of their child(ren)'s education (Browne & English, 1969). Butler Browne helped scores of students achieve their higher education goals, thus providing them with a means for better economic attainment, which leads to better personal and professional outcomes.

Similar to Butler Brown, evaluators strive to give participants a voice in the program. CRE evaluators make an effort to ensure that participants have a say in all aspects of an evaluation and that their opinions and observations are accurately reflected as the program is developed and implemented.

CONCLUSION

Exploration of evaluation through the eyes of the evaluator is a powerful notion, given the practical nature of the profession. Learning about the field from those who practice in it gives credence to personal experience and helps to inform future theory and practice. Although an emerging field in mainstream evaluation, elements of culturally responsive evaluation have existed for decades in the work of African American researchers and evaluators. However, many of their stories and/or works have been lost or forgotten. One explanation for this occurrence is that these early works were conducted during a time in American history when Jim Crow laws dominated the South, when race-based discriminatory views and practices were even more prevalent across the United States, and as women of all races began the journey to overcome oppressive political, economic, and social conditions. As such, for African American women, both racism and sexism contributed to how their work was viewed and utilized (or not) by those in positions of power.

Most well-known as the first African American woman to earn a PhD from Harvard University and for her work as an educator and administrator, Butler Browne is already a significant historical figure in her own right; however, her influence exceeds education. As presented in this chapter, her life and work have relevance to the field of culturally responsive evaluation. Although her story does not provide extensive examples of culturally responsive evaluation as it is presently conceptualized, her experiences, opinions, and accounts significantly contribute to our understanding of evaluation and especially to our conceptualizations in this field as defined by the ACESAS model. Her life work was anchored in a deep commitment to equality and justice for her people—and these remain the aspirations of CRE.

REFERENCES

Associated Press. (1986, December 5). Rose Butler Browne is dead; A Black pioneer in education. *The New York Times.* Retrieved from http://www.nytimes.com/1986/12/05/obituaries/rose-butler-browne-is-dead-a-black-pioneer-in-education.html
Brown v. Board of Education of Topeka, 347 U.S. 483 (1954).

Browne, R. (1939). *A critical evaluation of experimental studies of remedial reading, and the report of an experiment with backward readers.* Doctoral dissertation, Harvard University.

Browne, R. B., & English, J. W. (1969). *Love my children: The education of a teacher.* New York, NY: Meredith.

Collins English Dictionary-Complete and Unabridged. (n.d.). Social capital. *The Free Dictionary.* Retrieved from http://www.thefreedictionary.com/social+capital

Frazier-Anderson, P. N., Hood, S., & Hopson, R. K. (2012). Preliminary considerations of an African American culturally responsive evaluation system. In S. Lapan, M. Quartaroli, & F. Reimer (Eds.), *Qualitative research: An introduction to methods and designs* (pp. 347–372). San Francisco, CA: Jossey-Bass.

Frierson, H. T., Hood, S., & Hughes, G. B. (2002). Strategies that address culturally-responsive evaluation. In J. Fretchling (Ed.), *The 2002 user-friendly handbook for project evaluation* (pp. 63–73). Arlington, VA: National Science Foundation.

Hood, S. (2001). Nobody knows my name: In praise of African American evaluators who were responsive. *New Directions for Evaluation, 92,* 31–43.

Hopson, R. K., & Hood, S. (2005) An untold story in evaluation roots: Reid E. Jackson and his contributions toward culturally responsive evaluation at 3/4 century. In S. Hood, R. K. Hopson, & H. T. Frierson (Eds.), *The role of culture and cultural context: A mandate for inclusion, the discovery of truth and understanding in evaluative practice* (pp. 85–102) Charlotte, NC: Information Age.

Smith, B. (2007). Accessing social capital through the academic mentoring process. *Equity & Excellence in Education, 40,* 36–46.

Stone, C. N., Henig, J. R., Jones, B. D., & Pierannunzi, C. (2001). *Building civic capacity: The politics of reforming urban schools.* Lawrence: University Press of Kansas.

Tsering, T. (2010). Profile: Rose Butler Browne. *Psychology's Feminist Voices.* Retrieved from http://www.feministvoices.com/rose-butler-browne/

SECTION II

EVALUATORS' JOURNEYS OF INTROSPECTION
AND SELF-EXPLORATION

CHAPTER 5

CULTURE AND EVALUATION

From a Transcultural Belvedere[1,2]

Jennifer C. Greene
University of Illinois at Urbana-Champaign

**AMERICAN EVALUATION ASSOCIATION (AEA) STATEMENT
ON CULTURAL COMPETENCE IN EVALUATION (2011)**

Cultural competence is a stance taken toward culture, not a discrete status or simple mastery of particular knowledge and skills...

All evaluation reflects culturally influenced norms, values, and ways of knowing—making cultural competence integral to ethical, high-quality evaluation...

Cultural competence in evaluation requires that evaluators maintain a high degree of self-awareness and self-examination to better understand how their own backgrounds and other life experiences serve as assets or limitations in the conduct of an evaluation...

Culture has implications for all phases of evaluation—including staffing, development, and implementation of evaluation efforts as well as communicating and using evaluation results. (AEA, 2011)

---

*Continuing the Journey to Reposition Culture and Cultural Context
in Evaluation Theory and Practice,* pages 91–107
Copyright © 2015 by Information Age Publishing
All rights of reproduction in any form reserved.

AOTEAROA NEW ZEALAND EVALUATION ASSOCIATION (ANZEA)

Vision and Kaupapa

We "look to the maunga," we strive for excellence.
We recognize and value the cultures of all our peoples.
We honour their participation and we seek genuine partnerships.
Sharing exceptional skills and insightful knowledge,
we seek to support their aims and aspirations
for a healthy, prosperous and vibrant future.

The *tohu* and *whakatauki*, both integral to the identity of ANZEA, reflect our vision and core values.

The ANZEA *tohu* incorporates the poutama and tapa designs of Aotearoa and the Pacific.

The "tapa toru" (three sides) of the triangle design is an indigenous symbol of the "maunga" (mountain) which represents the search for higher meanings and the quest for self, individual and community wholeness . . .

The "niho taniwha" (teeth of the taniwha) are symbolic of strength.

The koru in the lettering symbolize generative energy and dynamic growth . . .

The *whakatauki*, "**He kura te tangata**" (People are precious) reflects the regard that we have for the intrinsic value of a human being and for the contribution of each person to the well-being of their *whānau*/families, their communities and their environment.

(ANZEA , 2013)

In this second decade of the 21st century, it is widely recognized that evaluation is a cultural practice. Nearly all agree that multiple and substantial threads of culture are interwoven into the program and context being evaluated, and most further acknowledge that key dimensions of culture (worldviews, values, customs) are also embedded in the stances, methodologies, and relationships engaged by the evaluator. This significant accomplishment reflects the expansive internationalization of evaluation over the past several decades (e.g., Ryan & Cousins, 2009) and its coming of age as an instrument of government and social change alike. This maturity of our field also reflects the fruits of the significant efforts of evaluation colleagues in all parts of the world and from all sectors of the evaluation community—too numerous to list, as the naming and claiming of culture in evaluation has been a global endeavor.

So, now what? What are the important challenges and opportunities for evaluators who deeply value and are attuned to the cultural dimensions of our craft, now that meaningful attention to culture in evaluation has been legitimized? How can we best advance the theory and the practice of culturally responsive and responsible evaluation?

I believe that guidelines, exemplars, and critical reflections that can meaningfully inform culturally responsive evaluation *practice* remain the highest priority. Clearly, the theory-practice dialogue for culturally responsive evaluation is well underway (e.g., Frierson, Hood, & Hughes, 2002; Hood, 1998; Hood, Hopson, & Frierson, 2005; Madison, 1992; McKegg & Wehipeihana, 2010; Mertens & Hopson, 2006; Smith, 2012; Thomas & Stevens, 2004; Thompson-Robinson, Hopson, & SenGupta, 2004). And I observe that many contributors to this conversation speak from their own experiences, engaged from their own particular standpoints. This, of course, is entirely sensible as we are each experts in our own life experiences and sense-makings thereof. But likely there are also cross-cultural perspectives and international dialogues of value to this conversation. This chapter adopts a cross-cultural lens to offer insights into the practical challenges of conducting culturally responsive and responsible evaluation and to encourage a spirited international dialogue.

I had the wonderful good fortune in 2012 to take my very first "traveling" sabbatical leave and to center this leave around a visit to Aotearoa New Zealand.[3] I was eager to learn about the recent cultural and political revitalization of the Māori people, catalyzed by the government's reaffirmation of the 1840 Treaty of Waitangi,[4] and I was especially eager to learn how this revitalization is showing up in the evaluation practices of my Māori and Pākehā colleagues.[5] Herein, I will share some of my experiences and initial insights from my visit to Aotearoa New Zealand and begin a conversation on how such insights might be adapted for culturally responsive evaluation work in the United States. I aim to contribute to the repertoire of *practical strategies* for culturally responsive evaluation in the United States, drawing on the experiences and wisdom of our Aotearoa New Zealand colleagues.

The adaptation that is most directly relevant for us in the United States is for our indigenous Native American peoples. Yet there are evaluators with significantly more expertise than I have in Indian ways of knowing and being, in Indian rituals of importance, *and* in making evaluation culturally responsive and relevant for Native American peoples. (See, for example, LaFrance, 2004; LaFrance & Nichols, 2010; LaFrance, Nichols, & Kirkhart, 2012; Nelson-Barber, LaFrance, Trumbull, & Aburto, 2005.) So my effort is to endeavor to think well about adapting the culturally engaged work of evaluators in Aotearoa New Zealand and to the contexts in which I work. These contexts characteristically are peopled by mainstream Americans and/or by traditional U.S. minority groups of African Americans, Latino/as, and immigrants, as well as people from families with limited economic means and people on other margins of our society.

LESSONS AND INSIGHTS FROM AOTEAROA NEW ZEALAND

This chapter will engage four principal issues, which are anchored in the particular experiences I had in Aotearoa New Zealand and chosen for their practical relevance to culturally responsive evaluation practice in the United States.[6]

1. With what rituals is evaluation conducted in Aotearoa New Zealand, and what do they contribute to evaluation practice in that country?
2. What approach to evaluation is dominant in Māori contexts and for what reasons?
3. What matters in evaluation practice in Māori contexts and how does it matter?
4. What political issues are salient in evaluation in Māori contexts and what influences do they have?

For each issue, I will describe what I observed in Aotearoa New Zealand, along with some initial thoughts about what we can learn from these experiences for culturally responsive and responsible evaluation in U.S. evaluation contexts.

Making Connections: Rituals in Evaluation Practice

In Aotearoa New Zealand, the Māori have a lovely traditional ritual of engagement and relationship building. It typically occurs at the beginning of meetings, workshops, classes, and even personal introductions. The Māori introduce themselves by identifying their tribe/s (*iwi*) and their tribal location(s) in relation to particular mountains, rivers, lakes, or other places of significance, such sites of canoe landings or battles. When there are Māori and Pākehā together, usually one Māori person will suggest that the group members introduce themselves to each other, and the Māori typically choose the introduction I just described. My colleagues from Aotearoa New Zealand tell me that this ritual has almost become normalized in New Zealand culture, most particularly when Māori and Pākehā come together, in everyday settings such as birthdays, weddings, and celebrations, as well as in more professional settings like evaluation contexts.

More formally, I experienced many government functions and professional meetings that began with a Māori ceremonial ritual of welcome (*powhiri*). The ritual includes a welcome by the hosts and a response by visitors, with songs of acknowledgment to the speakers interspersed throughout the ceremony, all followed by a bountiful tea. And at conferences around the world, after a presentation from a New Zealander, I have witnessed his or her colleagues from Aotearoa New Zealand come up to the front of the room and sing a song of appreciation for the speaker.

I cannot speak with any authority whatsoever about the meanings and functions of the Māori rituals of introduction and welcome, even though the words and songs were often translated for me, along with snippets of history. What *I experienced*, however, when greeted ceremoniously was a feeling of being genuinely welcomed into that space, even before anyone knew me. At times, this genuine welcoming feeling was quite profound. And I was told that the individual introductions of one's *iwi*, mountain, and river communicate kinship, community, and shared ideals and visions.

That is, I experienced these welcoming and celebratory rituals as vibrant elements of gatherings intended for interaction, meaning making, and collective sense making. Relationships, as explained to me, are at the heart of these rituals. The cultural practices are about connecting, reconnecting, and positioning who each person or group is in relation to their tribe, to places of tribal significance, to their history recent and past, to their work, and to their family and friends.

Perhaps more fundamentally, these introductory and welcoming rituals mark the gathering as a time of connection not just a time of work, a time for relating one to another as people not just talking formally as professionals, that is, a time of engagement with more than the professional countenance of those with whom we are meeting, for example, evaluation stakeholders. Or, as I have come to better understand, connections and relationships are not experiences that belong outside of work but rather constitute an integral part of work in Aotearoa New Zealand. Further, because these rituals are face-to-face, they can engage *all* of our senses (Kataraina Pipi, personal communication, 2013). The introductory and welcoming rituals in Aoteaora New Zealand thereby create a space for interactions of meaning and consequence—interactions grounded in relational trust and acceptance.

Culturally responsive and engaged evaluation is also fundamentally anchored in relational trust and acceptance. Without visible and palpable connections between evaluators and stakeholders, especially the program leaders, staff, and participants, our work has little chance of being meaningfully culturally responsive and thereby meaningfully consequential in that context.

So, with what kind of rituals might we in the United States initiate our evaluation work that would signal these value commitments of respect and acceptance and would begin to establish the relational trust and openness we seek in culturally responsive, responsible, and engaged evaluation? At the outset of a gathering, we often go around the room and introduce ourselves, typically offering our name and our job title or description. I wonder if we each also offered a snippet of personal history or an appreciation of some aspect of the gathering (in the spirit of appreciative inquiry; Preskill & Catsambas, 2006), we might begin to foster keener attention to relationships and stronger engagements with relational trust and acceptance?

I wonder also if more frequent progress updates on our evaluation work could offer occasions for building relationships as well as engaging in some thoughtful reflections on the data available and their implications for the program being evaluated (see Patton, 2008). A team of doctoral students and I recently evaluated a middle school summer math program aimed at increasing the number of students from underrepresented groups in advanced math courses.[7] The evaluation team's progress reports were central to the strong relationships developed in this context, relationships that have continued into new inquiry projects. We believe that one feature of our progress reports that helped foster meaningful and trusting relationships was our use of alternative ways of representing selected data and findings (skits, poems, graphics). These alternative presentations were intentionally evocative and were successful in catalyzing critical and thoughtful conversations and reflections about the program and its aspirations (Johnson, Hall, Greene, & Ahn, 2013).

I will now turn to the second of the four issues addressed in this chapter: the kind of evaluation I observed most frequently in Māori contexts in Aotearoa New Zealand.

Advancing Programs of Cultural Relevance and Consequence: Developmental Evaluation in Māori Contexts

I spent my time in Aotearoa New Zealand absorbing all I could from a variety of evaluation contexts that I had the privilege of learning about. I did this by reading materials, talking with evaluators over many cups of excellent New Zealand coffee, shadowing them on site visits, and sitting on the fringes of evaluators' *hui* (meetings) with project leadership and staff. I also spent whole days with both Māori and Pākehā evaluators listening in on their reflective conversations about evaluator roles and evaluator souls, about how to best engage the Māori revitalization in their work, and about their values and commitments. It was a most distinct privilege to be invited to observe and listen in.

One dominant observation throughout my time as an observer-learner in Aotearoa New Zealand is the common use of a form of *developmental evaluation* in contexts that involved an evaluation of a program targeted for Māori. Developmental evaluation is the evaluative process of working closely with program staff on the development, implementation, and critique of the underlying logic, activities, and implementation of a program toward attainment of desired outcomes. Developmental evaluation aims, in part, to support program staff and to develop their evaluative thinking and capacity. Recently, Michael Patton (2010) updated this idea to focus on developmental evaluation as supporting and guiding innovations under conditions of complexity. But more relevant to the Aotearoa New Zealand context, a developmental evaluation approach importantly enacts the kind of evaluation, and its role and contributions or uses, desired by the evaluators of these projects for Māori.[8] Developmental evaluation in Aotearoa New Zealand nurtures and supports program staff in their program work. Developmental evaluation also enhances the evaluative thinking of program staff and integrates an evaluative lens into ongoing program endeavors. Developmental evaluation aspires to contribute directly to programs that are significantly meaningful and consequential for program participants.

Signaling a core rationale for this widespread adoption of a form of developmental evaluation for Māori projects, many, many times I overheard a comment attesting to a fundamental shift in Māori program purpose and framework over the past decade or so. At root (though quite a bit more complex), the shift was from conducting and evaluating programs "for Māori" to conducting and evaluating programs "as Māori," that is, doing things in the Māori way. This shift was fully evident in the character of the programs I observed being evaluated.

To illustrate, one context I observed multiple times was an evaluation of a program funded by Sport New Zealand (NZ) and intended to encourage and support Māori youth and adults to participate in more physical activity. The director of He Oranga Poutama (HOP) observed that her program has been way ahead of Sport NZ in strategic and outcomes thinking. Sport NZ has seen HOP as a self-contained program with participation as its primary agenda and outcome. HOP staff see it as a political and cultural strategy, part of the wider Māori cultural revitalization, and are working to make it so. Here, practice precedes policy. As the evaluators, McKegg, Wehipeihana, and Pipi, (2013) wrote in their 2012 evaluation report,

> He Oranga Poutama (HOP) is a Sport NZ initiative that supports Māori well-being through sport and recreation. In 2009, the programme evolved from a focus on increasing the participation by Māori in sport, to one of participating and leading *as Māori* in sport and traditional physical recreation at community level. [That is, this revised focus emphasized not Māori participation in Western sport and physical activity, but rather Māori participation in traditional Māori sports and games, thus also serving as a cultural revitalization of these sport traditions.]

This shift in direction, to an *as Māori* focus, signalled that Sport NZ recognised the cultural distinctiveness aspect of the new programme goal and the importance of culturally distinctive pathways for sport and recreation if Māori were to participate as Māori. Sport NZ, along with other government agencies, was coming to realise that a strong and secure cultural identity for Māori, helps facilitate their access to wider society, as well as being vital to overall wellbeing, and were willing through the HOP initiative to invest in and enable, a stronger platform for Māori to participate as Māori. (p. 5)

Developmental evaluation, according to my kiwi colleagues, not only supports this political "as Māori" agenda for the HOP program (and others serving the Māori people), but also enables (gives permission to) the evaluators to partner with and actively support the program staff in the actual process of program development. This is in marked contrast, of course, to the common understanding of the evaluator as a neutral outsider. (Although the very wise Lee Cronbach opined decades ago that evaluators should only evaluate programs to which they are sympathetic; Cronbach et al., 1980.) Notably, as an observer of several planning meetings for an important weekend HOP hui, I watched two of the evaluators sit side by side with the project director as they collaboratively planned the hui. All three shared common principles and commitments, and common ends, notably to elevate the *cultural value and power* of this kind of project as part of the reaffirmation and revitalization of Māori culture. All three were co-collaborators in this shared venture.

Further, evaluators of HOP and other programs commented that developmental evaluation serves not only to affirm Māori values, but also their connections to the land as well as their connections to their *marae*.[9] Developmental evaluation helps them to create a sense of space, they said. I interpret this as meaning to create a safe, protected, *and affirming* space—a cultural, historical, and relational space—from which to assert Māori values and commitments and to serve as much as program supporters as program critics. As one evaluator said, "We do this [developmental-type evaluation] to live in a better world."

In sum, developmental evaluation is a favored approach in Aotearoa New Zealand for evaluations of Māori projects because it

- supports "as Māori" program thinking, acting, and reflecting, and supports conducting a program that serves Māori "in the Māori way";
- enables evaluators to fully partner with program staff in developing and enacting an "as Māori" program; and
- creates a safe and affirming space for the values and commitments that underlie these actions.

So, what lessons can we in the United States draw from selected Aotearoa New Zealand evaluators' embrace of developmental evaluation for our own evaluation practice, particularly in underserved communities with culturally different or marginalized peoples?

Herein I share three initial thoughts; thoughts that represent extant strands of culturally responsive and responsible evaluation or are fully consonant with the commitments and stances of this approach.

First, just as the "as Māori" evaluators in Aotearoa New Zealand adopt a developmental evaluation approach—in part because it enables, even demands, close attention to the consonance of the premises, design, and logic of the evaluand with Māori beliefs, values, and principles—we culturally responsive evaluators in the United States can also attend closely to the program's underlying design and premises. Many already do. But perhaps a renewed or reinvigorated focus on the program as designed is one important strategy to recommend, especially a renewed focus on the character and magnitude of the program's specific attention to and respect for the cultural ways of doing things both in the contexts at hand and also *as situated in the larger politics of culture in the United States.* One evaluation question that could accomplish this might be How well does the program design *genuinely and consequentially* respect and engage cultural diversity, even when there are political tensions or costs of doing so?

Second, many of the evaluation approaches and accompanying methods I learned about during my visit to Aotearoa New Zealand focused on programs exclusively for Māori participants. Some however were targeted for a diverse set of participants—Māori, Pākehā, Pasifika,[10] and others. Common to most of these that I observed was a concerted emphasis on assessing the program's success in serving those least well served in the contexts at hand, who were typically members of a cultural and/or a socioeconomic minority in the country. This emphasis went far beyond data disaggregation to include possibly different understandings of program participation and different definitions of program success for different groups. Culturally responsive evaluation, by definition, attends intentionally to the quality of the program experiences and outcomes of distinct cultural subgroups. Concerted attention to those subgroups least well served in the contexts at hand—attention mindful of possible *culturally specific understandings of and engagements with the evaluand*—could be an important evaluation strategy in some times and places. (See Greene, 2005, 2012 for further discussion of an equity focus in evaluation.)

And third, like "as Māori" evaluation in Aotearoa New Zealand, culturally responsive and responsible evaluation in the United States can be *importantly and intentionally affirming* to various program and evaluation participants. The staff of the sports program HOP (also nearly all Māori) expressed deep affirmation from the engagement of the evaluation team. The staff of a health-careers program, intended to attract and prepare more Māori young people for careers in health, expressed the same. This sense of affirmation and validation for one's own hard work can be a powerful lever of mobilization and change. We could work harder and smarter to create evaluation contexts that are deeply culturally affirming.

Fostering Relationships: Evaluation as a Social and Relational Practice

A Pākehā evaluator observed,

> Another thing you might find interesting in a small market [New Zealand has a total of 4.5 million people] is our very strong focus on relationships and building strong relational trust. It is a core kiwi value. We all know that there is probably only one to two degrees of separation between us and many of those we come in contact with.

"Relationships are not part of the work; they *are* the work," proclaimed one Māori evaluator. And a Māori program staff person said, "The emphasis on relationships [in this evaluation] has been key" to its effectiveness.

Distinct from the generally close-knit character of the New Zealand populace, the Māori culture itself is strongly *iwi* (tribal), *hapū* (kinship groups), and *whānau* or family based. As one Maori evaluator said, "We are iwi, hapū, whānau first and then professionals second. And our identities are whakapapa connected—that is, connected to our genealogy and family histories." Further, how many 2-day evaluation meetings with program staff have you experienced where all attendees sing traditional songs together in the evening, with guitar accompaniment, and *then* all sleep on cots in the one common room of the meeting house on the marae? This kind comfort, one with another, these kinds of close connections and relationships, I observed in many different Māori contexts throughout my visit to Aotearoa New Zealand.

These observations invoke the ideas of Tineke Abma, a health policy and evaluation expert extraordinaire from the Netherlands. Abma (2006) has said of the sociorelational dimensions of evaluation,

> The social relations among program people and other stakeholders in the evaluation setting are an integral part of the program being evaluated and thus directly involved in assessments of program quality.... The relations between the evaluator and program participants and others in the setting [further] influence the possibilities and constraints of the evaluative practice in that context. (pp. 185–186)

In my own recent work, the salience and importance of evaluation re-lationships surfaced strongly as our group worked to conceptualize, field test, and develop practical guidelines for meaningful *values engagement* in evaluation. In some reflections on our work (Hall, Ahn, & Greene, 2012), we offered the following:

> Our experience, both conceptually and practically, highlights the need for attention to the relational and communicative aspects of evaluation, as these [are the] aspects [of evaluation that shape and] influence the character of values engagement. [Close] attention [to evaluation's sociorelational dimensions] also positions evaluation as a moral-political practice, rather than a mere methodological undertaking. Focusing on these aspects has reinforced our belief that evaluators must assume responsibility for explicating and justifying the values being advanced in their work. (Hall, Ahn, & Greene, 2012, p. 206)

Tineke and I both agree with our Māori colleagues that the complex and contextual relational dimensions of evaluation are constitutive of the evaluator's presence on site, the values being advanced, and therefore the character of the data collected and the interpretations made.

Back to Aotearoa, Fiona Cram and colleagues have generated a set of seven Kaupapa (action-oriented) Māori evaluation principles and practices, presented in Table 5.1. To illustrate these in practice (drawing from the original table), the principle of "*Manaaki ki te tangata*: look after people" can be enacted by planning for evaluation participants to learn and share with one another as part of their engagement in the evaluation; developing participant-engagement activities that allow them to explore possibilities, inspire them to see bright futures, and also have fun; and considering thoughtfully how best to take care of participants with special needs.

So, what are the lessons herein for culturally responsive, responsible, and engaged evaluators in the United States? Here are three preliminary thoughts.

First, I believe that clear statements of the values that are guiding a given evaluation study, along with the rationale for these values, is an important step toward meaningful communication and authentic relationships. A clear values statement should become one of evaluation's commonplace or standard parts of our evaluative thinking, evident in our evaluation design, implementation, and reporting. In culturally responsive evaluation, clear statements of evaluator values offer articulated and public declarations of cultural respect and understanding, available for evaluation stakeholders to critique, support, or otherwise engage.

Second, I believe we need to take the social strands of our work more seriously and engage in them with greater intentionality. We are indeed already attuned to the importance of relationships, interactions, and communications in our work as culturally responsive evaluators. We are indeed

TABLE 5.1   Kaupapa Māori Evaluation Principles and Practices

Kaupapa Māori Principle	Explanation
Aroha ki te tangata: A respect for people	Allow people to define their own space and to meet on their own terms, using appropriate engagement processes and correct observance of protocols. Stay informed about previous activities in whānau/communities, and leave preconceived ideas at home.
He kanohi kitea: The seen face	"A voice may be heard but a face needs to be seen." This is about building personal relationships and becoming known to the whānau/community, using face-to-face approaches and investing the time it takes to become known.
Titiro, whakarongo…korero: Look, listen…speak	This is the fine art of watching, listening, and then, sometime later, talking. Allow whānau time to reflect on information provided, questions asked and responses given, and engage on-site within time frames that work for the whānau/community.
Manaaki ki te tangata: Look after people	This is about hospitality and reciprocity, enacted through kai, koha, training, capacity building, and the sharing of information. Also, be mindful of whānau obligations and resources, and do not take anything for granted.
Kia tupato: Be careful	This is about practitioners and whānau being culturally safe through the following of whānau protocols and customs.
Kaua e takahia te mana o te tangata: Don't trample on people's mana	Act in ways that are respectful and mana enhancing. Focus particularly on ensuring whānau participation at every stage.
Kia māhaki: Be humble	Act with humility, share knowledge, and provide opportunities for whānau and community empowerment/learning through engagement.

Source: Adapted from Cram (2009) and Pipi et al. (2004).

mindful of traditions and customs in varied contexts, or at least alert to the possible need to learn about these prior to entering and working in a given context. But, inspired by Fiona and our other Māori colleagues, I think many of us could use a set of articulated principles and guidelines for this relational work, and a set of concrete practices to accompany these principles. Multiple sets may be needed for different cultural groups and different settings. And we will always need an insider's specific assistance in guiding our evaluative pathway. But we ourselves can and need to get better at being *relationally* culturally responsive in our work so that our work can be of greater consequence.

And third, directly from Fiona Cram (with thanks), placing relationships as the foundation of a culturally responsive evaluation does *not* imply a relaxation of methodological rigor, strong warrants for evidence, or professional responsibilities. On the contrary, as Fiona's colleague Papaarangi Reid has said, "Māori deserve good science." So relational trust comes with accountability to the people in that context for work that is of consequence to them.

Being of Consequence: Engaging the Politics of Evaluation

And finally, following on my aspiration to be of consequence in our evaluation work, I wish to end with my modest observations and reflections on the politics of "as Māori" evaluation in contemporary Aotearoa New Zealand. Evaluation is intrinsically political as it serves some people's interests but not others, as it advances some people's values but not others, as it embraces some definitions of program quality but not others, and so forth. Culturally responsive evaluators already know this.

What did I observe about the political dimensions of "as Māori" evaluation during my study leave? I observed that the larger political context is centered on the core issue of Māori self-determination, accompanied by the complex issues of land and rights restitution for Maori *iwis*. I believe that these macro, cultural survival issues of political rights and of sovereignty are manifest in "as Māori" evaluation in both overt and more subtle ways.

Notably, overheard from Māori evaluators:

- It is NOT OK for non-Māori to do evaluation in Māori spaces on their own or without Māori guidance, no matter how much they know about Māori culture.
- It is important to always start from a position of Māori strengths.
- I do not do any multi-ethnic work or writing anymore because the Māori voice gets lost or watered down.
- There is a difference between culturally responsive evaluation and Māori/indigenous evaluation, a difference worth articulating more clearly.

Again, what lessons can we U.S. evaluators, working with diverse cultural groups in our society, draw from the contemporary Māori politics in Aotearoa New Zealand? Again, my initial thoughts.

First, our work as culturally responsive evaluators should not duck the complex and often-controversial political issues in the contexts in which we work, but rather engage respectfully and thoughtfully with them in our evaluation, as they are already there. In fact, a concerted focus on the politics of culture in the contexts in which we work can importantly anchor our work as culturally responsive and responsible evaluators.

Second, maintain vigilance and regard for cultural self-determination at least in our language. Learning from Veronica Thomas:

- There are no inherently "at-risk children, youth or families" in the United States. But there are many, far too many, people who are *placed at risk* by continuing structural inequities in our society.
- Similarly, children in our schools do not achieve or fail to achieve at a particular level according to remote standardized tests. Rather, children in our schools demonstrate some level of mastery of the material *that they have had the genuine opportunity to learn.*

And finally, I suggest that culturally responsive evaluation more explicitly and officially include the concept *and* the enactment of *culturally responsible* evaluation, a term I have used throughout this discussion. To me, the concept of cultural responsibility captures many of the assertive and proactive stances of "as Māori" evaluation I witnessed during my study leave. To me, the concept of cultural responsibility unmasks the muted hegemony of evaluation in especially government and public contexts and insists that evaluation serve, if not self-determination goals of cultural minority groups, then the more modest goals of democratizing voice, access, and judgment.

CLOSURE

Culture is an inherent and integral strand of the fabric of contemporary program evaluation, because culture is part of all human endeavors. Culture is embedded in the character of the problems and policies that catalyzed the intervention being evaluated, in the organizational systems and routines that shape the performances being assessed, and in the institutional norms and practices that define and bound these performances. Culture incorporates our worldviews, beliefs, traditions, values, customary ways of being and interacting, daily life routines, and more.

In the multicultural society that is the United States in the early 21st century, most contexts for evaluation are themselves inhabited by people and groups from a range of cultural backgrounds. A culturally responsive evaluation approach aspires to be morally and practically attuned to the varied cultures in the context and to craft an evaluation study that is respectful of and responsive to them. A culturally responsive *and responsible* evaluation approach holds us as evaluators accountable for these aspirations.

NOTES

1. An earlier version of this chapater was presented at the April 2013 inaugural conference of the Center for Culturally Responsive Evaluation and Assessment, University of Illinois, Urbana-Champaign.

   My sincere thanks to Fiona Cram for her thoughtful and useful comments on a draft of this presentation and to Fiona, Nan Wehipeihana, and Kate McKegg for their critical contributions to the cultural accuracy and appropriateness of my portraits of Māori customs and practices.

2. Belvedere—a building or part of a building positioned to offer a fine view of the surrounding area.

3. Aotearoa is one Māori name for New Zealand. Ngāi Tahu, the main South Island tribe, has other names for the country, prominently Te Waipounamu. Te Waipounamu today generally refers to the South Island, although in a traditional Māori lore, it was the mainland "o te waka a Maui," the canoe from which Maui fished up the North Island. Current government policy and convention is to call the country Aotearoa New Zealand.

4. The Treaty of Waitangi was originally signed by the British settlers, representing the crown, and hundreds of Māori chiefs. Disputes about its meaning and violations of its agreements continue to this day. The Waitangi Tribunal was established in 1975 to hear and research such breeches.

5. Pākehā is the Māori word for White settlers and colonists.

6. Among the omissions from this set of reflections is the widespread use of colorful graphics in "as Māori" evaluation practice. Visual portraits or diagrams were frequently used to represent a program's design. A popular professional development activity for program staff working with Māori featured an elaborately constructed and illustrated life pathway. The various purposes and roles of these and other graphics could be usefully explored.

7. This evaluation was part of a larger set of evaluations conducted as field tests of a values-engaged, educative approach to STEM education evaluation, funded by an Evaluation Research and Evaluation Capacity grant no. 0535793 from the U.S. National Science Foundation.

8. All such evaluation teams with whom I engaged were composed wholly or mostly of Māori evaluators.

9. In Māori usage, the *marae atea* (often shortened to *marae*) is the open space in front of the *wharenui* or meeting house (literally "large building"). However, the term marae is commonly used to refer to the whole complex, including the buildings and the open space. (Wikipedia, 2014)

10. Pasifika refers to New Zealanders of Pacific Island descent, currently numbering about 250,000.

REFERENCES

Abma, T. A. (2006). The social relations of evaluation. In I. F. Shaw, J. C. Greene, & M. M. Mark (Eds.), *The Sage handbook of evaluation* (pp. 184–199). London, UK: Sage.

American Evaluation Association (AEA). (2011, April 22). *American Evaluation Association statement on cultural competence in evaluation.* Washington, DC: American Evaluation Association. Retrieved from http://www.eval.org/p/cm/ld/fid=92

ANZEA. (2013). *Vision & Kaupapa.* Retrieved from http://www.anzea.org.nz/vision-kaupapa/

Cram, F. (2009). Maintaining indigenous voices. In D. Mertens & P. Ginsberg (Eds.), *Sage handbook of social science research ethics* (pp. 308–322). Thousand Oaks, CA: Sage.

Cronbach, L. J., Ambron. S. R., Dornbusch, S. M., Hess, R. D., Hornik, R. C., Phillips, D. C., . . . Weiner, S. S. (1980). *Toward reform of program evaluation.* San Francisco, CA: Jossey-Bass.

Frierson, H. T., Hood, S., & Hughes, G. (2002). Strategies that address culturally responsive evaluation. In J. Frechtling (Ed.), *The 2002 user-friendly handbook for project evaluation* (pp. 63–73). Arlington VA: National Science Foundation.

Greene, J. C. (2005). Evaluators as stewards of the public good. In S. Hood, R. K. Hopson, & H. T. Frierson (Eds.), *The role of culture and cultural context: A mandate for inclusion, truth, and understanding in evaluation theory and practice.* (pp. 7–20). Greenwich CT: Information Age.

Greene, J. C. (2012). Values-engaged evaluation. In M. Segone (Ed.), *Evaluation for equitable development results.* New York, NY: UNICEF.

Hall, J. N., Ahn, J., & Greene, J. C. (2012). Values engagement in evaluation: Ideas, illustrations, and implications. *American Journal of Evaluation, 33*(2), 195–207.

Hood, S. (1998). Responsive evaluation Amistad style: Perspectives of one African-American evaluator. In *Proceedings of the Stake Symposium on Educational Evaluation. Urbana-Champaign, IL: University of Illinois at Urbana-Champaign.*

Hood, S. L., Hopson, R. K., & Frierson, H. (Eds.). (2005). *The role of culture and cultural context: A mandate for inclusion, the discovery of truth, and understanding in evaluative theory and practice.* Greenwich CT: Information Age.

Johnson, J., Hall, J., Greene, J. C, & Ahn, J. (2013). Exploring alternative approaches for presenting evaluation results. *American Journal of Evaluation, 34*(4), 486–503.

LaFrance, J. L. (2004). Culturally competent evaluation in Indian Country. *New Directions for Evaluation, 102,* 39–50.

LaFrance, J., & Nichols, R. (2010). Reframing evaluation: Defining an indigenous evaluation framework. *The Canadian Journal of Program Evaluation, 23*(2), 13–31.

LaFrance, J., Nichols, R., & Kirkhart, K. E. (2012). Culture writes the script: On the centrality of context in indigenous evaluation. *New Directions for Evaluation, 135,* 59–74.

Madison, A. M. (Ed.). (1992). *Minority issues in program evaluation. New Directions for Program Evaluation, 53.* San Francisco, CA: Jossey-Bass.

McKegg, K., & Wehipeihana, N. (2010). *Developmental evaluation: A practitioners' introduction.* A workshop presented at the 2010 conference of the Australasian Evaluation Society, Wellington, ANZ.

McKegg, K., Wehipeihana, N., & Pipi, K. (2013). *He Oranga Poutama: What have we learned. A report on the developmental evaluation of He Oranga Poutama.* Wellington: Sport New Zealand.

Mertens, D. M., & Hopson, R. K. (2006). Advancing evaluation of STEM efforts through attention to diversity and culture. *New Directions for Evaluation, 109,* 35–51.

Nelson-Barber, S., LaFrance, J., Trumbull, E., & Aburto, S. (2005). Promoting culturally reliable and valid evaluation practice. In S. Hood, R. K. Hopson, & H. T. Frierson (Eds.), *The role of culture and cultural context in evaluation: A mandate for inclusion, truth, and understanding in evaluation theory and practice.* (pp. 61–85). Greenwich CT: Information Age.

Patton, M. Q. (2008). *Utilization-focused evaluation* (4th ed.). Thousand Oaks, CA: Sage.

Patton, M. Q. (2010). *Developmental evaluation: Applying complexity concepts to enhance innovation and use.* New York, NY: Guilford.

Pipi, K., Cram, F., Hawke, R., Hawke, S., Huriwai, TeM., . . . Tuuta, T. (2004). A research ethic for studying Māori and iwi provider success. *Journal of Social Policy, 23,* 141–153.

Preskill, H., & Catsambas, T. T. (2006). *Reframing evaluation through appreciative inquiry.* Thousand Oaks CA: Sage.

Ryan, K. R., & Cousins, J. B. (Eds.). (2009). *The Sage international handbook of educational evaluation* (pp. 323–340). Thousand Oaks CA: Sage.

Smith, L. T. (2012). *Decolonizing methodologies* (2nd ed.). London, UK: Zed.

Thomas, V. D., & Stevens, F. (Eds.). (2004). *Co-constructing a contextually responsive evaluation framework. New Directions for Evaluation, 101.* San Francisco, CA: Jossey-Bass.

Thompson-Robinson, M., Hopson, R. K., & SenGupta, S. (Eds.) (2004). *In search of cultural competence in evaluation. New Directions for Evaluation,* 102. San Francisco, CA: Jossey-Bass.

Wikipedia. (2014). *Marae.* Retrieved from http://en.wikipedia.org/wiki/Marae

CHAPTER 6

CULTURALLY RESPONSIVE EVALUATION AS A RESOURCE FOR HELPFUL-HELP

Hazel Symonette

PREFACE

My passion in developing and sharing this chapter's resources grew directly out of witnessing many problematic patterns during my 7-year tenure (1991–1998) as the first Policy and Planning Analyst in the former Office of Minority Affairs (now the Office of Inclusivity, Diversity, Equity and Student Success) of the University of Wisconsin System Administration (Symonette, 2004). These patterns have continued living large during my subsequent capacity-building work at the University of Wisconsin-Madison's Office of Quality Improvement, Office of Human Resource Development, Office of Equity and Diversity, and now the Division of Student Life (Symonette, 2006). They spotlight the woeful inadequacy of compositional/ structural diversity-focused initiatives when not accompanied by campus capacity-building initiatives and incentives for appropriately engaging diversity. Such myopia continues to result in a revolving door of marginalized involvement, attrition, and constrained success opportunities for diverse faculty, staff, and students. A change is needed.

Continuing the Journey to Reposition Culture and Cultural Context in Evaluation Theory and Practice, pages 109–129
Copyright © 2015 by Information Age Publishing
All rights of reproduction in any form reserved.

INTRODUCTION

The rising tide of insistent voices from the future summons us to ethical praxis and inclusive excellence, especially in making judgments about merit, worth, value, significance, and/or congruence. These voices are calling for empathy-grounded evaluators who can stand in other persons' perspectives in order to responsively engage in socioculturally appropriate and authentic communications and social relations (Bennett, 1998; Lustig & Koester, 2009).

Our social positioning, as well as our sociocultural lenses and filters, exert critical influences on the intervention and evaluation processes we design and implement, and ultimately on our interpretations and judgments about what is substantive and worthy of attention versus what is "noise" and thus extraneous variation. We are expected to ethically engage in "systematic data-based inquiry" in order to competently make judgments that are honest, respectful, fair, accurate, useful, and responsive to the general and public welfare (AEA, 2004; Yarbrough, Shulha, Hopson, & Caruthers, 2011). Who we are as knowers, inquirers, and engagers of others matters. We need to understand who we are as evaluators and how we know what we believe we know about others and ourselves. In this way, our evaluation practice becomes a resource for Helpful-Help, that is, help that moves beyond deficit-grounded presumptions of intrinsic brokenness and weakness toward conditional/situational reads of personal and social problems and limitations (Remen, 1999).

When evaluators provide Helpful-Help, they serve as contextually responsive channels and reliable/valid instruments for relevant data collection, analysis, and interpretation. Providing Helpful-Help requires that evaluators remain open, empathically learning-centered, diversity-grounded, and responsive in order to discern social structural conditions (especially the problematics) while engaging relevant social, psychological, and physical boundaries. Contextual discernment is especially important for evaluators because of their impactful judgment-making about merit, worth, value, significance, and congruence.

Such quality assurances require dynamic assessments of SELF-in-Context in the moment and across time. This involves intrapersonal check-ins (self-empathy) complemented by assessments from the vantage points of one's primary stakeholders (social empathy). The Integral Evaluator model, with its groundings in empathic perspective-taking, provides a systematic inquiry and reflective practice protocol that serves as a generative resource for this work

Our globally interconnected world is increasingly demanding diversity-grounded, equity-minded evaluators. At the same time, evaluator roles typically confer social powers to define reality and make impactful judgments about others. These judgment-making responsibilities place us among society's privileged authorities.

Privilege grants the cultural authority to make judgments about others and to have those judgments stick. It allows people to define reality and to have prevailing definitions of reality fit their experience. Privilege means being able to decide who gets taken seriously, who receives attention, who is accountable to whom and for what. (Johnson, 2001, p. 33)

Living up to and into these normative expectations requires evaluators to cultivate themselves as clear channels in order to look and actually see, to listen and actually hear, to touch and actually feel from multiple primary stakeholders' vantage points. We need to inquire about our own readiness, preparedness, and responsiveness for complex, interdependent—and often conflicting demands.

Because cultures and contexts are dynamic and ever-changing, one needs to proactively survey the shifting sociocultural and political terrain for action—social boundaries, borderlands, and intersections. Then identify relevant boundaries, from multiple stakeholder perspectives, and thus salient differences that make a substantive difference for access, process, and success opportunities in a given context. This boundary-spanning work is a lifelong process (Adams, Bell & Griffin, 1997; Cullinan, 1999). It calls for ongoing SELF-in-Context homework to assess and enhance one's portfolio of multicultural/intercultural resources and other boundary-spanning competencies. These are core prerequisites for what Karen Kirkhart called "interpersonal validity" in her 1994 Presidential Address at the American Evaluation Association annual conference: notably, "the soundness and trustworthiness of understandings emanating from personal interactions. . . . the skills and sensitivities of the researcher or evaluator, in how one uses oneself as a knower, as an inquirer" (Kirkhart, 1994, p. 4). I consistently modify Kirkhart's very useful concept by adding "engager": notably, what do we do with our boundary-spanning knowledge and inquiry skills to cultivate viable boundary-spanning social relations, processes, and practices.

As privileged authorities, especially in turbulent environments, how do we as evaluators honor the trust and normative expectations embedded and embodied in our social role as respectful, trustworthy answer-seekers and answer-makers? We must regularly check in: whose voices/views/vantage points am I privileging given my personal default perspectives and orientation? Without assiduously tracking, monitoring, and correcting (as needed) these predispositions, we may find ourselves inadvertently stifling, rather than summoning and nourishing, development of the full spectrum of human potential. We need to mindfully engage in ways that enhance prospects that our presence is facilitative rather than inhibitive and thus an engagement enhancer.

The increasing diversity and complexity of our world insistently challenges evaluators to use double-sided mirrors in order to ascertain our personal resources vis-à-vis the needs of our work agenda environment. This involves a clear-eyed assessment of our readiness and preparedness to provide Helpful-Help. More specifically, what does our self-assessment reveal about our capacity to design and provide evaluation services in ways that leave our primary stakeholders better off, both from their perspectives as well as our own?

This chapter introduces the Integral Evaluator model as a holistic framework for empathically assessing and exploring who we are in the context of who and what we are summoned to bring to our work as evaluators. Specifically, I am prioritizing evaluation in the service of enacting socially just interventions as well as enabling more socially just interveners. Living into this agenda foundationally involves the use of diversity-grounded, equity-minded assessment/evaluation processes to discern and configure robust contextually responsive opportunities for activating and supporting success.

My Integral Evaluator Quadrant model focuses on three multilevel developmental strands as resources for discerning and providing Helpful-Help: Calibrating SELF-In-Context, Knowing SELF-In-Context, and Activating SELF-In-Context. To mindfully cultivate our boundary-spanning capacities, we need to monitor and track ourselves in four key contexts: Relational (WHO is or should be present and involved—primary stakeholders?), Situational (WHAT is the work agenda and success vision?), Temporal (WHEN—time/timing?) and Spatial/Geographic (WHERE—physical and/or virtual environments?). My boundary-spanning model helps us unpack and engage the WHO? (relational) complexity at the heart of WHAT? (situational) agendas: notably, the human systems dynamics.

This chapter proceeds from a high-level overview of the Integral Evaluator Quadrant model (Figure 6.1) through an extensive set of probing quadrant-specific questions (Figure 6.2): *Self-to-Self/Looking Inward, Self-to-Self/Looking Outward, Self-to-Others and Self-to-Systems.* The final section further elaborates Figure 6.2 via four key tasks and next steps for mindfully jumpstarting and sustaining one's cultural competence agenda as a lifelong pilgrimage.

HELPFUL-HELP

Too often, well-meaning, well-intentioned initiatives have unintended problematic impacts that result in the social costs of accepting help being too high (Tuck, 2009). As Kaylynn Two Trees (2003) aptly puts it, "privilege is a learning disability." With little consequence for ourselves, we do violence to others' truths when we fail to develop and refine the self as an open, diversity-conscious, and expansively learning-centered, responsive instrument. Without such vigilant attention, our capacity to do excellent boundary-spanning work suffers greatly. Truly offering Helpful-Help requires expansion of our understandings of the self in dynamically diverse contexts within power and privilege/oppression hierarchies at a single point in time and also our understandings of the contexts embodied in the self across time (Harro, 2010).

To activate a Helpful-Help approach requires a focus on human systems dynamics. More specifically, we have to mindfully unpack and engage the WHO? complexity dwelling at the heart of culturally and contextually responsive interventions and evaluations:

- Who is to be helped via the intervention?
- Who are the primary helpers/interveners?
- Who do those primary interveners need to partner with to enact the success vision in ways that leave the target population better off?

Knowing and understanding the implied "theory of change" embedded within programmatic interventions moves them beyond presumptions and Black Box, random-scattershot strategies toward more explicit and mindful "If-then" tracking of the Who? and What? interconnections.

- For whom is what you are doing working in what ways, to what extent, and under what conditions?
  - Access: entry portal-screening criteria and results—Who is present?
  - Process: intervention-process congruence with whose needs/norms/rhythms for enacting and actualizing the success vision (notably, activities and outputs that scaffold the gap between what is and what is envisioned)?
  - Success: actual benefits and gains for whom?
- How do you know—data-grounded cues, clues, signposts?
- To what extent would which stakeholders agree with your assessments?

More specifically, what are participants actually exposed to and experiencing that is congruent with your (and their) visions of success and the intervention's outcome promises: notably, the actual scaffolding of the targeted outcomes gap? What is the Transformation Bridge that constitutes robust generative stimuli which then leads one to reasonably expect the desired participant outcomes?

This Helpful-Help orientation is similar to the expectations undergirding "Servant Leadership" as reflected in Robert Greenleaf's famous "Best Test" for living as a servant leader:

> Do those served grow as persons? Do they, *while being served*, become healthier, wiser, freer, more autonomous, more likely themselves to become servants?

And, what is the effect on the least privileged in society? Will they benefit or at least not be further deprived? (Greenleaf, 1977, p. 27; emphasis in original)

Helpful-Help is also similar to what Remen (1999) labels "serving" and thus distinctly different from her characterization of conventional helping and fixing.

Fixing and helping create a distance between people, but we cannot serve at a distance. We can only serve that to which we are profoundly connected....Serving is different from helping. Helping is not a relationship between equals. A helper may see others as weaker than they are, needier than they are, and people often feel this inequality. The danger in helping is that we may inadvertently take away from people more than we could ever give them; we may diminish their self-esteem, their sense of worth, integrity or even wholeness. (p. 1)

The primary contexts that one needs to mindfully track in order to offer Helpful-Help are Relational (Who?), Situational (What?), Temporal (When?), and Spatial/Geographic (Where?). To enact this success vision requires empathically assessing and reflecting on who you are—and perceived to be—as evaluator vis-à-vis appropriately engaging the right stakeholder voices and the right places, things, and timings. Cultivating SELF-in-Context as a Responsive Instrument increases prospects for cultural and contextual responsiveness and thereby expands opportunities for evaluators knowing how to provide Helpful-Help.

Cultivating SELF-In-Context as Responsive Instrument

My Cultivating SELF-In-Context as a Responsive Instrument model is an adaptation and elaboration of an Integral Ecology Quadrant Model (Esbjörn-Hargens & Zimmerman, 2009). Such models holistically spotlight relevant Individual versus Collective Level attributes in relation to relevant Interior versus Exterior Environment attributes. My approach promotes social justice while facilitating empowerment through supporting the integrity and boundary-spanning efficacy of service-sector practitioners, especially evaluators and educators, as they strive to walk the talk of their success visions. The resources shared in this chapter offer an explicit, contextually responsive systematic inquiry and reflective practice protocol—one that is grounded in dynamic multilevel developmental evaluation processes. To use it, practitioners need to regularly assess and engage SELF-in-Context as a responsive instrument from multiple vantage points. Doing so involves Calibrating SELF-In-Context, Knowing SELF-In-Context, and Activating SELF-In-Context.

Calibrating and Knowing Self are assessment inventory-type tasks. To infuse the dynamism needed to Activate SELF-in-Context, I have adapted Kurt Lewin's forcefield framework, which arrays change expediters/enhancers versus detractors (Mind Tools, 2014). The focus of these Forcefields of Readiness & Preparedness can range from micro to the more macro levels: notably, from the intrapersonal → interpersonal → systemic. These dynamic developmental evaluation processes correspond to my Self-to-Self * Self-to-Others * Self-to-Systems schema, respectively.

The core model undergirding my SELF-In-Context framework is Ken Wilber's Integral Quadrant model (Wilber, n.d.). Barrett Brown (2011) offers a relatively succinct explanation and a useful application to sustainability initiatives.

> In essence, the Integral framework seeks to weave together the many threads of human knowledge in an inclusive way. It attends to objective and subjective, and individual and collective, ways of knowing. At the same time, it is sensitive to the development of people and cultures over time and the impact this has on the way individuals and groups perceive the world. (Brown, 2011, para. 2)

> The quadrants are essentially four lenses that, when taken together, help us to comprehensively look at anyone, anything, or any event. By looking at a sustainability initiative through all of the quadrants, we're able to identify most—if not all—the major forces which influence the success or failure of that initiative. That's the key advantage of doing a quadrant analysis: you get a very comprehensive picture of all the dynamics at play that will either make or break your project. . . . Like unique windows on the world, the quadrants offer four unique ways of looking at the same thing, each of which reveals different dimensions or qualities of that thing. (Brown, 2007, paras. 5, 7)

My Integral Evaluator model provides a comprehensive framework for systematically calibrating, knowing, and activating self in situational and relational contexts, in particular. It builds upon and elaborates Wilber's (n.d.) Integral Quadrants; that is, (Interior versus Exterior Environments) X (Individual versus Collective Levels). This is described next. My approach also draws upon insights from the complexity sciences (Patton, 2011; Snowden & Boone, 2007), Integral Quadrant modeling (Esbjörn-Hargens & Zimmerman, 2009), program logic models (Funnell & Rogers, 2011), and Developmental Evaluation (Patton, 2011).

INTEGRAL EVALUATOR QUADRANT MODEL

Our perceptions yield culturally conditioned data, holding meanings that are not self-evident. The ultimate impact of these data is influenced by the clarity and depth of understandings of self-in-action within a particular sociocultural/sociopolitical context at a specific point in time. It is also influenced by understandings of the contexts embodied in the self; notably, one's social identities and roles that are derived through socialization and societal status allocation/distribution processes across time (Harro, 2010). Effectively doing SELF-in-Context development work requires a prioritizing focus on human differences that make a socially patterned difference; most importantly, those associated with privileged social identities. Consequently, one needs to hold in high consciousness the fact that privilege, like oppression (its tag-team partner), is a feature of a social system and not an intrinsic attribute of individuals.

> People have or don't have privilege depending upon the system they're in and the social categories other people put them in.... Privilege exists when one group has something that is systematically denied to others not because of who they are or what they've done, but because of the social category they belong to. (Johnson, 2001, p. 38)

Culture is a key metacontextual framework that informs and shapes all other major contexts—the relational, situational, temporal, and spatial/geographic contexts. As we engage in our work, how do we decide which sociocultural practices and processes within a service-delivery environment should be the focus of our attention: notably, which ways of being/thinking/saying/engaging inform doing the right things right from multiple vantage points? For example, which choices among teaching/learning strategies and resources gain our focus given the sociocultural predispositions we bring, whether by default or by design? Whose ways of being/doing/thinking/engaging are foregrounded and thus privileged? What messaging emerges as a result regarding WHO matters and belongs, or does not, whether it is intended or not?

Since 2008, I have used variants of Integral Quadrant modeling as a resource for contextually responsive interventions as well as assessment and evaluation processes; that is, for engaging contextualized WHO? factors: Who is served by whom, with whom embedded in situational, relational, temporal, and spatial/geographic contexts (Symonette. 2008)? At the heart of What agendas is the Who; that is, the human systems dynamics—notably, the interface between and among the primary stakeholders within the terrain of power and privilege/oppression and other salient dimensions of human differentiation.

Figure 6.1 provides an overview of my Integral Evaluator Quadrant model which displays four lenses for holistically cultivating self-empathy (row 1) and social empathy (row 2). Again, the quadrants are defined by the intersection of (Interior versus Exterior Environments) and (Individual versus Collective Levels):

- Upper Left Quadrant: Mapping Self as You Know Self
  Who Am I?
- Lower Left Quadrant: Mapping Self as You Perceive & Believe Others Know Self
  Where and With Whom do I Matter and Belong among Stakeholders?
- Upper Right Quadrant: Mapping Self in Self-Constructed Work Context.
  What Work Am I Being Called To Do?
- Lower Right Quadrant: Mapping Self In Self/Other-Constructed Work Context
  Whose Ways of Being/Doing/Engaging Matter and are thus Privileged? Who Authorizes, Decides, and How?

The Integral Evaluator model is a holistic systematic inquiry and reflective practice framework for crafting responsive programmatic interventions while simultaneously cultivating SELF-in-context as responsive instrument. It is a praxis-grounded adaptation and elaboration of my Integral Researcher-Self model (Symonette, 2008).

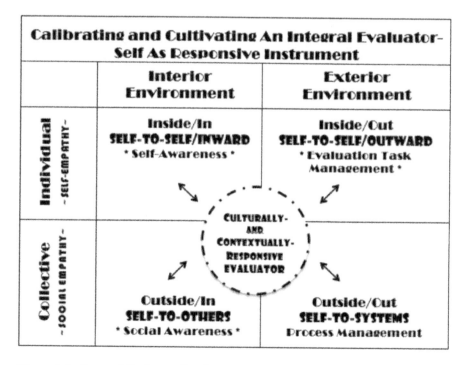

Figure 6.1 Integral Evaluator Quadrant model overview.

The double-headed arrows represent the interface between dynamic assessments related to "walking one's talk" (integrity check-ins) and "talking one's walk" (giving voice to the "raw data" of how one is actually living in and engaging the world). This Integral Evaluator Self-in-Context Model, when disaggregated and examined quadrant by quadrant, can serve as a resource for crafting a Who-focused logic model.

Mindfully walking around the quadrants will help inform and shape how we each can empathically design and support authentic inclusion and engagement strategies; notably, the configuration of communications and service delivery grace spaces. Such spaces embody the aspiration that we commit and strive to live into collaboratively constructed, mutually respectful, trust-enhancing physical and social environments. They encourage all to bring forward their BEST SELF in full voice to do their best learning, best engaging and best work. Deep 360-degree listening and discernment via regular applications of multilevel Forcefields of Readiness and Preparedness help guide us in more systematically assessing and addressing the needs of a services delivery agenda in order to increase prospects for Helpful-Help.

Boundary spanning is a foundational skill for service-sector practitioners, especially persons committed to helping individuals/groups/communities bring forward their best selves to do their best learning, best engaging, and best work. Who do I need to be in order to provide Helpful-Help? More specifically, in what ways do I need to cultivate myself as a responsive instrument in order to help them live into their success vision, given the relational, situational, temporal, and spatial/geographic contexts? What is my personal Forcefield of Readiness and Preparedness for that evaluation work agenda: notably, attributes that I embody or have available to build on (enhancers) versus work on (detractors)? Such assessments need to be conducted from both my vantage point (unilateral self-awareness) and from the vantage points of the stakeholders I am seeking to serve (multilateral self-awareness). The critical initial use of Forcefield assessments involves discerning patterns of convergence and divergence regarding one's Evaluator Portfolio: notably, variations in the relevant attributes that one is perceived to have, both to Work-WITH and to Work-ON.

Investment in SELF-in-Context development work helps us become a dynamic social relations barometer and compass for navigating and negotiating complex, often turbulent, human systems dynamics. Because cultures and contexts are constantly morphing, this is a lifelong systematic-inquiry and reflective-practice pilgrimage. During my intensive work in this domain for over 30 years, I have resolved, like many others, that sociocultural responsiveness and competence is a stance rather than a destination status or fixed state of being. And so for practitioners, this involves ongoing reflective conversations with self (and others) about one's ongoing journey path toward culturally and contextually responsive evaluation processes and practices. This is a special application of "Talking-My-Walk" vis-à-vis "Walking-My-Talk." (see http://www.heartintelligencecoach.com/walking-your-talk-or-talking-your-walk/)

I envision evaluators mindfully using their Forcefield of Readiness and Preparedness assessments to discern what the context is summoning from them vis-à-vis what their current Evaluator Portfolio has available to provide Helpful-Help. Systematically contrasting what is available versus needed/envisioned can help evaluators (and other service sector practitioners) more systematically "diagnose" and scaffold a personal development agenda: notably, a capacity-building bridge for emerging a more culturally and contextually responsive Evaluator Portfolio.

Dynamic SELF-In-Context assessments involve systematic calibration and understandings of SELF within relevant sociocultural/sociopolitical contingencies vis-à-vis key aspects of the intervention and service delivery environment. Cultivating SELF-In-Context as a Responsive Instrument in the service of socially just success visions involves three developmental strands.

1. CALIBRATE SELF-In-Context

Who are the right people/voices/vantage points and **What** are the right places, things and timings that help enliven/enable/enact **Why** a programmatic intervention has been created? This framework is informed by the ubiquitous Journalism and Quality Improvement protocol—the 5 W's and the 2 H's. My model zeros in on the 4 that represent contexts among the 7:

- Relational Context: Who?
- Situational Context: What?
- Temporal Context: When?
- Spatial/Geographic Context: Where?

2. KNOW SELF-In-Context

Who we are matters not simply as we know ourselves but, as importantly, as others "construct" us. We need not own others' images of us and our work; yet we surely need boundary-spanning awareness to start cultivating authentic communications and social relations from a place that resonates.

- Unilateral Self-Awareness
  As SELF knows SELF: **Self-Empathy**
- Multilateral Self-Awareness
  As OTHERS perceive & believe they know SELF: **Social Empathy**

3. ACTIVATE SELF-In-Context

The above inventory-type tasks lay a rich contextualized foundation for moving from discerning relevant information → insights → actions.

- Dynamic Multi-level Assessment
  - MICRO Forcefields of Readiness & Preparedness
    Intrapersonal and Interpersonal Domains
  - MACRO Forcefields of Readiness & Preparedness
    Systemic—Organizational/Institutional Domains
- Flexible Micro/Macro Zoom-Control powers

As the context requires, conscientiously zoom in for details—*mouse-eye view*—and zoom out for varying levels of a situated bigger picture vantage point: *moose-eye, giraffe-eye, and eagle-eye views.* Moving along that multilevel scaling, proactively acknowledge and own the discernment trade-offs associated with varying levels of magnification versus miniaturization.

The Integral Evaluator model provides a holistic grid for succinctly arraying key sensitizing concepts and questions. The embedded inquiry protocol guides us in systematic data-grounded assessments for regularly checking in with ourselves while doing boundary-spanning work to increase prospects for contextually/culturally responsive processes/practices that are both effective and appropriate from multiple vantage points.

DYNAMIC DEVELOPMENTAL EVALUATION

Such iterative assessments need to occur before, after, and during intervention development processes to check out one's self-in-action while being and doing self vis-à-vis one's service delivery and evaluation agenda. Most importantly, what are the relevant assets and resources in the Evaluator Portfolio—professional, intercultural, interpersonal, and intrapersonal— as well as the needs, challenges, blankspots, and blindspots? Again, I have adapted Kurt Lewin's (Mind Tools, 2014) Forcefield change framework to fuel ongoing inquiry that infuses some dynamism into this counterbalancing assessment process.

Zeroing in on the Inside/Out and Outside/Out Quadrants of the Integral Evaluator SELF-in-Context Model: What is the status of one's Forcefield of Preparedness and Readiness for the sociocultural context as well as for the tasks embodied in the intervention/evaluation agenda? This would be from the evaluator's own perspective and from his/her evaluative "read" of others' perspectives (see Figure 6.2).

Given a particular situational, relational, temporal and spatial/geographic context, how do the assets and resources in one's Evaluator Portfolio counterbalance the needs/challenges/ shortfalls? What does one have available to Work-WITH versus Work-ON? Given the intervention and the evaluation, which attributes should be foregrounded and amplified to foster boundary-spanning engagement and efficacy? To what extent would

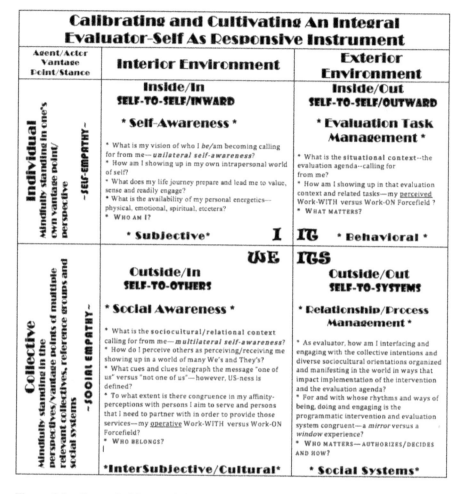

Figure 6.2 Expanded Integral Evaluator Quadrant model.

others agree? Who says so, given multiple voices, views, and vantage points. And how does one really know?

TASK 1. Priming Empathic Perspective-Taking: Inside/Out Reflections and Deliberations

The Integral Evaluator SELF-in-Context model offers a systematic inquiry and reflective practice protocol that fosters self-empathy and social empathy via mindfully discerning and standing in one's own perspective in addition to standing in and imagining relevant perspectives of primary stakeholders. Follow-on deliberative conversations with significant others would enhance and enrich these self-grounded assessments via opportunities to cross-verify and validate one's self-assessment insights. This would involve boundary-spanning dialogue and deliberations regarding patterns of convergence and divergence in one's own read of the relational and situational context vis-à-vis others' reads.

I encourage you to work from the inside/out—immersing oneself and gaining conscious clarity via self-grounded inquiry and reflections before expanding into broader deliberative circles for sharing, cross-validating, and elaborating insights. Lay the foundation with private brainstorming and reflections to excavate, honor, and harvest one's own insights and wisdom. Start with the Upper-Left *Who-Am-I?* Quadrant in preparation for mindfully walking around the quadrants to address the questions posed at the intersections (crossroads) of Individual and Collective Levels, for both the Interior and Exterior Environments.

Engaging in a systematic awareness-building, sensitizing process regarding one's own intrapersonal self should provide a robust foundation for more responsively discerning and exploring the WHO? agenda—the boundary-spanning work with human systems contours and dynamics—in the context of the WHAT? agenda.

TASK 2. Mapping the Human Systems Dynamics

Identify the key "WHO?" constituencies—notably, your intervention's primary stakeholders and their interconnections. Collaboratively brainstorm and prioritize among potential stakeholders. A 2 × 2 *High/Low* Stakeholder Mapping grid is a useful resource for prioritizing across the domain of persons who care about and can influence, positively or negatively, a programmatic intervention's destiny: *Levels of Investment* (time, money, etc.) × *Levels of Expected Impact.*

- **Who** are the persons served through participation in the intervention: notably, who is being engaged and transformed in what ways under what conditions?
- **Who** is crafting and providing the intervention activities? Who discerns and determines what is—and should be—learned/developed/transformed by whom based upon what?
- **Who** is doing the evaluative judgment making regarding the quality and depth of learning/development/transformation?

TASK 3. Engaging the Integral Evaluator Quadrant Model

The concepts and questions associated with each quadrant provide the beginnings of a comprehensive self-assessment framework, with heads-up alerts, for checking in with ourselves. The Integral Evaluator model is a systematic inquiry and reflective practice protocol for mindfully assessing and enhancing ethical praxis and inclusive excellence via increases in "interpersonal validity": notably, the soundness and trustworthiness of understandings warranted by one's uses of SELF as knower, inquirer, and engager of others vis-à-vis one's uses of evaluation tools, techniques, and strategies. To what extent is the evaluator looking and actually seeing; listening and actually hearing; touching and actually feeling? How does one know, and who says so? The prospects for culturally responsive, socially just, and inclusively excellent observations and evaluations are greatly enhanced with serious, ongoing consideration of these issues.

Use insights from one's *Who-Am-I?* Brainstorming to systematically walk around the quadrants vis-à-vis their sociocultural/sociopolitical meanings and implications for one's intervention agenda and associated assessment/ evaluation processes, practices, protocols, and products.

Upper Left Quadrant: Mapping Self as You Know Self

Individual *Interior* Environment—Unilateral Self-Awareness/Relational Context 1

Who Am I?
Self Empathy 1. Self-to-Self/Looking Inward

- What does my life journey prepare and lead me to value, sense, and readily engage?
- What is the *availability* of my personal energetics—physical, psychological, spiritual?
- What are my core Affinity-Discernment Criteria (informal/formal kinship and belonging) and my core Valuing-Judgment criteria?
- For which personal attributes and social identities do I hold a more ethnocentric versus a more open ethnorelative orientation? (Bennett, 1986)
- Who does my living persona radiate and message that I be and who/what I value?
- How do I know—cues, clues, signposts?

Lower Left Quadrant: Mapping Self as You Perceive and Believe Others Know Self

Collective *Interior* Environment—Multilateral Self-Awareness/Relational Context 2

Where and With Whom do I Matter and Belong Among Stakeholders? Social Empathy 1. Self-to-Others

- How do I perceive others as perceiving/receiving me showing up in a world of many We's and They's?
- What cues and clues telegraph the message "one of us" versus "not one of us"—however, US-ness is defined?
- For which personal attributes and social identities am I discerning and experiencing an ethnocentric versus an ethnorelative orientation among primary stakeholders? More specifically, in what ways and to what extent do my Affinity-Discernment Criteria (Who belongs?) and my Valuing-Judgment criteria (Who Matters?) converge ←o→ diverge with the configuration operating among primary stakeholders?
- What is the living operationalization of mattering and belonging—and thus community—within the relational context of the work agenda: e.g., the "Psychological Climate" and the Behavioral Climate." (Hurtado & Guillermo-Wann, 2013; Milem, Chang, & Antonio, 2005)
- To what extent is there congruence in my affinity-perceptions with persons I aim to serve and persons that I need to partner with in order to provide those services—my operative Work-WITH versus Work-ON **Forcefield**?

Upper Right Quadrant: Mapping Self in Self-Constructed Work Context.

Individual *Exterior* Environment—Situational Context 1

What Work Am I Being Called To Do? Self Empathy 2. Self-to-Self/Looking Outward

- What is the **situational context**—the evaluation agenda—calling for from me?
- How am I showing up in that evaluation context and related tasks— my perceived Work-WITH versus Work-ON **Forcefield** ?

Lower Right Quadrant: Mapping Self In Self/Other-Constructed Work Context.

Collective *Exterior* Environment: Institutional Structures & Social Systems—Situational Context 2

Whose Ways of Being/Doing/Engaging Matter and Are Thus Privileged?
Who Authorizes, Decides and How?
Social Empathy 2. Self-to-Systems

- As evaluator, how am I interfacing and engaging with the collective intentions and diverse sociocultural orientations organized and manifesting in the world in ways that impact implementation of the intervention and the evaluation agenda?
- For and with whose rhythms and ways of being, doing and engaging is the programmatic intervention and evaluation system congruent—a *mirror* versus a *window* experience? (Style, 1996)

The Integral Evaluator Model is a dynamic developmental evaluation resource that enhances the mindful uses of SELF-in-Context as a boundary-spanning, responsive instrument primed to provide Helpful-Help that more fully supports stakeholder success.

TASK 4. Embracing SELF-In-Context Work as a Lifelong Pilgrimage

The Integral Evaluator model is a developmental evaluation resource for ongoing systematic data-based inquiry and reflective conversations with self and others about alignment of aspirations/intentions and actions. This ongoing process would enable and enact an emergent intervention process—{Activities + Outputs = Transformation Bridge}—as well as a culturally and contextually responsive intervener. As noted earlier, this quadrant model provides a framework for sitting in the tensions of "Talking One's Walk" (giving voice to one's regular living realities) vis-à-vis "Walking One's Talk"—progress relative to aspirational intentions/success agendas such as becoming a Culturally Responsive Evaluator. The model is likely to be especially helpful in facilitating and supporting an emergent and evolving success-development process within complex, often turbulent, environments: one in which stakeholders are relatively far from agreement and there is relatively little certainty about what needs to be done (g-p training, 2007).

SOME EVOLVING AND EMERGENT JOURNEY-PATH REFLECTIONS

Investment in SELF-in-Context development work helps us become dynamic social relations barometers and compasses for navigating and negotiating complex, often turbulent human systems dynamics. Because cultures and contexts are constantly morphing, this is a lifelong systematic-inquiry and reflective-practice pilgrimage.

Our social positioning, as well as our sociocultural lenses, filters, and frames, exert crucial influences on the intervention and evaluation processes we design, their implementation, and ultimately our interpretations and judgments about what is substantive and worthy of attention versus what is "noise" and thus extraneous variation; who we are as knowers, inquirers, and engagers of others matters. As privileged authorities, evaluators especially need to mindfully honor the sacred trust embedded and embodied in our social roles as respectful, trustworthy answer-seekers and answer-makers. Normative expectations lead many to presume that professional evaluators will engage in ethical, socially just processes and practices for the public interest and the greater good.

Evaluators are one among the service-sector practitioners explicitly committed to the greater good. As such, we need to continually ask, How am I helping individuals/groups/communities bring forward their best selves to do their best learning, best engaging and best work? Who do I need to be to provide Helpful-Help? More specifically, in what ways do I need to cultivate myself as a responsive instrument to help them live into their success vision, given the relational, situational, temporal, spatial/geographic contexts? What is my Forcefield of Readiness and Preparedness for that work agenda, that is, what attributes do I embody or have available to build on (enhancers) versus work on (detractors)—both from my vantage point and from stakeholders' vantage points?

Empathically answering these questions requires that we stay open, light on our feet, expansively learning-centered, and responsive. These are core prerequisites for contextually responsive inquiry and engagement and thus for ethical praxis and inclusive excellence. To fully step into that charge, we are summoned to embrace 360-degree sensing, with clear channels, to activate the leaderly behaviors required for social justice and the greater good. We need to continuously examine the extent to which we are regularly activating ourselves for the greater good, given the configuration of our privileged versus nonprivileged identities and roles in a particular relational, situational, temporal, and spatial/geographic context.

To cultivate yourself as responsive instrument, actively embrace mirror-time stewardship with a double-sided mirror and regularly ask yourself these questions. In what ways and to what extent am I exercising 360-degree leaderly behavior—leading up, leading lateral, leading down—for the greater good? What is my Forcefield of Readiness and Preparedness for what the relational and situational context is summoning: notably, the configuration of assets and resources that I embody and have to work with vis-à-vis the needs/issues/challenges that I also embody which I need to work on?

In using forcefield assessments with a generative, appreciative mindset (Bushe, 2007), we can better understand how we might strategically foreground and amplify our assets and resources for the greater good while still working on our own limitations/problematics. What do you and I need to say and do and think for the best of all concerned?

The prospects for Helpful-Help—contextually responsive, socially just and inclusively excellent services—are greatly enhanced with serious ongoing consideration of the processes, practices and issues that this chapter addresses. Using my holistic Integral Quadrant framework, one can systematically cultivate Self as responsive instrument from one's own vantage point (unilateral self-awareness) as well as from primary stakeholders' vantage points (multilateral self-awareness). Especially crucial are the voices, views, and vantage points of the persons/groups/communities that we claim and aim to help. Accomplishing this involves dynamically assessing and *Calibrating* SELF-in-Context, *Knowing* SELF-in-Context, and *Activating* SELF-in-Context via mindful engagement of relevant forcefields of readiness and preparedness: self-to-self, self-to-others, and self-to-systems.

Sociocultural responsiveness and competence is a dynamic stance rather than a destination status or fixed state of being. For the greater good, I hope that we will energetically embrace lifelong reflective conversations with self—and others—about "Talking-My-Walk" vis-à-vis "Walking-My-Talk."

REFERENCES

Adams, M., Bell, L., & Griffin, P. (1997). *Teaching for diversity and social justice: A sourcebook*. London, UK: Routledge.

American Evaluation Association (AEA). (2004). *American Evaluation Association guiding principles for evaluators*. Retrieved from http://www.eval.org/p/cm/ld/fid=51

American Evaluation Association (AEA). (2011, April 22). *American Evaluation Association statement on cultural competence in evaluation*. Washington, DC: American Evaluation Association. Retrieved from http://www.eval.org/p/cm/ld/fid=92

Bennett, M. (1986). Towards ethnorelativism: A developmental model of intercultural sensitivity. In M. Paige (Ed.), *Cross-cultural orientation*. New York, NY: University Press of America.

Bennett, M. (1998). Overcoming the golden rule: Sympathy and empathy. In M. J. Bennett (Ed.), *Basic concepts of intercultural communication: Selected readings.* Yarmouth, ME: Intercultural.

Brown, B. (2007, February 20). *The four worlds of sustainability: Drawing upon four universal perspectives to support sustainability initiatives.* Retrieved from http:// nextstepintegral.org/wp-content/uploads/2011/04/Four-Worlds-of-Sustainability-Barrett-C-Brown.pdf

Brown, B. (2011). *Four quadrants of sustainability* [Blog post]. Retrieved from http:// integralthinkers.com/integral-theory/four-quadrants-of-sustainability/

Bushe, G. R. (2007). Appreciative inquiry is not (just) about the positive. *OD Practitioner, 39*(4), 30–35.

Cullinan, C. (1999). Vision, privilege and the limits of tolerance. *Electronic Magazine of Multicultural Education, 1*(2). Retrieved from http://jonah.eastern.edu/ emme/1999spring/cullinan.html

Esbjörn-Hargens, S., & Zimmerman, M. (2009, March). An overview of integral ecology: A comprehensive approach to today's complex planetary issues [White paper]. *Integral Institute.* Retrieved from: http://nextstepintegral. org/wp-content/uploads/2011/04/Overview-of-Integral-Ecology-Hargens-Zimmerman.pdf

Funnell, S. C. & Rogers, P. J. (2011). *Purposeful program theory: Effective use of theories of change and logic models.* San Francisco, CA: Wiley.

g-p training.net. (2007). *The Stacey matrix.* Retrieved from http://www.gp-training. net/training/communication_skills/consultation/equipoise/complexity/ stacey.htm

Greenleaf, R. K. (1977). Servant leadership: A journey into the nature of legitimate power and greatness. Mahwah, NJ: Paulist.

Harro, B. (2010). Cycle of socialization. In M. Adams, W. J. Blumenfeld, C. Castaneda, H. W. Hackman, M. L. Peters, & X. Zuniga (Eds). *Readings for diversity and social justice.* New York, NY: Routledge.

Hurtado, S., & Guillermo-Wann, C. (2013). *Diverse learning environments: Assessing and creating conditions for student success: Final report to the Ford Foundation.* Los Angeles, CA: Higher Education Research Institute.

Johnson, A. G. (2001). *Privilege, power and difference.* New York, NY: McGraw-Hill Higher Education.

Kirkhart, K. (1994). Seeking multicultural validity: A postcard from the road. *Evaluation Practice, 16*(1), 1–12.

Lewin, K. (1951). *Field theory in social science.* New York, NY: Harper and Row.

Lustig, M. W., & Koester, J. (2009). *Intercultural competence: Interpersonal communication across cultures.* Boston, MA: Allyn & Bacon.

Milem, J. F., Chang, M. J., & Antonio, A. L. (2005). *Making diversity work on campus: A research based perspective.* Washington, DC: Association of American Colleges and Universities.

Mind Tools. (2014). *Force field analysis: Analyzing the pressures for and against change.* Retrieved from http://www.mindtools.com/pages/article/newTED_06.htm

Patton, M. Q. (2011). *Developmental evaluation: Applying complexity concepts to enhance innovation and use.* New York, NY: Guilford.

Remen, R. N. (1999, September). Helping, fixing or serving? *Shambhala Sun,* pp. 25–27.

Snowden, D., & Boone, M. (2007). A leader's framework for decision making. *Harvard Business Review, 85*(11), 68–76.

Style, E. (1996). Curriculum as window and mirror. *Social Science Record, 33,* 35–42.

Symonette, H. (2004). Walking pathways towards becoming a culturally competent evaluator: Boundaries, borderlands and border-crossings. *New Directions for Evaluation, 102,* 95–109.

Symonette, H. (2006). Making evaluation work for the greater good: Supporting provocative possibility and responsive praxis in leadership development. In J. W. Martineau, K. M. Hannum, & C. Reinelt (Eds.), *The handbook of leadership development evaluation.* New York, NY: Wiley.

Symonette, H. (2008). Cultivating self as responsive instrument: Working the boundaries and borderlands for ethical border-crossings. In D. M. Mertens & P. E. Ginsberg (Eds.), *The handbook of social research ethics.* Thousand Oaks, CA: Sage.

Tuck, E. (2009). Suspending damage: A letter to communities. *Harvard Educational Review, 79,* 409–428.

TwoTrees, K. (2003). *7 directions practice.* Retrieved from www.7dp.org

Wilber, K. (n.d.). *Integral Institute scholars.* Retrieved from http://www.integral institute.org

Yarbrough, D. B., Shulha, L. M., Hopson, R. K., & Caruthers, F.A. (2011). *The program evaluation standards: A guide for evaluators and evaluation users* (3rd ed.). Berkeley Hills, CA: Sage.

CHAPTER 7

PEELING OPEN THE KIWI[1]

Reterritorializing (Pākehā/White) Evaluation in Aotearoa New Zealand

**Rae Torrie, Mathea Roorda, Robin Peace, Mark Dalgety,
and Robyn Bailey[2]**

Outside of Aotearoa, the term *Pākehā* has little resonance. In New Zealand, however, it is a term that is embraced by some as an identity position, a positive category descriptor, or both, whereas for others it is none of these. Research suggests that only 9.8% of New Zealanders of European descent preferred the indigenous name "Pākehā" (Sibley, Houkamau, & Hoverd, 2011, p. 208).

This chapter describes the journey of five self-identified Pākehā evaluators motivated to "engage in a meaningful, scholarly dialogue about the roles of culture and context in evaluation" (Hood, Hopson, & Frierson, 2005, p. 2), from a New Zealand evaluator perspective. We do not speak as any authoritative Pākehā evaluator voice in New Zealand, but rather as five evaluators seeking ways of working deliberately and appropriately in the cultural space. Pākehā is a term that has salience in our "Kiwi" evaluation practice: our engagement with the challenges associated with its use

*Continuing the Journey to Reposition Culture and Cultural Context
in Evaluation Theory and Practice*, pages 131–149

suggests it has potential to be transformative personally, politically, ethically, and professionally.

We each believe that working in the cultural space is implicit in all evaluation practice.[3] All policies and programs in Aotearoa New Zealand, be they social, environmental, or economic, have a cultural dimension. Furthermore, the cultural and political dimensions of government policies and programs in New Zealand are underpinned by present-day interpretations of the Treaty of Waitangi: the founding document of New Zealand signed on the 6th of February 1840, at a place called Waitangi, between the British Crown and rangatira (Māori chiefs) (Hayward, 2013, p. 1). While the Treaty has legal status under 62 separate Acts of Parliament, it has particular influence on government policy through the development of various sets of Treaty Principles (Hayward, 2013, pp. 2–5). It is the interpreted (and contested) Principles of the Treaty that most directly influence government evaluative work (see also Hayward, 2004).

As evaluators working in this context, we are particularly challenged to think about how a Treaty relationship, Māori colleagues, Māori-focused programs, and policies that require evaluation, all conduce toward a different understanding of our practice. We locate our discussion within Hopson's framing of culturally responsive evaluation as "a theoretical, conceptual and inherently political position that includes the centrality of and attunedness to culture in the theory and practice of evaluation" (Hopson, 2009, p. 431).

New Zealand is imbued with the ideas of territory central to the colonial projects of the British Empire that called into being the possibilities of both a place entity that could be surveyed and marked on maps as "New Zealand," and a destination for White settler colonists. In the metaphor of the surveyor, this chapter describes our pegging of the ground with some strings and markers for understanding and engaging in the cultural space of Aotearoa. We loosely use the concept of reterritorializing in the title and text to signal the theoretical as well as the geographical, historical, cultural, and political contexts that have shaped our thinking.

Our reference to concepts of "deterritorializing" and "reterritorializing" developed by two French academics, Gilles Deleuze and Felix Guattari (Deleuze & Guattari, 1987; Massumi, 1992) signals our awareness of processual change: that nothing is fixed, the process of change is fluid and displacing. However, rather than use these concepts to suggest we see ourselves as the "nomad subjects" who are "unmarked, unlocatable and disembodied" (Wuthnow, 2002, p. 186), we sought to identify and define that which situates our experience as a "ground for the production of knowledge and political action" (Wuthnow, 2002, p. 194). In the process of confronting the difference between our White selves and Māori in relation to evaluation practice, we have had to first, uproot ourselves (to deterritorialize) from habits of belonging and self-understanding in order to challenge notions of identity and hegemony. Through this uprooting, we have also engaged with decoding the patterns of actions that affect us as individuals in order to be reimplanted in a new context (Massumi, 1992, p. 51). On our journey, we were opening our own understanding (as individuals and as a small group) to "the politics of community, solidarity, identity and cultural difference" (Gupta & Ferguson, 1992, p. 68) to reconceptualize our own identity and cultural difference in the spaces of Aotearoa. By peeling open our own postcolonial settler stories, we hoped to understand more about the concept of being Kiwi-Pākehā, White settlers, new/newer migrants from Europe and what this means for who we are and what we do in the professional spaces of evaluation practice.

For Māori, the arrival of settler colonists and the signing of the Treaty of Waitangi was a deterritorializing moment (albeit in relation to tribal areas rather than the nation) through which preexisting spatial references were suppressed along with the language that expressed them. For the White settlers, the colony provided an opportunity for territorializing—making claims to space and economy, place and aesthetic—that would define the fabric of the imagined community (Anderson, 1991) and thereby of the emerging (White settler) nation state. As Rasack (2002, p. 3) suggests, "national mythologies of white settler societies are deeply spatialized" and power politics are inherent in the mapping (or what she calls the "unmapping" (p. 3) of colonized spaces. The intimate relationship between settler law and settler identity became a territorializing instrument through which space becomes dispossessed, renamed, and racialized.

We used a combination of tools and approaches from critical reflection (Argyris & Schön, 1974; Savaya & Gardner, 2012; Schön, 1983); auto ethnography (Ellis & Bochner, 2000); analytic autoethnography (Anderson, 2006); discourse analysis; and White studies (Borderlands e-journal, 2004; Engles, 2006; Hillman, n.d.) to develop a multimethod approach that structured a year-long discussion. We read, discussed, work-shopped, wrote vignettes, and drafted text informed by a series of four core questions:

1. Why is it difficult, amongst ourselves, to talk about what it means to be a Pākehā evaluator?
2. What does it mean to be Pākehā: Who are we?
3. What have we learned on the journey about being Pākehā evaluators?
4. Where to next?

From this point on, the chapter is divided into four sections, framed by these questions.

WHY IS IT DIFFICULT, AMONGST OURSELVES, TO TALK ABOUT WHAT IT MEANS TO BE A PĀKEHĀ EVALUATOR?

Despite observations for nearly two decades about the nervousness and tentativeness of Pākehā researchers and evaluators going into Māori space (Cram, 2009; Tolich, 2002), and challenges from Māori colleagues about how we might need to work differently with Māori, attempts to discuss being Pākehā evaluators have tended to result in those present talking at cross-purposes. We were keen to understand the dynamics of these crossed conversations, why they happened, and how to engage in a constructive dialogue about them that would be important both personally and professionally.

To understand this question, we focus briefly, first on New Zealand's colonial history and Māori-Pākehā relationships, and then on the development of a heuristic that helped us identify what seemed to make the conversation about being Pākehā evaluators complicated.

New Zealand's Colonial History and Māori-Pākehā Relationships

In Aotearoa, there are a number of cultural and contextual factors that have significant impact on the practice of evaluation. These include, but are not limited to, several important characteristics of the country that set it apart from three other White settler colonial nations: Australia, Canada, and the United States of America (Lawrence, 2010). While New Zealand is frequently compared with these other countries, it differs from each. First, in New Zealand, the history of colonization and the settlement of incomers is relatively recent (King, 2003). Second, state-sanctioned biculturalism underpins a relationship between the *tangata whenua* (indigenous "people of the land") and the *tangata tiriti* ("people of the treaty"; the incoming state agencies and their representatives, the Anglo-Europeans, with whom the Treaty was signed) (Ministry for Culture and Heritage, 2013). Third, New Zealand is now second only to Australia as one of the most culturally diverse Organization of Economic Development (OECD) countries in the world (Spoonley & Peace, 2012, p. 87). Finally, the overall size (both geographically and demographically) of the country, with a population of four and a half million concentrated in five main urban centers, means that degrees of separation between individuals, groups, communities, and government are very compressed, with high levels of interconnections. The country is often likened to a village, but a village in which cultural differences are defining and often awkwardly or weakly acknowledged, accommodated, or understood by the dominant culture.

Historically, research and evaluation in New Zealand was largely undertaken by the dominant, White settler culture, and the negative consequences of this research attention for Māori, Pasifika (settlers from the Pacific Islands), and other minority peoples have been documented (Cram, 1997; Smith, 1999). In recent years, as Māori have reemerged as larger players in the social, political, and economic landscape, Māori evaluators have increasingly asserted the self-determining principle of "by, with and for Māori" or "as Māori" (Wehipeihana, 2011). In so doing, Māori have strategically interpellated bicultural articulations of difference in relation to discourses of "honoring the Treaty."

This Māori renaissance has been also a watershed for Pākehā identity (King, 1985). As Māori evaluators have challenged the status quo, Pākehā evaluators have been prompted to reflect on whether it is appropriate to undertake projects focused exclusively or particularly with Māori and if so, under what conditions (Tolich, 2002; Torrie, 2009; Wehipeihana, Davidson, McKegg, & Shanker, 2010).

Māori evaluators have steadily clarified and strengthened their approaches to working in a *kaupapa* Māori way (Masters, 2002; Tauri, 2004; Wehipeihana, 2008, 2011), grown Māori evaluator capacity and capability, and assumed leadership roles in evaluations involving Māori. Many Pākehā evaluators have been slower to grapple with these sensitive and complex issues (Roorda & Peace, 2009), though some have actively participated with others to recognize the role of culture (Aotearoa New Zealand Evaluation Association, 2011).

There appear to be two main ways in which Pākehā evaluators engage with the conversation about working appropriately in the cultural space: reflecting on ourselves and our evaluator role in working with Māori, and identifying the skills and knowledge we need to become culturally responsive evaluators, including practical strategies for engaging appropriately with Māori colleagues, clients, and users in evaluation practice. There are no models or frameworks that systematize these approaches, which was the first challenge we set ourselves.

Developing a Heuristic

As a group (four evaluation practitioners and one academic), our journey toward identifying these two approaches came together after the Aotearoa New Zealand Evaluation Association's (ANZEA) national evaluation conference in 2012. At the plenary, an ANZEA *Taumata* or Council member challenged Pākehā evaluators about the need for bilingual fluency. In debates that followed from this challenge on the day, it became apparent that, as Pâkehâ, we were "talking past each other"[4] (Metge & Kinloch, 1978).

Whenever discussion began, people seemed to enter the debate from different starting points, with very different assumptions about what mattered and why. The framework presented in the octopus or *te wheke*⁵ heuristic (see Figure 7.1) was developed from an initial sketch of what we saw those entry points to be, and was then conceptually refined.

We drew on Hazel Symonette's "inside-out," "outside-in" paradigm for cultural competence (2004, p. 99). The concept of inside-out refers to the process of reflection on "self-as-instrument and self-in-context" (p. 99) and composes half of the territory that needs to be explored for cultural competence. Pākehā evaluators who enter the conversation from this direction are focused on *what it means* to be Pākehā, how this might shape practice, and what these things mean for whether and how we should engage with Māori. The three arms on the inside-out side focus first on identity and how we name and know ourselves culturally; second, on how that knowing shapes our sense of belonging and place and our understanding of the impact of culture and ethnicity; and third, on understanding our own personal motivations for choosing (or not) to highlight culture in evaluation practice. These motivations might include personal questioning, political pragmatism, a sense of social justice, a desire to improve practice, or all of these in different combinations.

Symonette's framing of outside-in involves "expanding and enriching one's diversity-relevant knowledge and skills repertoire and one's professional evaluator's toolkit" (2004, p. 99). Pākehā evaluators who enter the conversation at this entry point are focused on the Other, on acquiring skills and knowledge about Māori (or other ethnic groups), and ideas about *how* to work cross-culturally in order to traverse unfamiliar territory. The first two arms on the outside-in side are focused on learning Māori language (both to communicate and better understand Māori culture) and on learning about Māori *tikanga* (culture, custom, protocols) and the thinking, skills, and understanding about research and evaluation with Māori that shape the context for working cross-culturally. The third arm (bottom left) focuses on relationships with Māori colleagues with whom we might work, who can partner or assist us to carry out appropriate evaluations, how we might view and approach these relationships and our role in them, and how we might identify and troubleshoot issues of a cultural nature that arise. The fourth arm focuses on how we see our role, relationships, and responsibilities with our Pākehā colleagues, working together toward culturally responsive practice in Aotearoa.

We offer our heuristic here as a framework and language for facilitating a more focused discussion about working appropriately and consciously as Pākehā evaluators.

None of the process of arriving at the accomplished but still open framework was straightforward. Indeed, for the five of us involved, the process was the heart of the matter. In a sense, we began our own journey from the

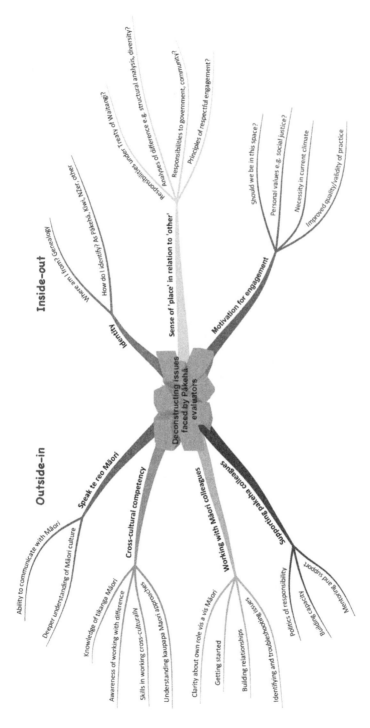

Figure 7.1   An initial framework for identifying issues faced by Pākehā evaluators developed by the authors.

inside-out (it is our sense, generally, that the inside-out questions have generally received less attention than the outside-in dimensions), and we use these inside-out insights to focus the next three questions.

WHAT DOES IT MEAN TO BE PĀKEHĀ: WHO ARE WE?

As indicated at the outset, the concept of Pākehā has its own divisive and challenging place in New Zealand. In this section, we briefly draw on literature and research to address the issue of defining Pākehā and then consider the impact of our own identity narratives on being Pākehā evaluators.

Defining Pākehā

In terms of definitions, we needed to understand the ways in which the concept of Pākehā is mobilized in Aotearoa and arrive at a working definition that suited our own views. We read scholarly definitions as well as some of the more public discourse (e.g., see Bell, 2006; Callister, 2011; King, 1999a, 1999b; Ramsden, 1995; Walker, 1996 for a range of perspectives).

None of these positions particularly capture how we see ourselves as Pākehā evaluators, although Bell's work certainly allows us to come closest to the idea of troublement with which we have engaged. Paraphrasing Bell, as Pākehā evaluators, we are not seeking to either "remember/forget" our individual or collective histories, in the "interests of *con*structing a unified and cohesive sense of identity," but rather, "through troubling our own sense of that identity to better understand the provisional, fluid, and entangled spaces we currently occupy" (Bell, 2006, p. 265).

Recent theses written on biculturalism or being Pākehā have challenged notions of Pākehā as an identity position that can unproblematically be assumed (e.g., see Barnes 2006; Bell, 2004; Campbell, 2005; Collins, 2004; Huygens, 2007; Jellie, 2001; McCreanor, 1995; Mitcalf, 2008; Walker, 1996). Mitcalf's research concludes with a statement that we, as individuals and a group, can identify with: "As 'ordinary' Pākehā, as bridge makers and border crossers on a journey of cultural identity making and of ethical, social and political concern and commitment, [we hope to engage with] . . . some of the prismatic and dilemmatic aspects of Pākehā identity" (Mitcalf, 2008, p. 110).

It is in the context of much being written and little understood that we began to work as a group choosing to look both at the wider politic and our positions within it. As with Mitcalf's (2008) research participants, we quickly established that "Pākehā identity can be seen to be dynamically diverse and constantly shifting" (p. 108) and that none of us is at any point of arrival in our understanding ourselves as Pākehā.

Being Pākehā Evaluators

Three key ideas emerged from our year-long process of discussion, debate, and self-reflection. First, we identified ways in which there is no easy, shared understanding of the idea of Pākehā but that it was possible to mobilize Pākehā as a sensitizing concept in relation to our work. Second, we recognized the profound degree to which affect (emotion) and identity are interwoven in our selves and in our work. Third, we considered the relevance of imported cultural evaluation terminology to our project. Each of these insights is discussed below in relation to the development of our understanding about what being a Pākehā evaluator asks of each of us.

Shared understandings.
We used a technique of vignette writing to capture and share our individual stories about growing up in New Zealand. In a series of group discussions, we shared and discussed the vignettes amongst ourselves and used them as a primary data source to identify commonalities and differences in our experiences. The personal disclosure of these stories held surprises and provided a platform for vigorous discussion. While all five of us were born in New Zealand in the 1950s and early 1960s, we grew up in very different communities, with different family, class, denominational, and educational backgrounds. Our parents worked as farmers, teachers, tradesmen, and homemakers. The narratives of origin (Irish, Scottish, English, Dutch) and arrival (from the early 1800s through to the late 1940s) created different stories of belonging. Catholic, protestant, and agnostic beliefs shaped different worldviews. It was our differences in particular that provided insight into why it is hard to hold the conversation about what it means to be a Pākehā evaluator. Assumptions of commonalities were not well founded. At one end of a continuum, some felt a profound sense of belonging associated with Pākehā identity; at the other, the term was an acceptable but not personally meaningful identity category. Being Pākehā seemed a necessary but not sufficient condition for understanding the political, ideological, and values dimensions of our work as evaluators.

What emerged as critical to the discussion of the political importance of our identity positions to our work was a shared consciousness and commitment to notions of fairness, social justice, a respect for diversity, and the importance of the Treaty of Waitangi as an agreement that should guide decision-making. There was a common awareness of White privilege (Lund, 2010; McIntosh, 1990) as it was represented in a New Zealand context, and a willingness to read literature that addressed the role of power and hegemony (Bell, 2004, 2006; Consedine & Consedine, 2005; Smith 1999). There were also shared experiences of being the Other, that is, in a minority and somehow disempowered, which we saw as an additional catalyst for engaging in this dialogical process. Collectively, we subscribe to the idea of evaluating social programs as a way of making a positive difference in the lives of the people involved or, as Greene puts it, "within a vision of evaluation conducted in the public interest, for the public good" (2005, p. 8).

The octopus framework (Figure 7.1) helped articulate how our shared political, ethical, and value orientations also drove our desire for evaluation quality. Against the call for "expanding and enriching one's diversity-relevant knowledge and skills repertoire and one's professional evaluator's toolkit" (Symonette, 2004, p. 99), we identified a range of practical strategies to enhance our commitment to at least doing no harm and ideally making a positive difference as external evaluators. In clarifying our own roles in relation to Māori, we actively choose not to pursue evaluation bids that have a primary focus on Māori, and to participate only if invited. When invited, we understand we work in partnership with Māori colleagues, seeking and listening to advice in the design of evaluations and in how to engage Māori informants. In developing cross-cultural awareness, we have a working fluency with common greetings, expressions, and *waiata* (songs) that may be sung at moments of greeting and farewell. We have learned to slow down and behave appropriately and respectfully in Māori spaces. Some of us have formally engaged in learning *te reo Māori* (Māori language).

Irrespective of the different ways that we personally identify, the term *Pākehā* has allowed us to reflect on how evaluation practice works in New Zealand in ways that are different from practice outlined in any standard evaluation textbook. It has also brought an increased awareness or consciousness of the consequences of hegemonic positioning implicit in our membership of the dominant culture and investments in Western knowledge paradigms. In the work we undertook to anlayze our process and reflect on the vignettes and literature, we have retrospectively come together around the idea of thinking about "Pākehā" as a sensitizing concept (Blumer, as quoted in Patton, 2002, pp. 278–279). That is, Pākehā is a term that we can use wittingly to frame arguments, identify positions, and reframe the debates in dialogue with each other and with others outside our group, in different contexts.

We have come to see the value of using the term very deliberately. It allows us to move through three spaces. First, we can acknowledge the contestation surrounding the term and choose to use it in a self-claiming way. Second, it provides us with a vehicle for postcolonial reflection and also acknowledges, through use of non-English terminology, our awareness of a relationship, indeed, many complex and fluid relationships between Māori and non-Māori. Third, in the context of evaluation, it allows us to focus our thinking on what it means to us and our practice to be biculturally constituted both through this term and our connections with our histories and the nation state. Being Pākehā evaluators is as much about "how" we are as "who" we are.

Affect and identity.

Our second insight was less well-anticipated and revealed a gap in our heurustic: a "recognizing the feelings that come into play" aspect of the model. We became increasingly conscious as we participated in our discussions that, at times, there was a strong emotional dimension present. We identified a range of responses to this affect-laden discourse and sought to decode its implications for our professional practice. First, we quickly came to see that it was not possible to explore this topic only from a safe professional, academic, or intellectual distance, and there were consequences from that. The emotional dimensions were powerful and important: we experienced and named shame, discomfort, uncertainty, anxiety, vulnerability, dislocation, defensiveness, anger, empowerment, intimacy, and trust.

Second, we recognized that this emotionality arose from expressing deeply held personal views and private experiences about ourselves, who we were, and how we perceived the world. We were uprooting ourselves (deterritorializing) from habits of belonging and self-understanding. We were unpacking and revealing hidden notions of ethnicity, race, and belonging, giving form to previously unexamined attitudes, some of which we found unpleasant or uncomfortable in ourselves. Making it ordinary, in the spaces of our talk, to sit with the sense of vulnerability and discomfort was important. We needed to accept as normal that feelings attended on sharing identity narratives. We also needed to acknowledge the anxiety and uncertainty we experienced being unsure about what were socially acceptable opinions both within and beyond our group. In saying things out loud that we were normally guarded about, we risked exposure to criticism of our attitudes or behavior.

Emotion was also present as we identifed and discussed the sense of discomfort, dislocation, and shame linked to our "Pākehā amnesia" (Consedine & Consedine, 2005 p. 172) about the past actions by settlers in Aotearoa New Zealand. There is no question that many Māori had land unjustly confiscated, and claims to the Waitangi Tribunal seeking redress for such grievances continue to increase our understanding of these events. All members of our group are on a personal journey of making sense of what this means for us and how we feel about it today. We have explored feelings of defensiveness (on behalf of our forebears), guilt, and sadness. Shame proffers complexity in the identity space as it sits between individual experiences and structured institutional and national histories. For one of the participants, the shame emanated from the sense of living alongside and not developing the facility to communicate in the language of the other—the hegemonic presumption always, that the other will speak to us.

Finally, this was a highly reflexive conversation investigating our positionings of self (be it conscious or unconscious) and exploring how this influenced our professional practice. The easist win was the realization of how the professional and personal strongly intersected for all of us. We also noted a strong uplift in energy and mood, a sense of freedom and mutual pleasure as we tackled subjects seen as taboo.[6] The emotional uplift was seen to proceed from being able to safely air contested and private opinions about culture and identity. As some of these subjects were decoded, some of the attached emotionality and tension seemed to diminish.

We came to see the capacity to be personally vulnerable with each other, to recognize the feelings that come into play, as an essential element to the substantive inside-out engagement. We observed that vulnerability and the ability to be intimate were attributes that appeared to facilitate deeper levels of learning and discernment for the participants. This intimacy emerged through the willingness to look and have some level of insight into our own values and ways of being. The dialogue required us to have care and consciousness for ourself and others. Interpersonal trust was indispensable. We sought to be respectful of others when eliciting their views and values and honed listening skills. Being open to multiple ways of seeing, including recognizing that there is no one way which is either right or wrong, were key ingredients for reimplanting ourselves in a new territory on knowing where head and heart were open to change. We found the ability to acknowledge not knowing the answers and starting the exploration from a place "inside of self" supported rich and safe dialogue.

Cultural evaluation terminology.

Over the course of our ongoing individual and group reflections, we spent a considerable portion of time seeking a language to describe the purpose of our journey. We found ourselves variously using the imported terminologies of cultural consciousness, competence, and responsiveness, even as these concepts did not sufficiently capture the particular challenge we had set ourselves. Central to what we were aiming to describe was a way of being, implied in the uprooting, decoding, and reimplanting journey we had embarked on, where the individual became more conscious, attentive, and present in the complex web of self and context. We felt the term *cultural consciousness* was useful but could imply a separation between mind and behavior—the idea that it is possible to to be conscious but not act. Similarly, the term *cultural competence* seemed positive but could imply separation of the relational, feeling-self from the range of skills, knowledge, and attitudes that might be instrumentally enacted—an arrived-at state of technocratic expertise. The *culturally responsive* concept, also useful and positive, could imply a reactive positioning—"you show me culture and I will respond." While all of these concepts alluded to self-awareness and the centrality of culture, our sense was that something more embodied and intersubjective was at play. What we recognized is that as with the troublesome identity concept of Pākehā, these concepts, in all their nuanced forms, are also sensitizing. They encourage us to reflect on what good evaluation practice might look like when we place culture at the center, but all are aspirational rather than definitive.

Where to Next?

Our final question remains open. The octopus heuristic helped us frame the different ways we see people engaging with and entering the discourse on being Pākehā and being Pākehā evaluators in Aotearoa. It opened up a space for us to participate in an enriched dialogue on the predominately inside-out arms of the octopus: our ethnic identity, our sense of place in relation to other, our motivation for engagement, and additionally, the need to recognize and honor the feelings and emotion that come into play. We anticipate the framework will prove useful in further discussions with colleagues and will be further modified over time.

CONCLUSIONS

We began this process with a desire to understand the difficult nature of conversations about Pākehā engagement with Māori in professional evaluation contexts. The octopus heuristic was our initial response to this—a framework through which we could decode the multiple starting points of engagement. Symonnette's (2004) framing was particularly useful as it drew our attention to the relatively underdeveloped inside-out space. We also responded to an invitation to prepare this chapter, and in doing so, committed ourselves to a longer and more complex journey to comprehend what being Pākehā entailed for the five of us.

The four questions we asked ourselves guided our progress. Our conclusions are clear. We recognized it was difficult, amongst ourselves, to talk about what it means to be a Pākehā evaluator because we lacked a shared understanding or common vocabulary of experience. We underestimated the powerful emotional investments in the "identity question" and needed to find ways to negotiate that. Having a methodology—a set of strategies and protocols for our engagement with each other as well as with the question—was invaluable.

We also came to understand that the question "What does it mean to be Pākehā: Who are we?" was fundamental to the more operational question of what it means to be a Pākehā evaluator. We recognized, profoundly, that working professionally in a cross-cultural space cannot simply be reduced to a set of professional prescriptions. Relationality is both implicit and explicit—not just between self and Other but with ourselves as Other.

What we learned on the journey was individually and collectively transformative. It was not ordinary for us, in our professional lives, to engage in personal disclosure. The process we engaged in was a significant investment in time, and hugely important. Through attention to the detail of how we talked with each other and the tools we chose and used to address our questions, we engaged in an intimate, trusting, circular, and deeply spiraling group process, which entailed talking, reading, writing, analyzing, and seeing ourselves and each other in new ways. We were able to reimplant ourselves in our settler contexts with deeper confidence and humility. The benefits of our process, focused on understanding ourselves as Pākehā evaluators, were gifts of insight about concepts, behaviors, attitudes, and emotional responses. It reaffirmed the need to pay as much, if not more, attention to the inside-out reflections on self-as-instrument and self-in-context.

The question of "Where to next?" is a reminder of the open-ended and fluid nature of social change. Culturally responsive evaluation signifies to us the need to take time to understand the "culturally influenced norms, values, and ways of knowing" (AEA, 2011, p. 1) of our own culture and context. Even though it was a hard and uprooting experience, it provided us, as Wuthnow (2002) suggested it might, with "ground for the production of knowledge and political action" (p. 194). We also recognize that this cultural exploration is territory traversed by many evaluators. It is a journey where the territory becomes progressively uncovered.

What It's Like

When someone asks you to explain
what's it like where you come from,
you say you're still finding out,
and it's not because you enjoy being
vague, or smart-arse, a sophist
if you like, it's just because it's true . . . .

Brian Turner[7]

NOTES

1. The *kiwifruit* (or *kiwi*; Actinidia deliciosa) arrived, deterritorialized, in New Zealand as a curiosity from China in 1904: brown skinned, green fleshed. Originally known as 'yang tao' (one version of a native name in the territory of Southern China), by the 1950s it was known as Chinese Gooseberries (its new colonial name referencing both its Chinese origins and what it was seen by English people to be culturally similar to). In 1959, the name "kiwifruit" co-opted the image of the flightless, brown, native New Zealand bird (the Kiwi) and the vernacular name for New Zealanders (*Kiwi*). *Pākehā* is a Māori

word, variously defined, that broadly refers to White settler New Zealanders of European descent. It is an exonym in the sense that it is "a name by which one people or social group refers to another and by which the group so named does not refer to itself" (see http://www.thefreedictionary.com/exonym). *Aotearoa* is the Māori name for New Zealand and is used interchangeably throughout the chapter.

2. The opportunity to be included in this volume came from an invitation from the editor via a Māori colleague, Nan Wehipeihana.

3. This is consistent with the central tenets of culturally responsive evaluation, which "recognize that demographic, sociopolitical, and contextual dimensions, locations, perspectives, and characteristics of culture matter fundamentally in evaluation" (Hopson, 2009, p. 431).

4. This term, which has entered the New Zealand lexicon as an expression of cross-cultural communication, was coined by Metge and Kinloch based on their experience of observing Māori and Samoan people in their dealings with Pākehā, where "a good deal of miscommunication occurs between members of these groups because the parties interpret each other's words and actions in terms of their own understandings, assuming that these are shared when in fact they are not—in other words, because of cultural differences" (1978, p. 8). It has long-standing use in Aotearoa as shorthand for miscommunication, particularly cross-cultural.

5. The heuristic developed its current form organically as we organized our thinking, and we then linked it to the idea of *te wheke*, or the octopus. This has a local "fit" as a well-known octopus model developed by Rose Pere (1984) in a public health context. As Lynne Pere (2006, p. 102) describes the *te wheke* health model: "The body and the head of the octopus represent the whole whanau unit, and each of the tentacles is symbolic of a particular dimension of health. All eight tentacles collectively contribute to waiora—the total well-being of the individual and the whanau. This is represented by the eyes of the octopus. The intertwining nature of the tentacles further reinforces the close relationships between each of the eight dimensions." This notion of a whole constituted by intertwined interdimensionality felt appropriate for us.

6. The word *taboo* came into the English language from James Cook's visit to the South Pacific in the 1770s. Its English meaning is informed by a common Polynesian (including Māori) word *tapu* (see http://www.britannica.com/EBchecked/topic/579821/taboo).

7. Brian Turner is a New Zealand poet and author.

REFERENCES

Anderson, B. (1991). *Imagined communities: Reflections on the origin and spread of nationalism* (Rev. & ext. ed.). London, UK: Verso.

Anderson, L. (2006). Analytic autoethnography. *Journal of Contemporary Ethnography, 35*(4), 373–395.

Argyris, C., & Schön, D. (1974). *Theory in practice: Increasing professional effectiveness.* San Francisco, CA: Jossey-Bass.

American Evaluation Association (AEA). (2011, April 22). *American Evaluation Association statement on cultural competence in evaluation.* Washington, DC: American Evaluation Association. Retrieved from http://www.eval.org/p/cm/ld/fid=92

Aotearoa New Zealand Evaluation Association. (2011). *Evaluator competencies.* Retrieved from http://www.anzea.org.nz/wpcontent/uploads/2013/05/110801_anzea_evaluator_competencies_final.pdf

Barnes, A. (2006). *Taku ara, taku mahara: Pākehā family experiences of kaupapa Māori and bilingual education.* Unpublished master's thesis. University of Waikato. Hamilton, New Zealand

Bell, A. (2004). *Relating Māori and Pākehā: The politics of indigenous and settler identities.* Unpublished Doctoral dissertation, Massey University, Palmerston North, New Zealand.

Bell, A. (2006). Bifurcation and entanglement? Settler identity and biculturalism in Aotearoa New Zealand. *Continuum, 20*(2), 253–268.

Borderlands e-journal. (2004). *Vol. 3*(2). Retrieved from http://www.borderlands.net.au/index.html

Callister, P. (2011). The construction of ethnicity and 'belonging' in New Zealand: Where we have come from and where we might be going. *Journal of New Zealand Studies, 10,* 115–137.

Campbell, B. M. (2005). *Negotiating biculturalism: Deconstructing Pākehā subjectivity.* Unpublished Doctoral Dissertation, Massey University, Palmerston North, New Zealand.

Collins, H. M. (2004). *Te putahitanga o nga tai e rua: The meeting of two tides—journeys of mixed heritage Māori/Pākehā towards identity strength.* Unpublished master's thesis, Massey University, Wellington, New Zealand.

Consedine, R., & Consedine, J. (2005). *Healing our history* (Revised & updated). Auckland, New Zealand: Penguin.

Cram, F. (2009). Maintaining indigenous voices. In P. E. Ginsberg & D. M. Mertens (Eds.), *The handbook of social research ethics* (pp. 308–322). Thousand Oaks, CA: Sage.

Deleuze, G., & Guattari, F. (1987). *A thousand plateaus: Capitalism and schizophrenia.* (B. Massumi, Trans.). Minneapolis: University of Minnesota Press. (Original work published 1980)

Ellis, C., & Bochner, A. (2000). Autoethnography, personal narrative, reflexivity: Researcher as subject. In N. K. Denzin & Y. S. Lincoln (Eds.), *Handbook of qualitative research* (2nd ed., pp. 733–768). Thousand Oaks, CA: Sage.

Engles, T. (2006) *Towards a bibliography of critical Whitenesss studies.* Urbana-Champaign: University of Illinois at Urbana-Champaign. Retrieved from http://cdms.ds.uiuc.edu/Research_CDMS/CriticalWhiteness/Index.htm

Greene, J. C. (2005). Evaluators as stewards of the public good. In S. Hood, R. Hopson, & H. Frierson (Eds.), *The role of culture and cultural context: A mandate for inclusion, the discovery of truth, and understanding in evaluative theory and practice.* Greenwich, CT: Information Age.

Gupta, A., & Ferguson, J. (1992). Beyond "culture": Space, identity, and the politics of difference. *Cultural Anthropology, 7*(1), 6–23. doi:10.1525/can.1992.7.1.02a00020a

Hayward, J. (2004). Flowing from the treaty's words: The principles of the Treaty of Waitangi. In J. Hayward & N. Wheen (Eds.), *The Waitangi Tribunal: Te roopu whakamana i te Tiriti o Waitangi* (pp. 29–40). Wellington, New Zealand: Bridget Williams.

Hayward, J. (2013). Story: Principles of the Treaty of Waitangi—ngā mātāpono o te tiriti. *Te Ara: The Encyclopedia of New Zealand.* Retrieved June 22, 2014, from http://www.TeAra.govt.nz/en/principles-of-the-treaty-of-waitangi-nga-matapono-o-te-tiriti/sources

Hillman, R. (n.d.). White me. *GriffithREVIEW.* Retreived https://griffithreview.com/edition-31-ways-of-seeing/white-me

Hood, S., Hopson, R., & Frierson, H. (2005). Introduction: This is where we stand. In S. Hood, R. Hopson, & H. Frierson (Eds.), *The role of culture and cultural context: A mandate for inclusion, the discovery of truth, and understanding in evaluative theory and practice.* Greenwich, CT: Information Age.

Hopson, R. K. (2009). Reclaiming knowledge at the margins: Culturally responsive evaluation in the current evaluation moment. In K. Ryan & J. B. Cousins (Eds.), *The Sage international handbook of educational evaluation.* Thousand Oaks, CA: Sage.

Huygens, I. (2007). *Processes of Pakeha change in response to the Treaty of Waitangi.* Unpublished doctoral thesis, University of Waikato, Hamilton, New Zealand.

Jellie, M. (2001). *The formation of Pākehā identity in relation to te reo Māori and te ao Māori.* Unpublished master's thesis, University of Canterbury, Christchurch, New Zealand.

King, M. (1985). *Being Pākehā: An encounter with New Zealand and the Māori renaissance.* Auckland, New Zealand: Hodder and Stoughton.

King, M. (1999a). *Pākehā: The quest for New Zealand identity.* Auckland, New Zealand: Penguin.

King, M. (1999b). *Being Pākehā now: Reflections and recollections of a white native.* Auckland, New Zealand: Penguin.

King, M. (2003). *Penguin history of New Zealand.* Auckland, New Zealand: Penguin.

Lawrence, B. (2010). Legislating identity: Colonialism, land and indigenous legacies. In M. Wetherell & C. Mohanty (Eds.), *The Sage handbook of identities* (pp. 508–525). Thousand Oaks, CA: Sage.

Lund, C. L. (2010). The nature of White privilege in the teaching and training of adults *New Directions for Adult and Continuing Education, 125*(18), 15–25.

Massumi, B. (1992). *A user's guide to capitalism and schizophrenia: Deviations from Deleuze and Guattari.* Cambridge: Massachusetts Institute of Technology Press.

Masters, B. (2002). *Developing a Kaupapa Māori evaluation model—One size fits all?* Hamilton, New Zealand: University of Waikato Māori & Psychology Research Unit Papers 127.

McCreanor, T. (1995). *Pākehā discourses of Māori/Pākehā relations.* Unpublished doctoral dissertation, University of Auckland, New Zealand.

McIntosh, P. (1990, Winter). White privilege: Unpacking the invisible knapsack. *Independent School, 49*(2), 31–49. Retrieved from http://people.westminster-college.edu/faculty/jsibbett/readings/White_Privilege.pdf

Metge, J., & Kinloch, P. (1978). *Talking past each other: Problems of cross-cultural communication.* Wellington, New Zealand: Victoria University Press.

Ministry for Culture and Heritage. (2013). *The Treaty in brief.* Retrieved from http://www.nzhistory.net.nz/politics/treaty/the-treaty-in-brief

Mitcalf, M. A. (2008). *Understandings of being Pākehā: Exploring the perspectives of six Pākehā who have studied in Māori cultural learning contexts.* Unpublished master's thesis, Massey University, Palmerston North, New Zealand.

Patton, M. Q. (2002). *Qualitative research and evaluation methods* (3rd ed.). Thousand Oaks, CA: Sage.

Pere, L (2006). *Oho Mauri: Cultural identity, wellbeing, and tangata whai ora/motuhake.* Unpublished doctoral dissertation, Massey University, Wellington, New Zealand.

Pere, R. (1984, March 19–22). *Te oranga o te whānau: The health of the whānau.* Hui-whakaoranga Māori Health planning workshop. Hoani Waititi Marae, Auckland, New Zealand.

Ramsden, I. (1995). Own the past and create the future. In K. Irwin & I. Ramsden (Eds.), *Toi Wahine: The worlds of Maori women.* Wellington, New Zealand: Penguin.

Rasack, S. (2002) When place becomes race. In S. Rasack (Ed.), *Race, space and the law: Unmapping a White settler society.* Toronto, Canada: Between the Lines.

Roorda, M., & Peace, R. (2009). Challenges to implementing good practice guidelines for evaluation with Māori: A pâkehâ perspective. *Social Policy Journal of New Zealand, 34,* 73–89.

Savaya, R., & Gardner, F. (2012). Critical reflection to identify gaps between espoused theory and theory-in-use. *Social Work, 57*(2), 145–154.

Schön, D. (1983). *The reflective practitioner: How professionals think in action.* London, UK: Temple Smith.

Sibley, C. G., Houkamau, C. A., & Hoverd, W. J. (2011). Ethnic group labels and intergroup attitudes in New Zealand: Naming preferences predict distinct ingroup and outgroup biases. *Analyses of Social Issues and Public Policy, 11,* 201–220. Retrieved May 27, 2013, from http://onlinelibrary.wiley.com/doi/10.1111/j.1530-2415.2011.01244.x/abstract

Smith, L. T. (1999). *Decolonising methodologies: Research and indigenous peoples.* London, UK; Dunedin, New Zealand: Zed/University of Otago Press.

Spoonley, P., & Peace, R. (2012). Social cohesion in a bi-cultural society: The challenges of immigrant diversity in Aotearoa/New Zealand. In P. Spoonley & E. Tolley (Eds.), *Diverse nations, diverse responses: Approaches to social cohesion in immigrant societies.* Kingston, Canada: Queen's School of Policy Studies, McGill-Queens University Press.

Symonette, H. (2004). Walking pathways toward becoming a culturally competent evaluator: Boundaries, borderlands, and border crossings. In M. Thompson-Robinson, R. Hopson, & S. SenGupta (Eds.), *New directions for evaluation: In search of cultural competence in evaluation: Toward principles and practices* (pp. 102, 95–109. San Francisco, CA: Jossey-Bass.

Tauri, J. (2004). *Key issues in the development of government agency guidelines for research and evaluation with Māori.* Wellington, New Zealand: Ministry of Social Development.

Tolich, M. (2002). Pākehā "paralysis": Cultural safety for those researching the general population of Aotearoa. *Social Policy Journal of New Zealand, 19,* 164–178.

Torrie, R. (2009). *Whether or not to go there: Pākehā evaluators and evaluations involving Māori*. Wellington, New Zealand: Unpublished paper.

Walker, S. (1996). *Kia tau te rangimarie. Kaupapa Māori theory as a resistance against the construction of Māori as the other*. Unpublished masters thesis, University of Auckland, New Zealand.

Wehipeihana, N. (2008). *Indigenous Evaluation—A journey beyond participatory and collaborative approaches in evaluation* Paper presented at the American Evaluation Association National Conference, 2008.

Wehipeihana, N. (2011). *Creating space for indigenous values, practices and leadership in evaluation: The Aotearoa New Zealand experience*. Keynote presentation at the 3rd Biennial South African Monitoring & Evaluation Association Conference, Johannesburg: SAMEA.

Wehipeihana, N., Davidson, E. J., McKegg, K., & Shanker, V. (2010). What does it take to do evaluation in communites and cultural contexts other than our own. *Journal of Multidisciplinary Evaluation, 6*(13), 182–192.

Wuthnow J. (2002). Deleuze in the postcolonial: On nomads and indigenous politics. *Feminist Theory, 3*, 183. doi:10.1177/1464700102003002344

CHAPTER 8

BEGINNING A CONVERSATION ABOUT SPIRITUALITY IN MĀORI AND PASIFIKA EVALUATION[1]

Vivienne Kennedy, Fiona Cram, Kirimatao Paipa,
Kataraina Pipi, Maria Baker, Laurie Porima, Pale Sauni
and Clark Tuagalu

ABSTRACT

For Māori (Indigenous peoples of Aotearoa New Zealand) and Pasifika (peoples from the Pacific Islands, Polynesia, who reside in Aotearoa New Zealand), spirituality is threaded through cultural beliefs, values, and practices. As an inherent part of daily life and cultural vitality, spirituality is embedded in Māori and Pasifika services and programs. This chapter contemplates the importance of spirituality in the everyday lives of Māori and Pasifika peoples, and begins a conversation about how Māori and Pasifika evaluators acknowledge, value, and represent spirituality in their evaluation work. As groundwork for this chapter, Māori and Pasifika evaluators shared their thoughts about spirituality in a traditional learning context, a *wānanga* (forum for discussion and learning). Key themes from the *wānanga* included being respectful of people, upholding their *mana* (status), having a love for people, and

*Continuing the Journey to Reposition Culture and Cultural Context
in Evaluation Theory and Practice*, pages 151–177
Copyright © 2015 by Information Age Publishing

sharing without concealment. Our hope is that our experiences will prompt other evaluators to contemplate how spirituality is woven into their culturally responsive evaluation practice.

INTRODUCTION

It wasn't a large gathering, but those who felt they needed to be there were there. We sat in more of an oval than a circle, constrained by space and other furniture. All the same, we were happy to be there, among friends who were known to us in various mixtures of personal and professional lives. We were led by one of us who we knew would keep us safe and lead us gently. She called upon us to pray together, with four people offering thanks for our gathering and asking for blessings for our time together and our sharing with one another. Then we began, with people talking one by one around the circle about what was on their minds and in their hearts to share about spirituality. There was attentive and respectful listening and at times tears and laughter, and sometimes both. This was how we began our journey together of speaking, listening, and being moved by spirit in our contemplations of the role of spirituality in our professional lives as evaluators.

Recently, a group of Māori (Indigenous peoples of Aotearoa New Zealand) and Pasifika (peoples from the Pacific Islands, Polynesia, who reside in Aotearoa New Zealand) evaluators gathered to share thoughts, feelings, and experiences about the spiritual dimension of evaluation. This chapter arises from that gathering. Our aim in writing it is to highlight the importance of spirituality in the everyday lives of Māori and Pasifika and the ways in which we, as evaluators, acknowledge, value, and represent this spirituality in our evaluation work. We encourage you to think along with us as we begin this conversation. We first explore both spirituality and evaluation. Themes that emerged from our *wananga* (forum for discussion and learning) are then described. (See Appendix for a description of the *wānanga* process and for a glossary of Māori words.) Finally we offer some concluding remarks.

SPIRITUALITY

For Māori and Pasifika, spirituality is threaded through cultural beliefs, values, and practices. Cleve Barlow (1991, p. 152) describes some of those beliefs: "*Māori* believe that all things have a spirit as well as a physical body; even the earth has a spirit, and so do the animals, birds, and fish; mankind also has a spirit."

Spirituality is an inherent part of daily life and cultural vitality, and something we have in common with many other Indigenous peoples. For Hawaiian scholar Manulani Meyer (2001), spirituality is about the relationship people have with their world. This is also expressed by African American scholar bell hooks (1990, p. 218), who writes, "For me spiritual life is not an interest, it's a way of life, of being in the world, the foundation of everything."

Spirituality is an integral part of Indigenous health and wellness (Cram, Smith, & Johnstone, 2003). For example, the connection Samoans have to their place of existence includes all things spiritual and physical, mental and emotional in relation to their place (Tamasese, Teteru, Waldegrave, & Bush, 2005). It makes sense then that for Māori and Pasifika, being culturally responsive in whatever we do, including evaluation, will include an element of spirituality (Hood, 2009).

Spirituality in Knowledge and Knowing

Spirituality is part of Indigenous ontology and epistemology; that is, part of our theory about the nature of reality or what is known, and part of our relationship as knowers with what is knowable. For Cree scholar Shawn Wilson (2008, p. 33), the ontological question is, "What is real?" and the epistemological question is, "How do I know what is real?" In Meyer's (2013) words, epistemology is about "knowledge" as both a noun and a verb. Of her relationship with epistemology, Meyer writes that everything in her life involves a consideration of her beliefs about knowledge. "I can see a dead frog on the road, and it relates to epistemology" (Meyer, 2001, p. 192). Samoan researcher Tuagalu (2013) writes that three epistemological principles are common across Pacific cultures: people are strongly connected to their community or collective; people are strongly connected to their spiritual, mental, physical, and emotional worlds, values, and beliefs; and knowledge is collectively owned. Linda Tuhiwai Smith (1999, p. 74) hones in on the importance of Indigenous concepts of spirituality within Indigenous knowledge and ways of knowing.

> The arguments of different Indigenous peoples based on spiritual relationships to the universe, to the landscape and to stones, rocks, insects and other things, seen and unseen, have been difficult arguments for western systems of knowledge to deal with or accept. These arguments give a partial indication of the different worldviews and alternative ways of coming to know, and of being, which still endure within the Indigenous world.

The role of spirituality within Māori and Pasifika services and programs needs to be seen and valued by non-Indigenous funders. To be culturally responsive, the evaluators of these services and programs have to be able to inquire about spirituality and then incorporate what they find out into their evaluation methodologies and reporting.

Evaluation

LaFrance and Nicols (2009, p. 26) write,

We must recognize that Indigenous knowledge does not always mesh with Western concepts of reality as something that is observable and measurable. Ceremonies and cultural protocols connect us to the spiritual aspects of our surroundings, as well as to our ancestors, whose energy remains with us. As program implementers and evaluators, we honor all these relationships through the thoughtful use of our own ceremonies, blessings, and celebrations.

Spiritual values are embedded within Māori and Pasifika services and programs and are often explicit in the assessments given by Māori and Pasifika evaluators about how effective or otherwise initiatives are. For example, in a Māori context, *kaumātua* (elders) may speak about the *mauri* (life essence) of a context changing so as to become more positive, more *tika* (right) (Cram, Kempton, & Armstrong, 1998). Women may speak of sacredness in relation to the body as a way of explaining their *whakamaa* (reticence) about getting Pap smears (Ministry of Health, 1997). Educators may speak of maintaining the *mana* (cultural authority) of the children and young people in their care (Ministry of Education, 2010). Victims of crime may speak of a courtroom as *paru* (unclean) (Cram, Pihama, & Karehana, 1999). Whatever the context and whomever the people, a discussion about the value and worth of an initiative will include the contemplation of an aspect of spirituality. This is also the case in evaluations of Samoan initiatives. Tuagalu (2013) maintains that an effective evaluation approach reflects the core values of the people and incorporates traditional knowledge about Samoan epistemology.

A WĀNANGA ON SPIRITUALITY AND EVALUATION

In the days of our ancestors, Māori considered the sharing of, learning of, and participation in the acquisition of knowledge as sacred. *Wānanga* traditionally described a body of knowledge shared with a group of people who were specifically selected to take part in the *wānanga*. Importantly, and equally as significant to the sharing of knowledge, was the environment in which the sharing took place, the selection of participants, and the purification ceremonies upon entering and leaving the "house of learning." Today, there are many perspectives on what is knowledge versus what is information, and what is considered sacred. *Wānanga*, too, has many interpretations and is used in a variety of contexts. *Wānanga* has been brought into the field of evaluation to consider topics of importance to Māori and

Pasifika evaluators and is seen as a fitting method to discuss *wairua* along-side evaluation practice.

EXPRESSIONS OF SPIRITUALITY

Seven themes emerged from the *wānanga* sharing. These are described below with *wānanga* participants identified by their first names when they agreed to this. The wishes of some to remain anonymous have been honored. Each theme provides an insight into the sharing of participants. We have not integrated this sharing any further than the thematic organization to honor the turn-taking rather than discussion style of the *wānanga*. Speech balloons highlight some of the essence of particular themes.

Mauri—Feeling Connected

The following experiences talk about being culturally and spiritually connected. This connection is linked to the essence of life itself—*mauri*. *Tihei Mauri Ora*—Behold, there is Life!

Kirimatao explained that for her feeling spiritually connected is about being connected not necessarily with God, but with the things that feel good inside and have good vibrations. This *mauri* (source of emotions) shows her when she is feeling good about things. Kirimatao elaborates,

> You know, my *mauri* lessens when I get stressed, and it's bloody up there when I need sleep and things are going on, and the *mauri* is running through my veins. And that passion for our people shows in that kind of way.

Angela talked about cultural practices being second nature in the things she does. As a weaver, she practices ancient processes of *karakia* (prayer) and *whakatauki* (proverbs) to connect those who've gone before with the process. If traditional practices of *karakia* and expressing gratitude when collecting *harakeke* (flax) are not carried out, there is a pervading sense that things have not been done right. Angela noted that processes in *mahi raranga* (weaving) maintain our *mana tangata* (prestige of the people) and *mana atua* (sacred power from the ancestors/ gods).

Maira spoke of being brought up with spirituality and the importance of passing on the teachings to the next generation. Her experience was one of being taught that there is an *Atua* (a God) and that whenever she got into a situation where she felt unsafe, in need of comfort, inspiration, or direction, she could *karakia* and everything would be okay. She feels that *karakia* is an important part of her life and that wherever we go, whatever we do, that we have *karakia*.

Debbie's understanding is that spirituality can be a connection to God that is a way of life. She acknowledges in our evaluation practice that there are things greater than us, beyond us, and that people have experiences of *wairuatanga* (spirituality) that are deeply profound and have significant meaning for them.

Clark shared how the religious aspects of spirituality have helped shape the person he is today. He talked of having a strong connection to God, particularly at times when he needed guidance and support to make decisions around work, relationships, and self-development. Spiritually, this researcher and evaluator has a strong sense of who he is, particularly in terms of engaging in work to improve health as well as social and education outcomes for his people in New Zealand. In terms of research and evaluation, he draws on his strong connection to God to guide his thoughts, feelings, and actions and to ensure everyone has the opportunity to express their concerns, interests, and issues. His spiritual connection embodies his cultural values around a number of principles, including respect, service, humility, reciprocity, inclusiveness, and altruism.

Pale explained that most Pasifika are church-goers (stemming from the strong influence of missionaries in the Pacific Islands from the 1830s), and they still rigidly follow Christianity today. Pale further said that although there are a few who believe in *Tangaroa* (God of the Sea) and *Io* (the Supreme God) and other traditional imageries—rivers, rocks, and stones—most Pasifika continue to go to church every Sunday.

Roxanne was brought up around her grandmother, who was "staunchly *Ringatu*" (of the *Ringatu* faith).[2] Roxanne acknowledges the spirituality of the *Ringatu* faith, although she admits to being unsure as to the nature of spirituality. She explains that she tends to feel her way around things, and she has a belief that time and place is synchronistic. Roxanne explains,

> I've ended up in some situations thinking, "Why am I doing this *mahi* [work]?" And I'll end up making a connection with someone who can join the dots and I'll think, "That's why I'm doing this!" I don't know if I'd call that spirituality.

Aroha ki te tangata—Respect for People

Aroha ki te tangata' literally translates as "love for the people." In our *mahi* with *whānau* (families), the perceptible experience we provide to *whānau* is that of striving to make a difference; not because it is our job, but because of our genuine interest in and love for the people. With love comes respect.

Kataraina spoke of the time she and Kirimatao were contracted to undertake a research project in which they interviewed 30 *whānau* who were affected by meth (methamphetamine). The *kaupapa* (agenda) was to look at the negative impact of meth, and *whānau* coping strategies. Kataraina and Kiri worked alongside two wonderful people based at Hoani Waititi *marae*[3] who work in the alcohol and drug addiction field and who helped them connect to *whānau* for this project. Kataraina felt that each one of the interviews they conducted was a *wairua* experience in itself, with the researchers experiencing amazing learning. She explained,

> We would sometimes spend up to six hours with individuals or *whānau*. You hear lots and lots of *kōrero* [discussion] in different places; you hear it, you feel it, you make sense of it in your head—it is a *ā wairua* [spiritual] and a *ā ngākau* [heartfelt] experience.

For Te Kapua, keeping safe in any circumstance is about being spiritually aware of other people's *āhua* (appearance), feelings, and emotions and seeing the unseen; that is, a person's spirit or *wairua*. In evaluation *mahi*, Te Kapua contends that *whanaungatanga* (relationships) are key, as they are the foundation of connecting with people in this way.

Laurie also mentioned the importance of relationships and having a genuine interest in the people who you represent and engage with. He counseled that if people see this attitude of care, they will welcome you; but if they see you just coming for the data, they will probably not be that open. Laurie advocated establishing a *wairua* connection with people through *whakapapa* (genealogical) and *whanaungatanga* links so that for the period you are together, you can enjoy a genuine relationship.

A *wānanga* participant spoke about visiting providers[4] whose research projects had not gone well. Her initial thoughts were ones of trepidation as to the openness of the reception they would receive. As it turned out, it was a wonderful meeting, as everyone went in with the right heart.

Viv referred in particular to *whanaungatanga* aspects of spirituality; namely, making familial linkages and connections by remembering and acknowledging her forbears and the knowledge, customs, beliefs, and values that they passed on through the generations to ensure that she, her relations, and colleagues continue to practice rituals of care, love, respect, and responsibility to others. Viv explained,

> The spiritual nature of our work includes our knowing as Indigenous people that behind each one of us are many generations—our forebearers nurture and guide us, and so they live on. Hence we never travel our journey of life alone.

Sharmaine mentioned the principle of respect and how it is the basis of our encounter. She spoke of the need to ensure that we, and those who we are meeting with, are safe and enabled to speak freely, and that each party's views are valued. Sharmaine also mentioned the principle of *whakaute* (to show respect), reminding us that w*hakaute* is important throughout the evaluation process and at all levels, not just in the encounter, but also in the recording, analyzing, and interpreting of the information. She advised that *whakaute* is important in retelling the stories to various audiences so that the integrity or truth (*pono*) of the stories is upheld (also see section 3 below, *Kaitiakitanga*—Guardianship).

Maria commented that an Indigenous researcher and evaluator should have knowledge and understanding in terms of *wairua* when working with their people, and that if someone claims to be an Indigenous researcher or evaluator, there is an expectation that she/he will be able to look after things pertaining to *wairua*. In order to do this, she/he will need to have experienced situations where *wairua* is present and explored what *wairua* means to her/him.

> The relationships between participants and Indigenous evaluators often reveal interrelational, fluid interconnectedness between people and physical and spiritual spaces. When seeking information, the process utilized by the Indigenous evaluator has purpose yet reciprocity and responsibility for taking care of the *kōrero* shared. (Maria)

Kaitiakitanga—Guardianship

An aspect of *kaitiakitanga* is that we understand and recognize the honor being accorded us from the gifts of *korero* (stories) that are being shared with us—the sacredness of the sharing and of that being shared. Maria explained,

> When you make a connection with somebody, be it a short-term occurrence or a one-off engagement, that [*wairua*] connection stays. In our line of *mahi*, there's a potential that people will share *kōrero* that possibly they've never shared before, so we as researchers and evaluators have an obligation to look after that. You have to honor that; you have to recognize it. Part of that, about looking after *wairua*, is about *kaitiakitanga*. We need to know how to look after that [*wairua* and interaction as researcher and participant]—and at the same time you have to look after yourself. That *koha* [gift] and giving back [reciprocating], there's a whole *mauri* in that, and I think that's a feeling of depth, life meaning, and of responsibility.

Fiona endorsed this, saying she that she is constantly amazed at what people share with her and the ways in which, for whatever reasons, they'll share things that are actually spiritual, and that there is a responsibility that goes with that.

Kirimatao commented that our work is not just about research and evaluation; it's about reciprocity and giving back to the people. She reflected,

> How does my spirit guide me in evaluation? It talks to me about koha and about giving back, it talks to me about reciprocity, it talks to me about shutting my mouth and listening. It's not just the research, it's not just the project anymore; it's actually a time when we can support our *whānau* to move and transform, just in that little space. And if we can give them that space, *ka rawe!* [fabulous!]

The following research experience portrays an example of *kaitiakitanga,* where we as researchers and evaluators become custodians of information, whether temporarily or otherwise. The experience was a reminder to the researchers and evaluators in the *wānanga* to *kia tūpato* (take care), and to look after that which we are entrusted with. It was also a reminder to be aware of the types and depth of information that projects may require researchers to collect, and whether we have or are able to develop the kind of relationships with research and evaluation participants that ensure we are comfortable doing that work.

A researcher spoke of her experience of holding onto data that was not included in the research project report for which it was gathered, as strong differences of opinion had arisen between the researcher and the research participant, who was a distant elderly relative. Nevertheless, the interviews with this relative had resulted in the compilation of information and knowledge that the relative's family would treasure. The researcher had thought to keep herself safe from any cultural transgressions by taking her father to all meetings so that he would carry out all the necessary traditional procedures and protocols, including *karakia.* So she was quite surprised when she encountered an experience that served as a reminder that she still had this material in her care. The experience occurred in the form of a pervading smell of a particular perfume that the relation's deceased wife used to wear.[5] The researcher recalled that the experience was not unnerving, but it was a reminder that she was holding onto information that needed to be returned to its rightful place. As a result, the researcher ensured that all the relevant information was returned to the family, complete with transcripts and tape recordings. The researcher ruminated on the nature of the relationship with the *whānau* involved and the learning from her experience: "I realized the other side of it; it was actually that whole realm of *wairua* that kicks in when you have a close association with people. That [experience] was my little wake up call."

Kia tūpato—Taking Care

It is important to ensure that as evaluators we are sufficiently prepared for whatever situation awaits us. Maria reminded us that we have to make sure that as evaluators, we are in a good state of mind and readiness before we go and do whatever the *mahi* is with people. We need to be prepared for whatever might eventuate by centering ourselves or by making sure that our frame of mind is right and by ensuing that we are experienced or are supported to undertake the work.

Fiona talked about taking time to be quiet and settled within oneself in order to be responsive in our research and evaluation work. She suggested we need to tune in to a quiet and settled place for ourselves to be so that we are neither leading nor directly influencing others about what they should be feeling, what they should say, or what they might think we want to hear or talk about. Fiona reflected,

> Part of finding this quiet place is about the rituals that take place in our encounters when I'm often asking people how they would like to begin. Part of this is about me not wanting to impose a spirituality on a situation that may be inappropriate, and part of it is about wanting to acknowledge the *rangatiratanga* [sovereignty] of those I'm with to both protect and direct the context.

Pale talked about *talanoa*. In Tongan and Samoan situations in particular, this is a way for Pasifika to *kōrero* (talk) safely. Pale counseled that up until recently "safe, cross-cultural, multilevel, cross-status, and cross-ethnic" used to be nice descriptions of *talanoa*. However, he questioned what that meant in terms of methodologies and confidentiality when he and his colleagues are conducting research and evaluation with their communities. He pondered an example of how *talanoa* fits a situation where people are disclosing sexual abuse in a men's group. He questioned that if *talanoa* is without concealment, will there be situations in the community where the perpetrator can sit with the 14-year old victim and have that *talanoa*, because it is without concealment? He conceded that perhaps the issue of confidentiality is contextual when it is inclusive in the *talanoa*. Pale explained that *talanoa* is also about who is in the room, what status the people have, and the nuances that flow between and within the *talanoa*.

Bryce explained the dilemma he had faced in his work with prisoners. When he went through *whakawhanaungatanga* (making kinship and other connections) with them, they would then literally *ruaki a wairua* (a form of spiritual regurgitation) on him, and some of their *kōrero* was too much to bear. Bryce felt in some ways that he was blessed to be privy to such personal revelations. However, in some ways, the aftermath was a curse. He recalls,

Figuratively, these people would *ruaki* [regurgitate—purge themselves through the telling of their story]. Just thinking about some of the *kōrero* now, [I would ask them] "Do you *karakia*?" [The reply was] "No, because when I was getting abused I called out for God [And where was God when I needed him?]" And, yeah, there were those sorts of occasions when I would think to myself, "What do I do with that?" But the . . . process for them was *rongoā* [cathartic].

Bryce then shared his story about ridding himself from the resulting *ngāngara* (dark negative energies). He tried all sorts of methods to *whakanoa* (cleanse the spirit) himself using cultural methods such as sprinkling or dowsing himself with water from his tribe's river. Bryce's colleague highlighted two things for him. The first was to emphasize that Bryce needed to recognize his limitations in terms of protecting himself against such forces, and the second was to ensure Bryce protected his *whānau*. This realization had a significant impact on Bryce, so much so that he felt it necessary to forgo this *mahi*. His decision was about being *tika* and *pono*; that is, being true and straight-up about his limitations.

Kellie shared her experience of conducting an evaluation of a rehabilitation program with male prisoners. She told of being physically ill the day following an interview with a prisoner, of being unable to work, and of the greenstone (jade) pendant she wore around her neck taking on a revolting smell. A discussion with her aunt revealed the need for Kellie to keep herself safe. Kellie was quick to point out that the negative effects emanated from the prison environment, and she contemplated the effects of this environment on inmates.

> If that is what the system does to me when I am in there for an hour and a half, what is that system doing to that *tane* [man] that I was talking to who was in there on a rehab program? Where is the space for us as evaluators to report that; that is, the impact of the environment and systems? If that's what it's like for us as evaluators and researchers, imagine what it is like for our people inside those systems on a daily basis.

Laurie talked about the importance of maintaining customary practices such as *karakia* (prayer) for the sake of maintaining traditional rituals, and because it is almost inherent in the things he does. He reminded us that similarly in our work, we do *karakia* before we start something, when we finish, and when having a *kai* (meal), so that we are firstly giving *mana* (status) to our hosts, and we are also keeping ourselves safe. He emphasized that this is about taking responsibility, making good decisions, and dealing with things.

Roxanne explained that for her, the concept of spirituality in *tikanga* (traditional cultural practices) is different from spirituality. She sees things need to be done *tika* (correctly), a value that she was brought up with, a belief that *tikanga* (custom) is embedded in something that is spiritual. In particular, she cited the importance of engaging in *karakia, mihimihi* (introductions), and *whakawhanaungatanga* processes when engaging with Māori providers for the first time during evaluations.

Whakanoa—Cleansing of the Spirit

Four ways of cleansing the spirit were described under this theme: *roimata* (tears), *mirimiri* (massage), *katakata* (laughter), and *waiata* (music and singing). *Wairua* here relates to indigenous evaluators finding balance to maintain their equilibrium and to ensure and promote their sense of harmony and well-being.

Roimata—Tears.
Louise explained that she uses tears as a form of cleansing, as a way to move her to a different place or space. Although she is reluctant to be that emotionally expressive in front of *whānau* in the course of her work, she notes that she sometimes shares emotionally to acknowledge what *whānau* are sharing. She also takes time to cleanse herself in a way that is safe for everyone so that she can move away from that time with *whānau* and come back when she needs to.

Mirimiri—Massage: Therapy for mind, body, and soul.
Kataraina mentioned *mirimiri* as a form of relief and release from the stressful work she commits to. She talked about the responsibilities involved in work she is often asked to undertake and the considerations in taking on the "hard to do" stuff with our *whānau* and communities who are in need. In undertaking this work, she reflected that the *wairua* needs to be cleansed and uplifted, and she pondered how people factor in the protection that is needed, including the need to balance the male/female element, the debriefing time that is required after each interview, and the *mirimiri* that is needed so that residual heaviness is lifted after the *mahi* is done.

In Pasifika communities, it is common for families to engage in *fofo* (Samoan word for massage). Pale explained that, as with the Māori, massage is therapeutic and spiritual. In some Pasifika contexts, massage is accompanied with song and rhythmic chanting to assist the healing and coordinating of the massage team.

Katakata—Laughter and humor (That is so part of the spirit).
During the *wānanga*, there was much laughter. Laughter makes us feel good and gives us strength. It is also a respite from pain and sadness. Such was the case after Pale's emotional sharing of the story of a pregnant Tongan

---

INTUITIVE PREPARATION

As an Indigenous evaluator one's tasks are to "listen" "observe" and "enquire." It would aid if you were holistically involved in the interaction. This means being well prepared prior to the interview or and being open to the possible expressions in the interaction that may be manifestations of your culture and of *wairua*.

---

woman who was found wandering the streets of Wellington, suffering from a malady. Pale then shared the following, which broke the tension of despondency from the experience shared and resulting questions that he had posed: "I love the ghost stories; I've got hundreds of those. I saw a ghost in Room 21 at 3 o'clock this morning." Laughter then flowed as *wānanga* participants realized Pale was referring to the friend and colleague he was colluding with until the wee hours of the morning.

The Samoan word for humor or fun storytelling and leg pulling is *faleaitu* or "house where the spirit lives and makes people laugh." Pale explained that most of this is done in the cultural language of the Pasifika community. Plays, drama acts, songs, role-plays, and enactments are an integral part of the performance. Weaved into the narratives are spiritual lessons and principles, and often biblical parables are acted out to underline the message they are conveying in the humorous way.

Tim recognized that laughter plays its part in lifting the heaviness of spirit. He reflected on a time when he attended the *tangi* (funeral) of a friend of his aunt. As well as *waiata* (song) to lift the spirit, there is also *katakata*. Tim recalled being at the *tangi* with it being a typical West Coast day where the rain thumped to the point that the floor of his car was absolutely soaking from having left the window slightly open. Whilst sitting in the garage afterwards with the *whānau*, one *kuia* (elderly woman) said, "When someone really beautiful dies, it rains because it's the tears of the old people; the *tipuna* are so sad." Then she asked, "What if it doesn't rain?" And the reply was, "Well, the *tipuna* probably didn't like them," to which there was laughter from the bereaved *whānau* and friends.

Bryce explained he has a very liberal approach to *wairua*. Although he respects *wairua*, he takes a jovial approach to it, recognizing that humor helps him to get through various situations. He explained that in terms of *wairua*, what sprang to mind for him in his work in prisons as a cultural assessor was *tika* (correct) and *pono* (true) and their variations. He described his work as going into prisons and talking with *whānau* about looking at cultural strength from a Māori perspective to create change. He recalled that there had been occasions when he had walked into a room with just the prisoner in there and yet the place felt crowded. So he related that they went through certain *whakanoa* protocols—*karakia* being one of them and others being having a *kai, korero,* and *kata.* Bryce then laughingly recalled one of his uncles saying, "And if those things don't work, then good luck to you boy; you're on your own; you're on your final frontier!" This elicited much laughter from the *wānanga* participants.

Waiata—Music soothes and uplifts the spirit.

One of Kataraina's and Pale's many gifts are that they are singers, composers, and guitarists as well as accomplished facilitators. Although Kataraina expressed that music has various uses, Viv asserts that to listen to Kataraina and Pale sing and play their guitars, and to witness them mesmerize and engage people through music and facilitation, is to experience *wairua* at work—to experience healing; soothing and uplifting of the spirit; effect communal sharing; evoke emotions, thoughts, and memories; and be entertained.

Tim talked of how his aunt was skillful at relieving his anxiety through singing. He reminisced that when he hears a beautiful *waiata,* it reminds him of the spiritual power of music. An example was the time he started doing research on the West Coast. He recalled that most of the *wairua* things that had happened to him occurred at Poutini.[6] As a child, he used to get chills every time he went there. He attributed the spooky feelings to the spirits of the old coal miners who had died, but his aunt dispelled that myth and explained that it had been a battleground where Tūmatakōkiri (a fierce tribe that dominated the northwestern quadrant of the South Island)[7] and their *whānau* had fought. After dispensing that information, Tim recalled his aunt then started singing, and although it was not traditional *waiata,* he felt completely cleansed and free of the spooky feeling.

Manaaki ki te tangata—Generosity and Sharing With People

Viv asserted that our aspirations are to advocate for our people in the hope that we can create positive and meaningful change that will have benefits for all, not just Māori and Pasifika. She talked of the idealism one of her *tupuna* (in this case, her mother's first cousin) demonstrated; namely, a commitment to caring for his people. Maria stated that this is about *mana ake*—giving *mana* to the *kaupapa* and the people whom we are evaluating. Viv and Maria recalled that when situations are particularly arduous, they remember the quote of that *tupuna* and elder Sir James Henare, which serves to motivate them:

Kua tawhiti kē tō haerenga mai, kia kore e haere tonu;
He tino nui rawa ō mahi, kia kore e mahi tonu.

You have come too far not to go further;
You have done too much, not to do more.

Viv explained that she feels there is spirituality in the work that she and her colleagues do with their people, such as working with them at the grassroots level in order to advocate for better outcomes at government and policy levels. She feels that they are supported and encouraged in their commitment by those who have gone before them, and this feeling is vindicated when things go well, such as the flow of the *korero*, the *āhua* (positive demeanor) of people they engage with, and fruitful exchanges. Conversely, Viv declared that, "When the going gets tough, we think of Uncle Jim and our forebearers, and we are inspired to continue on the path that they paved for us so long ago."

Louise explained that she is still building her understanding of the principle of *whakamana,* but she describes it as shared with her by Laurie Porima, "as embodying the process of empowerment, through respect, humility, and recognition of our innate talents, gifts, and abilities." Louise explained,

> When working with and for our people, we acknowledge and honor them and aim to create space to allow their aspirations to rise to the surface, take shape, and potentially begin to soar. This transformation also has the ability to be shared with others who may draw strength or inspiration to reignite or revitalize their own journeys.

Louise concurs with Laurie that being a part of this transformational process is truly a gift and therefore we must practice evaluation in *mana*-enhancing ways.

Laurie's view is that spirituality in evaluation is the individual's responsibility and that all need to be mindful of the spaces that their work takes them into. He explained that the *mana* (status) accorded to someone is earned from his/her attitude and deeds, thus Laurie came to the conclusion that it is about giving and receiving *mana.* He explained that if he gives *mana* by showing his face at *hui* (meetings), then he is deemed to be giving *mana* to the organizer. However, he contends that you cannot just make *mana*; it must be freely given, and it can easily be taken away. Laurie further clarified that if people come to his *hui,* then through *kanohi kitea* (showing their face—referring to someone attending in person), they give *mana* to him and his *whānau.* He points out that if we maintain that attitude and relate it back to our evaluation and research *mahi,* then it is about making sure we know who we are, we are secure in who we are, we know why we are there, and at all times we are respectful.

Mōhiotanga, mātauranga, and māramatanga— Knowledge, collective wisdom, and enlightenment

Wikuki reflected on perceptions of *wairua* in terms of science and ecology, and the evolvement of *wairua* from ancient times and what that might mean in terms of evolving ecology and theology. He posits that work in the United States talks about spiritual capital and spirituality in science. Therefore, he suggested that considerations for us as evaluators would be whether evaluation is an art or science.

> What spirituality do we have as Māori and Pacific people, and [what does that mean in terms of] how the word is encoded in science and ecology? *Wai* [water] was the original mirror in the old days. That's what [our ancestors] did; looked at their reflection in the water. You're looking back at yourself, at your own *wairua*. This potential mechanism that we have is imbued within us because we have *mauri*—the life force. Because we have a life force, we automatically have *tapu* [sacredness]. The challenge for our people is to keep spirituality at its core.

Pale talked about the intuitive ways that Pasifika work, and that if researchers and evaluators don't know their position on spirituality, then they miss out on how to engage with Pasifika. He reflected on the importance of recognizing and maintaining customary rituals and of noting those things as being part of the methodology of working with Māori and Pasifika. Pale then queried how we validate, measure, report on, and give effect to these cultural and spiritual experiences:

> Even our very first wave of engagement with those communities, they are so still the same—it's the prayer, it's the recognizing of the status in the room; all those things are connected to that same story. So if we do anything less than that as evaluators, then I think we've missed a huge methodology, or a huge outcome that we then have to write about. I think it's a great thing to talk about and get a sense of when in our spaces, not to be afraid.

REFLECTIONS ON THE WĀNANGA

Wānanga participants were asked to share their reflections of the *wānanga*. Most comments affirmed the *wānanga* as a great opportunity to share thoughts and experiences around the topic of spirituality that is so inherent in the work that we do in the research and evaluation space, with participants looking forward to further discussion on the *kaupapa*. Louise talked about the *wānanga* as a fantastic opportunity to come together and share our experiences of spirituality and how they inform our practice as evaluators. She thought it was a beautiful, loving, safe environment, and she felt at peace to share, and was humbled by those who shared their *whakaaro* (thoughts) so freely. Fiona expressed that she enjoyed the *wānanga* as an initial coming together and sharing of personal and professional experiences (that are often so intimately intertwined). She thought we had just scratched the surface. Having said this, the reason she contends we managed to even scratch the surface is because we know and trust one another. Fiona views the *wānanga* as just a beginning step. Viv felt the *wānanga* was a great opportunity to start exploring the huge *kaupapa* of *wairua* in relation to culture and evaluation, in a safe environment with like-minded people. She thought it was a privilege to share and to hear of others' experiences. Viv looks forward to more *wānanga* and to refining the process to ensure that the spirituality and sacredness of the space in which we *wānanga* this *kaupapa* is maintained. Tim felt it was a privilege to work in this way. He contends that by adding that which we know (*mōhiotanga*) to the collective wisdom (*mātauranga*), we build understanding (*māramatanga*). Tania commented that it would be a challenge to reflect the *wānanga* discussions on paper, to write what we were talking about and feeling. She is often conscious of the privilege of being with all this information and the connections developed from it. She described it as not tangible but that "you feel it, so it'll be a challenge to get that *wairua* onto paper." Kirimatao then responded with a wise crack, "We'd better get some ghost writers in, get some ghost busting on this job" (that elicits laughter from the *wānanga* participants). Kim expressed her gratitude for all that we do for our *whānau*. She loved listening to the stories and feeling the spirit that journeys with us in those stories.

> Inherent in this perspective of being an Indigenous evaluator, you will have spent time exploring, learning, and reflecting upon wairua knowledge and understanding what wairua may mean amongst your own people. (Maria)

CONCLUDING REMARKS

This chapter has presented the themes arising from our *wānanga*, where Māori and Pasifika evaluators met to consider *wairua* within evaluation. Hood (2009) writes about the importance of evaluators sharing in the lived experiences of the communities they work in, as these experiences build the capability of evaluators to be culturally responsive. In this regard, Māori scholar Māori Marsden (1992, p. 136) writes,

> The reality we experience subjectively is incapable of rational synthesis...Remembering that the cultural milieu is rooted both in the temporal world and the transcendent world, this brings a person into intimate relationships with the gods and his universe.

For us, culturally responsive evaluation takes this into account. It is not our task as evaluators to try and make the spiritual elements of programs more rational. Rather, we need to weave into our assessments of program value and merit our subjective understandings of how spirituality is an aspect of a program's vision, design, implementation, and success. We desire our evaluation work to be infused with the sophisticated concepts of spirituality and cosmology that were noted in Māori by early explorers, traders, and missionaries to Aotearoa (Smith, 2012). The *wānanga* was our way of sitting with one another, almost as a form of peer supervision, to reflect upon and validate the legitimacy and achievability of this desire.

Fox (1991, pp. 11–12) writes, "Spirituality is a life-filled path, a spirit-filled way of living...A path is not goal oriented. A path is the way itself, and every moment on it is a holy moment; a sacred seeing goes on there."

This reflects the sentiments of many *wānanga* participants; namely, that spirituality is a way of life. It is about knowing and being sourced from within our cultures; knowing and being that are fundamental, Indigenous, inherited, ingrained, and characteristic of who we are. Spirituality is some or many of these things for each of us. Spirituality is therefore in the things we do, including research and evaluation. It is part of our shared, lived cultural experience.

Wānanga participants were asked to keep three questions in mind when considering the experience(s) they wished to share. Few *wānanga* participants spoke directly to these questions in this first outing. We therefore offer some reflections on them now that we have examined our *wānanga* experience further in the writing of this chapter.

Keeping Safe and Protected

How do we conduct ourselves so that protocols are adhered to and everyone involved in an evaluation is safe and protected, not only ethically and morally, but also spiritually?

Many participants' stories referred to protocols (traditional customs and practices) and principles they maintained and/or observed because they grew up knowing them or they had learned them in adult life. Some were customary practices that were passed on as part of a living culture; others were learned in the course of their professional duties or in the course of life itself. Adherence to protocols generally ensured safety and protection. When there was a lack of use or awareness of protocols, safety was compromised. We therefore need to create and maintain an ethic of care to ensure we are aware of what is required to keep us safe, including necessary and relevant protocols, and that we cover each others' backs. As culturally responsive evaluators we "should always be guided by the principle of *tika* which is the very basis of the word *tīkanga*" (Mead, 2003, p. 318, italics added); in other words, guided by the principle of doing what is right, appropriate, just, and true, as this is the foundation of custom. In doing so, we should examine our own expectations and assumptions about spirituality, ensure we are well supported, and remain courageous (Ormond, Cram, & Carter, 2006).

Respectfully Representing Spirituality

How do we take into account and respectfully represent the spiritual nature of initiatives within our evaluations?

Wānanga participants felt comfortable sharing because we were a reasonably small group of people who largely knew one another. We therefore trusted that the information being shared would be respected. Even so, some participants were apprehensive about the *wānanga* and what would happen to the information gleaned from the *wānanga*. Our conclusion from this one small experience is that the topic of spirituality/*wairua* should be approached with caution. We used the term *Kia tūpato* for one of the *wānanga* themes, and we reiterate its meaning here: Be careful. We need to carefully consider how to inquire into and share about the spiritual nature of the programs we evaluate, especially about how this information may be perceived and utilized by stakeholders. In the introduction to this chapter, we described how interviewees in a project on the needs of Māori victims of crime described a courthouse as *paru* or unclean. They did not mean the courthouse was dirty, but rather that it was spiritually unclean. In order to be culturally responsive, we must seek to represent the lived experiences of those involved in our evaluations; for example, explaining this uncleanliness in a way that provides an avenue of possible redress (e.g., blessing the courthouse) by those responsible if they too wish to be culturally responsive. This responsive representation of the spiritual nature of initiatives we are evaluating opens pathways that will undoubtedly challenge government funders of programs and services (see below). Even so, the spiritual aspects of Māori and Pasifika culture need to be explicit in our work.

Funders' Capacity to Understand

How do we build the evaluation capacity of funders so that they understand, accept, and value feedback in relation to spiritual aspects of initiatives? Evaluation capacity building with a focus on government agencies and other funders of Māori and Pasifika initiatives will help strengthen their readiness for evaluations that incorporate spirituality. Duignan (2002) identified three key elements of building evaluation capacity in the social policy sector in this country: appropriate evaluation models, a culture of evaluation, and the strategic prioritization of evaluation questions. The more responsive each element is to Māori and Pasifika cultures, including spirituality, the more valid the evaluations of Māori and Pasifika initiatives they undertake and commission will be (Hood, 2009). The infiltration of Māori and Pasifika models of health and wellness into social policy and health sectors has increased tolerance for the inclusion of the spiritual, even if their capacity to understand what this is remains limited. As Māori and Pasifika evaluators, our role is to take funders on a cultural journey of how we do evaluations and what we find. In other words, our communications, including reports, should seek to represent communities and organiz`ations well, and take readers on a journey that enhances their understanding. By opening up this window on our worlds, we are inviting people to connect on a spiritual level. We will also be acknowledging that our customs and traditions are important in the lives of our people; that we strive to uphold these things as valid, characteristic, and commonplace; and that there is a sacredness in maintaining and valuing these practices and beliefs.

In conclusion, we reiterate that the experiences shared in the *wānanga* were by no means exhaustive and are only some of the myriad cultural and spiritual practices utilized in the course of our professional commitments. It was not intended that this chapter provide a comprehensive definition of *wairua* and *tikanga* in evaluation; we have only just started on an explorative journey of this *kaupapa*. What we do know is that the scope of *wairua* is so vast that this *kaupapa* warrants further discussion. This chapter concludes with a quote of Sir Apirana Ngata, a leader of the Māori people and a prominent politician in the 20th century, whose words were encouragement to a young woman to further her education.

> E tipu e rea, mō ngā rā o tōu ao;
> Ko tō ringa ki ngā rākau ā te Pākehā, hei ara mō tō tinana;
> Ko tō ngākau ki ngā taonga ā ō tipuna Māori, hei tikitiki mō tō māhuna;
> Ko tō wairua ki tō Atua, nāna nei ngā mea katoa

> *Grow up and thrive for the days destined to you;*
> *Your hands to the tools of the European New Zealanders to provide physical sustenance;*
> *Your heart to the treasures of your Māori ancestors as a diadem for your brow;*
> *Your soul to your God, to whom all things belong.*

APPENDIX
Glossary

āhua	appearance, state of being
Aotearoa	New Zealand
Aroha	Love
Atua	God, deity
faleaitu	humor, fun story telling, leg pulling
fofo	massage
harakeke	flax
hui	meeting
kai	food, meal, to eat
kaitiaki	guardian, custodian
kaitiakitanga	guardianship
kanohi kitea	be seen to be actively involved
karakia	prayer, grace, blessing, chant, acknowledgement
katakata	laugh, laughter
kaumātua	elder
kaupapa	topic, agenda
koha	gift, donation, contribution
kōrero	talk, speak, discussion, stories
kuia	elderly woman
mahi	work, job, activity
mana	status, cultural authority, prestige, esteem
manaaki	support, take care of, protect
manaakitanga	hospitality, support, kindness
marae	meeting place where formal greetings and discussions take place
māramatanga	enlightenment, understanding
mātauranga	wisdom
mauri	life force, source of emotions, living essence
mirimiri	massage, rub, soothe
mōhiotanga	knowledge, understanding
ngākau	heart, seat of affections
ngāngara	dross, creepy crawly
Pākehā	New Zealander of European descent
paru	unclean, dirty, soiled
Pasifika	Indigenous peoples of the Pacific Islands, Polynesia, now residing in Aotearoa New Zealand

pono	truth
pōwhiri	welcoming ceremony
pūtake	purpose
rangatiratanga	sovereignty, self-determination, autonomy
raranga	weave, plait
rawe	excellent
reo	language
rongoa	remedy, cure, medicine
ruaki	vomit, retch
talanoa	conversations and sharing without concealment
tane	male, man
tangata	person, people
tangi	mourning and funeral process
tapu	sacred
tika	true, correct, just
tikanga	custom, practice, procedure
tinana	physical (in terms of a component of health)
tipuna/ tupuna	ancestor, grandparent (male or female)
tūpato	take care, be wary, be cautious
wai	water
wairua	spirit
wairuatanga	spirituality
wānanga	forum for discussion and learning, learning sessions
whakaaro	thought, opinion, idea
whakamaa	reticence, shame, embarrassment
whakamana	empowerment
whakanoa	cleanse, to remove tapu
whakapapa	genealogy, lineage, descent
whakatauki	proverb, saying
whakaute	show respect
whakawhanaungatanga	relationship building
whānau	family, families, family members—immediate and extended
whanaungatanga	relationship(s), kinship

WĀNANGA METHODOLOGY
An Invitation to the Wānanga

A total of 21 people chose to participate in the *wānanga*.[8] Participants were asked to keep in mind that the intention was not to define spirituality, but rather to portray aspects of spirituality that Indigenous researchers and evaluators consider when working in a culturally responsive manner with their people. They were asked to consider the following three questions in preparation for the *wānanga*:

- How do we conduct ourselves so that protocols are adhered to and everyone involved in an evaluation is "safe" and "protected," not only ethically and morally, but also spiritually?
- How do we take into account and respectfully represent the spiritual nature of initiatives within our evaluations?
- How do we build the evaluation capacity of funders so that they understand, accept, and value feedback in relation to spiritual aspects of initiatives?

Participants were also asked to prepare for the *wānanga* by thinking about an example of spirituality in evaluation that they would be happy to share with their peers as well as in an international audience.

Wairua Wānanga Process

The processes followed for the *wānanga* are described below. This set the tone for the sanctity of the sharing that took place.

Karakia o Ngā Hau e Whā—Blessings From the four winds

Chairs were positioned in an oval setup in the center of the room so that all participants would be seated together without the barrier of conference desks, thus creating an informal and more personalized space where everyone could see and hear each other. Kirimatao, as facilitator of the *wānanga*, chose four people to say a *karakia* (blessing) by virtue of their geographical position within the oval seating, as symbolically representing the coming together of people from *Ngā Hau E Whā* (the Four Winds)—from the four corners of the world—north, south, east, and west.

Tikanga o te Wānanga—Personal Behavior

Kirimatao emphasized the personal considerations expected of participants:

- That our mind, our heart, and good will is focused on the speaker and that technology interferes with this.
- That people leaving and entering without permission will distract from the focus.
- People speak from their truth without fear of judgment, and that there are no rights, no wrongs.
- Everyone would have the opportunity to speak.

Pūtake o te Wānanga—Purpose of the Forum

Kirimatao then outlined the nature of the *wānanga* process:

- That the stories that come from within this space are sacred to and owned only by the people who shared them.
- That we all trust the process of the *wānanga* and the reasons it was called, and we therefore entrust our stories to be cared for in the sacred way that they are presented within the *wānanga* space.
- We give permission for our spirit to be captured in writing for the sole purpose of contributing to the Culturally Responsive Evaluation chapter[9] on spirit and evaluation.
- We trust that a respectful process will occur and further permissions will be sought, if and where specific stories are used verbatim.

Writing the Chapter

The way in which this chapter was to emerge from the *wānanga* was discussed before and after the *wānanga*, including during the continuation of the *wānanga* on the second morning of the workshop. It was during these discussions that we decided to share what was said during the *wānanga*, grouping people's sharing around key principles about the role of spirituality within evaluation practice. This honors people's contributions while not seeking to prematurely shape answers to the three questions we had set ourselves. Our realization at the end of the *wānanga* was that we are journeying toward answers to these questions, with this journey needing to be given time and space.

Discussion from the *wānanga* was audio taped with consent from the participants, and the recording was transcribed. One person who did not sit in on the *wānanga* provided a written account of her experiences and thoughts, which have been incorporated into this chapter. Each *wānanga* participant was then sent their transcribed narrative, which they could add to, amend, or delete from to ensure that it was a true reflection of what they wished to share. Participants were also asked to reflect on their narrative and highlight one or two key principles or practices from their narrative that they wished to share in the chapter, and to also provide a few sentences about what they were thinking in relation to the principles or practices. Some participants managed to do this within the time frame offered; others did not. In the development of the next section, narratives were grouped under expressed principles, and context was provided as required to tell participants' stories. The draft chapter was then sent to all *wānanga* participants for their feedback and consent as to the presentation of their narratives.

NOTES

1. We express gratitude and appreciation to our friends and colleagues who, in the interests of exploring what it is we do culturally in the research and evaluation space in terms of spirituality, generously shared their knowledge and experiences. *Nga mihi nui ki a* Maira Daymond, Tepora Emery, Debbie Goodwin, Te Kapua Hohepa-Watene, Wikuki Kingi, Sharmaine Nolan, Tim Rochford, Kim Smith, Roxanne Smith, Kellie Spee, Bryce Turner, Angela Wallace, Louise Were *rātou ko* Tania Wolfgramm. *Ngā mihi aroha*—with greatest sympathy, Angela passed after a long illness June 26, 2014.
2. *Ringatu* faith was a Maori religious movement founded in the 1860s by Te Kooti Arikirangi.
3. A *marae* is a communal meeting place or area that these days is commonly referred to as the communal facility and place of belonging for Māori, that consists of a carved meeting house, dining hall, cooking facilities, and the *marae atea*—the sacred space in front of the meeting house. Hoani Waititi *marae* is an urban pan-tribal community meeting place in West Auckland at which various services including social, justice, educational, and cultural services are provided.
4. Providers in this context refers to nongovernmental organizations that provide health and social services.
5. This form of extrasensory perception in the field of parapsychology is known as clairalience—sense of smells/ scents.
6. Westland Tai Poutini National Park is located halfway down the South Island on the West Coast
7. See www.theprow.org.nz/ngati-tumatakokiri/#.UZgh4ILe468
8. Unfortunately, not all action researchers were advised of the *wānanga* before the day on which it was held. When it came time to start the *wānanga*, it became apparent that some people were not comfortable with discussing the

kaupapa (topic) in this forum, especially as they had not had enough time to ruminate on the *kaupapa* and their possible contribution. Several people therefore chose not to participate.

9. Dr. Stafford Hood had liaised with Dr Fiona Cram about New Zealand evaluators contributing chapters to the second edition of this volume.

REFERENCES

Barlow, C. (1991). *Tikanga whakaaro: Key concepts in Māori culture.* Auckland, New Zealand: Oxford University Press.

Cram, F., Kempton, M., & Armstrong, S. (1998). *Te Whare Tirohanga Māori, Hawkes Bay Regional Prison—Evaluation Report.* Wellington, New Zealand: Department of Corrections.

Cram, F., Pihama, L., & Karehana, M. (1999). *Meeting the needs of Māori victims of crime.* Wellington, New Zealand: Te Puni Kōkiri & Ministry of Justice.

Cram, F., Smith, L., & Johnstone, W. (2003). Mapping the themes of Māori talk about health. *New Zealand Medical Journal, 116.*

Duignan, P. (2002). Buildng social policy evaluation capacity. *Social Policy Journal of New Zealand, 19,* 179–194.

Fox, M. (1991). *Creation spirituality: Liberating gifts for the peoples of the earth.* New York, NY: HarperCollins.

Hood, S. (2009). Evaluation for and by Navajos: A narrative case for the irrelevance of globalization. In K. E. Ryan & J. B. Cousins (Eds.), *The Sage handbook of educational evaluation.* Thousand Oaks, CA: Sage.

hooks, b. (1990). *Yearning—Race, gender and cultural politics.* Boston, MA: South End.

LaFrance, J., & Nichols, R. (2009). *Indigenous evaluation framework: Telling our story in our place and time. Written for the American Higher Education Consortium.* Alexandria, VA: American Indian Higher Education Consortium.

Marsden, M. (1992). God, man and universe: A Māori view. In M. King (Ed.), *Te Ao Hurihuri—Aspects of Maoritanga* (pp. 117–137). Auckland, New Zealand: Reed.

Mead, H. M. (2003), *Tikanga Māori: Living by Māori values.* Wellington, New Zealand: Huia.

Meyer, M. A. (2001). Acultural understandings of empiricism: A Native Hawaiian critique. *Canadian Journal of Native Education, 25*(2), 188–198.

Meyer, M. A. (2013). The context within: My journey into research. In D. M. Mertens, F. Cram, & B. Chilisa (Eds.), *Indigenous pathways into social research—Voices of a new generation.* Walnut Creek, CA: Left Coast.

Ministry of Education. (2010). *Tū Rangatira: Māori medium educational leadershiop.* Wellington, New Zealand: Ministry of Education.

Ministry of Health. (1997). *A brief narrative on Māori women in the national cervical screening programme.* Wellington, New Zealand: Ministry of Health.

Ormond, A., Cram, F., & Carter, L. (2006). Researching our relations: Reflections on ethics and marginalisation. [Special supplement] *Alternative: An international Journal of Indigenous Scholarship,* 180–198.

Smith, L. T. (1999). *Decolonizing methodologies: Research and indigenous peoples.* New York, NY; Dunedin, New Zealand: Zed/Otago University Press.

Smith, L. T. (2012). *Decolonizing methodologies—Research and Indigenous peoples* (2nd ed.). London, UK; New York, NY: Zed.

Tamasese, K., Teteru, C., Waldegrave, C., & Bush, A. (2005). Ole taeao afua, the new morning: A qualitative investigation into Samoan perspectives on mental health and culturally appropriate services. *Australian and New Zealand Journal of Psychiatry, 39,* 300–309.

Tuagalu, C. (2013, May 16). Samoan ways of knowing. *Whānau Ora Research.* Retrieved June 5, 2013, from http://whanauoraresearch.co.nz/news/samoan-ways-of-knowing/

Wilson, S. (2008). *Research is ceremony. Indigenous research methods.* Black Point, Nova Scotia, Canada: Fernwood.

CHAPTER 9

CULTURAL REACTIVITY VS. CULTURAL RESPONSIVENESS

Addressing Macro Issues Starting With Micro Changes in Evaluation

Dominica McBride

ABSTRACT

The process of evaluation dictates the product. If the process is invalid or tainted, then the product and outcomes of an evaluation will also be compromised. Human dynamics can profoundly influence this process, despite attempts to be objective. Psychology and cultural neuroscience show the universality of these dynamics and the importance of addressing them in our professional work. These disciplines provide research that identifies ways in which human nature can inadvertently affect evaluation practice. Given that evaluation can have major implications for participants and communities, it is paramount that evaluators are aware of the human phenomena that influence practice, product, and outcomes. These influencing factors include, but are not limited to, brain functioning, past experience, culture, and associations. They affect our interactions and relationships, values, and decisions, all of which have substantial consequences for the evaluation.

Continuing the Journey to Reposition Culture and Cultural Context
in Evaluation Theory and Practice, pages 179–202
Copyright © 2015 by Information Age Publishing
All rights of reproduction in any form reserved.

The ultimate goal of evaluation is the greater public good (Greene, 2005a) and social justice (House, 1990). If the field is to realize this ideal, it is integral that we further attend to the process and the human facets that affect it, as these factors can either derail an evaluation or optimize its impact. Culturally Responsive Evaluation (CRE) has identified a path for evaluation to achieve the larger macrogoal of social justice and ways in which we can address human bias through inclusion, relationships, and an orientation to context. Adding a focus on the psychological/affective factors influencing the process will help to further hone CRE practice and achieve these marcolevel goals. This chapter highlights integral aspects of evaluation and their intersection with psychology and cultural neuroscience, identifies how these intersectional variables can affect evaluation, and pulls from these disciplines to hone evaluation practice and further enact CRE.

INTRODUCTION

Injustice anywhere is a threat to justice everywhere.
—Martin Luther King Jr. (1963)

Social injustice has plagued the United States since its nascence. Through wars and movements, disparity has persisted and manifested in health, education, criminal justice, and politics—many areas where evaluation plays (or should play) a significant role. However, even in evaluation, injustice can be perpetuated given human intrapersonal and interpersonal dynamics. Human nature is multidimensional, consisting of biology, experience, thoughts, and emotions (Flay, Snyder, & Petraitis, 2009). It is shaped before we are born and continues to be molded throughout our lives. Although human nature can be adaptive and protective, it can also be a barrier in work and relationships. If we do not attend to these human dynamics, it can compromise the validity of our evaluations. It can even end in adverse consequences for those who we may be trying to help. Part of human nature is the brain's tendency to create stereotypes, make associations, and send signals to the body, which then reacts to those generalizations (McBride & Bell, 2013). Given the malleability of the brain, it is shaped by experiences and exposures, including parenting, peer preferences, and the media. Thus, on a subconscious or conscious level, we encode these messages and act on them through decisions and behaviors. For example, to some degree, all of those exposed to repeated racist messages have a stereotype of the group that has been the target of those messages. These stereotypes, even if subconscious, can negatively affect our interactions and decisions in working with a particular group, especially in the absence of antithetical experiences. I label these automatic, subconscious thoughts and subsequent actions cultural reactivity. Cultural reactivity can compromise validity, interfere in relationships, cloud values, and influence decision-making. Culturally Responsive Evaluation (CRE) is one theoretical orientation that substantively addresses the effects of ignoring culture and context and places emphasis on the injustice in the larger sociopolitical landscape. However, the importance of and methods that address cultural reactivity have not been delineated.

In this chapter, I pull from psychology and cultural neuroscience to address these psychological and affective factors and further CRE's process and objectives. The purpose of this chapter is to help hone evaluation practice and impact through providing knowledge and skills that address cultural reactivity. This chapter first delineates various aspects of evaluation that are affected by our psychology and brain functioning. These disciplines highlight the relevance for and importance of all evaluators attending to cultural reactivity. It then describes the extant dimensions of CRE and provides an overview of a psychological/affective dimension constructed to address psychological and neurological variables affecting evaluations. It describes the skills that constitute this dimension and how to hone these skillsets. Figure 9.1 presents the overarching model described throughout this chapter for how this dimension fits into the greater picture of CRE and its relation to macrogoals.

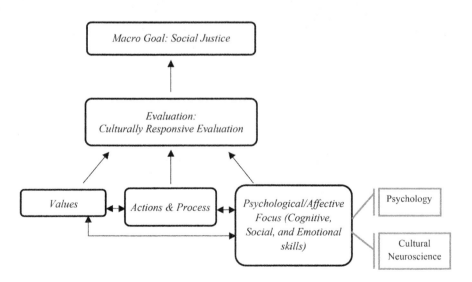

Figure 9.1 Framework for how microchanges influence evaluation and a macrogoal.

EVALUATION AS A HUMAN PROCESS

Evaluation, inclusive of the process of judging or placing a value on a program, policy, product, and so forth, can be seen as a process of decision-making (Kundin, 2010) and subsequent actions, and influenced by our values (Greene, 2005a; Greene, DeStefano, Burgon, & Hall, 2006), relationships (Greene, 2005a; Patton, 2008), contexts, and culture (Frierson, Hood, & Hughes, 2002). From planning and designing to implementing and reevaluating, evaluation is colored by us as evaluators, as human beings (Kitayama & Park, 2010). I highlight the obvious because, in evaluation, our humanness and the humanness of others that influence the evaluation is too often overlooked. Being human encompasses our biology, including our brain, as well as emotions, experiences, life lessons, behavior patterns, cognitions, and cultural influences. Experiences, lessons learned from parents, peers, teachers, media, and emotions shape thinking and behavior (Flay et al., 2009). Brain scanning technologies have revealed even more about being human. Neurological research has shown that much of our thinking goes on below the surface level of consciousness and deliberateness and thus is automatic or subconscious (Haynes et al., 2007). This "thinking" leads to most of our actions and behaviors. We are influenced by the subconscious parts of our brain much more than the scientific community ever realized prior to these new technologies. Evaluation is not immune to the influence of our subconscious. Even potentially harmful lessons and experiences can shape our perspective and values, guide our decisions, and even dictate our actions (Johnson et al., 2002; Kitayama & Park, 2010). They can influence our judgments and, thus, can impact others (Johnson et al., 2002). Due to our susceptibility and the significant consequences of some of our decisions (see House, 1990), attending to this dynamic in evaluation is of central importance. There are three main facets of evaluation that can dictate both the process and the outcome of evaluations, including values, decisions, and relationships. These aspects can determine the validity of our data, shape the perception of the evaluation and findings, and influence how or if the findings are used. The sections below highlight the importance of these components.

Values

In evaluation, values are central (Greene, 2005a) and affect the focus of the evaluation (Hall, Ahn, & Greene, 2012) and, consequently, the products, outcomes, and effects. Values can intentionally or unintentionally manifest through decisions and actions (Bardi & Schwartz, 2003). We have values—some of them known and others unknown—that are evident in our evaluation choices. The centrality of values and their influence on decisions is not only a claim of some evaluation scholars but is also a psychological phenomenon (Weber & Morris, 2010). If we value something, which may be subtly learned by observing our parents (Bandura, 1977) or watching television, we will act on that value in some way. We often choose objects and life experiences (or stakeholders to participate and evaluation designs) that coincide with our values regardless of it being the best choice or not (Wright & Wright, 2013).

Decisions

Decision-making is another core activity of evaluation practice (Kundin, 2010). We decide whether to undertake a particular evaluation project or not, who to include on (or whether to even create) an evaluation team, who to consult, the methodologies, and how to employ the methods (e.g., who does the interviewing, in what locations, where surveys are completed). In addition, we also decide how to interpret findings, if the evaluand has value and in what ways, whether to take context and culture into account, what recommendations to offer, and more. These examples do not include the "in-the-moment," unexpected decisions that also need to be made. Regardless if the process is premeditated or spontaneous, decision-making is another area in which our past experiences, culture, and biology influence our process and outcomes (Gladwell, 2005).

Relationships

Similarly, relationships are at the core of evaluation practice. We have relationships with those who hire us, program personnel, other beneficiaries, and maybe even those in the community where the evaluand operates. Relationships are integral in understanding the program, its context, and its stakeholders. Through relationships, we can infuse community voice and support empowerment. Strong relationships can also support increasing evaluation use, improving programs, and enhancing organizations. High-functioning relationships and constructive interactions help to obtain valid data (Kirkhart, 1995). Relationships characterized by accountability, respect, cultural sensitivity, openness, and trust necessary in effective and fruitful interactions help to obtain better data and increase the likelihood of evaluation use (Patton, 2008). The challenge here is that even our relationships are influenced by automatic, subconscious processes (Beukeboom, 2009; Xu, Zuo, Wang, & Han, 2009) that can lead to power differentials and mistrust.

In short, these integral aspects of evaluation are deeply influenced by our psychology and biology, and affect the validity of our data and effects of the evaluation on the program, organization, or policy, and most importantly, the people. Ultimately, whether valid or not, evaluation products can have implications for the larger social goals of contributing to the greater public good (Greene, 2005a) and realizing social justice (House, 1990).

Culturally Responsive Evaluation

Social equality is often obstructed by challenging barriers, including a biased social structure that shows up in and is guided by policies, programs that do not address root causes of problems, and programs delivered in a culturally insensitive way, leaving behind groups and communities. CRE is one theoretical orientation that was developed to address these obstacles. In essence, it is constituted by political and value commitments to and actions toward cultural integrity, community empowerment, and sociopolitical change. Thus, values, decision-making, and relationships are integral to the process, ultimately feeding into achieving social justice.

It has been developed to counter the potentially negative consequences of invalidity due to ignoring culture and the exclusion of historically silenced voices in the evaluation process. It maintains that culture cannot be disentangled from the understanding of a program, policy, or initiative and the impact it has on people (Frazier-Anderson, Hood, & Hopson, 2011; Frierson et al., 2002). The CRE process comprises studying the context, history, and culture of the program and participants, and including participants and other community stakeholders in decision-making throughout the evaluation (Frazier-Anderson et al., 2011). This is to ensure that the tools used to gather data are culturally sensitive, the community has a voice, and the process supports empowerment. Harken back to the quote that started this chapter; CRE strives to address social injustice both within its process (e.g., involving community) and by its products (e.g., decisions, evaluation reports), hence, using the process as part of the cure and evaluation as an intervention.

There appear to be two dimensions of CRE in the current literature: values commitments and actions/steps (see Table 9.1). The values dimension is constituted by commitments to social justice, inclusion, empowerment, and cultural respect. This dimension is the foundation for the second aspect: the recommended actions or steps of CRE (Frazier-Anderson et al., 2011; Frierson et al., 2002). Together, these two dimensions should, ideally, contribute to social justice through accurately capturing the impact of programs from the perspective of those participating in them, and improving or sustaining effective programs for communities that have been

TABLE 9.1   Dimensions of Culturally Responsive Evaluation

Dimension	Description
Values Commitments	• Social justice • Empowerment • Inclusion • Cultural respect
Actions	• Analyze context and examine sociopolitical assumptions • Develop an evaluation team with evaluators from the group of focus • Include those affected by the program and from the community • Develop/adapt culturally sensitive measurement tools • Consider/integrate culture of participants • Convene a CRE review panel
Psychological/Affective	• Regular critical self-reflection • Enhancing cognitive skills • Honing social and emotional intelligence

marginalized. However, given human nature, these two dimensions may not be enough to actualize validity and sufficiently advocate for the change needed to achieve social justice. I present a third dimension focusing on intrapersonal and interpersonal dynamics to advance the application of CRE. This third dimension will further support validity (especially multicultural validity; Kirkhart, 1995, 2013), the development of authentic and transformational relationships (where the synergy leads to something greater), and stronger movement toward the greater public good and social justice. It can be characterized as the psychological or affective dimension, which focuses on the human part of evaluation. It highlights our human nature, including biology, emotion, life experiences, behavior and thought patterns, and cultural influences and how they either hinder or help our evaluation practice. In honing this dimension, we become aware of our natural and often unknown barriers to accurately perceive a situation, evaluand, or person, and enhance our ability to correctly discern. Thus, we will make more valid claims, interpretations, conclusions, and recommendations through a more effective, relational, and humane process (Goleman, 2006). We will also form stronger relationships and foundations for achieving macrogoals.

The Need for a Psychological/Affective Focus

Unfortunately, the process of the evaluation, even if performed by someone from the community of focus, can be harmful instead of beneficial due to our psychology and neural functioning. The brain develops from bottom to top and inside to out. On average, it takes approximately 26 years for the frontal lobes (the seat of reason, discernment, and executive decision-making) to fully form (National Research Council and Institute of Medicine, 2009). Life experiences, repeated exposure, and thought and behavior patterns form our neural connections and general neural matrix (Wright & Wright, 2013).

Our brains are built for automaticity, which means that they are wired to conserve energy through creating automatic processes and associations (Spunt & Lieberman, 2013). Therefore, instead of spending time and energy wondering if it is safe to sit in a chair, we automatically sit in it because our brain has created a stereotype of a chair which is now an automatic association which leads to an automatic behavior—sitting down (Fiske, 1992). This way, we can save our energy for something more important, like fighting or fleeing in a dangerous situation. Due to automaticity, most of our brain functioning and thus cognitions take place below our conscious awareness. This means that most of what we do comes from those automatic or patterned ways of doing and seeing (Haynes et al., 2007; Mason & Morris, 2010). Think of a time when you have driven home and not even remembered driving there. You had taken that route so often that it had become a neural pattern and thus an automatic process. Dr. Michael Ryce (2013) uses the metaphor of vision to illuminate this automatic neurologic phenomenon. Our retinas take in the light particles that are reflected off of what we are seeing (a tree, a person), creating a picture in our brains. We then "see" the picture our brain has created. We never actually see what is in front of us. This dynamic is often manifested in our professional lives. It does not suddenly stop as we walk through the doors of our office or an organization. This process continues as long as our brains are alive and working. Therefore, the implications for us as evaluators is that our perception of what is in front of us, be it a person or program, will, at times, be tainted.

Cultural neuroscience, a discipline that studies how culture influences neurological functioning and thought patterns, provides greater depth and nuance to this picture (Ames & Fiske, 2010; Kitayama & Park, 2010). Findings from cultural neuroscience studies suggest neurological universalities and cultural differences relative to the brain. We now know that culture deeply influences brain patterns and the way people live, think, decide, perceive, and problem-solve (Ames, & Fiske, 2010; Kitayama & Park, 2010; Weber & Morris, 2010). All of these mental processes play important roles in evaluation.

HOW CULTURAL NEUROSCIENCE AND PSYCHOLOGY MATTER TO EVALUATION, ESPECIALLY TO CRE

Despite their relevance and influence in the evaluation process, cultural neuroscience and psychology are two disciplines rarely discussed in evaluation as it relates to how they impact practice. The model presented in Figure 9.1 shows where these disciplines influence evaluation. Actions and process (e.g., choosing and engaging stakeholders, developing questions) are at the center of the model because they are the most central aspects of the evaluation. They end in the product, which should contribute to the macrogoal. For better or worse, the actions and process are deeply influenced by the values and psychological/affective dimensions. Figure 9.2 shows how psychology and cultural neuroscience influence the process through the values exhibited, decisions made, and relationships and interactions formed. Values, decisions, and relationships can make an evaluation process valid and potent or invalid and powerless in having influence in improving a program or changing a policy. Thus, it is integral to optimize the process for optimal impact. Reflexivity and proactively honing a particular set of psychological and affective skills can help achieve this objective.

Figure 9.2 also demonstrates the interconnectedness of relationships, values, and decision-making. Given our psychology and their interdependence, they often cannot be disentangled from each other. Latent or explicit values influence who we engage or form relationships with and how we interact with certain people or groups. They also influence our decisions. We lean toward what we value, be it deliberately or inadvertently. The relationships we form and interactions we engage in can affect what we decide and may further shape our value system. Our decisions also affect our values and can strengthen or weaken relationships. Each of these aspects has been discussed in extant literature; however, this section focuses on what lies at the intersection and how cultural neuroscience and psychology can inform our understanding of the interpersonal and intrapersonal factors influencing them. The following section highlights the neurological and psychological phenomena that influence each of these aspects of evaluation with a focus on those factors that subtly yet deeply affect them, including stereotyping, empathy, and attribution/interpretation.

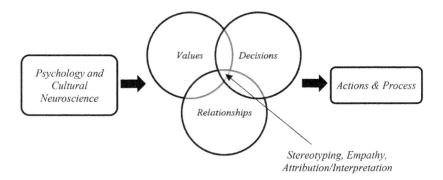

Figure 9.2 How psychology and cultural neuroscience influence evaluation practice.

Stereotyping, Empathy, and Attribution: What Lies at the Intersection

Relationships, decisions, and values in evaluation greatly influence if and how the process contributes to macrogoals. Unfortunately, strong relationships characterized by trust, openness, accurately seeing, and being accurately seen are quite difficult to achieve (Yalom, 1989). Our neural matrix complicates this process with perceptions, stereotypes, behavior patterns, projections, and assumptions, most of the time unknown to us without diligent and critical self-reflection. These mental phenomena influence our nonverbal communication (Goleman, 2006), the manner in which we treat others, and the level of empathy in a given interaction (Brewer, 2004; Johnson et al., 2002; Xu et al., 2009). They also affect our value system and the decisions we make. Each of these facets can have profound implications for the impact of evaluation or the harm or benefit it can have on the people involved.

Stereotyping.

Stereotyping is one mental function that can hinder a process, stagnate relationships, and prevent fruitful interactions. It influences nonverbal communication, treatment of others, and empathy. It also affects our valuing and decisions. Stereotyping in general is not something that can be avoided, as it is a natural neurological function. Our brains are repeatedly shown biased stimuli (e.g., media), freely absorbing information that contributes to the racist, sexist, classist beliefs or values all who are exposed have to some degree. These associations are encoded in our brains and become automatic, subconscious thoughts influencing our decisions, behaviors, and interactions (Greenwald & Banaji, 1995; Sue et al., 2007). For example, if an evaluator has a latent stereotype of a group as incompetent, she/he is likely to decide (even inadvertently) to exclude that group from a decision-making process. Even if included, the evaluator may unintentionally insult those from the group based on the stereotype.

A microaggression (Pinderhughes, 1979) is an example of when automatic, implicit thoughts influence actions and relationships. It is an often unintentional slight against a person due to her/his group status (Pinderhughes, 1979; Sue et al., 2007). For example, a patient in a hospital may mistake a female professional as a nurse instead of a physician. Often times, people in marginalized groups face myriad of these interactions throughout their lives (Sue et al., 2007; Thompson-Miller & Feagin, 2007). These slights encroach on a person's mental and physical energy (Pinderhughes, 1979; Sue et al., 2007). They can impinge and derail an evaluation process if done with members of an evaluation team, interviewees, or other stakeholders. Microaggressions have been identified as contributing to disparities in education (Gordon & Johnson, 2003); health (Betancourt, Green, Carrillo, & Park, 2005; Gilmore, 2007; Langer, 1999); employment (Gordon & Johnson, 2003); and the criminal justice system (Alexander, 2010). These micro-offenses can take the form of ignoring a group's history and context, condescension (Sue et al., 2007), or unfair targeting (e.g., by police [Alexander, 2010] or special education). Hence, there have likely been myriad microaggressions in evaluation, especially in ignoring a group's history or context. Possibly the most challenging aspect of this phenomena is that it is simultaneously insidious, unintentional, and subconscious. Usually, people are not aware they are perpetrating microaggressions, which allows them to continue. Ultimately, everyone interacting with another group does this to some degree. Due to the subtlety and lack of intentionality in microaggressions, the receiver is often confused about the offense and unsure of how to react (Sue et al., 2007). This silent and invisible dance leaves both parties in limbo, where there is no movement toward a deeper, more truthful relationship. Fortunately, interactions and relationships can be repaired; however, the person engaging in microaggressions must catch their microaggression and attempt to mend the breach. For this correction to happen, the person must be self-aware. Part of this self-awareness includes identifying the thoughts and emotions influencing interactions.

These tacit assumptions and associations often sprout from fear on the part of the doer of microaggressions. Ronquillo et al. (2007) found that European Americans in their study had greater activity in their amygdala (the part of the brain involved in experiencing emotions, especially fear) when viewing darker toned faces—the darker the tone, the greater the fear response. This fear response can influence interactions, as it is nearly impossible to completely hide one's emotional state (Goleman, 2006). These affects and dynamics also affect the preference or valuing of a group and their related cultural norms, beliefs, and traditions (Barrett, 2005; Blumenfeld & Raymond, 2000). These cultural preferences and values can influence an evaluator's perception of the evaluation, evaluand, and participants.

Stereotyping and subsequent valuing can also affect validity. Beukeboom (2009) found that open nonverbals (e.g., smiling, open posture, leaning forward) elicit more interpretive and subjective discussion and descriptions, whereas responses to people with closed nonverbals (e.g., frowns, leaning away, folder arms) were void of this freer expression. Consequently, closed listeners are more likely to inhibit the speaker from sharing their deeper thoughts and opinions. In evaluation, this has implications for data collection and validity. Participants, interviewees, or focus group members may describe what happened in a program and provide concrete examples to closed listeners. However, they would be less likely to talk subjectively, stating what the program meant to them, how it affected their lives, how they liked the program, or how they think it would impact others. According to the findings of Beukeboom's study, interviewees would also refrain from interpretive statements, despite the value of learning and including stakeholders' interpretations of the program, data, and findings. When we are not aware of our implicit associations or stereotypes, we may be unintentionally closed in our interactions (which is how the mind-body interaction works). For instance, if we have a subconscious stereotype of a poor person as lazy, crazy, or dangerous, our facial expression and body posture will likely convey feelings associated with this stereotype (Gladwell, 2005), such as repulsion or fear, to some degree (Ames & Fiske, 2010). Thus, instead of automatically leaning in and having an open posture, we may lean away or close our arms, leading to the interviewee being less forthright with information and descriptive of his subjective experience.

Empathy.

Empathy also profoundly influences our interactions with others, how much we value a person or culture, and our subsequent decisions. It is the cornerstone of relationships, compassion, and benevolence (Goleman, 1995, 2006). Without empathy, there would be no altruism, collective efficacy, community, or working relationships. Team functioning would be compromised (Moriarty & Buckley, 2003). We would miss the healing power of positive relationships (Levey & Levey, 1998), and there would be no true understanding of one another (Goleman, 2006). On the other hand, empathy fosters trust, strong working alliances, functional teams, and interpersonal understanding. This subtle yet potent social dynamic is at the center of social intelligence (Goleman, 2006) and a product of emotional intelligence (Goleman, 1995). Both of these intelligences are necessary ingredients for social cohesion, leadership, and much of one's professional success (Goleman, 1995, 2006). As evaluators, it can affect our data, interpretations, and recommendations. In evaluation, empathy is necessary in developing a deep understanding of the meaning and experience of the participants and other stakeholders. A deeper understanding also influences validity, contributes to compassionate and thoughtful decision-making, and increases the likelihood for more positive social outcomes (Brewer, 2004; Martin, 1993).

Neuroscience, again, provides further insight into human capacity for empathy. Research shows that in the brain, "mirror neurons" (Rizzolatti & Craighero, 2004) are partly responsible for empathic responses (Keysers, 2011). Mirror neurons were discovered when observing the brain activity of a viewer watching another conduct an activity (e.g., picking up a pencil); in this moment, the same parts of the viewer's brain activate as if the viewer was doing the activity (Restak, 2003; Rizzolatti & Craighero, 2004). This empathic neurological reaction also applies to facial expressions, including those of emotions. Typically, when we see another's emotional expression, we feel the emotion within ourselves, even unknowingly (Goleman, 2006). It would seem that the brain would function the same way regardless of who is being viewed. Surprisingly, the most primal level of empathy—physiological empathy—has been shown to decrease when interacting with or witnessing certain out-groups (Johnson et al., 2002; Xu et al., 2009).

Xu et al. (2009) conducted a study examining neurological reactions to the pain of another ethnic group. They included pictures of Caucasian and Chinese faces and Caucasian and Chinese participants showing pictures of faces with a needle piercing them. Participants were shown faces representing their own ethnic group and the other ethnic group. They found that activity in the anterior cingulate cortex (the seat of pain sensory in the brain) was activated when viewing faces with the needle penetrating those of their own ethnic group. However, this empathic reaction severely diminished when viewing faces with the needle penetrating members of the other ethnic group, therefore suggesting that people from one group typically did not "feel the pain" of those from the other group.

Another study by Chiao et al. (2008) measured the brain's response to ethnic out-groups' fearful facial expressions. They found that the bilateral amygdala (the part of the brain that lights up when we feel fear) responded more when witnessing the fear in one's own group than in another group. Differences in facial memory have also been found based on gender as males are more likely to remember male faces rather than female faces (Pinkham et al., 2008). Most striking and disturbing is the neurological reaction to the "least-esteemed" groups in American society, such as people who are homeless or addicted to drugs (Ames & Fiske, 2010). Harris and Fiske (2007) found that the activity in the medial frontal cortex, a part of the brain active in social cognition (when perceiving another human), significantly decreases when perceiving the "least-esteemed" groups. This suggests that they may be dehumanized by others (Ames & Fiske, 2010), hence, devalued and objectified.

This automatic response can have pivotal consequences in decision-making. For example, in a jury process, Brewer (2004) found that those judging a defendant within their ethnic group were more empathic and receptive to mitigating evidence, thus, more likely to make a fair decision. The implications for evaluation are tremendous. Our decisions potentially affect many currently and to come, as programs and policies can be either cut or expanded based on evaluation results or recommendations.

Interpretation and attribution.

Likewise, our interpretations and attributions can also reflect and influence relationships, values, and decisions. Our interpretations and attributions, as in most other mental processes, are influenced by culture, rearing, and experiences (Ames & Fiske, 2010; Kitayama & Park, 2010;

Weber & Morris, 2010). Research in cultural neuroscience also contributes to understanding automatic attributions and interpretations. Research in this field has found that people reared in independent-oriented (often Western) cultures tend to have an automatic tendency to disregard or devalue the contextual or situational aspects influencing a person's behavior and focus on disposition. However, those from more interdependent-oriented cultures (often Eastern) tend to automatically place more focus on the context or situation and its influence on behavior (Nisbett, 2003). Kitayama and Park (2010) stated,

> One basic pattern that can be gleaned from the cross-cultural studies on person perception is that person as a figural object (vis-à-vis situational information) stands out in social perception of North Americans. For Asians and Asian Americans, however, the figural object seems more embedded because it is tied more closely to situational constraints or affordances. (p. 117)

These processes are not only shown in behavior or outward choice but they first show up neurologically in particular areas of the brain (Kitayama & Park, 2010; Kobayashi, Glover, & Temple, 2007). Interpretations reflect automatic perceptions of the individual and neurological functioning. For independent-oriented cultures, this proclivity toward dispositional attribution persists despite research concluding that context influences behavior in many situations (Baumer & South, 2001; Brown et al., 2010; Cohen et al., 2000; Gladwell, 2000). For example, Cohen et al. (2000) found that gonorrhea rates correlated with the number of broken windows in a neighborhood, potentially signifying that community disregard can lead to risky behavior. Gladwell (2000) described how crime decreased with merely cleaning New York subways in the 80s to 90s. Some neuroscience research has reached similar conclusions. They have found the longer a person lives in a context or is influenced by a set of cultural mores, the stronger the tendency to exhibit particular ways of thinking and patterns of behavior, resulting in neurological changes (Maguire et al., 2000). In healing, helping, and social professions, this is critically important and can have substantial consequences. If medical doctors fail to understand the context affecting their patients, their treatment may be ineffective, resulting in the inability of the patient to follow medical advice (Langer, 1999; Tang, Fantone, Bozynski, & Adams, 2002). For example, if a patient is to buy healthy foods, it may be a challenge for one living in a food desert with little access to transportation. For mental health professionals, not considering context can easily result in misdiagnosis (Chien & Bell, 2008), the wrong treatment, continuation of the symptoms, or possibly exacerbating symptoms (Bell, 2008). Similarly in evaluation, forgoing context has implications for understanding programs and their participants, analyzing and interpreting data, and making appropriate recommendations. If we decide (be it deliberately or by default) to forgo contextual analysis, we will miss important information influencing the participants and the root causes of the problem. For example, someone may tacitly value independence and autonomy and, unaware of this value, overlook the value of collectivism or group cohesion. Therefore, the evaluator may focus on individualistic outcomes and miss opportunities to integrate a community asset or program facet that could transform the social condition. Misattribution can also negatively affect a relationship with a person or community. For example, I work on the south and west sides of Chicago, where there is disproportionate rates of violent crimes. If I were to attribute the violence to disposition as an evaluator, I would not only be inaccurate, I would also fray my relationship with the communities. Many community members correctly have a contextual orientation and perceive and experience how context influences their lives, decisions, and behavior. If I were to devalue and understate the role of context, the community may not trust me or think I understand or listen to them.

Effects of Cultural Reactivity

Consequently, neglecting the influence of our psychology and neurology can have deleterious effects for marginalized communities. In 2005, Brekke, Nakagami, Kee, and Green studied cross-ethnic differences in the ability to perceive emotion in people with schizophrenia. They found that people of color scored lower in their perception of emotion and concluded that they, therefore, had lesser ability in this area. However, there was one major oversight. People of color were only shown White faces. Pinkham et al. (2008) corrected this mistakes in their research by using the faces of both African Americans and Caucasians to study differences in facial processing by African American and Caucasian people with schizophrenia compared to those with no mental disorder. This study found that African Americans did not have an emotional deficit in their ability to recognize and process emotions. Brekke et al.'s (2005) research methods and conclusion provide examples of cultural reactivity, automatically concluding, deciding on, or behaving based on subtle, subconscious, or overt cognitions and affects (e.g., stereotypes, cultural associations), especially without critical reflection and/or conscious thought around other possibilities. Cultural reactivity can manifest as verbal or nonverbal reactions (facial expressions, body posture, decisions) based on mental associations about an individual or cultural group (see Table 9.2).

Research shows that cultural reactivity has had adverse social and medical consequences, including premature termination in mental health treatment (Wade & Bernstein, 1991), health disparities (Agency for Healthcare Research and Quality, 2011; Burkard & Knox, 2004), incarceration

TABLE 9.2 Cultural Reactivity Versus Cultural Responsiveness

Cultural Reactivity	Cultural Responsiveness
Making decisions without considering other possible underlying drivers	Critically self-reflecting on decisions and having open communication about possible drivers
Interacting without self-observation or reflection	Honing social and emotional intelligence
Acting without examining assumptions	Engaging in self and team processes around assumptions on project, self, others, etc.

(Alexander, 2010; Kirk, 2008), and police-involved shootings (Correll et al., 2002, Payne, Lambert, & Jacoby, 2002). Theoretical orientations in evaluation, such as CRE and Empowerment Evaluation, have attempted to minimize these consequences of individual human bias through inclusion of participants and other stakeholders in the evaluation planning and implementation. However, even here, the brain is still at work and evaluators' automatic reactions will ensue with participating stakeholders if unexamined. Without self-awareness and a proactive stance toward personal growth, cultural reactivity will continue to influence evaluation practice and impact. Increasing the number of evaluators of color has been one initiative to help solve this problem of offending and perpetuating oppression (Frazier-Anderson et al., 2011). While this increase is helpful, it alone does not solve the problem of cultural reactivity. Even those within group, while likely more empathic toward people in their group, still hold stereotypes that affect their interactions with them (Gladwell, 2005).

For those of us living in the United States, we are "swimming in the same waters" of media and history. In the 1940s, Kenneth and Mamie Clark conducted their famous "doll study," finding that African American children preferred Caucasian over African American dolls. In 2005, Kara Davis replicated the study and filmed these conversations (Davis & Reel Works Teen Filmmaking, 2005). She spoke with 21 African American children, placing a Caucasian doll and an African American doll in front of them and asked them which they preferred. The majority of youth (15 out of 21) chose the Caucasian doll, showing that little had changed with regard to the effects of racism on youth in over 60 years. Even in the case of educated adults within marginalized groups, it may be very likely that the findings in Harris and Fiske's (2007) study (i.e., dehumanizing the "least-esteemed") manifest within group. Even if one believes she/he is "culturally competent," there is still a need for continual expansion and refinement. The literature on cultural competence does not adequately attend to the specific and prescribed set of skills needed to counter the aforementioned neurological challenges. Thus, regardless of ethnic group or level of cultural competence, we must all recognize the importance of developing our understanding of and skills within the psychological/affective dimension in our work as evaluators.

How to Address the Problem

There are three particular skillsets that address stereotypes, empathy, and attribution/interpretation. They will help us more easily recognize and dictate our values, form strong relationships and engage in fruitful interactions, and make sound and just decisions. These skillsets include cognitive, social, and emotional skills.

Cognitive Skills

While neuoscience teaches us that our brains are shaped by our experiences and exposures, it also provides us with a path for reshaping our brains (Harris & Fiske, 2007; Price, Ramsden, Hope, Friston, & Seghier, 2013; Wright & Wright, 2013). Along with automaticity, the neurological phenomenon of "neuroplasticity" (Draganski et al., 2004) is the ability of our brain to change and reform. We can play an active role in reshaping our brain by establishing new thinking and behavior patterns that create new neural patterns. We can take what was once automatic and make it conscious. For example, Harris and Fiske (2007) found that the tendency of the brain to objectify members of an outcast group changed when activating a cognitive empathic process, such as intentionally thinking of another's preference for something. When participants engaged in this mental activity, the social part of the brain activated and reversed objectification. If we intentionally repeat this process, it is possible that over time a more empathic thought pattern will become automatic, resulting in a more open and welcoming stance. However, this change often requires first identifying the automatic thought before we can deliberately change it and establish a different pattern (Wright & Wright, 2013).

Cognitive skills encompass the ability to identify conscious and underlying thoughts (Wright & Wright, 2013) and change our cognitions and thought patterns (Catalano, Berglund, Ryan, Lonczak, & Hawkins, 2004). These skills will help in perceiving and changing our stereotypes, preconceived notions, and other associations. For example, Dr. David Williams, sociologist and expert on addressing racism, suggested exploring and identifying the stereotypes within a person and proactively substituting those thoughts with more positive characteristics of the group (Wilkerson, 2013). One way to identify group preferences and stereotypes is through the Harvard's Implicit Association Test (see www.implicit.harvard.edu). This test allows people to learn their implicit group biases, by age, gender, religion, ethnicity, weight, socioeconomic status, and mental health status. We can also hone these skills through practicing focusing exercises, like mindfulness meditation or cognitive behavioral techniques (see Boyes, 2012). Wright and Wright (2013) advocate for an "assignment way of living," where one practices a skill or new behavior repeatedly to establish a new pattern. One way this could be applied to cultural reactivity is to practice identifying one's associations or automatic thoughts that arise in a conversation or when passing a stranger on the street. The assignment could be to name three thoughts that arose when walking past a Hispanic woman, an Arabic man dressed in a thawb, or a Black child, for examples. These skills and practices also help to guide us in examining our related emotions that influence our values, decisions, and behavior.

Emotional and social intelligence.

Emotions also deeply affect our interactions, relationships, and conceptualizations, whether we are aware of them or not (Goleman, 1995). Recognizing, identifying, expressing, and regulating emotions help us to uncover subconscious thoughts and deliberately shape our interactions for stronger relationships and more open, truthful interchanges (Goleman, 1995, 2006; Wright & Wright, 2013). Emotional intelligence is the ability to feel, identify, express, and manage our emotions (Goleman, 1995; Wright & Wright, 2013). Emotions are often mistakenly thought to cause irrationality, thus, having no place in the workplace or decision-making. Contrary to this opinion, emotional intelligence has been found to be essential in good decision-making, integral in comprehension and communication (Beukeboom, 2009), necessary for rationality, and a cornerstone of academic and professional success (Cherniss, Extein, Goleman, & Weissberg, 2006; Goleman, 1995; Wright & Wright, 2013).

Emotional intelligence is also a prerequisite for social intelligence. Social intelligence is the ability to cultivate strong working alliances and high-functioning teams. It also helps in comprehending social complexity (Goleman, 2006). It includes awareness and facility in social situations. Social awareness constitutes primal empathy, attunement, empathic accuracy, and social cognition. It means that a person "feels with" another and understands their nonverbal communication, listens completely and is fully present, accurately identifies the experience of the other, and is able to understand broader social systems (Goleman, 2006, p. 84). This conscious living contributes to other aspects of social awareness such as social facility, which encompasses synchrony, self-presentation, influence, and concern (Goleman, 2006, p. 84). With these abilities, a person is able to be nonverbally in sync with others, accurately and authentically convey and portray themselves, intentionally create a desired outcome, and show concern about and respond to others' needs in their best interest (Goleman, 2006). In evaluation, emotional and social intelligence can enhance our decision-making and awareness of our tacit values, curb our tendency to be culturally reactive, improve our interviewing and facilitation, and hone our interpretations and recommendations. This skillset alone can change the face and reputation of evaluation and more strongly contribute to social justice.

To hone emotional skills, start attending to feelings. Practice identifying, labeling, and expressing your emotions (see Wright & Wright, 2013). For social skills, you can improve your empathy and practice fully attending to the person with which you are engaged. Dr. Paul Ekman has conducted significant research on facial microexpressions (Ekman & Friesen, 2003) and has a training tool (the Ekman Micro Expression Training Tool 3.0) designed to enhance emotional recognition and therefore empathy (Goleman, 2006). Finally, the development of positive intercultural relationships also helps to decrease prejudice (Dovidio, Gaertner, & Kawakami, 2003; Smith, 1994) and may help to enhance neurological and interactional empathy. There are myriad ways to hone the skills of cultural responsiveness and the aforementioned are merely a few.

CONCLUSION

Cultural reactivity can damage relationships, taint data, and lead to deleterious social consequences. This neurological and psychological process is automatic, and we are all doing it to some degree, given the nature of being human. However, with consciousness, self-awareness, self-reflection, and deliberate action, we can curb our cultural reactivity and hone our cultural responsiveness. Although our life experiences shape our brains and behavior, we can consciously change both to enhance our evaluation practice. Through honing the psychological/affective dimension of cultural responsiveness, we can develop stronger relationships and working alliances. We can create social environments for openness and better data, perceive and interpret more accurately, make better decisions, and form stronger, more constructive relationships. This journey of further cognitive development and social and emotional intelligence is a challenging one. However, it can have major personal and societal consequences and increase the likelihood of reaching the macrogoal of social justice.

REFERENCES

Agency for Healthcare Research and Quality. (2011). National healthcare disparities report. Retrieved June 2, 2013, from http://www.ahrq.gov/research/findings/nhqrdr/nhdr11/nhdr11.pdf

Alexandar, M. (2010). The new Jim Crow: Mass incarceration in the age of colorblindness. New York, NY: New Press.

Ames, D. L., & Fiske, S. T. (2010). Cultural neuroscience. Asian Journal of Social Psychology, 13, 72–82.

Bandura, A. (1977). Social learning theory. Englewood Cliffs, NJ: Prentice Hall.

Bardi, A., & Schwartz, S. (2003). Values and behavior: Strength and structure of relations. Personality and Social Psychology Bulletin, 29, 1207–1220.

Barrett, K. H. (2005). Case examples: Addressing racism, discrimination, and cultural bias in the interface of psychology and law. In K. H. Barrett & W. H. George (Eds.), Race, culture, psychology, & law (pp.19–29). Thousand Oaks, CA: Sage.

Baumer, E. P., & South, S. J. (2001). Community effects on youth sexual activity. Journal of Marriage and Family, 63, 540–554.

Bell, C. C. (2008). Should culture considerations influence early interventions? In M. Blumenfield & R. J. Ursano (Eds.), Intervention and resilience after mass trauma (pp. 127–148). Cambridge, UK: Cambridge University Press.

Betancourt, J. R., Green, A. R., Carrillo, J. E., & Park, E. R. (2005). Cultural competence and healthcare disparities: Key perspectives and trends. Health Affairs, 24, 499–505.

Beukeboom, C. J. (2009). When words feel right: How affective expressions of listeners change a speaker's language use. European Journal of Social Psychology, 39, 747–756.

Blumenfeld, W. J., & Raymond D. (2000). Prejudice and discrimination. In M. Adams, W. J. Blumenfeld, R. Castaneda, H. W. Hackman, M. L. Peters, & X. Zuniga (Eds.), Readings for diversity and social justice (pp. 21–30). New York, NY: Routledge.

Boyes, A. (2012, December 6). Cognitive behavioral therapy techniques that work. Psychology Today. Retrieved June 1, 2013, from http://www.psychologytoday.com/blog/in-practice/201212/cognitive-behavioral-therapy-techniques-work

Brekke, J. S., Nakagami, E., Kee, K. S., & Green, M. F. (2005). Cross-ethnic differences in perception of emotion in schizophrenia. Schizophrenia Research, 77, 289–298.

Brewer, T. W. (2004). Race and jurors' receptivity to mitigation in capital cases: The effect of jurors', defendants', and victims' race in combination. Law and Human Behavior, 28, 529–545.

Brown, S. C., Flavin, K., Kaupert, S., Tapia, M., Prado, G., Hirama, I.,...Pantin, H. (2012). The role of settings in family-based prevention of HIV/STDs. In W. Pequegnat & C. Bell (Eds.), Families and HIV/AIDS: Culture and contextual issues in prevention and treatment (pp. 69–93). New York, NY: Springer.

Burkard, A. W., & Knox, S. (2004). Effect of therapist color-blindness on empathy and attributions in cross-cultural counseling. Journal of Counseling Psychology, 51, 387–397.

Catalano, R. F., Berglund, M. L., Ryan, J. A. M., Lonczak, H. S., & Hawkins, J. D. (2004). Positive youth development in the United States: Research findings on evaluations of positive youth development programs. The Annals of the American Academy of Political and Social Science, 591, 98–124.

Cherniss, C., Extein, M., Goleman, D., & Weissberg, R. (2006). Emotional intelligence: What does the research really indicate? Educational Psychologist, 41, 239–245.

Chiao, J. Y., Iidaka, T., Gordon, H. L., Nogawa, J., Bar, M., Aminoff, E., . . . Ambady, N. (2008). Cultural specificity in amygdala response to fear faces. *Journal of Cognitive Neuroscience, 20,* 2167–2164.

Chien, P. L., & Bell, C. C. (2008). Racial differences and schizophrenia. *Directions in Psychiatry, 28,* 285–292.

Clark, K. B., & Clark, M. P. (1950). Emotional factors in racial identification and preference in Negro children. *The Journal of Negro Education, 19,* 341–350.

Correll, J., Park, B., Judd, C. M., & Wittenbrink, B. (2002). The police officer's dilemma: Using ethnicity to disambiguate potentially threatening individuals. *Journal of Personality and Social Psychology, 83,* 1314–1329.

Cohen, D., Spear, S., Scribner, R., Kissinger, P., Mason, K., & Wildgen, J. (2000). "Broken windows" and the risk of gonorrhea. *American Journal of Public Health, 90,* 230–236.

Davis, K., & Reel Works Teen Filmmaking (2005). *A girl like me.* [Documentary]. Retrieved December 1, 2014 from http://www.youtube.com/watch?v=z0Bx FRu_SOw

Dovidio, J. F., Gaertner, S. L., & Kawakami, K. (2003). Intergroup contact: The past, present, and the future. group processes. *Intergroup Relations, 6,* 5–21.

Draganski, B., Gaser, C., Busch, V., Schuierer, G., Bogdahn, U., & May, A. (2004). Neuroplasticity: Changes in grey matter induced by training. *Nature, 427,* 311–312.

Ekman, P., & Friesen, W. V. (2003). *Unmasking the face: A guide to recognizing emotions from facial expressions.* Los Angeles, CA: Malor.

Fiske, S. (1992). Thinking is for doing: Portraits of social cognition from daguerreotype to laserphoto. *Journal of Personality and Social Psychology, 63,* 877–889.

Flay, B. R., Snyder, F., & Petraitis, J. (2009). The theory of triadic influence. In R. J. DiClemente, M. C. Kegler, & R. A. Crosby (Eds.), Emerging theories in health promotion practice and research (2nd ed., pp. 451–510). New York, NY: Jossey-Bass.

Frazier-Anderson, P., Hood, S., & Hopson, R. (2011). Preliminary considerations of an African American culturally responsive evaluation system. In S. D. Lapan, M. T. Quartaroli, & F. J. Riemer (Eds.), *Qualitative research: An introduction to methods and designs* (pp. 347–372). San Francisco, CA: Jossey-Bass.

Frierson, H. T., Hood, S., & Hughes, G. B. (2002). A guide to conducting culturally responsive evaluations. In J. Frechtling (Ed.), *The 2002 user-friendly handbook for project evaluation.* (pp. 63–73). Arlington, VA: National Science Foundation.

Gilmore, J. A. (2007). Reducing disparities in the access and use of Internet health information. A discussion paper. *International Journal of Nursing Studies, 44,* 1270–1278.

Gladwell, M. (2005). *Blink: The power of thinking without thinking.* New York, NY: Time Warner.

Gladwell, M. (2000). *Tipping point: How little things can make a big difference.* New York, NY: Back Bay.

Goleman, D. (1995). *Emotional intelligence: Why it can matter more than IQ.* New York, NY: Bantam.

Goleman, D. (2006). *Social intelligence: The revolutionary new science of human relationships.* New York, NY: Bantam.

Gordon, J., & Johnson, M. (2003). Race, speech, and hostile educational environment: What color is free speech? *Journal of Social Philosophy, 34,* 414–436.

Greene, J. C. (2005a). Evaluators as stewards of the public good. In S. Hood, R. Hopson, & H. Freirson (Eds.), *The role of culture and context: A mandate for inclusion, the discovery of truth, and understanding in evaluative theory and practice* (pp. 7–20). Greenwich, CT: Information Age.

Greene, J. C. (2005b). A value-engaged approach for evaluating the Bunche-Da Vinci Learning Academy. *New Direction for Evaluation, 106,* 27–45.

Greene, J. C., DeStefano, L., Burgon, H., & Hall, J. (2006). An educative, values-engaged approach to evaluating STEM educational programs. *New Directions for Evaluation, 109,* 53–71.

Greenwald, A. G., & Banaji, M. R. (1995). Implicit social cognition: Attitudes, self-esteem, and stereotypes. *Psychological Review, 102,* 4–27.

Hall, J. N. Ahn, J., & Greene, J. C. (2012) Values engagement in evaluation: Ideas, illustrations, and implications. *American Journal of Evaluation, 33,* 195–207.

Harris, L. T., & Fiske, S. T. (2007). Social groups that elicit disgust are differentially processed in mPFC. *Social Cognitive and Affective Neuroscience, 2,* 45–51.

Haynes, J. D., Sakai, K., Rees, G., Gilbert, S., Frith, C., & Passingham, R. E. (2007). Reading hidden intentions in the human brain. *Current Biology, 17,* 323–328.

House, E. (1990). Methodology and justice. *New Directions for Evaluation, 45,* 23–36.

Johnson, J. D., Simmons, C. H., Jordan, A., MacLean, L., Taddei, J., & Thomas, D. (2002). Rodney King and O. J. revisited: The impact of race and defendant empathy induction on judicial decisions. *Journal of Applied Social Psychology, 32,* 1208–1223.

Keysers, C. (2011). *The empathic brain* [Kindle E-Book].

King Jr., M. L. (1963). Letter from Birmingham Jail. Unpublished document.

Kirk, D. S. (2008). The neighborhood context of racial and ethnic disparities in arrest. *Demography, 45,* 55–77.

Kirkhart, K. (1995). 1994 conference theme: Evaluation and social justice seeking validity: A postcard from the road. *American Journal of Evaluation, 16,* 1–12.

Kirkhart, K. E. (2013, April). *Repositioning validity.* Plenary panel presented at the Inaugural Conference of the Center for Culturally Responsive Evaluation and Assessment (CREA), Chicago, IL.

Kitayama, S., & Park, J. (2010). Cultural neuroscience of the self: Understanding the social grounding of the brain. *Social Cognitive and Affective Neuroscience, 5,* 111–129.

Kobayashi, C., Glover, G. H., & Temple, E. (2007). Cultural and linguistic effects on neural bases of "theory of mind" in American cultural neuroscience of the self and Japanese children. *Brain Research: Cognitive Brain Research, 1164,* 95–107.

Kundin, D. M. (2010). A conceptual framework for how evaluators make everyday decisions. *American Journal of Evaluation, 31,* 347–362.

Langer, N. (1999). Culturally competent professionals in therapeutic alliances enhance patient compliance. *Journal of Health Care for the Poor and Underserved, 10,* 19–26.

Levey, J., & Levey, M. (1998). *Living in balance: A dynamic approach for creating harmony and wholeness in a chaotic world.* Berkeley, CA: Conari.

Maguire, E. A., Gadian, D. G., Johnsrude, I. S., Good, C. D., Ashburner, J., Frackowiak, R. S., & Frith, E. A. (2000). Navigation-related structural change in the hippocampi of taxi drivers. *Proceedings of the National Academy of Sciences of the United States of America, 97,* 4398–4403.

Martin, C. (1993). Feelings, emotional empathy, and decision making: Listening to the voices of the heart. *Journal of Management Development, 12,* 33–45.

Mason, M. F., & Morris, M. W. (2010). Culture, attribution and automaticity: A social cognitive neuroscience view. *Social, Cognitive, and Affective Neuroscience, 5,* 292–306.

Moriarty, M., & Buckley, F. (2003). Increasing team emotional intelligence through process. *Journal of European Industrial Training, 27,* 98–110.

McBride, D. F., & Bell, C. C. (2013). Culture competency. In K. Yeager, D. Cutler, D. Svendsen, & G. Sills. (Eds), Textbook of modern community mental health work: An interdisciplinary approach (pp.155–169). New York, NY: Oxford University Press.

National Research Council and Institute of Medicine. (2009). Preventing mental, emotional, and behavioral disorders among young people: Progress and possibilities. In M. E. O'Connell, T. Boat, & K. E. Warner (Eds.), Washington, DC: National Academies Press.

Nisbett, R. E. (2003). The geography of thought: How Asians and Westerners think differently . . . and why. New York, NY: Free Press.

Patton, M. Q. (2008). *Utilization-focused evaluation* (4th ed.). Thousand Oaks, CA: Sage.

Payne, B. K., Lambert, A. J., & Jacoby, L. L. (2002). Best laid plans: Effects of goals on accessibility bias and cognitive control in race-based misperceptions of weapons. *Journal of Experimental Social Psychology, 38,* 384–396.

Pinkham, A. E., Sasson, N. J., Calkins, M. E., Richard, J., Hughett, P., Gur, R. E., & Gur, R. C. (2008). The other-race effect in face processing among African American and Caucasian individuals with schizophrenia. *American Journal of Psychiatry, 165,* 639–645.

Pinderhughes, C. (1979). Differential bonding: Toward a psychological theory of stereotyping. *American Journal of Psychiatry, 136,* 33–37.

Price, C. J., Ramsden, S., Hope, T. M., Friston, K. J., & Seghier, M. L. (2013). Predicting IQ change from brain structure: A cross-validation study. *Developmental Cognitive Neuroscience, 5,* 172–184.

Restak, R. (2003). *The new brain: How the modern age is rewiring your brain.* Emmaus, PA: Rodale.

Rizzolatti, G., & Craighero, L. (2004). The mirror-neuron system. *Annual Review of Neuroscience, 27,* 169–192.

Ronquillo, J., Denson, T. F., Lickel, B., Lu, Z., Nandy, A., & Maddox, K. B. (2007). The effects of skin tone on race-related amygdala activity: An fMRI investigation. *Social, Cognitive, and Affective Neurosceince, 2,* 39–44.

Ryce, M. (2013). *Why is this happening to me . . . again?* Retrieved June 2, 2013, from http://www.whyagain.org/index.php/en/

Shephard, G. (2006). *How to be the employee your company can't live without: 18 ways to become indispensable.* Hoboken, NJ: Wiley.

Smith, C. B. (1994). Back and to the future: The intergroup contact hypothesis revisited. *Social Inquiry, 64,* 438–455.

Spunt, R. P., & Lieberman, M. D. (2013). The busy social brain: Evidence for automaticity and control in the neural systems supporting social cognition and action understanding. *Psychological Science, 24,* 80–86.

Sue, D. W., Capodilupo, C. M., Torino, G. C., Bucceri, J. M., Holder, A. M. B., Nadal, K. L., et al. (2007). Racial microaggressions in everyday life: Implications for clinical practice. *American Psychologist, 62,* 271–268.

Tang, T. S., Fantone, J. C., Bozynski, M. E. A., & Adams, B. S. (2002). Implementation and evaluation of an undergraduate sociocultural medicine program. *Academic Medicine, 77,* 578–585.

Thompson-Miller, R., & Feagin, J. R. (2007) Continuing injuries of racism: Counseling in a racist context. *The Counseling Psychologist, 35,* 106–115.

Wade, P., & Bernstein, B. L. (1991). Culture sensitivity training and counselor's race: Effects on Black female clients' perceptions and attrition. *Journal of Counseling Psychology, 38,* 9–15.

Weber, E., U., & Morris, M. W. (2010). Culture and judgment and decision making: The constructivist turn. *Perspectives on Psychological Science, 5,* 410–419.

Wilkerson, I. (2013, September). No, you're not imagining it. *Essence.* pp. 132–137.

Wright, J., & Wright, B. (2013). Transformed: The science of spectacular living. New York, NY: Turner.

Xu, X., Zuo, X., Wang, X., & Han, S. (2009). Do you feel my pain? Racial group membership modulates empathic neural responses. *The Journal of Neuroscience, 29*(26), 8525–8529.

Yalom, I. D. (1989). Love's executioner. New York, NY: HarperCollins.

SECTION III

APPLICATIONS OF CRE IN GLOBAL AND INDIGENOUS
SCHOOL CONTEXTS

CHAPTER 10

CULTURE CHANGES, IRISH EVALUATION AND ASSESSMENT TRADITIONS STAY THE SAME?

Exploring Peer- and Self-Assessment as a Means of Empowering Ethnic Minority Students

Joe O'Hara, Gerry McNamara, Kathy Harrison

ABSTRACT

The past two decades in Ireland have been marked by significant political, social, economic and cultural change. During this period, Ireland moved from being an isolated, comparatively closed and culturally relatively homogenous society to one of the most economically liberal and socially diverse countries in Europe (Devine, 2012). From 1996 to 2007, the Irish economy was one of the fastest growing in the world and, for perhaps the first time in its history, Ireland experienced large-scale immigration. Demographic and cultural stresses apart, in 2008, every aspect of Irish life changed further. This time

Continuing the Journey to Reposition Culture and Cultural Context in Evaluation Theory and Practice, pages 205–231
Copyright © 2015 by Information Age Publishing

the change was triggered by the banking debacle and subsequent political and financial fallout, the effects of which have been felt by the entire Irish population (e.g., see McWilliams, 2010; Williams, 2013). Government austerity measures continue to affect everyone, with the result that all public services, including education, continue to struggle with the consequences of expenditure cuts.

In parallel to these economic and demographic upheavals, there has also been a significant drift toward secularism. While Roman Catholicism continues to be the predominant religion (CSO, 2011a), there is already a demand for greater diversity in school provision. All of these changes, together with the growth of cultural diversity in the country and the classroom, bring great pressure to bear on educational provision and pedagogical practice in Ireland.

This chapter focuses on how the traditional practice of educational assessment in Ireland has been impacted by the rapidly changing context outlined above. Specifically, it explores the pressure on the school system to adapt to the presence of learners from a diverse range of cultural backgrounds and the system's response, from the viewpoints of both learners and teachers. Ireland is not new to managing the complexity of minority groups within the population. The Irish Travelling community has been an indigenous but distinct population throughout Irish history with its own discrete culture. Descended from a traditionally nomadic population who followed herds of cattle and later lived by selling their own skills and crafts, most Travellers today live settled lives in houses, but endeavor to remain true to their heritage and customs.

This chapter looks in particular at one example of a class comprising Traveller and other students where they joined the teacher in assessing their learning. Through a process of Peer- and Self-Assessment, the students assessed themselves and each other. It examines the cultural responsiveness of the assessment and its impact on the inclusion of all students, including members of the Travelling community, from student and teacher perspectives.

> *What we now call multicultural education . . . is a composite. It is no longer*
> *solely race, or class, or gender. Rather, it is the infinite permutations that come*
> *about as a result of the dazzling array of combinations human beings recruit*
> *to organize and fulfill themselves.*
> —Gloria Ladson-Billings (2004, p. 50)

The study was prompted by the Culturally Responsive Evaluation and Assessment (CREA) development centers situated in the College of Education in the University of Illinois at Urbana-Champaign (UIUC) and in the School of Education Studies at Dublin City University (DCU). It is an attempt to present an innovative, learner-centric, teacher-learner partnership, intercultural style of assessment that is more in line with multicultural inclusion: a form of assessment that presents a level playing field for immigrants, Travellers, and all citizens who are served by Irish education service providers.

Irish Travellers are an indigenous minority group. Validating their ethnicity, Hough (2011) reports that DNA testing of a group of Travellers indicates that they split from the general, settled Irish population between 1,000 and 2,000 years ago. Fay (2011, p. 2), points out that

> their [Traveller] culture, values, religious practices, and customs have been profoundly shaped by their unique traditions and history. Nomadism was an integral part of Traveller culture, but many Travellers are no longer nomadic, either by choice or due to lack of support for and criminalisation of nomadism. Travellers also have their own language; however due to lack of recognition and support, this is gradually dying out.

That the nomadic heritage is on the wane is borne out by the 2011 Irish Census figures, which show that only 12% of Travellers live in caravans or mobile homes (trailers), compared with one in four in 2006 (CSO, 2011a). In an audit of 442 primary schools across Ireland, 2.4% of enrolled students were from the Traveller community. In individual clusters of schools (a cluster being typically five to ten schools with between 1,000 and 5,000 students), the number of students from the Traveller community enrolled varied from none to over 14%. In the geographic area covered by this study, there were individual schools audited which reported 22% and 33% Traveller enrollment (DES, 2007).

The study is located in the existing body of knowledge of culture, cultural competence, cultural sensitivity, and assessment, all of which are used to underscore the justification for carrying out this particular research.

The implementation of the research (which specifically includes students from Ireland's Travelling community) is described. The methodology employed is detailed and the findings, from both the study in the early school leavers center and from interviews with the other participants, are discussed within the background already defined. Finally, conclusions are outlined together with recommendations.

CONTEXT AND BACKGROUND

Being sensitive to the reality that "context is everything" (Jolly, 2013), this chapter embeds the research in the emerging Irish context. A look at the background reveals that recent rapid demographic change in Ireland has resulted in a multicultural society and for the first time Ireland has experienced a swing from emigration to immigration. During the period from 2002 to 2011, Ireland witnessed an increase of 143% in the number of immigrants resident in the country (CSO, 2011c). In relation to education, the CSO (which records Irish population statistics collected by census) states that about 10% of people in Ireland under the age of 15 were born outside

Ireland, thus, it is not unreasonable to assume that about 10% of students at elementary level are nonnational. However, this figure is, of course, not evenly distributed across all schools, and in many schools there are much higher concentrations of immigrant students. It is noteworthy that an elementary school teacher involved in the study reported 70% of students were nonnational in origin (although some of the children may have been born in Ireland to immigrant parents).

Traditional methods of teaching and learning which have served a mainly homogenous society are under stress to accommodate the new multicultural classroom, which seeks to provide a learner-centric educational environment. As a way of addressing some of the shortcomings of traditional (monocultural) teaching, and to accommodate increasing religious and cultural diversity, a movement initiated by parents with one school in 1978 has grown to include some 60 multidenominational elementary schools under the Educate Together umbrella (Dalkey School Project National School, 2013).

A further area which is in need of review in Ireland, and which has also been found difficult to deal with elsewhere, is the *assessment of student learning*. To begin with, Frierson, Hood, Hughes, and Thomas (2010) contend that "there are no culture-free...educational tests." An example of the complexity involved in this seemingly simple problem is provided by Stobart (2005), who points out that while assessment may be seen as a technical issue, *fairness* in assessment is a sociocultural construct with intertwined quantitative (equality of outcomes) and qualitative (equity and justice of outcomes) strands, which cannot be divorced from questions of fairness in curriculum and pedagogical practice. This current study shows that the traditional style of assessment does not address the above questions of culture, nor of fairness as equality of outcomes, nor as equity and justice. This is corroborated by MacCraith et al. (2012, p. 2), who submitted a report on the Irish school Leaving Certificate examination and progression to tertiary education to the Minister for Education and Skills. In that submission, they state that, "while equitable in the transparency and incorruptibility of the assessment and selection process, it promotes significant inequity through the capacity of the more advantaged to game the system."

The traditional style of assessment used in Irish education can be described as having two aspects:

- *formative* (assessment *for* learning), left largely to the teacher and, although it may aspire to become more learner-centric, it is constrained by lack of resources such as teacher time and in-service training. As a result, it tends toward a standardized, inflexible model based on teacher questioning and assessing home- or classroom-produced assignments, and

- *summative* (assessment *of* learning), which is dominated by formal state-run examinations, culminating at the end of second-level education in the high-stakes, centralized, state-set, public Leaving Certificate examination.

By its nature, traditional Irish school assessment does not serve the "new" Irish adequately. In fact, this form of assessment is still at a loss as to how to serve its own Irish ethnic minority group, the Travelling community. The evidence (see Figure 10.1) shows that, when compared to the general population, Travellers are not generally faring well in the current education system.

On another level, traditional assessment practice inculcates the habit of overdependence on authority—the teacher or assessor—and as a consequence, hinders the development of self-reliance and initiative in the learner (Harrison, 2011). This is substantiated by an evaluation carried out in another early school leaver center by the DES (2006; especially section 4.2). The evaluation concluded that, in many instances, the proclivity of the teacher to take the lead prevented students from having the chance "to take initiatives and be proactive in their own learning and in the progression of their work."

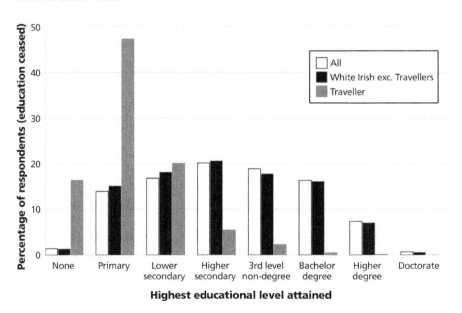

Figure 10.1 Census 2011 figures for the highest level of education attained by those who reported having ceased education. Data shown are (a) all Irish residents, (b) those identifying as "White Irish" (*except* for those identifying as members of the Travelling community), and (c) those identifying as White Irish members of the Travelling community.

In a more general sense, the traditional Irish school Leaving Certificate examination (matriculation, by the scoring of a prerequisite number of *points*, for entry into Higher Education) is a regimented form of assessment. Students are ushered toward this examination by educationalists from approximately 4 to 18 years of age. It is a rite of passage which has been relentlessly assessing the learning of Irish students for generations, with little change, and the ambition of students, teachers, and families alike is for the student to achieve the requisite number of *points*. These *points* open the door to Higher Education programs, which ultimately allow entry to the professions. It is clear that there is an urgent need for more inclusive, flexible assessment practices to replace the competitive *personal* drive to achieve *points*.

The Travelling Community

The National Consultative Committee on Racism and Interculturalism (NCCRI) (2004, p. 4) claims that, according to Travellers themselves and others, they can be identified "as people with a shared history, culture and traditions including, historically, a nomadic way of life on the island of Ireland." In addition, under Irish Law (Employment Equality Acts, 1998, 2004; Equal Status Acts, 2000 to 2004), Travellers are afforded protection against discrimination under one of the nine grounds laid down by these Acts (sources of discrimination, identified as gender, marital status, family status, sexual orientation, religion, age, disability, race or membership of the Traveller community). Discrimination has been defined as "the treatment of a person in a less favourable way than another person has been or would be treated in a comparable situation. The legislation prohibits discrimination, including indirect discrimination and discrimination by association" (Barry, 2004 p. 8). However, a culturally sensitive look at the two Acts reveals an ambiguity toward the ethnicity of Travellers. Discrimination because of a person's ethnicity is prohibited under the "ground of race" (one of the nine discriminatory grounds). However, when it comes to Travellers, discrimination does not come under "the ground of race" as with other cultures: Travellers are protected from discrimination under a different heading referred to as "the traveller community ground" (Employment Equality Act, 1998 s.6; Equal Status Act, 2000 s.3).

Notwithstanding this protection, Travellers currently fare considerably worse than the general population in terms of their educational attainments, as illustrated in Figure 10.1. Education is not the only area where the Traveller experience is out of line with the rest of the Irish population; as Table 10.1 (see second column 'Irish Traveller Ethnic Minority') indicates, Travellers also experience significant deficits in the field of health welfare.

Shift in Irish Culture

According to Dublin City University (DCU) Equality Office (2013), "diversity in Ireland contributes to the richness, resourcefulness and innovation that makes society flourish." However true this may be, exploiting and accommodating the diversity of culture in an educational context is not simple. The reality as mentioned previously is that immigration has dramatically increased in recent years (CSO, 2011c). It is clear that meeting and satisfying the demands of the "new" Irish multicultural classroom with a mix of children from Irish, migrant, and Traveller families is taxing educators at all levels of the Irish educational spectrum as they endeavor to come to terms with this multicultural student population, as noted by Darmody, Smyth, and McCoy (2012). This is also borne out by Smyth, Darmody, McGinnity, and Byrne (2009, p. xiv), who point out that, despite the accrued benefits, "immigration has posed challenges for schools with little prior experience of dealing with cultural and linguistic diversity."

The emotional strain of this paradigm shift is identified by MacLachlan (2003, p. 32) with his observation that living in Ireland at this time in its history can be "uncertain...frightening and disorientating." Reporting from his perspective as a member of the Traveller ethnic minority group, Collins (1997) claims "the situation of Travellers in Ireland today can be best described as one of exclusion and oppression." Although only representing one view (Collins'), and from one perspective (a Traveller's), this suggests that inclusion and equality are still not widely practiced in multicultural Ireland. Addressing the curriculum and placing importance on education for Travellers and other minority cultural backgrounds, Collins maintains that multicultural education is well advanced in Europe, but strongly argues that this is not happening in Ireland. Collins is not isolated in his thinking nor in his linkage of Travellers to other ethnic and cultural groups. Writing on discrimination from a more general perspective, Fanning (2002, p. 174) claims that, despite political awareness of discriminatory behavior and inequalities suffered by Travellers, there has been a lack of momentum in addressing their issues and points to a corollary, arguing that "a past unwillingness to acknowledge or challenge institutional racism is likely to contribute to the marginalization of new minority communities within Irish society. Such dangers are particularly acute given the lesser rights of many members of these communities." Without such strong voices challenging and attempting to redress all forms of discrimination and racism, social justice will continue to present as an elusive and intangible target. One reason, both obvious and very simple, is provided by Pusch (2009, p. 71): "it is hard to see your own culture when you are in the midst of it."

Multicultural Ireland

The greatest inward population movement in Ireland's history occurred during the economic boom of the last two decades, introducing many new cultures. The emerging face of this new Irish *culture* is clearly evident in classrooms, particularly at the elementary level. Many of the immigrants of this boom time come from Eastern Europe, Africa, and Asia, and many now have children progressing through the Irish education system. Widely reported, these demographic changes mean that approximately 10% of elementary school students in Ireland are nonnational (slightly less in second-level education), with 17% of Irish residents having been born outside the country (Hough, 2012; Murray, 2011). These are nationwide averages, but the reality is shown by an example from this research where, in one elementary teacher's classroom, fewer than half of the students were Irish.

It is *culture* and in turn *cultural identity* which defines every citizen who resides in a country or who is a member of a particular cultural group. Cognizant of the challenges presented to educators new to meeting the needs of the growing blend of cultures in Ireland, the *Intercultural Education Strategy 2010–2015* (Ireland Dept. of Education and Skills, 2010, p. 3) recommends "research to establish what progress is being made towards ensuring that all students, including immigrants, are achieving to their full potential." This provides a rationale for research such as this study. The research findings will contribute to informing future evaluations both in the value of culturally responsive assessment and in the cultural sensitivity needed in conducting an evaluation.

MULTICULTURAL EDUCATION

Education, which includes learning in all of its various forms, is paramount in securing and maintaining a multicultural society founded on social justice (CREA, 2013). Further, a multicultural education must provide a service which "fosters the public good and overarching goals of the commonwealth" (Banks, 1997, p. viii). To do this successfully, each and every learner must be treated with respect and dignity throughout their lifelong education. All learners, including Travellers, other native Irish, and immigrants, must be provided with learning experiences that promote equality, access, and inclusion to support them in reaching their full potential as active citizens capable of contributing effectively to their communities. The consequence of failing in this task is highlighted by Banton (1994, p. 6), who claims "patterns of inequality established in one generation are easily transmitted to subsequent generations because people grow up regarding them as right and natural."

TABLE 10.1 Ethnic Minority Experiences in Ireland

Irish Immigrant Population	Irish Traveller Ethnic Minority
"Immigrants do not fare as well on average as Irish nationals in the Irish labour market in 2010, with the results varying according to nationality and ethnicity" (Kingston, O'Connell, & Kelly, 2013). "Black African, Ethnic Minority EU and EU New Member State (NMS) groups fare worse than other national-ethnic groups in terms of both objective labour market outcomes (e.g., employment and unemployment) and in their experience of discrimination" (Kingston et al., 2013).	The All Ireland Traveller Health Study (2010) reports that in 2008, the average Traveller life expectancy at birth was 61.7 (male) and 70.1 (female) compared with 76.8 male and 81.6 female in the general population (deficits of 15.1 and 11.5 years). These compare with 1987 life expectancies of 61.7 (male) and 65.3 (female) when the corresponding general population figures were 71.6 and 77.2 (deficits of 9.9 and 11.9 years). Infant mortality is 14.1 per thousand live births among the Traveller community compared with 3.9 in general population. The suicide rate for a Traveller male is almost seven (6.6) times higher than in the general population (the rate for females is over five times higher but, due to the small numbers, cannot be said to be significantly different from the general population).

TABLE 10.2 Multicultural Ireland

Resident in the Irish State						
White Irish—not Traveller		White Irish—Traveller		Other		Total population
Number	% Total population	Number	% Total population	Number	% Total population	Number
3,682,958	83.63	28,843	0.65	691,926	15.71	4,403,727

Source: CSO, 2011d

Table 10.1 illustrates cases of present-day cultural inequalities in relation to social and health issues which immigrants and Travellers have to contend with.

The ethnic breakdown of Irish residents in Table 10.2 in relation to Travellers and immigrants (included in the column headed "Other") from the 2011 Irish Census clearly shows a great many people are, or stand to be, impacted by the result of decisions made by Irish education policymakers.

TRADITIONAL ASSESSMENT IN IRELAND

The educational system in Ireland has in itself built up a strong *culture*, which tends to favor certain practices for the assessment of learning outcomes. However, it is widely recognized that these practices can often pay greater deference to the culture of the system than they do to the cultures of the learners and the culture of the society which is their context (Boud & Falchikov, 2007). The practice of fitting learners into an existing system of learning and student compliance with the system of learning and assessment remains a perennial concern.

It can be argued that the education process continues to perpetuate a standardized summative assessment (Leaving Certificate examination) which is not only the antithesis of cultural sensitivity and responsiveness, but has been historically a marker of difference between lower and higher socioeconomic classes. This concurs with the National Council for Curriculum and Assessment's *Submission to the National Strategy for Higher Education* (2009). The submission acknowledges that the main value placed on the Leaving Certificate examination is the accrual of points for entry into Higher Education. The ready acceptance of a points system to place value on the grades achieved at this level underlines the perceived intention and use of the assessment—to select for preparation for the professions. That is not to imply the policy intent behind the introduction of points was to be divisive or elitist, but that appears to be the outcome (see MacCraith et al. [2012] above). In the *Submission*, the National Council for Curriculum and Assessment stresses that one of the original aims of the Irish Leaving Certificate examination was to recognize achievement, but that this has been displaced by a competition for points: it accepts that although rote, shallow learning is not an aim of second-level education; there is a tacit acceptance that it is what is needed to maximize points. This use of assessment as a selection tool rather than as a learning methodology is accepted by the National Council for Curriculum and Assessment as being out of balance (NCCA, 2009).

CULTURALLY RESPONSIVE EVALUATION AND ASSESSMENT

Hood (1998a, p. 194), in addressing culturally responsive assessment, argues that "the first priority of efforts to develop culturally responsive assessments is to determine whether the tasks and criteria developed with this goal in mind are congruent with the targeted domain and learning outcomes." It would appear that the traditional approach to assessment used in Irish education is remiss in this area because it does not consider cultural differences sufficiently, if at all, an observation which may be attributable to its monocultural heritage.

Culturally Responsive Evaluation and Assessment (CREA) is a concept in its infancy in Ireland. Equally early in its formation is the concept of intercultural competence, which according to Spitzberg and Changnon (2009,

p. 7) is "the appropriate and effective management of interaction between people who, to some degree or another, represent different or divergent affective, cognitive and behavioral orientations to the world." CREA being such a new concept in Irish education is recognized as a challenge for educationalists. This is evidenced by the National Council for Curriculum and Assessment guidelines, *Intercultural Education in the Post-Primary School* (2006, p. 91), which states, "There is a growing awareness of the special difficulties associated with assessing the students from minority and immigrant populations." Difficult as it may be to ensure culturally sensitive assessment practices, it is evident that multicultural education requires a more flexible approach than the traditional assessment style, which is incongruent with serving the needs of a Ireland's new learning population.

PEER- AND SELF-ASSESSMENT

Defining P&SA, Fautley and Savage (2008, p. 51; author emphasis) state that "*peer-assessment* involves students assessing the work of other students, their peers; while *self-assessment* involves each individual in a consideration of their own work." This empowers learners to be actively involved in the assessment of their own learning through sharing ownership of the assessment process with the teacher.

Hopson (2013) presents a challenge, questioning whether assessment can be a *liberating* experience. P&SA is one way of meeting this challenge, as both forms (peer- and self-) of assessment are learner-driven, learner-centric, and have been shown to be learner-friendly (Cheng & Warren, 2000; Fawcett, 2005; McDonald & Boud, 2003). These forms of assessment have been held in high regard by many generations of practitioners, for example, from Jardine (1818), Falchikov (1986), Sluijsmans, Brand-Gruwel, and van Merriënboer (2002), Bryan (2006) to Bouzidi and Jaillet (2009).

The benefits reported from the aforementioned authors, and others, include P&SA being perceived as a fair means of assessment with the capacity to sustain lifelong learning.

In successfully fulfilling their duty of care by employing learner-centric assessment methodologies, educational service providers will support each student in reaching his or her full potential—self-actualization (Maslow, 1954). This is in accordance with culturally responsive evaluation and assessment, which is to "increase the likelihood that social and educational policies and practices are more socially just (fair, equitable, [and] respectful of human dignity)" (CREA, 2013). Put succinctly, educational service providers will satisfy the needs of the learner through engaging the learners in the assessment process.

THE RESEARCH

The research involved a pilot project implementing Peer- and Self-Assessment (P&SA) across the educational spectrum. It consisted of a multicenter, cross-sectional study, spanning the educational levels from elementary (4 years plus) through second (13–18 years) and third-level (18 years plus) in mainstream education and early school leavers (including students from the Traveller community) in Further Education (Further Education in Ireland relates to education outside the mainstream. Usually students are older than school age, but they can include early school leavers [those who leave education whilst still of compulsory school age], studying below degree level: sometimes called continuing education in the United States). The participating educational institutions were in city, urban, and rural locations.

P&SA involves the learner partnering the teacher in the assessment process. It involves the learner in assessing the work of other students in the class (peer-assessment) and their own work (self-assessment).

Research Questions

The objective of the research was to ascertain the cultural sensitivity of P&SA as an intervention in Ireland's evolving multicultural classrooms. Specifically, it asks,

1. Can Peer- and Self-Assessment empower ethnic minority students?
2. Do Peer- and Self-Assessment adhere to the principles of social justice and human rights?
3. Are Peer- and Self-Assessment inclusive, and can they respond to the indigent, migrant, and Traveller cultures in Ireland's learning population?

Context of Study

This research spans the whole continuum of education, including elementary, secondary (urban and rural), Further, and Higher Education. Among the participating centers across the spectrum of learning, the Further Education center (YouthReach), which provides second-chance education for early school leavers, included a majority of students from the Traveller community. As an ethnic minority group, Travellers have not fared well in education generally. This particular early school leaver class comprised mixed-gender students ranging from approximately 15 to 18 years of age. It is to be noted that a core principle of the YouthReach program mandates that the learner be placed at the center of all teaching and learning methodologies (YouthReach, 2011), a principle which appears to have a positive effect in attracting learners from a culture where most people have traditionally left education by the end of elementary school (CSO, 2011b).

Sample

Purposive or judgmental sampling (Berg, 2004) or stratified purposive sampling (Kemper, Stringfield, & Teddlie, 2003) was considered best suited to the this study, where participants are chosen because they cover certain levels or categories of a property or properties of the participants (in this case all possible ages and educational levels). In total there were 366 participating students and 14 participating teachers/coordinators. Prior to these studies, none of the students, the teachers, or their organizations had experienced P&SA (this necessitated the presence of one of the researchers in the centers during the implementation of the P&SA).

Data Collection and Quality

Data were gathered through meetings and semistructured interviews, which included questions on the cultural impact of P&SA. Students and staff were interviewed following the P&SA project to ascertain their perspectives on the assessment. The teachers of the participating students were interviewed to determine whether they viewed P&SA as a culturally responsive form of assessment. Data were gathered from a number of different viewpoints and using multiple tools to gather data with the same focus provided methodological triangulation.

Methodology

This qualitative study took the form of a phenomenological, interpretative inquiry (the knowledge was constructed and contextual). The aim of the study was to investigate the experience of different teachers with their learners as a result of implementing P&SA (Patton, 1990). The focus, in particular, was on the common, shared, and lived assessment experience of the students and teachers as advocated in Husserl's (1931) Interpretative Phenomenological (IP) approach.

THE P&SA INTERVENTION

According to circumstances, the teachers had been using a combination of traditional, teacher-led assessment methods including individual or group studies, written papers, oral or written tests, and terminal examinations.

In all studies, the assessments were based on students working in small groups. The format and P&SA implementation conditions were kept the same in each center to help conserve consistency in the studies. Keeping each study as consistent as possible improved effectiveness in collaborating with each teacher. Also, eliminating as many variables as possible helped maximize the validity and reliability of the research.

The P&SA marking templates were discussed and agreed with teachers/coordinators. The concept of P&SA was introduced to each class with assessment format and sample criteria, and the ethics of assessment were introduced to the learners. The learners were randomly assigned to small groups (3–8). Each group selected its own assessment criteria (generally five), facilitated by the teacher and one of the researchers.

A workshop was held to present P&SA procedures for learners, including the criteria they had selected following discussions with the teacher. The students had a practice P&SA session, including calculation of marks. Some time after this practice, the students carried out their peer- and self-assessment. On completion of their assessment, the teacher provided the students with their final overall mark (grade) and their formative feedback (how well they performed against each of the criteria).

P&SA Design

The design of the assessment process was influenced by Brown and Smith (1997); Race (1998); Brown, Bull, and Pendlebury (1997); and Biggs (1999), and especially by the discussion by Lejk and Wyvill (2002) on holistic and category-based approaches.

P&SA Implementation

The P&SA was conducted anonymously (under examination conditions) with the students having the right to appeal, as advocated by Willis et al. (2002), the teacher acting as final arbiter. The implementation took one term/semester in each case. This chapter pays specific attention to the cultural aspects of the P&SA experience, particularly those reported by participating students from the Travelling community in the early school leavers' center, and that center's coordinator and teachers.

In implementing P&SA, teachers allocated students to groups to work on a project and provided the task to be assessed. For example, in one case, it was a collage based on the sporting and leisure facilities within the locality. The teacher appraised the standard of the collage produced. The students looked at the process of producing the collage. Among themselves in their group, they decided what would be important in working together to get the collage finished. To do this, these students came up with five key areas (criteria) for the process of completing the project. The criteria comprised *be pleasant, listen to everyone's opinion, include everyone, do the work,* and *attend every meeting.* This aspect of the students' assessment was to provide feedback on how well the chosen criteria had been achieved, which ranged from none to excellent. This formative assessment also became the informal rubric by which the students could judge their own and each others' overall contribution to the process. The students then awarded themselves and each other a summative mark for their overall contribution to the process, ranging from 0 to 4, which contributed to their individual grade (mark). The calculation is shown in Equation 10.1.

$$\text{Mark} = \frac{[\text{tutor mark for presentation}] \times [\text{student's mark}]}{[\text{highest student's mark in the group}]} \tag{10.1}$$

The students worked on a team project that was already part of the class curriculum. The assessment comprised two parts: a formative component, with criteria for the provision of feedback to be selected by the students; and a summative component for the students to assess overall individual contribution.

For the *formative component,* each group of students selected and agreed to criteria which they believed to be important elements in the process (e.g., mutual respect, equal division of work, quality of work, attendance at meetings, sense of humor, punctuality). Each student marked her/himself and peers in the group on a 5-point Likert scale: none, poor, fair, good or excellent. (For the purpose of giving feedback only, each of these scale-points was assigned a score of 0 to 4, which was averaged and rounded for each student in each criterion).

The *summative component* consisted of two parts: a tutor mark based on how well the *product* (the presentation) met the objectives; and in each group, each student awarded a mark for the contribution to the *process* from each member (including her/himself) on a scale of: 0 = *none,* 1 = *poor,* 2 = *fair,* 3 = *good,* and 4 = *excellent contribution.* This provided a weighting factor calculated by the student's mark divided by the highest student's mark in the group. Each group member received a *pro rata* mark, which would consist of the tutor's mark for the product multiplied by the weighting factor and rounded up. (The group member(s) with the highest mark received the tutor mark). The calculation of marks is summarized in Equation 10.1.

As an example of the calculation of marks, one class group worked on a project and handed in a collective assignment at the conclusion of the project. The teacher marked the finished assignments (*product*) and awarded the group a mark of 76%. Each student then filled in a P&SA mark sheet by giving self and each peer in the group a mark (summative) for their overall contribution to the project (*process*). The P&SA marks were then totalled from all sheets for each student, which provided each student's P&SA mark.

For instance, Student A in the group attained a P&SA mark of 32 (the highest in the group); by the formula in Equation 10.1, Student A's final mark was $(76 \times 32)/32 = 76\%$. In the same group, Student B was given a P&SA mark of 25. Again as illustrated in Equation 10.1, the mark was calculated as $(76 \times 25)/32 = 59.375$, which was rounded up to give Student B a final mark of 60%. This calculation was followed for each member in each group.

RESEARCH FINDINGS

Perspectives on the Traveller Experience

From the perspective of facilitating the learning of Travellers, speaking on his impressions of P&SA, the coordinator of the early school leaver center thought that this form of assessment would help learners start to understand the concept of "collective responsibility" and that it would provide them with the opportunity and ability to receive and provide constructive criticism. He said it was a platform where students, the majority of whom were Travellers, could co-`operate and "learn from each other." Stressing the positive experience gained through the ownership felt in large part from the selection of the P&SA criteria, he maintained that students gained an advantage from collaborating and deciding upon their assessment criteria together as a collective body. The coordinator observed students displaying greater tolerance of and empathy with their peers, speaking about how the "exchange of values" reduced suspicion as they began to know and have a greater insight into each other's way of working. He saw this aspect as important because it was a way of tackling the fear and stereotypical perspectives which can occur when one is faced with new, unfamiliar, different people. He concluded that his students were also "more connected with the work, more motivated, and more interested than they would have been in previous times."

Although he had been hesitant to join the research on P&SA, he suggested this was due to the uncertainty of the students' response and a fear that they would fail to engage with the process. However, despite this initial reluctance, the coordinator acknowledged that by the end of the study, the students had actively engaged with their group project and the assessment. He observed that the process had "worked to be constructive rather than counterproductive." This was important to him because previously, his Traveller community students had enjoyed few positive learning experiences in their prior education. Referring to his observation of students' active engagement in their assessment and group project, he reported that students attended their classes and remained until the end of class. He also observed that he had not been asked to intervene with students at any stage of the study, and no student had raised any issue with him or with any member of staff during this time. The coordinator pointed out that this was not something to be taken for granted as this was not always the case. He believed the lack of issues was due to the students' positive engagement with the project as a result of their involvement with and ownership of their assessment process.

The teacher in the center believed the students had warmed to P&SA because "for once in the whole education system they're asked what do they think." She observed that this was something very new. She reported being surprised that the students liked taking responsibility, which she had not fully appreciated before their P&SA. She also observed that the students welcomed receiving feedback from their peers; she was aware of the importance of feedback to learners, but said "I didn't realise how important it was to them."

The students from the early school leavers center echoed the coordinator's observations in their own remarks, describing how they had a better understanding of the students they worked with: "where they're coming from and who they are." They explained that working together and marking each other helped them to "get to know the group well and to get to know each other in a different way" and that they could identify with students they would not normally have spoken to. Expecting "easy marks," they were surprised at the fairness and honesty of their marking, showing the increased engagement (both with the work and with their peers) as they noted that wanting good marks from their peers, they put in more effort. One Traveller student concluded, "You'd fly through life with assessments like that," indicating that if he had an input into his assessment, he would be able to contribute to shaping his own progress, helping him through his education and throughout his life.

Teacher Perspective

The current Irish policy aspiration in relation to lifelong learning is laid out by the DES (2000, p. 31) as a "holistic curriculum, . . . [which] reflects cultural and community context and experience; . . . a view of the student

TABLE 10.3 Teachers' Definitions of Culturally Responsive Assessment

- We take into regard the present situation with different people ... the life situation of others [should be] taken into consideration in assessment.   (*Elementary*)

- Is assessment based on values critical, important to a child's culture ... I should find out about the child's culture, tailor my assessment to that.   (*Second-level: Urban*)

- Take into consideration ... circumstances and level of English.   (*Second-level: Urban*)

- Take into account ... topics relevant to student or country.   (*Second-level: Rural*)

- Taking into account cultural differences ... respond by interventions set up to recognize this.   (*Further Ed: early school leavers*)

- Embracing and valuing what we bring together through intercultural links ... making sure [it is embraced] as part of learning.   (*Higher/Further Ed: senior learners*)

- Is necessary [but] the tools aren't there ... one test fits all ... accommodate children to get onto this ladder here.   (*Elementary*)

as a self-directed, self-motivated learner; ... learning as construction rather than as instruction.... preparing the learner for a life of learning rather than for a terminal, end-of-learning examination." The reality from the perspective of the teachers surveyed in this research is quite different.

When asked about how they would define the notion of culturally responsive assessment from a theoretical perspective, teachers in this study offered the following range of ideas, quoted in Table 10.3.

In contrast, however, when asked to describe their experience of the reality of assessment as they experienced it in their classrooms, the responses were very different, as the following quotations illustrate: "[Assessment] is neither responsive nor sensitive ... we are trained as teachers to get students through a particular examination ... predominantly Irish ... it's just so related to Irish culture ... every child no matter where from has to be assessed on the same model ... we treat our students like they are numbers ... do not believe that we are trained to take into account the diversity of cultures ... we have one blunt tool ... whether you're from China or Carrick-on-Shannon." It was also felt that basic needs of immigrant students were not being adequately met in one school. One teacher said that

> students in our school whose first language is not English and who struggle in this with the instruction from the teacher in the classrooms, I think that is a form of abuse. I'm sorry, that is strong language, but I think those students have a right to understand what the teacher is saying, and I think it is up to the school to provide for the needs of those students so that they do understand, and at the moment that is not happening because they are all put in together.

It is clear that in the perception of the teachers interviewed for this study there remains a substantial gap between rhetoric of assessment policy aspiration and the reality in schools. This research makes clear that teachers who took part in P&SA found the process to be an effective methodology for bridging this gap between rhetoric and reality. Teachers found P&SA to be compatible with their concepts of what constitutes culturally responsive assessment. All participating teachers took this view. There were no dissenters.

Much of the data reported in the early school leaver center by both the students and the coordinator were reflected in other schools. For example, a teacher in an urban secondary school reported about the class coming "together as a whole . . . students assessing each other, sharing that with the teacher." A teacher in an elementary school said that "it would lead to explanation of their own ideas between the students themselves; they are very good at understanding each other when that happens." She also observed that the level of engagement within a small working group, with each individual giving an opinion, facilitated a deeper level of communication, which she believed would result in increased collaboration, understanding, and integration for the new immigrants. She commented on the level of understanding and interaction she had witnessed with one of her pupils who experienced difficulty in the class. The teacher remarked on the help this pupil received from her peers, saying, "Sometimes the penny never drops, but the girls in her group have been so kind to her. I have never seen that before."

In second-level education, two teachers from separate schools expressed surprise at their own previous overinvolvement in directing student learning. Comments included how they were taken aback at having done "so much to show the students everything and tell them what to do" and how they normally invest a considerable amount of time directing their work. Commenting on how their students' motivation had been affected by the process of P&SA, one teacher reported that "this is the first time I left the work entirely to the group." Teachers in both schools expressed satisfaction with how their students stepped up and "pushed themselves" during the P&SA project. One of the teachers reported an increase in motivation and interaction, saying that some students who "may have probably sat back and let the leaders take charge, actually did a lot more than they would have done and interacted and made their voice heard as opposed to just sitting there." Another teacher believed P&SA would foster integration because

> students learn from each other; not alone learn from each other but actually understand their differences, or that some people learn one way and some people learn another. They could actually see it firsthand, the different ways people have of approaching a problem and solving it . . . it's bound to deepen their knowledge, their understanding of it.

In Higher and Further Education, the current approach to the quality of treatment of Ireland's Travellers was raised. One teacher claimed, "We still have a lot of prejudice or mindsets to change around the Travelling community." Put in an educational context, it is also highlighted by the coordinator of the early school leaver center who described his Traveller students as "mostly having a negative experience" in their encounter with learning to date. He went on to explain that many of the families of these students may have finished their education at elementary level (12 to 13 years of age) and that to overcome this negative experience, a key challenge is to get "the importance of education through to them." This is supported by the data already introduced in Figure 10.1, where it can be seen that the majority of Travellers left education at or during primary (elementary) level.

Although there are gradual shifts in thinking by policymakers, some teachers expressed the view that, "it would have to involve curricular change or syllabus change before formal assessment could take account of cultural diversity." Also, a major stumbling block to inclusion was seen to be Ireland's lack of non-Irish teachers in elementary school. This was attributed by a teacher in Higher Education to the requirement of having an Irish language qualification and was foreseen as a major issue for current and future debate.

Table 10.4 below contains a synopsis of the teachers' views of P&SA. The table compares P&SA with the traditional Irish assessment procedures from the perspective of the constituent underpinnings of cultural responsiveness, namely, equality, access, inclusion, and social justice (which incorporates

TABLE 10.4   Comparison of Traditional Assessment With Peer- and Self-Assessment With a Focus on Cultural Responsiveness

Traditional Assessment		Peer- and Self-Assessment Culturally Responsive	Equality	Access	Inclusion	Social Justice
rigid		constructivist (Bruner, 1996)			X	
static		holistic, dynamic		X	X	X
demotivates		motivates			X	
isolation		interdependence	X		X	
competitive		collaborative	X		X	
self interest	incompatible with culturally responsive assessment	teambuilding	X		X	
static, finished		sustainable		X		X
indifference		empathy			X	
silence		communication			X	
self pursuit		shared learning	X		X	
authoritarian		shared responsibility	X		X	X
singular identity		pluralist		X	X	
one-size-fits-all		individual recognition	X		X	X

democratic values of responsibility, accountability, and trust). The table also outlines how the traditional assessment is a source of student demotivation as it is a source of isolation with no input into the assessment process when compared to P&SA, which facilitates student ownership and collaboration. The authoritarian approach is replaced with the learner sharing responsibility with the teacher and peers during P&SA. Indifference to "my neighbor" gives way to an interdependence and a building of empathy between peers. The preponderance of individual competitiveness is subsumed into a cooperative team spirit, and the natural element of competition is expressed, if at all, as friendly team rivalry between different groups of learners. The singular identity of traditional assessment transforms to a pluralist identity under P&SA, which is more in line with the requirements for active citizenship in a diverse society.

Table 10.5 illustrates the advantages that emerged from the collected data classified into two categories: those characteristics fostered through the process of P&SA, which directly facilitate inclusion, and those characteristics which build strength of character with capacity to generate empathic, tolerant behavior and attitudes. The personal attributes of self-esteem, confidence in self, and self-determination are what make the difference in being in a position to make a worthwhile difference to one's own life and to the life of others who will also share in the well-being and fortune of the country.

TABLE 10.5   Emergent Themes

Advantages	Elementary	2nd level	Early School Leavers	Further Ed	Higher Ed
Self-esteem, -confidence—"opinion matters"—more vocal		X	X	X	X
Encouraged cooperation/interactivity (help those in difficulty)	X	X	X		X
Fosters self-reliance, responsibility		X	X	X	X
More student control, self-determination—agree criteria		X		X	X
Student ownership of learning, independence, self-direction		X	X		X
Encourages/needs/show openness, honesty		X	X		X
Encourages introspection, "you," self-improvement				X	X
Showed good judgement—become nonjudgemental	X	X			
Fosters critical thought, judgement					X
Demands maturity					X

Note: **Bold text** indicates traits fostering inclusion. *Italicized text* indicates traits fostering self-reliance. Both types of traits are needed for successful intercultural inclusion and integration.

Overall, there were no dissenting voices as to the value of adopting P&SA as both learning and assessment tools, although it was reported by teachers that P&SA were labor intensive and time consuming. Nevertheless, they considered this style of assessment worthwhile, and recommended that P&SA be adopted into the Irish educational curriculum.

CONCLUSION

We know what it is to be strangers in a new land, to feel lost, to be the butt of racism and sectarianism. But we also know that, generously and humanely addressed, inward migration brings opportunities to create a culturally richer and more dynamic society for the future.

—President of Ireland, Mary McAleese (2003 p. 7)

Clearly, as it stands, Ireland's rigid assessment culture is not fit-for-purpose in assisting in the provision and sustenance of the life and social skills needed to flourish as an active and contented citizen in 21st century multicultural Ireland. This is primarily because of its narrow, one-size-fits-all view of learners and its overreliance on teachers and examiners. More innovative, flexible, inclusive, learner-centric forms of assessment are called for to provide a platform where ethnic majority, immigrant, and Traveller learn and work together. This will promote the creation of a future rich in the necessary skills and resources to create and sustain personal and collective employment, social endeavor, and spiritual outlets to serve the common good. For this to happen, there has to be a more urgent shift away from the competitive nature of a standardized Irish Leaving Certificate test where students struggle to achieve personal points as a rite of passage to a future career and life built on *individualism* (Seligman, 2006). A suite of more holistic, culturally sensitive, and responsive assessment practices should now take precedence. It is evident from the findings of this study that involving learners in the assessment and decision-making process with the teacher/assessor has made the assessment more learner-centric, flexible, and culturally responsive; it facilitates a deeper form of learning while cultivating a more inclusive environment. Adopting this type of approach best serves diverse ethnic groups, including Travellers and immigrants, in taking ownership of their educational progress and assessment, and in a wider sense, involvement and inclusion in society. In answering the research questions, the findings clearly show P&SA to be inclusive and responsive to the cultural needs of Travellers, as well as migrants and indigenous learners. Based on democratic principles, P&SA adhere to the tenets of social justice and human rights, empowering all, including ethnic minority students.

That said, it must be acknowledged that teachers found involving learners in their assessment places a heavy toll on time. This is the cost of introducing any new learning methodology. In addition to preparation, delivery, and monitoring aspects, there are also other demands on time. These include, for example, teacher familiarization; learner induction into the program; training, including practice runs; scaffolding for support and guidance; and continuous explanation, clarification, and monitoring. This demand on resources and time can be ameliorated in part by the use of technology (Wood, 2009) to aid in the assessment itself and in the practice and training aspects of the assessment.

Ensuring culturally sensitive assessment requires partnership and collaboration, which is a move away from individualism toward the greater strength of collective, interdependent thinking. Cultural responsiveness in assessment calls for openness and a commitment to more sensitive forms of assessment. In short, it means total reform of Ireland's traditional standardized assessment and a fresh approach with newer, learner-oriented styles of assessment (Harrison, 2011; Hood, 1998b). This chapter has identified one such culturally responsive practice: Peer- and Self-Assessment.

In summary, traditional practice of educational assessment in Ireland does not have the capacity to serve Ireland's multicultural learner. In truth, traditional assessment has never met the needs of its own indigenous ethnic minority group—the Traveller community—and unless there is an urgent overhaul of this outdated system of punitive learning, Ireland's immigrants will join the Travellers in their suffering.

REFERENCES

All Ireland Traveller Health Study. (2010). *Summary of findings.* UCD-led All Ireland Traveller Health Study research team. Dublin, Ireland: Department of Health and Children; Health Service Executive; University College Dublin; Dublin City University; and Belfast: Department of Health, Social Services and Public Safety.

Banks, J. A. (1997). *Educating citizens in a multicultural society.* New York, NY: Teachers College Press.

Banton, M. (1994). *Discrimination.* Buckingham, UK: Open University Press.

Barry, E. (2004) Legislation—An overview. In A. Lodge & K. Lynch (Eds.), *Diversity at school.* Dublin, Ireland: Institute of Public Administration (for Equality Authority).

Berg, B. L. (2004). *Qualitative Research Methods for the social science* (5th ed.). Boston, MA: Pearson.

Biggs, J. (1999). *Teaching for quality learning at university: What the student does.* Buckingham, UK: Society for Research into Higher Education/Open University Press.

Boud, D., & Falchikov, N. (2007). Assessment for the longer term. In D. Boud & N. Falchikov (Eds.), *Rethinking assessment in higher education: Learning for the longer Term.* Oxford, UK: Routledge.

Bouzidi, L., & Jaillet, A. (2009). Can online peer-assessment be trusted? *Educational Technology & Society, 12*(4), 257–268.

Brown, G., Bull, J., & Pendlebury, M. (1997). *Assessing student learning in higher education.* London, UK: Routledge.

Brown, S., & Smith, B. (1997). *Getting to grips with assessment. SEDA Special No.3.* Birmingham, UK: Staff & Educational Development Association.

Bruner, J. (1996). *Towards a theory of instruction.* Cambridge, MA: Harvard University Press.

Bryan, C. (2006). Developing group learning through assessment. In C. Bryan & K. Clegg, (Eds.), *Innovative assessment in higher education.* Lonedon, UK: Routledge.

Central Statistics Office (CSO). (2011a). *This is Ireland: Highlights from Census 2011, Part 1.* Dublin, Ireland: Stationery Office

Central Statistics Office (CSO). (2011b). *Profile 7: Religion, ethnicity and Irish Travellers–Ethnic and cultural background in Ireland.* Dublin, Ireland: Stationery Office

Central Statistics Office (CSO). (2011c). *Profile 6: Migration and diversity.* Dublin, Ireland: Stationery Office

Central Statistics Office (CSO). (2011d). *Statistics.* Retrieved April 1, 2013, from http://www.cso.ie/en/statistics/population/personsusuallyresidentandpresentinthestateoncensusnightclassifiedbynationalityandagegroup/

Cheng, W., & Warren, M. (2000). Making a difference: using peers to assess individual students' contributions to a group project. *Teaching in Higher Education, 5*(2) 243–255.

Collins, M. (1997). Travellers in Ireland. In O. Egan (Ed.), *Minority ethnic groups in higher education in Ireland—Proceedings of Conference held in St. Patrick's College, Maynooth, 27 September 1996.* Cork, Ireland: Higher Education Equality Unit, University College Cork. Retrieved May 17, 2013, from http://www.ucc.ie/publications/heeu/Minority/minority.htm

Culturally Responsive Evaluation and Assessment (CREA). (2013). *Conference theme: Repositioning Culture in Evaluation and Assessment.* Champaign: College of Education, University of Illinois at Urbana-Champaign. Retrieved April 10, 2013, from http://education.illinois.edu/crea/conference/theme [QA: URL does not work.]

Dalkey School Project National School. (2013). *Our school.* Retrieved May 24, 2013, from: http://www.dspns.ie/about-us/about/

Darmody, M., Smyth, E., & McCoy, S. (2012). *School sector variation among primary schools in Ireland.* Dublin, Ireland: Educate Together/Economic and Social Research Institute.

DCU Equality Office. (2013). *Diversity charter.* Retrieved May 18, 2013, from http://www.dcu.ie/equality/diversity_charter.shtml

Department of Education and Science (DES). (2000). *Learning for life: White paper on adult education.* Dublin, Ireland: Stationery Office.

Department of Education and Science (DES). (2006). *Evaluation of youthreach centres.* Retrieved March 15, 2013, from http://www.education.ie/en/Publications/

Inspection-Reports-Publications/Evaluations-of-Centres-of-Education-List-/ report1_Y__71590B.htm

Department of Education and Science (DES). (2007). *Audit of school enrolment policies* by *Regional Office Services (Summary)*. Retrieved September 3, 2013, from http://www.education.ie/en/Parents/Information/School-Enrolment/des_ enrolment_audit_report.pdf

Devine, D. (2012). *Immigration and schooling in the Republic of Ireland: Making a difference?* Manchester, UK: Manchester University Press

Employment Equality Acts, 1998 and 2004. Acts number 21 of 1998 and 24 of 2004. Dublin, Ireland: Stationery Office.

Equal Status Acts, 2000 to 2004. Acts number 8 of 2000 and 24 of 2004. Dublin, Ireland: Stationery Office.

Falchikov, N. (1986). Product comparisons and process benefits of collaborative peer group and self-assessments. *Assessment and Evaluation in Higher Education, 11*(2), 146–166.

Fanning, B. (2002). *Racism and social change in the Republic of Ireland.* Manchester, UK: Manchester University Press.

Fautley, M., & Savage, J. (2008). *Achieving QTS: Assessment for learning and teaching in secondary schools.* Exeter, UK: Learning Matters.

Fawcett, L. (2005) *Developing peer-assessment skills in hospitality management students.* Retrieved May 4, 2013, from http://www.heacademy.ac.uk/assets/hlst/documents/case_studies/ developing_peer_assessment_skills.pdf [QA: URL not viable.]

Fay, R. (Ed.). (2011). *Irish Travellers and Roma shadow report: A response to Ireland's third and fourth report on the International Convention on the Elimination of all Forms of Racial Discrimination (CERD)*. Dublin, Ireland: Pavee Point Travellers Centre.

Frierson, H. T., Hood, S., Hughes, G. B., & Thomas, V. G. (2010) A guide to conducting culturally responsive evaluations. In J. Frechtling (Ed.), *The 2010 user-friendly handbook for project evaluation* (pp 75–96). National Science Foundation.

Harrison, K. (2011). *Re-thinking assessment philosophy and practice: Peer- and self-assessment.* PhD thesis, Dublin City University, Dublin, Ireland.

Hood, S. L. (1998a). Culturally responsive performance-based assessment: Conceptual and psychometric considerations. *Journal of Negro Education, 67*(3), 187–196.

Hood, S. L. (1998b). Assessment in the context of culture and pedagogy: A collective effort, a meaningful goal. *Journal of Negro Education, 67*(3), 184–186.

Hopson, R. (2013, April 2–3). *Keynote address.* CREA Inaugural Conference, Chicago, IL.

Hough, J. (2011, May 31). DNA study: Travellers a distinct ethnicity *The Irish Examiner.*

Hough, J. (2012, March 30). Poles outnumber British nationals as families re-unite. *The Irish Examiner.*

Husserl, E. (1931). *Ideas pertaining to a pure phenomenology and to a phenomenological philosophy* (W. R. B.Gibson, Trans.). New York, NY: Collier. (Originally work published 1931)

Ireland Dept. of Education and Skills.(2010). *Intercultural education strategy 2010-2015*. Dublin, Ireland: Department of Education and Skills and the Office of the Minister for Integration.

Jardine, G. (1818). *Outlines of philosophical education, illustrated by the method of teaching the logic, or first class of philosophy, in the University of Glasgow*. Glasgow, Scotland: A. & J. M. Duncan; Edinburgh: Anderson & MacDowall; London: Longman, Hurst, Bees, Orme, & Brown.

Jolly, E. (2013, April 21–23). *Keynote address*. CREA Inaugural Conference, Chicago, IL

Kemper, E. A., Stringfield, S., & Teddlie, C. (2003). Mixed methods sampling strategies in social science research. In A. Tashakkori & C. Teddlie (Eds.), *Handbook of mixed methods in social & behavioral research*. Thousand Oaks, CA: Sage.

Kingston, G., O'Connell, P. J., & Kelly, E. (2013). Ethnicity and nationality in the Irish labour market: Evidence from the QNHS Equality Module 2010. *Equality Authority and the Economic and Social Research Institute*. Retrieved May 17, 2013, from http://www.esri.ie/UserFiles/publications/BKMNEXT230.pdf

Ladson-Billings, G. (2004). New directions in multicultural education: Complexities, boundaries, and critical race theory. In J. A. Banks & C. A. M. Banks (Eds.), *Handbook of research on multicultural education* (2nd ed.). San Francisco, CA: Jossey-Bass.

Lejk, M., & Wyvill, M. (2002). Peer-assessment and contributions to a group project: Student attitudes to holistic and category-based approaches. *Assessment and Evaluation in Higher Education, 27*(6), 569–577.

MacCraith, B., Browne, J. J., Nolan, P., Prendergast, P., Murphy, M., Brady, H.,... Costello, N. (2012). Communication from the IUA Council to Minister for Education and Skills, Mr Ruairi Quinn TD on the matter of: Reform of selection and entry to university in the context of national educational policy. *Irish Universities Association*. Retrieved May 15, 2013, from http://www.iua.ie/press-publications/publications/iua-submissions/

MacLachlan, M. (2003). Cultural dynamics: Transition and identity in modern Ireland. In *Mosaic or melting pot?—Living with diversity: Proceedings of a conference on Cultural Diversity, Dublin 2003*. Dublin, Ireland: Irish National Committee, European Cultural Foundation and Royal Irish Academy.

Maslow, A. (1954). *Motivation and personality*. New York, NY: Harper and Row.

McAleese, M. (2003). Foreword. In *Mosaic or melting pot?—Living with diversity: Proceedings of a conference on Cultural Diversity, Dublin 2003*. Dublin, Ireland: Irish National Committee, European Cultural Foundation and Royal Irish Academy.

McDonald, B., & Boud, D. (2003). The impact of self-assessment on achievement: The effects of self-assessment training on performance in external examinations. *Assessment in Education, 10*(2), 209–220.

McWilliams, D. (2010, June 10). Elite is preparing to sell country down the river. *Irish Independent*. Retrieved October 18, 2010, from http://www.independent.ie/opinion/columnists/david-mcwilliams/david-mcwilliams-elite-is-preparing-to-sell-country-down-the-river-2366359.html

Murray, N. (2011, March 22). Non-English speaking pupils failed by schools. *The Irish Examiner*.

National Consultative Committee on Racism and Interculturalism (NCCRI). (2004). *The importance of recognising Travellers as an ethnic group: Submission to the Joint Oireachtas Committee on Human Rights.* Dublin, Ireland: NCCRI.

National Council for Curriculum and Assessment (NCCA). (2006). *Intercultural education in the post-primary school.* Retrieved April 2, 2013, from http://www.ncca.ie/uploadedfiles/publications/Interc%20Guide_Eng.pdf

National Council for Curriculum and Assessment (NCCA). (2009, June). *Submission to the National Strategy for Higher Education.* Retrieved February 21, 2011, from http://www.ncca.ie/en/NCCA_submission_to_the_National_Strategy_for_Higher_Education.pdf

Patton, M. Q. (1990). *Qualitative evaluation and research methods* (2nd ed.). Thousand Oaks, CA: Sage.

Pusch, M. D. (2009). The interculturally competent global leader. In D. K. Deardorff (Ed.), *The Sage handbook of intercultural competence* (pp. 66–84). Thousand Oaks, CA: Sage.

Race, P. (1998). Practical pointers on peer-assessment. In S. Brown (Ed.), *Peer-assessment in Practice. SEDA Paper 102.* Birmingham, UK: Staff and Educational Development Association.

Seligman, M. E. P. (2006). *Learned optimism: How to change your mind and your life.* New York, NY: Vintage.

Sluijsmans, D. M. A., Brand-Gruwel, S., & van Merriënboer, J. J. G. (2002). Peer-assessment training in teacher education: effects on performance and perceptions. *Assessment and Evaluation in Higher Education, 27*(5), 444–454.

Smyth, E., Darmody, M., McGinnity, F., & Byrne, D. (2009). *Adapting to diversity: Irish schools and newcomer students.* Dublin, Ireland: Economic and Social Research Institute.

Spitzberg, B. H., & Changnon, G. (2009). Conceptualizing intercultural competence. In D. K. Deardorff (Ed.), *The Sage handbook of intercultural competence* (pp. 2–52). Thousand Oaks, CA: Sage.

Stobart, G. (2005). Fairness in multicultural assessment systems. *Assessment in Education, 12*(3), 275–287.

Wood, D. (2009). A scaffolded approach to developing students' skills and competence to participate in self and peer assessment. In J. Milton, C. Hall, J. Lang, G. Allan, & M. Nomikoudis (Eds.), *ATN Assessment Conference 2009: Assessment in Different Dimensions: Conference proceedings.* Melbourne, Australia: Learning and Teaching Unit, RMIT University.

Williams, P. (2013, June 25). Abuse the bank guarantee, don't get caught—David Drumm. *Irish Independent,* pp. 1–2.

Willis, S. C., Jones, A., Bundy, C., Burdett, K., Whitehouse, C. R., & O'Neill, P. A. (2002). Small group work and assessment in a PBL curriculum: A qualitative and quantitative evaluation of student perceptions of the process of working in small groups and its assessment. *Medical Teacher, 24*(5), 495–501.

Youthreach (2011) About Youthreach [online]. Curriculum Development Unit, Department of Education and Science. Available from http://www.youthreach.ie/aatopmenu/AboutYR/about.html [Accessed 30 May 2011]

CHAPTER 11

IMPLEMENTING CULTURALLY SENSITIVE ASSESSMENT TOOLS FOR THE INCLUSION OF ROMA CHILDREN IN MAINSTREAM SCHOOLS

S. Mitakidou, E. Tressou, and P. Karagianni
Aristotle University of Thessaloniki

Omitting the centrality and relevance of culture in the context of evaluation leaves open the distinct possibility that too many variables are not understood and in many cases misunderstood.
—Hopson & Hood (2005, p. 87)

The evaluative process described in this chapter has been developed within the framework of the European Union Program "Education of Roma Children in the Regions of Central Macedonia, Western Macedonia, Eastern Macedonia and Thrace"; that is, a large part of Northern Greece. It is a program focused on the education of Roma children, in particular, their inclusion in school, their uninterrupted attendance, and their successful completion of school. Its field of operation includes approximately 4,000 Roma and non-Roma children, 102 schools, as well as 26 settlements and 14 camps. Evaluation is ingrained in every aspect of the program. For the

Continuing the Journey to Reposition Culture and Cultural Context in Evaluation Theory and Practice, pages 233–250

purposes of this chapter, we focus on the assessment of one specific part of the evaluative process, the children's performance in a selected number of classes, the so-called *classes of main intervention.*

THE CASE OF ROMA

In Europe

Roma constitute the largest and oldest minority in Europe, with a population of 10 to 12 million.[1] Despite the fact that they have lived in Europe since the 14th century, they still suffer from severe poverty and exclusion; in fact, an estimated 90% of the Roma population live well below the poverty level. Life expectancy is 10–15 times lower than that of the non-Roma population; birth rate is higher but infant mortality is reported to be two to six times higher than that of the non-Roma population. There are certainly cross-country variations; nevertheless, no European country can claim fully successful inclusion of their Roma citizens (Commissioner for Human Rights, 2012, p. 11).[2]

In Greece

In Greece, Roma are not identified as a minority, because their associations oppose the minority status. Rather, they are Greek citizens, and data collection based on their ethnic lineage raises ethical concerns. Since the Greek population censuses do not distinguish the Roma from the overall population, there are no accurate demographic statistics on their numbers.[3] They can only be identified on the basis of their concentration in certain areas and their lifestyle as a "Roma" community. Estimates of the size of the Roma population in Greece are imprecise and vary from 50,000 to 500,000! For example, the Roma Network in Greece estimates their numbers to be approximately 250,000.[4] At the same time, the Council of Europe 2012 report estimates the Roma population to be between 50,000 and 300,000, suggesting that they could represent as high as 1.55% of the total Greek population (11,319,048).[5]

It would be inaccurate to consider our target group as a homogeneous group in any aspect, when, in fact, they represent a very wide spectrum of in-group, often in-family, variability. In terms of their variations, Greek Roma are mainly Christian or Muslim (in Thrace) and they speak Romani (an oral language), Greek, and Turkish (in Thrace), as well as combinations of these three and other languages. They are divided in subgroups,[6] such as tsigganoi, fitsiria, gyftoi, tourkogyftoi, katsiveloi, and athiganoi, according to their geographical descent, dialect, occupation, and settlement (Lydaki, 1998). The umbrella term for all of these subgroups and equally numerous subgroups in other European countries is Roma.

The living conditions of Roma vary. The majority live in settlements composed of built houses or less sturdy prefabricated constructions, mostly in distinct areas within a city or town. A smaller number of them live in camps with makeshift constructions or tents or even more wretched living conditions, usually at the edge of cities or towns. Further, some Roma families live in neighborhoods and homes comparable to typical mainstream standards. Contrary to common belief, 70% of Greek Roma are permanently settled in houses, 22% live permanently in camps, 5% live between two different residences, and only approximately 3% are still nomads (Papadimitriou, Mamarelis, & Niarchos, 2011).[7]

Despite in-group differences, Roma share several significant similarities. They maintain and observe traditions, they preserve their home language (Romani), and they rely on family (often extended family) ties (Lydaki, 1998).

Roma and Education

The educational experiences of Roma children in Greece have persistently demonstrated unsuccessful trajectories. School attendance and performance has been reported erratic for Roma children all over Europe. According to the European Monitoring Centre on Racism and Xenophobia (EUMC, 2006),

> Low attendance and high absenteeism rates could indicate on the one hand that pupils and parents are not convinced of the importance of education and on the other hand that schools tend to have a more permissive attitude towards their attendance. (p. 8)

Interpretation of the reasons for this problematic relation between the school and Roma families is exceptionally complex, and beyond the scope of this chapter.

Identifying and recording the percentage of Roma children in public schools in Greece is as difficult as is the documentation of the size of the overall population. Our data indicate that Roma children in Central Macedonia represent an approximate 1.69% of the total school population at the primary level and 0.38% at the compulsory secondary level.[8]

According to the European Union Agency for Fundamental Rights (FRA & UNDP, 2012), less than 10% of Greek Roma children are reported to attend preschool or kindergarten, and approximately 37% of the Roma children aged 7–15 do not attend school. Further, the summative evaluation report of the previous EU program for the education of Roma children (2006–2008) raises the dropout rate of Roma students enrolled in primary schools to 77% (Mitsis, 2008).

Illiteracy rates among the Roma population are high. In our own research in the designated areas of operation (Northern Greece), out of a sample of 8,137 Roma, 23% reported they had finished primary school, 4% compulsory secondary school, and 1.7% stated having finished senior high school. A widespread explanation why Roma children do not attend or fail at school is based on a common belief that "they are not fit for school" (Mitakidou & Tressou, 2007). However, an excluded community cannot be held responsible for failing to partake in the institutions of a society that has persistently deprived it of its basic rights to social resources, notably education, and relegated members of this excluded community to inhumane and undignified living conditions (Mitakidou & Tressou, 2007).

From the beginning of our involvement with the Roma Program, we sought to collect data that would give us insight into the sociocultural factors that importantly influence the Roma educational experience and allow us an informed basis for designing, implementing, and assessing educational interventions. We knew that we had to understand the context, consider the social and political forces that influence education, and account for culturally specific factors. "The understanding of the complexity of community context supports the trustworthiness of the data gathered and their interpretation" claim Nelson-Barber, LaFrance, Trumbull, and Aburto (2005, p. 73).

The idea of education as an end in itself has not gained significance and value for Roma as they continue to be dramatically excluded from access to public and social funding, leaving them with considerably limited resources to insure their very survival. The promise of education to afford Roma with the same opportunities as non-Roma Greeks has yet to be realized.

The Program

The Program "Education of Roma Children in the Regions of Central Macedonia, Western Macedonia, Eastern Macedonia and Thrace," (2010–2014), is a program funded by the European Social Fund (ESF), and it is the third in a series of Greek cross-cultural education programs for the Roma since 1997. It aims primarily at supporting and enhancing the access, regular attendance, and progress of Roma children, including disabled children, in the lines of an inclusive paradigm that promotes their equal, quality, and fair participation in school. The target groups are Roma students at primary and secondary compulsory education level, Roma adolescents and young adults, teachers, Roma communities, and the wider mainstream community.

The three authors of this chapter serve as the scientific and coordinating team of the program. Along with our collaborators, we mediate between the Roma population, the school, and the wider community, not in order to surrogate but in order to

- coordinate and empower the Roma community by identifying and accentuating their strengths and by working to establish behaviors and attitudes that will help them function more effectively and independently in society;
- empower teachers in their role of critical practitioners;
- help change attitudes and behaviors of the wider community by deconstructing the predominant prejudiced image they hold for Roma; and
- create a common space of interface between Roma and non-Roma populations where terms of equality, justice, and dignity prevail.

Educational interventions of the Program have been designed to address mixed student populations; that is, Roma and non-Roma children, so that all children develop cognitive and social skills through cross-cultural interaction. Additionally, Roma children receive academic and psychosocial support inside and outside of school.

Program psychologists and social workers work daily in the field (i.e., Roma settlements, schools, public services) in an effort to empower the Roma population and assist them in dealing with legal and practical pendencies, mostly the ones that put obstacles in the way of children's school attendance (i.e., vaccinations, registration at civil registers, birth certificates, etc.); in short, working to build alliances between Roma and non-Roma adults and children.

At the same time, program teachers and other practitioners (i.e., theatre and music artists) collaborate with class teachers to design, organize, and implement in-school activities in order to support the children's attendance by creating an attractive, cooperative learning environment where cross-group interactions are promoted and learning becomes a meaningful process for all.

Support instruction (for primary and secondary education students) is the only educational intervention addressed exclusively to Roma children, who often lack the knowledge and skills necessary to attend classes corresponding to their age. The lessons are offered at school—within or after the school program—and in Roma settlements. In addition, there are summer lessons to support students in the transition from one level of education to the next.

Circles of Collaboration

The context where we operate is multilayered and complex in terms of the diversity of the different sites involved; the diversity of needs; the diversity of the schools, institutions, and agencies serving the population in these settings; the diversity of the formal and informal educational sites where our interventions take place; and the diversity of the views, attitudes, sensitivity, responsiveness, drive, and enthusiasm of all stakeholders involved in the task. Evaluation is ingrained in every aspect of the Program as a means of enlightening and making sense of the complexity of the context so that we may operate effectively along the lines of its diversity and intricacy.

The Roma population itself is very diverse, as previously reported. In addition to Roma, schools and their professionals constitute another context to understand and consider as part of our task. Teachers we cooperate with are a mixed group in terms of knowledge, training, experience, awareness, and empathy.

Collaborators in our Program represent another significant element of diversity in this context, not only due to their professional identities but also to their differing ideologies and agendas. The Program collaborators are composed of academics, administrators, psychologists, social workers, Roma mediators, teachers, and specialists in drama, dancing, music, and the environment. Collaboration is based on the premise that all participants function as both "problem-framers and problem solvers" (Darling-Hammond, 1994), therefore they are invited to use their acquired knowledge and experience to enter the field but be accepting of and responsive to the cultural context as a valuable learning opportunity that can inform their practice and increase their effectiveness.

As the coordinating team of the Program, the three authors of this chapter may serve as an intermediary and unifying cross-contextual force, but we also represent another context, due to our different professional expertise and personalities, thus adding contextual variables to the complex equation that constitutes this Program.

The need to address the multiple layers of this contextual diversity in a meaningful and culturally responsive manner has led to the need to seek culturally relevant evaluative means inclusive of all different perspectives. This has a twofold value: evaluation is enriched with all stakeholders' input, and stakeholders are allowed a deeper understanding and appreciation of their milieu, which holds promise for repositioning their/our practice in the lines of a more sensitive and refined paradigm.

THE EVALUATIVE PROCESS

Current Assessment Practice

In Greece, efforts were made in the 1990s to free assessment from the psychometric paradigm and to also remove the comparison of scores through arithmetic grades (Solomon, 1999). The paradigm shift for assessment is succinctly presented in the official national curriculum (DEPPS, 2003), where the innovation for students' assessment involves "the instrumental combination of assessment and self-assessment at every aspect of the teaching process. Varied assessment and self-assessment forms are introduced, depending on the specifics of each subject matter and each student" (DEPPS, 2003, Introductory note; our translation). Current mandates view assessment as one of the most important tools for educational change, associating it with both student progress and teacher success. "The basic purpose of pupil assessment is to provide feedback about both pupil progress and teacher success (or in other words, about learning and teaching processes) and also to identify learner strengths and weaknesses" (DEPPS, 2003, General part, p. 29). In the official national curriculum, special reference is made to the assessment of the students' critical ability and creativity, motivation for learning, problem-solving strategies, and metacognitive and self-evaluation skills (DEPPS, 2003, General part, p. 30).

A mixture of diagnostic, formative, and summative types of assessment is suggested by the Institute of Educational Policy of the Ministry of Education, with a distinct preference given to formative assessment. The implications of these directives make assessment one of the most important means of teaching and learning evaluation and eventually educational change, thereby also informing teachers' decisions about educational tools and teaching strategies.

Research studies concerning assessment choices made by teachers (Bagakis, 2001; Mavromatis, Zouganeli, Kafka, & Stergiou, 2007; Rekalidou & Papaemmanouil, 2006) have revealed that the open spirit of the assessment suggested in the national curriculum has not filtered down into schools, and that teachers prefer a self-created type of informal assessment. A study conducted by the Institute of Educational Policy (Mavromatis et al., 2007) revealed that a significant number of primary school teachers assessed their students using their own assessment tools and strategies, rather than an official tool. The teachers' preferred assessments were daily oral examinations of students (91%), teacher-made informal tests (89%), check of students' daily homework (78%), and student observation (51%). The students' behavior in class was also assessed and played a critical role in teachers' evaluation.

Findings also confirm that the most difficult challenge for teachers is to employ assessment results in designing educational approaches and teaching material. Teachers fail to use assessment results for improving their teaching, mainly because they are not trained in assessment or data use. Further, they do not take advantage of formative forms of assessment; thus, the most popular and generally recognized form of assessment remains the summative assessment (Mavromatis et al, 2007; Rekalidou & Papaemmanouil, 2006). In other words, assessment is not transformed into a tool that could trigger change of the teaching practice.

Setting the Scene

The various tools we have created and used so far compose one multidimensional evaluative mechanism, the main purpose of which is to help us gain a holistic picture of our field of action and the attempted interventions.

The example we refer to here draws from the assessment practices in six schools, the so-called schools of *central intervention,* which were selected among the 102 in our field of operation, on the basis of the percentage of Roma children enrolled in them and their geographical location. The criteria for inclusion were that the schools enrolled a significant percentage (higher than 40%) of Roma children and were located in areas representative of the Roma living settings. Five of the six schools had more than 40% of Roma children enrolled with only one school with a less than 40% Roma students enrolled (30%). This school was selected because of the children's' diverse backgrounds (immigrants from many countries, repatriates, poor Greek children) and because it was the only school in the city of Thessaloniki. Two schools were in neighboring Thessaloniki municipalities, and the other three in different areas of Northern Greece. The idea behind this intervention in the six selected schools is that if Roma children receive full cognitive and sociopsychological support in the first crucial years of their schooling (K–2), the likelihood of their staying at school is increased.

For the purposes of this chapter, we examine 11 first- and second-grade classes and 150 students.[9] The teachers in these 11 classes agreed to accept a second teacher assigned by the Program to cooperate with them in a collaborative team-teaching process, an unusual teaching scheme in Greek schools. The teachers in all of the schools were non-Roma Greek and so were the Program teachers. In fact, to the best of our knowledge, in our area of operation, there are not any teachers of Roma origin.[10]

The Program teacher collaborated with the main class teacher to design cross-curriculum holistic activities, create and use extra teaching materials associated with the national curriculum goals, and implement and assess these additional teaching materials and activities. The main intention of this intervention was to support and enhance the everyday praxis of the regular teacher in order to make teaching more appealing, empowering, and effective for their diverse students. The Program teacher's role was not restricted to supporting Roma students alone but rather to addressing the needs of all students in their classes. This was the plan, and there were several training meetings to ensure there was a common understanding as to the intervention's purposes in terms of teaching and assessment practices.

Based on the Program teachers' daily reports, we realized that despite their valuable contribution to the smooth inclusion of Roma children in the classroom learning community, they were absorbed by the day-to-day routine and failed to inform, reflect on, and improve their practice with the immediate feedback of their students' performance. In the same vein, they did not provide the children with feedback on their performance. After a discussion with the Program teachers in one of our regular after-class meetings, it was decided that we would collaborate with them to prepare formative assessment tools to monitor their students' learning and simultaneously gain awareness of their own professional development (Kalantzis & Cope, 2012; Nicol & Macfarlane-Dick, 2004; Stiggins, 2005).

For low achievers, such as Roma children, traditional testing only confirms significantly lower performance compared with their classmates, resulting in their tendency "to question their own capabilities as learners...depriv[ing] them of the emotional reserves needed to continue to take risks" (Stiggins, 2005, p. 325). In order to counterbalance the detrimental effects of assessment on low achievers, assessment *of* learning should be coupled with assessment *for* learning (Stiggins, 2005, p. 325).

The Tools

It was a challenge to find ways to assess Roma students' learning in the classes of main intervention so that the assessment process could generate feedback beneficial to students and to teachers. Our epistemological beliefs underlying the design of the assessment tools included

- Assessment approaches are inherently related with the assessors' views about teaching and learning.
- Assessment is most meaningfully used formatively to provide feedback as to the efficacy of the attempted interventions so that they can be monitored and improved. Therefore, assessment is used in ways that serve to inform teaching and learning.
- Participation of teachers in the process of assessing, i.e., both in the design and the interpretation of the results, secures authenticity.

- Triangulation of sources and reflection on data allows for informed interpretation because, as Moss (in Gipps, 1994) argues, "A hermeneutic approach to assessment involves holistic integrated interpretations of performance that aim at contextualized understanding of real attainments" (Gipps, 1994, p. 371).

Six tools are examined for the purposes of this chaper: (a) Attendance rate tool, (b) Teachers daily professional journals, (c) Language assessment tool, (d) Mathematics assessment tool, (e) Social skills tool, and (f) Teachers' self-reflection tool. The tool contents were agreed upon in close collaboration with the Program teachers.

All of the assessment tools described here were completed by Program teachers so that they could contextualize children's performance and associate it with their own practice.

We followed a process of evaluation of these that was divided into two phases: "the discovery phase" (Guba & Lincoln, 2001), which included the first two tools, and the "implementation phase," which included the remaining four tools (see Figure 11.1).

The type of the Program, the established routines of all circles of collaborators and the design of this evaluative process have allowed us to meet the trustworthiness and authenticity criteria (Guba & Lincoln, 2001). In terms of credibility, we have relied on thick description, triangulation, active participation, peer debriefing, and prolonged engagement. Signs of transferability are provided through the expressed interest of cooperating schools to learn about our tools and use them. Our methodological decisions and choices are being evaluated by external evaluators for dependability and confirmability.

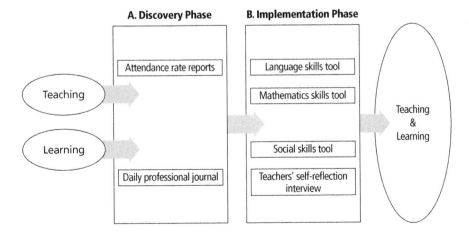

Figure 11.1 Assessment tools.

Discovery Phase

Attendance rate report.

    Use: Exploratory-Formative

    Form: Checklist of students' daily, weekly, monthly attendance reports (3 levels of attendance: 0–30%, 30%–60%, and 60%–90%)

Content: Individual students' daily, weekly, monthly attendance reports

We were aware of previous reports (FRA & UNDP, 2012; Ministry of Employment and Social Security, 2011; Mitsis, 2008) that confirmed the low attendance rate of Roma children. However, we wanted to undertake a research project that created an updated data base to investigate whether there is relationship between Roma students' inconsistent school attendance patterns and their academic failure, and if these data could contribute to improving the school attendance of these students.

Daily professional journal.

    Use: Formative

    Form: Descriptive detailed report of daily practice.

Content: Balancing time and turn taking in teaching, subjects taught, and case studies of children who face difficulties.

From the beginning of the Program, participating teachers maintained a professional journal as a descriptive-reflective tool of their daily practice. Our review of approximately 1,070 journal entries by Program teachers revealed that they primarily provided descriptions of surface classroom routines and the content that had been covered, but failed to provide any reflections that could build on the strong interrelation between teaching and learning. This seemed to suggest the need for the use of supplementary formative tools to assist Program teachers in identifying the connection between their teaching and their students' academic progress. As a result, in addition to the two previously mentioned tools, four additional tools were developed in the areas of: Language, Mathematics, Social development, and Teacher self-reflection.

Implementation Phase

Language tool.

    Use: Exploratory-Formative

    Form: Checklist consisting of 34 items to be answered on a scale of 1–4 (1. Almost never; 2. A Little; 3. A lot; 4. Almost always). A separate column for comments on each of the items was also incorporated with the suggestion to include context bound information.

Content: Curriculum objectives on language (comprehension, oral, speaking, and writing) skills and ability in pragmatics

Thick observation and documentation of the students' learning was suggested before completing the checklist. Program teachers completed the checklists for all students (Roma and non-Roma) based on their observations, students' written work, their responses to teaching material, and participation in classroom discussions. The checklist items covered fairly comprehensive areas of the students' language growth, avoiding fragmented and isolated pieces of knowledge. This information contributed to the Program teachers' ability to identify children's strengths and weaknesses in core curriculum areas as well as language tasks, providing clarification of students' progress toward the expected learning outcomes and helping Program teachers relate these results to their teaching.

Mathematics tool.

Use: Exploratory-Formative

Form: Checklist consisting of 36 items to be answered on a scale of 1–4 (1. Almost never; 2. Little; 3. A lot; 4. Always). A separate column for comments on each of the items was also incorporated, with the suggestion to include context-bound information.

Content: Curriculum objectives on mathematics, including counting, measurement, the concept of number, problem-solving, and mathematics skills in context

The completion of the mathematics checklist followed the same protocol as the language checklist. The items of the tool covered core curriculum areas associated with real life problem-solving situations.

Social skills tool.

Use: Exploratory-Formative

Form: Checklist consisting of 36 items to be answered on a scale of 1–4 (1. Almost never, 2. Little, 3. A lot, 4. Always). The teachers could also comment on each of the items in a separate column.

Content: Social language skills, familiarization with school culture, and students' social image

Again, the same protocol was used. In this particular tool, the students' social-skills profile is further associated with their background (conditions of living, parents' educational level, and economic situation), as it is completed in the checklist. The main items of the tool cover areas of the students' class participation, self-organization, relationships with the others, ways of engaging with others, ways of engaging with the teachers, and ways of using the language for social interactions.

Teachers' self-reflection interview.

Use: Exploratory-Reflective

Form: open questions

Content: Reflection, expectations, intentions, teaching methods, and materials.

The interview consisted of three main axes, including the teachers'

- views of their role (teaching methods, relationship with the cooperating teacher, and use of differentiated methods and materials, intentions, changes)
- emotions (satisfaction, self-fulfillment, disappointment, frustration, ambivalence/uncertainty)
- relationships with other members of the school staff.

To complete the circle of student evaluation, we sought to explore Program teachers' self-perceived role and self-evaluation of their praxis. The interview mainly functioned as a springboard for reflection.

Discussion

An assessment, Darling-Hammond (1994) maintains, will fulfill its purposes when it becomes "a recursive process of self-reflection, self-critique, self-correction and self-renewal" (p. 5). This participatory, collaborative evaluative practice has proved to be a dynamic, rewarding, and empowering process, in that it informed teaching and motivated learning. For example, in the written reports of the main classroom teachers, their initial skepticism of the collaborative scheme has been gradually replaced with recognition and appreciation of the Program teachers' marked contribution not only in increasing Roma children's attendance rate and creating a class community conducive to learning but also in helping them link teaching with continuous formative assessment. As Nelson-Barber et al. (2005) claim, "Planning for change and implementing change are very important aspects of the work, and the process itself may have unexpected benefits in terms of learning" (p. 69).

These types of assessments are used to identify curriculum issues while also providing sufficient and rich data on children's performance, as well as on teachers' instructional methods and their interrelationship. The information generated from these tools can be used as a personal "bank" for Program teachers. Processing their daily reports, four areas of growth of their practice emerged. On the basis of the insights gained by their involvement with this evaluative process, the Program teachers recognized that they were able to

- understand better the context of their practice;
- check their judgments, validate good practices, and discard unsuccessful choices;
- fairly evaluate their students in an unthreatening manner; and
- be able to defend their choices as being evidence based.

In summary, we did not aspire to create yet more performance assessment tools, even if they were culturally appropriate, but to use assessment as a unifying force between teaching and learning. For example, we chose to monitor Roma children's attendance rates in order to demonstrate how a perceived cultural trait that admittedly poses barriers to Roma children's school progress; that is, their erratic school attendance could actually be used by teachers as a springboard for reflecting on and adapting their teaching practice accordingly. Interpreting Roma children's attendance rates with teachers, we discussed possible ways of encountering the difficulty by adopting teaching choices (i.e., creating differentiated teaching material based on the national curriculum contents) that would make the learning environment functional, relevant, and attractive for Roma and non-Roma children alike.

Working toward the same end, we created the language-, mathematics-, and social-skills tools that aimed at revealing the teachers' own estimates of Roma and non-Roma children's cognitive and social profiles. We cross-examined those results with the data drawn from the teachers' daily journals and interviews. We then collaborated with them to create learning material and a learning environment that was more congruent with the needs of the students in their mixed classes. Therefore, our tools were culturally appropriate in the sense that they catered to the needs of the specific classroom culture and aimed at enhancing both performance rates and teacher responsiveness to classroom needs.

The assessment mechanism we have developed (ongoing, context-bound, longitudinal) points to an emerging qualitative and open typology. The methodological choices and processes can easily be replicated, if not the tools themselves as they are context-specific. This typology can act as a bridge for teachers who want to create their own teaching tools: it can offer an alternative to the vague suggestions of the national curriculum and traditional decontextualized assessment practices. As Darling-Hammond and Snyder (2000) believe, teachers must be empowered and facilitated to "develop strategies that are both powerful and practical for the evaluation of contextualized teaching" (p. 543).

It is an assessment process that encourages reflection, reconceptualization, and reconstruction of our assessing practices. On the other hand, we were able to identify limitations that demand redesign. Specifically it is important to include parents and children as active participants in the evaluation process (Swadener, Lundy, Blanchet-Cohen, & Habashi, 2013).

Processes such as thick description, peer debriefing, and external evaluation require a disproportionate amount of time, human potential, and resources. This can be a drawback if the assessment is the responsibility of individual teachers rather than the shared responsibility of the entire school. In other words, the school must be motivated and inspired to share and assume more responsibility for the assessment, with the academic team facilitating change in the process when necessary. If not, the question of sustainability of good practices will remain.

The process described here has had positive effects on teacher growth and consequently on student learning. In their self-reflection interviews, the 11 Program teachers reported gains at different levels:

- They became aware and articulate as to the learning goals needing to be pursued for their students.
- They adjusted their teaching and differentiated syllabus material to better serve their students' needs.
- They were able to translate their aspirations and expectations into assessment procedures that were relevant and appropriate for their students.
- They became a learning team that relied on collaboration and reflection to improve their practice.

The main teachers also reported benefits:

- They were introduced to a formative assessment process in the making.
- They recognized its value and realized its effectiveness in that it did not disempower and categorize students.
- They described the process as a learning in-service training process.

The students benefited as the Program teachers' daily reports indicate

- The teaching methods and materials were differentiated to be adjusted to the diverse Roma and non-Roma students' needs.
- Students' confidence in themselves was strengthened.
- Roma students realized the direct relationship between attendance rates and their academic success.

CONCLUDING REMARKS

This chapter has argued that a contextualized, continuous, reflective, and open type of assessment is viable. Being an intrinsic part of the classroom culture, assessment can have significant implications for student learning. Traditionally, assessment has served to sort children according to their performance, widening instead of narrowing the performance gap between low and high achievers. Working with diverse student populations, our challenge has been to find ways to turn negative assessment implications to formative evaluative feedback so that assessment could serve the children's best interests: teachers could see the promise of success in all of their students and acquire the skills and power to build on them in order to disrupt the learning dynamics. It is an effort that involves interrupting the (vicious) circle of failure that low achievers find themselves trapped into and use assessment to support and enhance student learning. Developing a continuous flow of evidence of their students' performance and analyzing these evidence cues reflectively, teachers can use assessment as a motivator; that is, as a means of improving their students' learning opportunities as well as their own teaching.

Assessment, very much like other aspects of teaching, must be culturally relevant to secure gains for students and teachers. This involves designing and administering contextualized assessment material as well as engaging students (and parents) so that they have a clear and timely picture of their current level of performance and the expected goals. Engaging children and parents in this assessment process was neglected, and we fully recognize that this must be addressed in the future.

Given the strong influence of assessment on teaching and learning and on shaping school policies and practices, we can be hopeful that by working for the establishment of culturally appropriate assessment practices, we are working toward ameliorating the unequal distribution of educational resources among students.

NOTES

1. Data drawn from http://www.errc.org/article/roma-rights-2013-national-roma-integration-strategies; www.dosta.org; http://hub.coe.int/what-we-do/human-rights/roma-and-travellers; and http://www.coe.int/t/dg3/roma travellers/Default_en.asp
2. http://www.coe.int/t/commissioner/source/prems/prems79611_GBR_CouvHumanRightsOfRoma_WEB.pdf
3. The last Greek census that included questions on ethnicity and mother tongue was in 1951: Dragonas with Mylonas (2012) Roma mothers and their young children, Country Report: Greece. Bernard Van Leer Foundation, unpublished report.

4. Management Organisation Unit of Development Programs, Intermediate Management Body, 2012. http://www.mou.gr/en

5. http://hub.coe.int/web/coe-portal/roma

6. Fara (clan) or phyli (race) as Roma themselves call these subgroups.

7. An older national survey of the General Secretariat of Popular Education of the Ministry of Education recorded that 72% of the Greek Roma live in houses, 22.3% in tents, 14.7% in makeshift shacks, and 0.9% in old buses (Lydaki, 1998).

8. This is the percentage of the Roma children enrolled in school. However, in a research study conducted at the exploratory phase of our program, we found a significant percentage, 18%, of children who had never enrolled in school.

9. The first-grade class of the school in Thessaloniki had only one Roma child in the second year of this intervention, so it was not selected.

10. As explained before, it is hard to identify a teacher's (or student's) origin unless they are self-identified.

REFERENCES

Bagakis, G. (2001). *Assessment of educational programs and the school.* Athens, Greece: Metehmio.

Commissioner for Human Rights. (2012). Human rights of Roma and Travellers in Europe. Strasbourg, France: Council of Europe Publications.

Darling-Hammond, L. (1994). Performance-based assessment and educational equity. *Harvard Educational Review, 64*(1), 5–30.

Darling-Hammond, L., & Snyder, J. (2000). Authentic assessment of teaching in context. *Teaching and Teacher Education, 16*, 523–545.

DEPPS-APPS. (2003). A cross thematic curriculum framework for compulsory education. *Diathematikon Programma. Official Gazette issue B, nr 303/13-03-03 and issue B, nr 304/13-03-0.* Translated by members of the Pedagogical Institute.

European Monitoring Centre on Racism and Xenophobia (EUMC). (2006). *Roma and Travellers in public education: An overview of the situation in EU member states.* Vienna, Austria: EUMC.

FRA & UNDP. (2012). *The situation of Roma in 11 EU member states. Survey results at a glance.* European Union Agency for Fundamental Rights. Luxembourg: Publications Office of the European Union.

Gipps, C. (1994). *Beyond testing.* London, UK: Falmer.

Guba, E. G., & Lincoln, Y. S. (2001). Guidelines and checklist for constructivist (a.k.a. Fourth Generation) evaluation. *Evaluation Checklists Project.* Retrieved April 5, 2013, from www.wmich.edu/evalctr/checklists

Hopson, R., & Hood, S. (2005). An untold story in evaluation roots: Reid E. Jackson and his contributions toward culturally responsive evaluation at three quarters of a century. In S. Hood, R. Hopson, & H. Frierson (Eds.), *The role of culture and cultural context.* Greenwich, CT: Information Age.

Lydaki, A. (1998). *Gypsies in town. Growing up in Saint Barbara.* Athens, Greece: Kastaniotis.

Kalantzis, M., & Cope, B. (2012). *New learning* (2nd ed.). New York, NY: Cambridge University Press.

Mavrommatis, Y., Zouganeli, A., Kafka, D., & Stergiou, P. (2007). Student assessment. *Review of Educational Matters, 13,* 84–98.

Ministry of Employment and Social Security. (2011). *National strategic framework for Roma.* Retrieved from http://ec.europa.eu/justice/discrimination/files/roma_greece_strategy_en.pdf

Mitakidou, S., & Tressou, E. (2007). *Let me tell you how they'll learn how to read and write. Gypsy women speak for the education of their children.* Athens, Greece: Kaleidoskopeio.

Mitsis, N. (2008). *Assessment of the project Inclusion of Gypsy children in school.* Athens, Greece: Omas Synergon.

Nelson-Barber, S. LaFrance, J., Trumbull, E., & Aburto, S. (2005). Promoting culturally reliable and valid evaluation practice. In S. Hood, R. Hopson, & H. Frierson (Eds.), *The role of culture and cultural context.* Greenwich, CT: Information Age.

Nicol, D., & Macfarlane-Dick, D. (2004). Rethinking formative assessment in HE: A theoretical model and seven principles of good feedback practice. Retrieved from http://www.heacademy.ac.uk/assessment/ASS051D_SENLEF_model.doc

Papadimitriou, D., Mamarelis, A., & Niarchos, G. (2011). *Measures to promote the situation of Roma EU citizens in the European Union.* Country Reports. Greece. In European Parliament. Directorate General for Internal Policies. Policy Department C: Citizens' Rights and Constitutional Affairs. Brussels: European Parliament (pp. 142–162). Retrieved from http://www.europarl.europa.eu/studies

Rekalidou, G., & Papaemmanouil, D. (2006). Teachers' speculations and views about assessment and the family's role in formulating assessment results. In D. Kakana, K. Botsoglou, N. Chaniotakis, & E. Kavalari (Eds.), *Assessment in education: Educational and practical dimensions.* Thessaloniki, Greece: Kyriakidis.

Solomon, I. (Ed.). (1999). *Internal assessment and programming of the educational work in the school unit.* Athens: Pedagogical Institute, Assessment Unit, Ministry of Education.

Stiggins, R. (2005). From formative assessment to assessment for learning. *Phi Delta Kappan, 87*(4), 324–328.

Swadener, E. Lundy, L., Blanchet-Cohen, N., & Habashi, J. (Eds.), (2013). *Children's rights and education.* New York, NY: Peter Lang.

CHAPTER 12

EVALUATING ALCH'I'NI BA/ FOR THE CHILDREN

The Troubled Cultural Work of an Indigenous Teacher Education Project

Carolyne J. White and Guy Senese

"One must choose words carefully and mean what we say. Words are very powerful, spiritually and practically....What if everything we said to each other was similar to a prayer?" Speaking primarily in the Diné language, Navajo Council delegate, Thomas Walker, Jr., provides an intervention in the convention of the Eurocentric university environment. He shares traditional knowledge with the participants of the Alch'i'ni Ba (For The Children) Navajo Teacher Education Program. He invites them to cling to their cultural heritage, to remember the importance of their relationship with people, with nature and with the divine. He tells them that their participation in Alch'i'ni Ba is a high calling, saying, "When I read the grant proposal, I was very moved that this was a project to do teacher education differently, Navajo specific. I stand in moral support of the program."

—White, 2006, p. 215

This chapter is a discussion of an evaluation and subsequent academic journal article which concluded that a collaborative Navajo teacher education

Continuing the Journey to Reposition Culture and Cultural Context in Evaluation Theory and Practice, pages 251–272
Copyright © 2015 by Information Age Publishing

program failed to deliver its promise to provide a culturally responsive education. Worse, the evaluation and article claim that the project continues the assimilationist, cultural colonialist education which characterizes so much of Native American history. We, two of the co-directors of this program, reflect on Mr. Walker's comments above and choose our words carefully as we inquire into the practice of culturally responsive evaluation. We begin with a context for this inquiry.

A Context for this Inquiry

A collaboration with the Navajo Nation, Little Singer Community School in the Bird Springs community on the Navajo Nation, and Northern Arizona University, Alch'i'ni Ba set out in the summer of 2004 to prepare twelve Native American (Diné/Navajo) students to enter the field of elementary and secondary school teaching and to serve children in schools on the Navajo reservation.[1] Funding from the Office of Indian Education, within the U.S. Department of Education, paid students' tuition, fees, books, and monthly stipends to assist with their living expenses. To qualify for participation, students needed to have completed enough college coursework to be able to graduate within 2 years. A one-year induction program supported their first year of teaching. Two Navajo women, Lucinda Godinez and Etta Shirley, principals at Little Singer School, co-directed this 3-year project.

We, nonindigenous theorists and practitioners, entered into this project as co-principal investigators in collaboration with the Navajo Nation from our career-long concerns that Hopi and Navajo children, in whose communities both of us have lived and worked for a combined 75+ years, deserved stronger cultural and political preparation as students and the implied improved opportunity to learn from strong indigenous teachers. This critical and collaborative cultural education engagement built upon earlier successfully completed projects involving Hopi students in Northern Arizona (see White & Hermes, 2005; White, Paymella, & Nuvayouma, 2003).

As the Alch'i'ni Ba project was ending in 2007, we contracted for an evaluation. At the time, we viewed the evaluation as a fulfillment of what we had written in the grant proposal and as an opportunity for a new colleague to gain valuable professional experience. We anticipated that it would celebrate the project's accomplishments and strengthen future collaborative engagement; and to be honest, we expected that only a few people would actually read the report. Following a year of data collection, in 2008 we received the evaluation report and to our surprise, it was highly critical of the project's level of cultural responsiveness. While disappointed with this, we had no intention of interfering with the evaluation, which we assumed was conducted in good faith. In 2012, we were further surprised to discover the words that we had given IRB consent for use in the evaluation *only*, re-visioned into a "research project" for publication in a journal article with a minimal effort to disguise the identity of the project, co-directors, student participants, and the faculty and staff. From Anonymous (2012),

> The story of Southwestern University's ITP program shows that even if a pro-gram attempts to reject efforts to be everything to everyone, if it continues to allow the rule of the oppressor, it will be sucked back into the very system that it set out to reject. I walk the reader through this argument by illustrating how colonialism can be seen in the intent and development of the ITP program, throughout its implementation and in its outcomes. (p. 5)

> SU [Southwestern University] is a public institution with approximately 20,000 students that graduates significant numbers of certified teachers in the state. The institution also claims a commitment to serving diverse populations and has a specific goal of better meeting the educational needs of Indigenous students and tribal communities. (p. 6)

Researchers acknowledge the difficulty of truly providing anonymity to research participants and sites, but Anonymous (2012) writes, "I worked at SU during the time I served as the external evaluator for the ITP program" (p. 7), and the end of the article identifies her place of employment as Northern Arizona University (NAU).

We failed to anticipate the ways our colleague could approach this work or the multiple ways evaluation activity can go awry. Gerald Vizenor (1995) speaks to our experience with the evaluation report, and the journal article that followed, with these words: "The woodland dream songs and trickster stories that would bear the humor and tragic wisdom of tribal native experi-ence were superseded in the literature of dominance" (p. 68).

Our experience invites useful meditation on the following list of sig-nifiers: colonialism, pure and hybrid culture, community, Whiteness, op-pression, solidarity, ethic and cultural essentialism, state control of teacher education, tribal sovereignty, and state teacher certification. Within what follows, we write both together and separately. Rather than naming our evaluator and citing the journal article, here we use "Anonymous" because of our desire that this inquiry remain focused upon what can be learned from this experience rather than drawing attention to our colleague. We use selected text from both the evaluation report and the journal article, and draw from our lived experience, to discover something new about the conduct of culturally responsive evaluation. From this inquiry, we reflect upon how it could have gone differently and suggest practices that may enhance the conduct of evaluation work. Along the way, we consider the following questions, not with the intention to thoroughly answer them, but rather to have them guide our inquiry:

1. What is our responsibility for the distance between our understanding of and students' access to cultural experiences which were designed as part of the program?
2. Regarding the institution's constraints on teaching toward cultural responsiveness, should or could we have done more, including more to ensure that required education courses were more culturally responsive?
3. How might one judge, or is it even appropriate to judge, students' cultural knowledge? When does nonmembership in a cultural group disqualify one for the purposes of being culturally responsive? What is the issue of "essentialism" regarding who speaks for culture?
4. What ethical issues emerged in the conduct of this evaluation and subsequent publications that warrant attention by multiethnic evaluators when conducting culturally responsive evaluation work with Indigenous populations?

Here we confront the complexities of gaining access to any cultural high ground from which to mount a critique.[2] Thus, in this chapter, we "evaluate" a project evaluation from the first-person perspective of our lived experience, not from the third-person grandstands of theoretical distance. However we performed, we were part of the event. In the teacher education project, we worked toward solidarity with Native American students and their communities' educational aspirations. For 3 years, we hovered, worked the phones, had meetings, traveled to sites, planned cultural and political education experiences, and watched as 12 of the 14 Navajo student participants matriculated and graduated from college. Shortly thereafter, most began teaching in their communities, and some are currently engaged in graduate study. This is our story.

Autobiographical Flashbacks/Pointing Toward Positionality

From the journal article, Anonymous (2012) wrote,

As a White woman I was very much outside the Navajo community. My various identities certainly impacted, and continue to impact my work (p. 7).... As a White woman, there are important limits on the extent to which I can (and should) adopt frameworks such as TribalCrit and CRT. I use these frameworks as analytic and explanatory tools in order to better understand institutions, policies, and practices impacting Indigenous communities ... However, I do not claim to adopt the epistemological positions undergirding these frameworks, nor do I attempt to engage in counter-storytelling ... A full discussion of my own positionality, including the complicated issue of white researchers working with/in/for Indigenous communities, is beyond the scope of this paper. (p. 18)

To fully exercise a critique, while stating that there are "important limits" to it, without discussing those limits, is disingenuous. It is as if being a "White researcher" earns one a privileged place to "qualify" and limit one's responsibility. My (Guy Senese) main goal has been to respect the people I worked with, to avoid patronizing them, to apply myself to the work, and to take responsibility when I blundered into mistakes in those areas. When I failed, I failed there. No discussion, however simplistic, of my "positionality" is ever going to undo it. But let me interrupt with a short story about my own involvement, and *some* roots of my values. And then Carolyne will tell her story.

My "culture" is like many, wildly hybrid, influenced randomly. True, I am a White man, and I take responsibility for everything, including that and including that I cannot pretend to understand the many ways that being a White man inevitably complicates my research and practice. I can't begin to argue that this doesn't matter. But it's not for me to say how. I just don't know. But I was there, and I am here, telling this story, and working to describe my "respons/ibility" without any attempt to exclude myself due to my identity, especially when I did not exclude myself in reality. I admit it. I showed up in Native America 35 years ago and did some work. And, truly, there is no "full discussion" is there?

But let's go beyond assuming how being White is important. For, as a White Italian American it might make me less of a colonialist than an opportunist, working in a conspiracy to advance my career, at the expense of people who have no other choice: that is, a racketeer. That would be a good job for me, the rackets. As an Italian American, my cultural essentials would cook down nicely, like a good red wine reduction for a red spaghetti gravy. My essentials, vis-à-vis a Native American community, would make me a likely colonialist racketeer, like Columbus, who was also lost. I could have even more fun with this identity essentialism, but the subject is really too serious, so for my part, I'll keep close watch on sarcasm. The essence here derives from the world-historical essence—that indigeneity and tribal identities are crystalized in the practice of colonialism and genocide. Native American "identity" is politically centered in resistance to genocide and forced assimilation. My own ethnic identity is freighted with the inheritance of my own family moving through and putting in the past the struggles of immigrant second-class citizenship.

After graduating college in 1975, I spent a couple of years in Alaska working with Tlingit-Haida youth in a juvenile home. There I first learned of Native people in a real world, living lives in a place far from what I knew. I developed a great curiosity regarding Native American community life and particularly, community democracy and self-determination. I pursued graduate study at the University of Illinois and it was from there in 1979 that I jumped at the chance to teach at the Rough Rock Demonstration School, where educational self-determination, with local curriculum, pedagogy, indigenous language and culture classes, community control, were first piloted in a sustained manner. My few years there changed my and my family's life. What followed was 30+ years of engagement in and commitment to community democracy and education, following Native American education policy history.

Native American communities provided for me and nourished my early work. Later I returned to Illinois to complete my doctorate with advanced study in Native Education Policy Studies. My career was again defined and advanced by the publication of a book I worked on for almost 10 years on the mixed promise of Native American Self-determination (Senese, 1991). If there is any meaningful connection with my "positionality," it would not start with some vague reference to stereotypic ethnic or race assumptions, but with consciously assumed values of my own family. So whenever I had the chance to "give something back" or pay respect to this community and the extended relations of Native America, I have done it.

In 1997, my family had the chance to come back west to work at NAU. When I got the chance to work on the grant project with Carolyne, my first thought was that here was a chance to help develop a dozen new Navajo teachers for reservation schools. We would emphasize commitment to Navajo teaching and leadership development toward authentic self-determination and educational sovereignty. Carolyne and I had much in common regarding early connections between our family lives and Native communities, and a shared experience in intellectual support at the College of Education at the University of Illinois, where social commitments and the social foundations of education were symbiotic.

My (Carolyne White) family's roots are in England, France, and Germany. My parents grew up in Utah within the Mormon religion. From "pioneer stock," one of my ancestors kept a journal of the historic Mormon migration in the middle 1800s and another was a Pony Express rider. As a child, our family moved often because my father was a sergeant in the Air Force. I learned to study new social environments in order to adapt quickly. The only Mormon at some of my schools, I was different, felt marginal. The eldest of 10 children, asked to be responsible, I was mostly lost. As a girl, high school occurred to me as something to survive in order to get to the next stage of life, being married and having children.

In 1968, following the inherited trajectory of my family's religion, I married in the Mormon temple and went to work because my husband was a college student. Hired as the secretary for an Upward Bound Program that encouraged and supported Navajo and Hopi high school students to aspire to and prepare for college attendance and graduation, that was when I too aspired to be a college graduate. It was there, in Cedar City, Utah, that I began *learning with* indigenous peoples.

A few years later, I encountered my first feminist book and entered a new world. I left the Mormon church, pursued a college education, divorced, and in 1978, after completing a master's degree, was asked to direct that same Upward Bound Program. Some of the former students who were now teachers in schools in the Navajo and Hopi Nations worked with me as staff members. In 1988, I returned to the Navajo and Hopi Nations to conduct dissertation research with some of these same people. In 1998, when I accepted a position at NAU, a former Upward Bound student, staff member, and collaborator in my dissertation research said, "I prayed you here. I need someone to advise my dissertation research." Guy and I co-directed her dissertation.

In 2005, as I was saying good-bye to colleagues in the NAU College of Education prior to moving to New Jersey, I encountered Cheryl Yazzie Singer (former Upward student, staff member, and collaborator in my dissertation research, who is married to a former Upward Bound student, staff member, and collaborator in my dissertation research, and the mother of two daughters who were participants in Alch'i'ni Ba). She said, "This is not good-bye. Your umbilical cord is buried here. You will return." I bring these experiences and many, many more to this writing. While I have no coherent sense of an independent self, I believe that the Mormon religion, the military, gender socialization, and exposure to transformative possibilities that included Upward Bound and feminism, contribute to my being committed to all people having access to authoring fulfilling lives of joy and passionate contribution. Regarding work in indigenous education, I assert that there is no uncontaminated space of innocence, rather only ongoing contested and troubled spaces as we negotiate the ruins of colonialism.

I can imagine the possibility of writing words about the colonial nature of the university and teacher education, words very much like the words written in the evaluation report and journal article. Yet, from this space of having been written about, without the opportunity to review a draft of the documents prior to publication, without the opportunity to correct erroneous information, and without the opportunity to challenge what I read as simplifications of incredibly complex cultural phenomenon, I experience newly the dangerous landscape of research. I now hear more clearly Linda T. Smith's (2012) caution that "The word itself, 'research', is probably one of the dirtiest words in the indigenous world's vocabulary" (p. 1). And, as I revisit my relationships with Cheryl, Thomas, and Guy, I return to Barad's (2007) explanation of entanglement in quantum theory: "To be entangled is not simply to be intertwined with another, as in the joining of separate entities, but to lack an independent, self-contained existence. Existence is not an individual affair, rather individuals emerge through and as part of their entangled intra-relating" (p. ix).

As I discover quantum physics' entanglement, with St. Pierre (2011), I enter new possibilities for describing "human being." I reconsider the indigenous concept of "All My Relations" and the primacy of being in a caring and supportive relationship with all human beings. From this perspective, I consider carefully the words we use to write about the texts produced by our colleague, the person we chose to conduct this evaluation.[3] Ideally, this chapter would have been written as a conversation among the three of us and would also have included the perspectives of our primary collaborators, Lucinda Godinez, Etta Shirley, Joann Wood, and Thomas Walker, Jr.

Reviewing Alch'i'ni Ba Through the Words of an Evaluator

This chapter is about "culture" and "responsiveness" as interpreted through different lenses. In what follows, we wonder about what is signified when we speak the words "culture," "responsiveness," and "evaluation." Early in the evaluation report (Anonymous, 2008), comes the "good news":

> There were a number of other program strengths or successes that were identified by just one or two interviewees. From participants, these included the clarity of the courses and requirements needed for graduation, the relationships formed within the group, and getting to see the Hawaii immersion school. And from program staff, these included seeing the participants get along in the new and diverse context of NAU, taking participants to speak with legislators and other teachers about their work and thus being real "teacher leaders," and working with participants on research and conference presentations and "seeing themselves as real thinkers about this process of teaching and learning." (p. 4)

Later, Anonymous (2008) cites a quote from an interview, where a student describes his or her understanding of the program as follows:

> [The project goal was] "trying to give them [our future students] a perspective through the Navajo culture while we teach them. So that's what I got from it. Even though I am not traditional or anything like that, I did look at it where, you know, there are a lot of kids who are traditional and I need to be able to pull some of what they know and their language and connect it to, you know, modern education so they can get it." ...A few of the participants articulated a similar perspective on what they believed the goal of the program was, but more of them noted that they thought the goal was to increase the number of teachers "who could speak Navajo" and "who could integrate the language." While culture and language are obviously intimately related, some educators and scholars believe it is possible to focus on culture without language integration. The AB participants who discussed their belief

that the goal of the program was more teachers who could speak Navajo also expressed frustration that not all of the program participants were, in fact, fluent (or even near fluent) in Navajo. As I discuss later, this distinction was a significant source of tension within the program. (p. 3)

In any tribal community where language and culture loss has been described as "catastrophic," it would not be surprising that 14 Navajo students would not share a similar acquaintance with the Diné language. It would be exceptional and rare if they did. We knew of, and dealt explicitly with, this expected diversity of religious and cultural background. From our perspective, ongoing discussions about culture and its obvious relationship to language opened an opportunity for program participants to consider their cultural preparation, including knowledge of the language, and how what was missing could hamper their effectiveness. It is then relatively easy to imagine a student participant leaping to the simplistic conclusion that the program was about language. This is incredibly complex cultural territory. The words of Mary Hermes (2005), writing from an Objibwe context, are instructive:

> The reclaiming of language could propel the gains of the culture-based movement far beyond superficially adding fragmented pieces of cultural knowledge to the existing structure...Language is an equalizer, not a prize for competition. Students who are successful in learning their Indigenous language will not be competing against those who do not learn the language. Our language must be shared in order to survive...Language has a generative, creative power that is currently missing from the teaching of culture in schools. (p. 53)

The graduation rate is rightfully celebrated in the evaluation: graduating 13 of 14 Navajo students from college, when college attendance and retention records are generally so dismal among Native peoples.[4] Many students reported that without the program, they would not have graduated. Just increasing the number of children who would be taught one day by teachers from Navajo backgrounds is a degree of cultural responsiveness that should need no elaboration. Also celebrated was the unique partnership between the Little Singer elementary school at Birdsprings on Navajo and the project. The evaluation reads,

> By far, the most discussed aspect of the program that "worked well" was the collaboration between Little Singer and NAU that allowed Ałchini Bá participants to work in the classrooms at Little Singer. As one participant explained, "probably the best part was working with the kids at Little Singer." And as one staff explained, "a great thing about the program was seeing them just come alive around children." A few of the participants also talked about the importance of learning "how they do things in a rural community school"

and seeing how involved community members were in the schooling of their children in the Bird Springs community. In a related vein, another staff member felt like one of the successes of the program was a successful collaboration between a university and a reservation community school, which ultimately was good for the program participants as well as the school. A couple staff members specifically identified the professional development school model in which program participants took courses and learned in a community school as a key strength of the program. (Anonymous, 2008, p. 3)

The evaluation continues:

> Another commonly cited success of the program was the ability to "convey the importance of infusing culture to students who never thought of it before." Similarly, another staff member noted, "we were consistent in the goal to blend traditional public education curriculum and institutional strategies with consistent open-mindedness regarding other ways of looking at education from a Navajo perspective." Although the staff identified this as a strength of the program, most of the participants wanted more in this area. Most participants agreed that the program was successful in conveying the importance of being culturally responsive teachers, but they felt there was less success in helping them see how to make this a reality. As one participant said of this issue, "it wasn't finished," and as another explained, "it was connected and discussed but not applied." (Anonymous, 2008, p. 3)

On one hand, we agree, and we wish that more of the cultural experiences and teaching from a tribal perspective, including instruction from elders, formal and informal instruction in Navajo language, "counted" as part of a complete teacher education. However, the tight constraints of state certification standards, particularly at the elementary level, put severe limits on this option. In the article drawn from the evaluation, the writer argues that we might have applied the Navajo tribal standards and included these experiences. This deserves to be quoted in full before comment:

> SU and the ITP program might turn to the Navajo Nation as a sovereign entity for guidance about how to conceptualize and implement a teacher preparation program that is culturally responsive and relevant to Dine communities. Indeed the Office of Dine Culture Language and Community Service provides clear direction in its mission statement:
>
> > "The human resources of the Navajo Nation are its most valuable resource. The Navajo Tribe, as a sovereign nation, has a responsibility to oversee the education in whatever schools or school systems they are being educated, to assure their education provides excellence in the academic program and high, realistic expectations. An appropriate education for all Navajo people is one that fosters the formulation of age, grade and or

developmentally appropriate competencies in all basic areas of academic and cognitive skill;

a. Competence in English language skills and knowledge of American culture;

b. Competence in Navajo language skills and knowledge of Navajo culture;

c. Development of Navajo and U.S. citizenship;

d. Self-discipline and positive self-concept;

e. Preparation for lifetime responsibilities in the areas of employment, family life, recreation and use of leisure; and

f. An attitude toward education which encourages lifetime learning.

The Dine Cultural Content Standards are predicated on the belief that firm grounding of native students in their indigenous cultural heritage and language is a fundamentally sound pre-requisite to well-developed culturally healthy students... the standards are basically designed to convey principles and to place values on the meaning of Dine K ehgo Nitsahakeesgo Bee lina', so that learners will be empowered to comprehend and respect their cultural heritage through self-identity." ... These standards could guide the curriculum pedagogy and programming for ITP. This would result in a teacher preparation program that looks very different from the standard program offered at institutions like SU across the country. (Anonymous, 2012, pp. 17–18)

We agree that the standards are important, and we actively collaborated with the Navajo Nation as the program was conceptualized and implemented. It is worth noting that during the evaluation process, neither of us was asked by the evaluator if we had worked to include these standards in the project. In fact we had been in numerous conversations with the Navajo Department of Education regarding the future of these standards to perhaps someday, if not yet, trump Arizona state content and pedagogy standards. Tribal sovereignty over education has been a significant part of our work and its complex development an essential part of Guy's academic study (Senese, 1991). Tribal spokespersons described tribal sovereignty as a work in progress, as were the standards, which, when we were doing the grant, had not yet been formally adopted, even by the tribe. Tribal members also described the effort as "symbolic" on the way to enforcement. The Navajo standards are a rhetorical exercise in using language to create a new possibility in the future. The standards were not at that time a functioning force that could have served as leverage for a different program outline. In the one course that was required and reflected our goals, School and Society, I (Guy) altered the syllabus and assigned the Navajo standards to review and discuss. The evaluation makes note of a student comment on how we talked more about "politics" than culture. That's true. I was always concerned that "culture" as a construct was heavy on life-ways, fraught with oversimplified assumptions, and light on analyses of power. I maintain this concern in thinking about cultural responsiveness writ large.

The Problem With Appearances

Here we reflect on a comment in the evaluation about the appearance of classrooms visited by the evaluator and the signatures of neocolonialism.

> The intended and unintended consequences of the ITP program provide yet another space where colonialism rears its head. . . . I was struck by how similar many of the classrooms looked and especially by the " typicality" and White-ness of most of the classroom décor. (Anonymous, 2012, p. 15)

These were classrooms led by Navajo teachers in the Navajo nation. The evaluator mourns that of the seven classrooms she visited, only one had any significant Navajo décor, and this somehow becomes a program problem, not one for the Navajo education office. We appreciate this observation, but are also aware that one of the cultural values expressed in Native school board meeting after meeting is intertwined with a political economic goal and is the nearly desperate desire to see their children compete for a share in the opportunities of the dominant culture. This, coupled with tremendous cultural pride, presents a terrible impasse: an expressed assumption is that in a zero-sum credential and achievement competition, more time on culture and language sacrifices more dominant culture skills that are needed for success in higher education and a way out of the desperate precariousness of poverty or near poverty. Yet dominant culture skills can also become a one-way ticket to family and culture estrangement. This reality does not fit neatly into many White liberal academics' list of approved cultural expressions, for it is deeply entwined in the complex process of parents' calculations about the relationship between what schooling is and the life chances of their children. Academics say, "It's not a zero-sum game, you can have culture and language *and* have better standard education." Many bilingual educators agree and their arguments have not been ignored by Navajo politicians and education opinion leaders. Yet the politics on the ground are not so simple.

We agree that what is endangered is the dream that students, through culture and language, could learn what they need for cultural, political, and employment success. We spent 3 years in a best effort to encourage that within serious constraints. But Navajo politics is not homogenous or some indigenous dream world, unaffected by the lived histories of all involved. It's easy to look for Indian art on bulletin boards, but not so easy to find it in a deep relationship, bordering on two worlds, among a child, a parent, and a Diné teacher, during and after school, expressing all the nuances of lived culture in the now. It's not easy to put in an article either, and maybe not the proper place of an outsider to say what represents culture.

Our dream amidst the realities we faced was interpreted as cultural neglect by the evaluator. It was presented in the article not as a fluid pathway being created, but as a road not taken, and evidence of the colonialist, Eurocentric identity of two of the four co-PIs. The actions of our Navajo partners, advancing the same goals, who also had to contend with state standards, were not mentioned.

Outer Limits of Identity

The following extended quote from the evaluation (Anonymous, 2008) is pointed and, we believe, not disingenuous:

> The most frequently cited weakness in the program cited by Ałchini Bá participants was the lack of information about how to be culturally responsive teachers who were able to integrate Navajo language and culture into their classrooms. Almost every participant mentioned this concern and their desire to have more of this emphasis within the program. (p. 6)

Anonymous (2008) concludes,

> This is obviously an area that would require cooperation and buy-in from other faculty at NAU who teach courses, but if a future grant is pursued and the program is set up so that students enroll in all the same courses at the same time, this could open up very powerful opportunities for scaffolding across the teacher preparation curriculum. (p. 7)

We agree. A complete reorganization of the teacher education program toward these goals is required. To do so takes presence, time, and politics. Anonymous (2012) provides the following:

> The ITP program would have needed cooperation and buy-in from other faculty at SU who teach education courses. This kind of cooperation could have opened up powerful opportunities... Unfortunately, rather than seizing these opportunities, the SU teacher preparation program remained unchanged.... we might think of this as a sort of programmatic assimilation. (p. 12)

When the initial indigenous teacher preparation grant, the Hopi Teachers for Hopi Schools Program, was written, I (Carolyne) was the chair of the department that housed the teacher education program. Creating buy-in from the existing faculty members for the creation of more culturally responsive teacher education courses was one of my goals. This kind of institutional change is not simple to create nor is it simple to see the changes that have been occurring when one is a relatively new faculty member. To begin to access this institutional change, one would need to, at a minimum, speak with each faculty member. It is easy to pronounce that this *should have* happened, not so easy to acknowledge how it is *already happening* within pockets that can be easily overlooked when one of the places from which you look is a realized theoretical ideal rather than a process of *becoming*.

During the implementation of Alch'i'ni Ba, we too wished for more faculty, including Native faculty, engagement in the project. We had to contend with the potential damage done in required courses taught by faculty who were unrepentant antimulticulturalists, with advertisements to that effect in their course syllabi and on their office doors. Advising students to avoid such faculty when possible and mitigating racism were parts of our work in the project.

Waiting for Superprogram and What We Got

We did and do wish that there were undergraduate formal classes and integral parts of the teacher education program which could be developed for credit and that would be intensive in the culture teaching discussed above. It would require more than a scaffold. One of us, Senese, spent several years working on a campus committee in solidarity with Indigenous faculty and others to develop an Indigenous Studies program. Despite much lobbying, hours of meetings, and campus politicking, our efforts to connect this new major to the education program did not succeed. To fulfill our ideal of an Indigenous teacher education program would be a project for a generation and would require a radical reinvention of a teacher education certification process that is more flexible and more connected to an ideological shift away from standardized "evidence-" or "research-" based competencies toward cultural competence that is not added on but integral to teacher excellence. We share that dream. We worked to incorporate this impulse wherever we could. We continue to work toward this possibility, now in separate settings, against what was then a rising and is now, in 2013, a cresting tidal wave of curricular conformity, especially in those courses which meet state and "professional" certification standards.

Rightful is the criticism of a college that pays lip service to Native Education but is largely numb to any approaches which challenge the status quo, especially in the lockstep undergraduate curriculum. However, except for a few courageous teachers, most are subservient to the homogeneity of neoliberal standardization agendas which have outlawed a true bilingual education.

Another recommendation reads as follows:

SU and the ITP program might turn to the Navajo Nation as a sovereign governmental entity for guidance about how to conceptualize and implement a teacher preparation program that is culturally responsive and relevant to Diné communities. (Anonymous, 2012, p. 17)

The Navajo Nation was a partner in the project, and a Diné community school was a partner in the project. Both partners were actively involved in the creation and implementation of the project.

We will list just a few of the extracurricular experiences designed to bring the importance and value of Navajo culture home to the program participants. We offered a special section of the required social foundations of education course, where the entire focus of the course was upon dimensions of tribal history and the politics of sovereignty. In hindsight, that might have been used better as a time to teach Navajo history and culture. We might have further stretched the boundaries of the course description beyond what other students were getting.

We did several weekend sessions in a ceremonial space on campus (hogan)[5] where the school board president, and medicine man for the Birds Springs area, lectured in traditional manner to the students. In hindsight, we might have requested that more of these lectures were done in English. Yet I recall more fluent students saying that the frustration of not knowing the language in these sessions might be a spur to some, and they might have more desire to pursue formal and informal study and practice of their mother language.

Students attended several school board meetings at Little Singer. They had considerable interaction with Navajo children and parents at school events, before and after school. That informal time was built in to reinforce the importance of community and culture. The school itself was selected because of its congruence with our goals. It was and is different from many of the other local schools in that its mission was explicit regarding local control of curriculum to the extent practical and possible. It was up front regarding the importance of Navajo culture in school and in activities which had always included exposure to Navajo music, dance, ceremony, and values.

We made a special effort to connect students to a more global sense of indigenous schooling. We created an extended visit to *Annuenue*, a Hawaiian-language immersion school. In preparation for this visit, we had many discussions regarding the different trajectory of Native Hawaiian and Native American schools, including their own, regarding language "immersion," teaching entire academic subjects in the indigenous language. We remember the powerful day we spent with the principal of that school touring the classrooms where not a single word on the boards was in English. We tried not to read too much into the symbolism of décor, but we could not ignore the school lessons in science and language that were written in the Hawaiian language alone. We are strengthened by the memory of awe expressed by students for whom this was unforgettable.

Within this chapter, we have not provided an exhaustive list of the efforts that were made to "respond" to culture in the program. We share with the student quoted above the frustration that too many of their academic courses in education did not provide adequate experience in culture. We accept the notion that we might have made some different choices to maximize the limited instructional and informal time we had. We reject however the usefulness of a critique that rests on a foundation of a naïve understanding and misapplication of the colonial experience, assimilationism, and cultural essentialism, and is numb to the nuances and complexities of cross-cultural community building, not to mention more "academic" dimensions of hybridity, heteronormativity, and cultural contingency.

We also note, sadly, that more detail about the efforts, over and above the standard curriculum, to foster culture and community were ignored in the effort to fit this "research" into a simplistic theoretical and practical "shoe." We worked under federal project guidelines and within the confines of teacher accreditation in the state of Arizona. Anonymous (2008) reflects on the confines and "pressures" that accompany such an effort:

> The Alch'i'ni Ba program, like its counterparts across the country, suffers from a number of inherent potential tensions...This difficulty was articulated by one staff member in the following way: "we're trying to take students where they are and invite them to problematize all the things they take for granted.... How do you rethink what it means to teach in a way that is culturally compatible and culturally honoring?"...In two short years, though, how much "more" is really possible given the challenges involved in a program like Alch'i'ni Ba? (Anonymous, 2008, p. 19)

Anonymous (2012) continues with what becomes the central and surprising conclusion in the journal article:

> From the very beginning of the ITP program's conceptual development, the program already was struggling to fully reject the dominant teacher preparation paradigm. In other words, even through its goals and development, the ITP program was "struggling to fully reject, while exuding and advancing assimilation and colonialism." (p. 10)

We felt put in a category that includes the Indian Boarding School pioneers or someone like, say, Kit Carson, "Struggling to fully reject." No, we simply were working hard to get more Navajo teachers in the classroom to honor and accelerate learning in otherwise disregarded elements of culture, and help them learn and graduate. As for "exuding and advancing colonialism," mostly I (Guy) remember struggling to fully reject the fact that the phone was ringing at midnight and I had to meet Security to vouch for a student who was locked out of his/her apartment. Mostly I just remember trying to keep up, while busily helping plan weekly organizational meetings, picking up the vegetable tray, or running interference with department chairs to get somebody a class overload.

I (Carolyne) work to subvert the dominant teacher education paradigm. It is impossible to *fully reject* a paradigm that all of us are always already inside of; the state education standards our graduates are legally bound to teach toward are clearly embedded in this paradigm. The work of teachers requires *negotiation* of this paradigm, not simple rejection. It requires developing a vision through the dark glass of political and educational opportunity under a sun that, without the colonial legacy, would shine very differently.

And a memory on the complexity of developing such "vision" within a Navajo cultural context: The old minibus that carried our (Guy's) family from Illinois, died in Gallup 200 miles from our destination, Rough Rock, where we were heading to teach. The school sent a couple of men out to help us. My wife, myself, and our cranky 1-year-old rode back with them. I remember how helpless I felt, and grateful that they were willing to do this. I also remember going out jogging a few weeks after arriving past a place called "Cone Hill." That day running, one of those same guys, who would become a friend, stopped his truck and told me not to go near the hill. "Why not?" I shouted back, smiling gamely. He laughed and said, "Because you could go blind." He drove off. "Superstition," I thought. Two years later, I was going nowhere near it. And without a doubt, 33 years later, regarding culture and memory, there are things I can see and things I can't.

Contracting for a Culturally Responsive Evaluation

We did not give enough careful thought and attention to the evaluation of Alch'i'ni Ba. We now see that a contract that delineated all of our expectations could have created a different outcome. We could have required that this be a collaborative process that included crafting the inquiry together as a "situated response" (see Hermes, 1998), grounded in the community. We could have worked collectively to craft authentic inquiries with the project participants, and those inquiries could have had an intent of being *educative* and *transformative* rather than the conventional practice of interviewing that leaves participants *describing* and *reporting upon* opinions that may not have been critically considered and yet through the interview and reporting process become reified. What if culturally responsive evaluation activity functioned more in the domain of "stretching the mind?" Instead of "getting comfortable with our learned frameworks," Jamshed Bharucha (2008) issues a provocative invitation:

> Learn to keep stretching your mind, keep stepping outside your comfort zone, keep venturing beyond the familiar, keep trying to put yourself in the shoes of others whose frameworks or cultures are alien to you, and have an open mind to different ways of parsing the world. Before you critique a new idea, or another culture, master it to the point at which its proponents or members recognize that you get it. (p. 1)

Genuinely "Informed" Consent

Rather than extending the "informed" consent of all who agreed to be interviewed for the program evaluation into using our words in a journal article, why was our colleague unable to see the necessity of asking us about using our words for a new purpose? What blinded her to the harm created when we read our words, our work, and our career-long commitments to indigenous self-determination, refashioned and thrown into a theoretical framework that defined all of it as colonial, turned into fodder to support an academic argument with no acknowledgement of the impossibility of "confidentiality" when she writes that this is a program housed at the university where she works? McTaggart (1991, p. 15) asks, "Should the public's 'right to know' take precedence over the individuals' rights to 'own the facts about their own lives?'" A different possibility of engaging an evaluation inquiry while writing an article collaboratively, inviting a larger academic community into our different perspectives, and doing no harm, could be pursued. This approach could provide the opportunity for *dialogue* among stakeholders "through which the *real* or authentic *interests*, as compared to the perceived interests, of diverse stakeholders are identified" (Greene, 2006, p. 123). Such dialogue increases the likelihood of evaluation being "relationally responsible practice" (see Abma & Widdershovem, 2011).

"All Our Relations"

What if culturally responsive evaluation work were grounded in a space of relatedness to a community of stakeholders seeking more equitable and culturally honoring practices? From an indigenous perspective, *trust, relatedness,* and *community* trump a Eurocentric focus upon scientific evidence. Conducting evaluation work from *relatedness,* what might be different? (See Martin & Glesne, 2002.)

Being Navajo is an ongoing, moment-to-moment creation. There is no definitive way to be Navajo or to be a culturally responsive Navajo teacher or to conduct a culturally responsive evaluation. Let us consider our *listening* when we engage in evaluation work. What if the program participants' requests for more preparation for being culturally responsive teachers was heard as a program success, understood from an appreciation of what it takes to generate that kind of commitment with students who have been educated in predominantly Eurocentric public schools and often taught by teachers who give no value to "cultural responsiveness?" What if the Alch'i'ni Ba participants had been listened to as powerful educators who are literally creating what "culturally responsive teaching" can be every day in their classrooms? This is a creative, transformative process of *discovery* that cannot be taught like information. The complex reality of being a culturally responsive Navajo teacher includes the possibility of teaching to 30 different "cultures" in a classroom of students who all say they are Navajo. This is the space of artistic creation, a space similar in kind to the difference between the discourse of a grant proposal where you are imagining what you plan to deliver and the discourse of the practice you are able to deliver within the unpreviously imagined constraints and possibilities of life as it is lived.

Working Against Colonialism

This is a cautionary tale regarding critiques of "dominant culture" influence in indigenous community programming which involves "dominant culture institutions," which themselves emerge solidly from within the same institutional confines. These are the same environments that spawn, in their production-model research requirements, rushes to research judgment, distortions of evaluation data, doing double duty, like a reversible belt, as both evaluation results and research findings. While laboring to criticize a project for its culturally responsive weaknesses, and "White," "colonialist" collaboration, by providing an oppositional, unidimensional critical perspective, such research is itself a colonial production. It is confrontational yet secretive, conforming to a standard drawn from a theoretical world, a perfect model of academic production efficiency.

CONCLUSION: "GENUINE SERVICE REQUIRES HUMILITY"

Yes it does. A mix of the good news and the bad news characterizes the evaluation. The research article that followed the evaluation report is more serious and problematic. First, it represents the troubling publication of evaluation results without knowledge or permission of the project stakeholders and investigators. Thus, the evaluation data are now in public view, accompanied by claims and opinions of the author without the benefit of other perspectives. Beyond that, the article itself exposes a certain evasion if not outright dishonesty in the evaluation. There the reasons to celebrate cited in the evaluation disappear in an effort to expose what the author believes is the investigators' neglect of the "assimilationist" and "colonialist" approaches that the program, despite its goals, was "sucked back into." (Anonymous, 2012, p. 5).

In a final quote from the journal article:

> But if Indigenous teacher preparation efforts are to truly reject colonialism and advance sovereignty and self-determination within tribal communities, they cannot be constrained by larger systems of assimilation, White supremacy, and imperialism. It may be tempting, then, to throw our hands up in despair and conclude that the goal of preparing culturally responsive Indigenous teachers for Indigenous schools is impossible. This, however, is not what I am suggesting, nor is it what TribalCrit and my data suggest. Instead, I want to suggest that "genuine service requires humility" and recognition that good intentions and symbolic or surface-level changes are not enough to change centuries-old systems of colonization. Thus when programs like ITP operate within systems led and defined by predominantly white institutions, they cannot lead to the transcendent change required by TribalCrit and needed by the Dine. But if we keep in mind the words of the ITP graduate who explained they "prepared me to be a teacher, but not a culturally responsive Navajo teacher for Navajo kids" and we center the Navajo Nation's ideas about what Dine education ought to look like, programs such as ITP may come closer to fulfilling the goals of culturally responsive schooling and, ultimately, facilitating tribal nation' goals of self-determination through self-education. (Anonymous, 2012, p. 18)

We all stand somewhere amid the ruined blend of greed, desperation, ignorance, desire, fear, and evil that characterizes human exploitation and dispossession—that legacy of the colonial. Even so, we are compelled to do whatever we can do and working within that space, we did what we did, however imperfectly. We truly hope those 12 students, and the hundred, perhaps thousands, they will impact, go on to do well, and good, with political and cultural energy that, without this program, would likely not have existed.

NOTES

1. The Project Goals included
    a. Initiate a culturally responsive site-based undergraduate program and one-year intensive induction program leading to degree and certification for Navajo elementary and middle school educators.

    b. Provide training for preservice teachers and mentors in collaborative methods of teaching, mentoring skills, and teamwork practices.

    c. Develop an integrated, experiential, elementary and middle school teacher education curriculum for preparing culturally reflective practitioners for Navajo schools.

    d. Disseminate the results of the project to relevant international, national, state, and local audiences.

2. Here we acknowledge the generous assistance of our friend and colleague Corrine Glesne for thoughtful critique and feedback.

3. We acknowledge the generous assistance of our friend and colleague, Corinne Glesne, in helping us to navigate these risky waters. She read several drafts of this chapter and lovingly guided us in choosing our words carefully.

4. According to the U.S. Department of Education (2009), National Center for Educational Statistics, the college dropout rate among Native American students is nearly 60%. Regarding high school matriculation and the possibility of higher education, the national public school graduation rate for the class of 2010 reached 74.7%, rising nearly 2 full percentage points from the previous year and 8 points in the past decade. Much of the nation's improvement since 2000 has been driven by strong gains for historically underserved groups. Graduation rates for Latino students have skyrocketed 16 percentage points over this period, reaching 68% for the class of 2010. Rates for Black students, now at 62%, have risen 13 points. Graduation rates for White and Asian students—now at 80% and 81%, respectively—have increased at a slower pace. In a partial exception to the general upward trend, Native American students have experienced only modest improvements since 2000 and have seen their rates decline since 2008.

5. The word *hogan* means"home" or "the home place." It is a one-room, traditional Navajo structure built of logs and mud with an entrance that faces east.

REFERENCES

Abma, T. A., & Widdershoven, G. A. M. (2011). Evaluation as a relationally responsible practice. In N. K. Denzin & Y. Lincoln (Eds.), *The Sage handbook of qualitative research* (pp. 669-680). Thousand Oaks, CA: Sage

Anonymous. (2008). *A final evaluation discussion of the Alchini Ba program.* Unpublished evaluation report.

Anonymous. (2012). *Article with data from the Alch'i'ni Ba evaluation.* Unpublished evaluation report.

Barad, K. (2007). *Meeting the universe halfway: Quantum physics and the entanglement of matter and meaning.* Durham, NC: Duke University Press.

Bharucha, J. (2008). Education as stretching the mind. *Edge World Question Center.* Retrieved from http://www.edge.org/q2008/q08_16.html#bharucha

Greene, J. (2006). Evaluation, democracy and social change. In I. Shaw, J. Greene, & M. Mark (Eds.), *The Sage handbook of evaluation* (pp. 118–140). Thousand Oaks, CA: Sage.

Hermes, M. (1998). Research methods as a situated response: Towards a First Nations' methodology. *Qualitative studies in education, 11*(1), 155–168.

Hermes, M. (2005). "Ma'iingan is just a misspelling of the word wolf": A case for teaching culture through language. *Anthropology and education quarterly, 36*(1), 43–56.

Martin, P., & Glesne, C. (2002). From the global village to the pluriverse? "Other" ethics for cross-cultural qualitative research. *Ethics, Place and Environment, 5*(3), 205–221.

McTaggert, R. (1991). When democratic evaluation doesn't seem democratic. *Evaluation Practice, 12*(1), 9–21.

Senese, G. B. (1991). *Self-determination and the social education of Native Americans.* New York, NY: Praeger.

Smith, L. T. (2012). *Decolonizing methodologies: Research and indigenous peoples* (2nd ed.). London, UK: Zed.

St. Pierre, E. A. (2011). Refusing human being in humanist qualitative inquiry. In N. K. Denzin & M. D. Giardina (Eds.), *Qualitative inquiry and global crisis* (pp. 40–55). Walnut Creek, CA: Left Coast.

U.S. Department of Education. (2009). *The condition of education 2009* (NCES 2009-081). Washington DC: National Center for Education Statistics.

Vizenor, G. (1995). Measuring my blood. In G. Vizenor (Ed.), *Native American literature: A brief introduction and anthology* (pp. 299–336). Berkeley: University of California/HarperCollins College.

White, C. J. (2006) Humble and humbling research: A modest witnessing. In N. K. Denzin & M. D. Giardina (Eds.), *Qualitative inquiry and the conservative challenge.* Walnut Creek: CA: Left Coast.

White, C. J., & Hermes, M. (2005). Learning to play scholarly jazz: An exploration into indigenous methods for a culturally responsive evaluation. In S. Hood, R. Hopson, & H. Frierson (Eds.), *The role of culture and cultural context: A mandate for inclusion, the discovery of truth and understanding in evaluative theory and practice.* Greenwich, CT: Information Age.

White, C. J., Paymella, H., & Nuvayouma, D. (2003). Hopi teachers for Hopi schools: Collaborating to seed educational change. In D. McInerney & S. Van Etten (Eds.), *Sociocultural influences and teacher education programs: Research on sociocultural research on motivation and learning* (pp. 85–100). Greenwich, CT: Information Age.

SECTION IV

CLAIMING NEW TERRITORIES OF CRE:
CULTURALLY SPECIFIC METHODS, APPROACHES,
AND ECOLOGIES

CHAPTER 13

A TRANSFORMATIVE FRAMEWORK FOR CULTURALLY RESPONSIVE EVALUATION

Donna M. Mertens
Independent Consultant

Heather Zimmerman
Gallaudet University

Given that many evaluations are conducted on programs that are designed to address disparities in indicators of quality of life (e.g., health, education, safe environments), evaluators have become more aware of the need to integrate a strong stance on social justice into their work. In this chapter, we explore philosophical, theoretical, and methodological contributions by scholars who engage with the issues associated with culture and social justice in the context of evaluation by means of a broad philosophical tent that encompasses the tenets of culturally responsive evaluation (Hood, Hopson, & Frierson, 2005) and can be used to organize diverse theoretical and methodological stances that emanate from multiple cultural positionalities. As part of this ongoing

Continuing the Journey to Reposition Culture and Cultural Context
in Evaluation Theory and Practice, pages 275–287
Copyright © 2015 by Information Age Publishing
275

conversation, we offer the transformative paradigm as one organizing framework for philosophically grounding evaluation work that addresses equity and strives to create positive social change by consciously addressing racially based discrimination as well as discrimination based on other dimensions of diversity. The transformative paradigm provides an overarching philosophical umbrella that incorporates dimensions of diversity that are used as a basis for discrimination and oppression; culturally responsive evaluation is an approach to evaluation that is commensurate with the philosophical assumptions of the transformative paradigm (Mertens & Wilson, 2012). However, culturally responsive evaluation grew out of a focus on race/ethnicity and has not explicitly tackled the intersectionality of discriminatory dimensions of diversity. Thus, the territory shared by the transformative paradigm and culturally responsive evaluation is large; the additional perspectives gained from putting culturally responsive evaluation in conversation with a transformative philosophical framework is the subject of this chapter.

Philosophical frameworks for thinking about evaluation provide a way to organize assumptions about the meaning of ethics and the nature of reality, knowledge, and systematic inquiry. The evaluation world operates with several philosophical frameworks that are associated with different branches of evaluation (Alkin, 2012; Mertens & Wilson, 2012). The transformative paradigm is associated with the Social Justice branch of evaluation and provides a framework that is rooted in the ethical principle of human rights, thus leading to methodological implications that are commensurate with a culturally responsive approach to evaluation. The basic assumptions of the transformative paradigm in terms of axiological, ontological, epistemological, and methodological concepts are explained, and linkages are provided between the philosophical assumptions and application of culturally responsive evaluations. Sample studies provide illustrations of how the transformative paradigm is used to frame evaluations that use a culturally responsive approach based on evaluations in the deaf community and in international development contexts.

Social justice should not be limited to one branch of or approach to evaluation. We argue that social justice should be incorporated into all evaluations regardless of one's philosophical approach. However, members of marginalized communities make clear that they have not experienced evaluation as it was practiced on them to be responsive to the power differentials and political contexts that sustain an oppressive status quo (Chilisa, 2012; Cram, 2009; Mertens, Cram, & Chilisa, 2013; Mertens & Wilson, 2012). Social justice is a human rights issue and calls for individuals within our interconnected global society to take social responsibility and address injustice, oppressive privilege, and inequity by employing culturally responsive methodologies. Culturally responsive evaluation is commensurate with transformative philosophical assumptions, as can be seen in this description of CRE:

CRE is a theoretical, conceptual, and inherently political position that includes the centrality of and attune to culture in the theory and practice of evaluation. That is, CRE recognizes that demographic, sociopolitical, and contextual dimensions, locations, perspectives, and characteristics of culture matter fundamentally in evaluation. Those who use CRE understand and value lived experiences that help to (re)define, (re)interpret, and make sense in everyday life. By privileging notions of lived experiences and especially regarding communities and populations of color or indigenous groups, new explanations and understandings of evaluands, programs, and phenomena of study emerge. (Hopson, 2009, p. 433)

Thus, the overlap between the transformative assumptions and CRE tenets are clear in terms of the emphasis on culture, value attached to lived experience, sociopolitical and contextual dimensions, and challenging deficit perspectives. However, CRE grew out of attention to issues of race and ethnicity, thus its focus has been on addressing those dimensions of diversity. The transformative paradigm, on the other hand, encompasses issues of race and ethnicity, but also raises up other dimensions of diversity that are used as a basis of discrimination, such as gender, disability, deafness, religion, economic status, immigrant/refugee status, and age. CRE can be considered an approach or a model and as a "system or culmination of practical strategies and frameworks that attend to culture during the various stages and phases of an evaluation" (Hopson, 2009, p. 433). The transformative paradigm in contrast is a philosophical framing for evaluation that is made up of assumptions that guide thinking about evaluation from a human rights and social justice perspective and is commensurate with theories and approaches that hold similar values. Thus, this exploration of the overlap and differences between the transformative paradigm and CRE provides a platform for advancing understandings of how evaluators can be responsive to the intersectionality of dimensions of diversity that are used as a basis for discrimination.

TRANSFORMATIVE PARADIGM AND CRE: CONNECTIONS AND COMMITMENTS

Guba and Lincoln (2005) provided the evaluation community with a useful framework for depicting the philosophical assumptions that undergird decisions about ethics and methods in evaluations in the form of paradigms. Paradigms are constituted by four sets of assumptions:

- Axiology about the nature of ethics
- Ontology about the nature of reality

- Epistemology about the nature of knowledge and the relationship between the evaluator and the stakeholders
- Methodology about the nature of systematic inquiry.

This structure is used to organize a description of the transformative paradigm and to discuss the methodological implications of this paradigm for culturally responsive evaluation practice.

Axiology

The transformative axiological assumption begins with explicit acknowledgement that the role of evaluation is to support human rights and social justice. To this end, evaluators are called upon to act in ways that are respectful of the diversity of cultural groups involved in the evaluation. The American Evaluation Association's *Guiding Principles* (2004) and their *Statement on Cultural Competence* (2011) clearly establish the responsibilities of evaluators in this regard. AEA revised its Guiding Principles to include specific reference to include the following statement with regard to competence:

> To insure recognition, accurate interpretation and respect for diversity, evaluators should ensure that the members of the evaluation team collectively demonstrate cultural competence. Cultural competence would be reflected in evaluators seeking awareness of their own culturally-based assumptions, their understandings of the worldviews of culturally-different participants and stakeholders in the evaluation, and the use of appropriate evaluation strategies and skills in working with culturally different groups. Diversity may be in terms of race, ethnicity, gender, religion, socio-economics, or other factors pertinent to the evaluation context. (AEA, 2004)

AEA (2011, para. 2) extended its commitment to cultural competence in its cultural competency statement in which it states, "Cultural competence in evaluation theory and practice is critical for the profession and for the greater good of society." This theme is continued in the policy statement in terms of the recommended practices for evaluators that include acknowledging the complexity of cultural identity and recognizing the dynamics of power.

These practices are mirrored in the transformative axiological assumption in that cultural respect is paramount; by implication, evaluators need to be cognizant of the cultures in which they are working and the diversity of ways that culture is manifest. This understanding provides the basis for using the evaluation process to identify and address inequities in order to support human rights. In addition, the transformative paradigm calls upon the evaluator to give consideration to how the evaluation can further social change in the name of justice. A part of this consideration includes giving thought to reciprocity; that is, what do the stakeholders gain as a result of participating in the evaluation? Culturally responsive evaluators have led the way in understanding the meaning of working in communities marginalized because of race, ethnicity, and indigeneity (Cram, 2009; Hopson, 2009). The transformative framework stimulates discussion about the meaning of culture in other types of communities such as the deaf community and disability communities. This would lead to such questions as, how can evaluators work with members of these marginalized communities in culturally appropriate ways for social change? And, how do we justly honor culture and indigenous ways of knowing, especially in contexts in which cultural practices are oppressive to human rights? A cultural practice that oppresses the right to communication in their own language is seen in the denial of access to sign language for deaf people because some hearing people believe deaf people should read lips and vocalize. Other examples of cultural beliefs that are oppressive are those that condone violence against women and deny access to education for people with disabilities.

Ontology

Ontology is the branch of philosophy that addresses the nature of reality. Is there one reality that is out there waiting to be discovered or measured? Or are there multiple socially constructed realities that require interactions between evaluators and stakeholders in order for them to be known? The transformative paradigm holds that there are multiple versions of reality and that these versions come from different societal positionalities. Versions of reality are influenced by such characteristics as race/ethnicity, poverty, gender, sexual identity, disability, deafness, indigeneity, immigration status, religion, age, and many other factors. CRE has brought to visibility the differences in competing explanations of disparities between dominant and marginalized racial and indigenous communities (Cram, McCreanor, Smith, Nairn, & Johnstone, 2006; Hopson, 2009).

Based on the transformative ontological assumption, the crucial responsibility for the evaluator is to design methods that are sensitive to the different versions of reality and that make these visible along with the consequences associated with giving privilege to one version of reality over another. For example, some hearing people say to deaf people, "Why don't you just get a cochlear implant?" This version of reality reflects the hearing person's assumption that it is better to be hearing and that everyone wants to be hearing. Some deaf people have a strong cultural identity with the deaf community and feel that a question such as that posed above is equivalent to asking a Black person, "Why don't you bleach your skin so you can be White?" From this example, it is apparent that there is a sense of superiority and privilege associated with the dominant culture. The evaluator has a responsibility to understand reality from the perspective of all stakeholders and to bring to light the inherent audism, racism, or other isms present in some versions of realities and the harm that they can do.

Epistemology

The transformative epistemological assumption builds on the prior assumptions in that the experiences of all stakeholders, especially those from marginalized communities, need to be considered at every stage of the evaluation, from the conceptualization of the intervention to the diversity of the target population, to decisions about data collection, analysis, interpretation and use. CRE scholars deepened understandings about working in communities marginalized on the basis of race and ethnicity by bringing in the lenses of critical theories and decolonizing epistemologies (Hopson, 2009). Indigenous scholars have also expanded understandings of culturally, historically, and contextually rooted epistemologies in their own lands (Chilisa, 2012; Cram, 2009). Thus, the transformative epistemological assumption is enhanced by the specific race and indigenous contributions in terms of epistemology; these expanded understandings of the nature of relationships that create knowledge lead to specific implications for methodological decisions.

Based on both the transformative paradigm and CRE, evaluators need to adopt strategies that allow them to address inequities and to do so in a culturally respectful manner through the development of an interactive, honest, and trusting relationship with stakeholders. This brings to the fore questions of the identity of the evaluator in relation to the community. CRE raises questions about the importance of the evaluator sharing racial, ethnic, or indigenous roots. However, the transformative paradigm asks a broader set of questions, such as: Which salient characteristics of the community are shared with the evaluator; which are not? What are the implications of these similarities and differences? Is there more than one preferred language in the community? If so, who uses which language? If the evaluator is not skilled in the nondominant language, what steps are taken to insure that effective communication is possible? Thinking that having an interpreter in such cases is sufficient to address this issue oversimplifies the issue (Harris, Holmes, & Mertens, 2009). There is a need to address issues of power and trust and to recognize the historical and social location of knowledge.

Methodology

No specific methodology is associated with the transformative paradigm; however, there are principles that can guide evaluators in this regard.

Methodologies need to be able to be responsive to the complexity of cultures and to contribute to social change. Therefore, a dialogic process is useful at the beginning and throughout the methodology of an evaluation. By meaningful and appropriate dialogue with community members, evaluators can establish the context and the factors within specific contexts that require attention. This leads to decisions about the best type of data to collect in a cyclical manner; results of those decisions are fed back into representative groups of community members in order to inform next steps. This is akin to the process used in action research, although the mechanisms for feeding back information and the constitution of the groups may change at different points in the life cycle of the program.

Commonly, the use of mixed methods in the form of combining quantitative and qualitative data collection is found to be helpful for transformative evaluations. For example, identification of cultural complexity at the early stages of the project can be informed by looking at statistical data in the form of demographics and incidence disaggregated by various groups, as well as by qualitative approaches involving interviewing and observing members of the community. This first stage of data collection and analysis can be used as the basis for developing a pilot intervention that is culturally appropriate as well as for refining data collection methods that are also appropriate to the diverse cultural groups.

CRE and indigenous scholarship have contributed to understandings of methodologies that are responsive to cultures, languages, and social practices (Hopson, 2009). This has taken the form of indigenous communities exercising more control over who can do evaluations, establishing ethical guidelines and protocols, and incorporating reciprocity and capacity building in evaluation partnerships. These aspects of methodology align with those supported within the transformative paradigm. Members of the American Sign Language community have also developed methodologically based terms of reference that define culturally responsive evaluation practice in their community (Harris et al., 2009).

In the next section, we provide examples of two evaluation studies that illustrate the application of the assumptions of the transformative assumptions with reference to alignment with CRE principles to the evaluation of programs conducted with members of marginalized communities. These include Promundo and colleagues' program in Brazil that uses a school-based approach for engaging boys and girls in reducing gender-based violence and promoting greater support for gender equality (Barker et al., 2012); and a cultural and economic development program for deaf women in India (Kiyaga, 2003).

TRANSFORMATIVE CULTURALLY RESPONSIVE
EVALUATION STUDIES

Gender Inequality in Brazil

Barker et al.'s (2012) evaluation of Promundo, the International Center for Research on Women, and CARE International's school-based programs included programs in Brazil, the Balkans, and India. We use the evaluation in Brazil to illustrate the application of the transformative paradigm's principles by extending approaches beyond cultural responsiveness as emphasized in CRE to include gendered beliefs and practices that result in inequalities. The program and evaluation in Brazil began with an explicit gender justice and social justice lens, in keeping with CRE and the transformative paradigm's axiological assumption.

The school-based interventions were based on a review of contextual factors related to gender and culture, as well as on the results of prior evaluations of community-level programs that had been carried out with the same lens in the same countries. Hence, the cycle of evaluation began with the use of mixed methods data collection; qualitative data were collected on gender and cultural norms, while quantitative data were collected on the number of boys and girls completing school and the relationship between school completion and attitudes toward gender equity, along with the degree of effectiveness of the community-based interventions. The evaluators employed a "culturally relevant validated evaluation model (the GEM Scale—Gender-Equitable Men Scale) that seeks to measure the degree to which young men and women change their attitudes as a result of interventions" (Barker et al., 2012, p. 143) to measure changes in attitude toward gender equity. Results of the earlier evaluations supported the adaptation of the community-based strategies for the school-based interventions. These earlier evaluation results confirmed the importance of understanding that gender norms are not written in stone and can be challenged in the name of social justice. Thus, the evaluation helped make visible the versions of reality that exist in Brazil in terms of gender roles and how young people can, through activism, challenge those gender roles that are oppressive. A second example of versions of reality surfaced in the evaluation when the responses of young men and women were compared on the topic of the type of person young women would go out with. The young men worried that if they became more sensitive and gender equitable, young women would not want to go out with them because women prefer to date "bad boys." Data gathered from the young women confirmed that the young men were accurate in their concerns. The program developers used this information to add a segment to the young women's intervention that engaged them in critical discourse around this topic. This information from the evaluation became a critical piece of the puzzle for further development of the school-based intervention.

Epistemologically, young people were engaged in the evaluation in order to include an assessment of their engagement in activism and the extent to which they were able to use "their own preferred sources of information and cultural outlets in the community and craft messages—in the form of radio spots, billboards, posters, postcards, and dances . . . to be more gender-equitable" (Barker et al., 2012, p. 143). The evaluators thus showed respect for the young people, recognized their strengths, and used qualitative analysis of their information and messages as data to support the effectiveness of the program. They were able to provide data that "These campaigns encourage young men and women to reflect about how they act as men and women and enjoin them to respect their partners, not to use violence against women, and to practice safer sex" (Barker et al., 2012, p. 143). Given the findings from this part of the evaluation, the program developers agreed to adapt the strategies used in Brazil to the cultural contexts of other countries in the South, including India.

Methodologically, the evaluation expanded during the school-based intervention to incorporate evaluation of teacher training, youth participation, school campaigns by youth to promote nonviolence and reflections about gender norms, and 20 workshops with students over 10 weeks. The evaluation data confirm that

> jointly designing and implementing activities with teachers and students in schools generates a greater sense of ownership of the process, and enables programs to become institutionalized in the school curriculum. Part of this work has included transforming the culture of the classrooms to encourage collaborative learning that allows youth to question norms and behaviors, as well as to openly discuss sensitive issues (around sexuality and violence) with teachers and their peers. (Barker et al., 2012, p. 144)

In addition, transformative principles in the program and in its evaluation led to sharing results with policymakers, yielding accreditation by the Brazilian Ministry of Education for inclusion of this intervention in the curriculum. Ongoing evaluation results are shared with government and health officials to inform discussions about educating youth about sexuality (including HIV/AIDS) and gender norms. This focus on social transformation is an expansion of CRE and becomes possible because of the deep immersion within the culture of the communities in which the interventions and evaluation occur.

Deaf Women Foundation in India

In 2003, Nassozi Kiyaga from Uganda, a hearing graduate of Gallaudet University's International Development MA program, evaluated the Delhi Foundation of Deaf Women (DFDW) program. Kiyaga spent a total of 3 months evaluating the grassroots socioeconomic program. Indian deaf women founded the DFDW in 1973 in order to address the socioeconomic needs faced by deaf women in the Delhi area (Kiyaga, 2003). DFDW provides services such as matrimonial matchmaking for deaf women and deaf men; vocational artesian development; information, technology and computer training; early intervention services for deaf youth; and sociocultural activities for community members.

In keeping with CRE and the transformative paradigm, Kiyaga immersed herself in Indian deaf culture to learn Indian deaf cultural mores, norms, and Indian Sign Language (ISL) prior to conducting the study. She framed the study through a lens of human rights and social justice, with an awareness of power differences and diversity in the stakeholder groups involved in the program. In accord with CRE, she was particularly responsive to the linguistic differences in the stakeholder groups and demonstrated this by learning ISL and using multilingual interpreters who were competent in ASL, ISL, and spoken Hindi, Bengali, and Punjabi.

Kiyaga's use of qualitative methods illustrates the principle of CRE to privilege lived experiences. Her use of a multilingual approach and her use of ISL allowed deaf and hard-of-hearing respondents to express their experiences of the DFDW programs via the least restrictive language. Such commitment between the evaluator and stakeholders allowed Kiyaga to gain greater insight into systemic and cultural oppressive barriers deaf females experience within the metropolis. Moreover, Kiyaga designed all interviews with a sensitivity to reflect the heterogeneous experiences of participants, a principle of the transformative paradigm. For example, she considered the degree of hearing loss, age, length of involvement in DFDW, skills developed or not developed through DFDW, additional disabilities, religion, gender, vocational/educational background, and linguistic diversity. Furthermore, through using the transformative paradigm and culturally responsive approach, the evaluator was able to see the resourceful and creative determination deaf women demonstrated in constructing space for them to have meaningful participation in the community.

During the cultural-linguistic immersion period prior to Kiyaga's study, she observed participants' relationships and their interaction in their environment, which exhibited a "close-knit" and highly interactive society. In order to be culturally responsive, Kiyaga conducted focus group interviews (2 to 3 people per group). Kiyaga notes this method was almost always employed regardless of the hearing status of the evaluation participants.

Moreover, Kiyaga allowed participants to choose their preferred mode of communication during interviews. All interviews were hand-recorded or audiotaped dependent on the language used and were immediately transcribed after each session. Additionally, member checks were conducted with all participants. Each interview took approximately 90 minutes for two people to two hours for three people. Furthermore, to ensure accurate exchange and documentation during interview focus groups, Kiyaga employed two interpreters fluent in both the native sign language and English (the language of the study) during each interview. Interview respondents indicated that they received a range of benefits from the DFDW program. The highest of these was personal development (defined as confidence, self-esteem, identity, and independence), followed by communication mastery in Indian Sign Language, and employment (defined as self-sufficiency and earned wages).

By using qualitative methods, deaf women were provided a space to voice their stories and share them with focus group participants. The study documented this as a highly beneficial, affirmative, and inspirational aspect of focus groups. This study strongly exhibits how the evaluator used a transformative framework to develop the program theory and inquiry approach (Mertens, 2009). Additionally, the study demonstrates a keen observance and sensitivity to heterogeneous factors within the evaluand (see summary of study in Table 13.1). CRE scholarship aligns with the cultural issues raised in terms of Indian origin and use of appropriate languages, however, this perspective is enhanced by the transformative lens that raised issues related to deafness as a culture and how an evaluator can be responsive within that culture.

CONCLUSIONS

The transformative paradigm provides a philosophical framework that serves to guide thinking in evaluations with a goal of addressing issues of social justice and human rights. When evaluators start with this goal in mind, it influences each of their decisions throughout the conceptualization, planning, implementation, and use of evaluation findings. CRE approaches align with the philosophy of the transformative paradigm in that emphasis is placed on human rights. However, CRE is rooted in race/ethnicity and indigeneity as dimensions of diversity to be prioritized in evaluation practice. The theory and practice of CRE is highly relevant in the transformative paradigm and enriches thinking about how to address cultural complexity. In both CRE and the transformative paradigms, methodological decisions are made with a keen understanding of the need to be responsive to the complexity of the cultural context in which the evaluation takes place. This

TABLE 13.1 Transformative Assumptions and Delhi Foundation Evaluation

Transformative Paradigm and CRE	Delhi Foundation of Deaf Women (DFDW) program
Axiology	Evaluator took time to develop relationships with participants, observe/practice cultural mores, and learn Indian Sign Language. This demonstrates importance of cultural responsiveness and deaf people's rights to communication in their native language.
Ontology	Evaluator notes systemic and assumptive factors impacting oppression experienced by deaf women. Oppression can be culturally based and/or based on a person's inability to hear. Combining CRE and transformative lenses allows both aspects of oppression to surface and be made visible.
Epistemology	Evaluator recognized the need to establish a trusting relationship with participants and interpreters, as all were needed to work in tandem in order to gather data. CRE supports this type of relationship; transformative takes into account aspects of gender and deafness that might not surface otherwise.
Methodology	Employed qualitative methods such as focus groups of 2 to 3 interviewees per session to allow for ample time to gather accurate depictions of data and honor cultural norms. Both CRE and transformative support contextual analysis, which was very important in this study; in addition, transformative provides guidance for inclusion and support of deaf members of linguistic minority communities.

means that evaluators must establish respectful relationships based on trust with members of the community. The evaluation studies summarized in this chapter illustrate the methodological implications of the CRE approach when informed by the more expansive criteria for inclusion associated with the transformative paradigm. Evaluators took time to learn about the communities, establish respectful relationships and engage with community members to design appropriate evaluation strategies, review results, and facilitate the use of the results for positive social change.

If culture can be constructed in ways that are adverse to human rights and social justice, then transformative evaluators can work collaboratively to use evaluative ecologies as a platform for cultural deconstruction. Transformative culturally responsive evaluations go one step further to not just honor cultural ways of knowing and marginalized voices but seek to deconstruct the asymmetrical hegemony that prevents those voices from being heard and listened to.

The beauty of exploring the expanding boundaries of culturally responsive evaluation within the umbrella of the transformative paradigm rests in the potential to make visible aspects other than race, ethnicity, and indigeneity as cultural determinants. As illustrated by the case studies included in this chapter, evaluations that focus on cultural practices that discriminate on the basis of gender and international development with deaf communities increase the potential for evaluators to be part of a broader social change process.

REFERENCES

Alkin, M.C. (Ed.). (2012). *Evaluation roots* (2nd ed.). Thousand Oaks, CA: Sage.

American Evaluation Association (AEA). (2004). *Guiding principles for evaluators.* Washington, DC: American Evaluation Association.

American Evaluation Association (AEA). (2011, April 22). *American Evaluation Association statement on cultural competence in evaluation.* Washington, DC: American Evaluation Association. Retrieved from http://www.eval.org/p/cm/ld/fid=92

Barker, G., Verman, R., Crownover, J., Segundo, M., Fonseca, V., Contreras, J. M.,...Pawlak, P. (2012). Boys and education in the global south: Emerging vulnerabilities and new opportunities for promoting changes in gender norms. *Journal of Boyhood Studies, 6*(2), 137–150.

Chilisa, B. (2012). *Indigenous methodologies.* Thousand Oaks, CA: Sage.

Cram, F. (2009). Maintaining indigenous voices. In D. M. Mertens & P. Ginsberg (Eds.), *Handbook of social research ethics* (pp. 308–322). Thousand Oaks, CA: Sage.

Cram, C., McCreanor, T., Smith, L., Nairn, R., & Johnstone, W. (2006). Kaupapa Māori research and Pākehā social science: Epistemological tensions in a study of Māori health. *Hūlili, 3*, 41–68.

Guba, E., & Lincoln, Y. S. (2005). Paradigmatic controversies, contradictions, and emerging confluences. In N. K. Denzin & Y. S. Lincoln (Eds.) *The Sage handbook of qualitative research* (3rd ed., pp. 191–216). Thousand Oaks, CA: Sage.

Harris, R., Holmes, H., & Mertens, D. M. (2009). Research ethics in sign language communities. *Sign Language Studies, 9*(2), 104–131.

Hood, S., Hopson, R., & Frierson, H. (Eds.). (2005). *The role of culture and cultural context in evaluation: A mandate for inclusion, the discovery of truth, and understanding in evaluative theory and practice.* Greenwich, CT: Information Age.

Hopson, R. (2009). Reclaiming knowledge at the margins: Culturally responsive evaluation in the current evaluation moment. In K. Ryan & B. Cousins, (Eds.), *The Sage international handbook on evaluation* (pp. 431–448). Thousand Oaks, CA: Sage.

Kiyaga, N. (2003). *A qualitative study of grassroots community programmes for Indian deaf women in Delhi.* (Master's thesis, Gallaudet University, Washington DC)

Mertens, D. (2009). *Transformative research and evaluation.* New York, NY; London, UK: Guilford.

Mertens, D. M., Cram, F., & Chilisa, B. (2013). *Indigenous pathways into social research.* Walnut Hills, CA: Left Coast.

Mertens, D. M., & Wilson, A. T. (2012). *Program evaluation theory and practice: A comprehensive guide.* New York, NY; London, UK: Guilford.

CHAPTER 14

BEING CULTURALLY RESPONSIVE THROUGH KAUPAPA MĀORI EVALUATION

Fiona Cram, Vivienne Kennedy, Kirimatao Paipa, Kataraina Pipi, and Nan Wehipeihana

ABSTRACT

Kaupapa Māori (i.e., a Māori way) takes for granted the right of Māori (Indigenous New Zealanders) to be Māori; treasures Māori language and culture and embeds them within evaluation processes; and upholds and facilitates Māori control over Māori aspirations and destiny. A *Kaupapa Māori* paradigm sees being Māori as normal, thereby avoiding a victim-blaming mentality and promoting a structural analysis of Māori disparities. A *Kaupapa Māori* paradigm allows us to acknowledge that the evaluation we undertake as *Māori* evaluators has different ontological, epistemological, and axiological foundations than Western-oriented evaluation. *Kaupapa Māori* evaluation methodology is prescribed in cultural terms and makes moral and cultural sense. The Māori world is *whakapapa* (genealogy), and it is through the process of *whanaungatanga* (relationships, kinships) that we know our world. Our accountability for our evaluation work is primarily to our relations and, as such,

*Continuing the Journey to Reposition Culture and Cultural Context
in Evaluation Theory and Practice*, pages 289–311
Copyright © 2015 by Information Age Publishing
289

our evaluation practice addresses real issues so as to inform and promote real solutions that will facilitate Māori well-being and societal transformation. An important aspect of *Kaupapa Māori* evaluation is respectful dialogue across disciplinary and methodological boundaries to ensure mutual understandings and good science in the service of a *Māori kaupapa*. This chapter will explore *Kaupapa Māori* Evaluation (KME) as an example of local, Indigenous culturally responsive evaluation (CRE).

INTRODUCTION

A religious order works its ministry in a deprived suburb of a city in Aotearoa New Zealand. The suburb has a large population of Māori (Indigenous peoples of Aotearoa New Zealand) and Pasifika peoples (Indigenous peoples of the Pacific who now reside in Aotearoa New Zealand), and the order is committed to doing whatever they can to assist and support people who are too often marginalized from institutions and services by virtue of being both brown and poor. As part of their voluntary work in the suburb, one of the Sisters of the order has visited with a Māori woman each week for a cup of tea and a chat. After a year of visiting, the woman enrolls in a sewing course run by the order. When this course finishes after 3 months, the woman enrolls in the next sewing course being run and persuades her cousin to join her. For the Sisters, this is a moment of triumph; the relationship they have forged with this woman is bearing fruit in terms of her growing confidence and skill development. Her invitation to her cousin provides confirmation for the Sisters that their sewing course is appropriate and engaging. However, the Sisters receive some funding from a government agency to recruit Māori women, prepare them for work, and then get them into work—all within 6 months. There is a mismatch between the Sisters' knowledge of the needs and aspirations of the Māori women targeted for funding, which they have gained from living and working in this suburb, and the expectations of a government agency funder of what outcomes might be achievable and worthy of celebration within a short timeframe. This mismatch is particularly ironic because at the time the agency is making these outcome demands the suburb and its immediate surroundings are work-poor; in other words, there are little if any locally available employment opportunities for out-of-work, underskilled Māori women.

If you think the Sisters should not have signed a funding contract that contained what they should have known were unrealistic expectations, you may be right. But let's move past that for now, as it will divert us into a conversation about government contracting processes, out-of-touch bureaucrats, and nongovernment organizations (NGOs) just trying their best to deliver whatever services they can, both voluntarily and funded, to benefit their communities. As evaluators, we have often found ourselves in positions where programs or services that should never have been contracted for, have been, and NGOs have struggled to meet the demanding contractual obligations, even though the funding they have received has been put to good purpose and some outcomes have been achieved. Too often these outcomes fall short of funder expectations, even if they lay a firm foundation for longer-term outcomes that funders unrealistically assumed could be achieved within short time frames.

Evaluators who are caught up in these circumstances can and should argue for a theory of change like the Sisters' approach—a theory that acknowledges, values, and celebrates the (often foundational) outcomes that are attained, while also connecting them to the outcomes required to meet contractual accountabilities. For example, building interpersonal relationships and allowing Māori women to experience successful skill acquisition on a short, practical course lays a foundation of connectivity, esteem, and agency that is a prerequisite to more formally named preparation for paid employment. This example, and many others we have encountered in our work, calls for an evaluation approach that is anchored in an understanding of the context within which those working in Māori communities operate. This includes understanding what culturally responsive implementation of services and programs looks like, knowing the time frames needed to achieve outcomes, and assessing how well informed the contracting between a funder and an NGO has been. Such an evaluation will help manage expectations about the pace of change and provide feedback on the reasonableness of program goals (Alkin & Christie, 2004). In addition, evaluators of these programs and services will understand that the Māori world is premised on relationships (Williams, 1990), and that relationships infect the cultural milieu of programs and services that wish to respond to Māori needs, priorities, and aspirations. For example, a high-level theory of change developed by a group of Māori health providers during a *hui* (gathering) with Fiona Cram was simply three connected boxes that described how *whanaungatanga* (kinship)[1] leads to *whanaungatanga* that, in turn, leads to *whanaungatanga*. Their point was that positive change in the people they worked with rested upon the growth of their sense of connection and belonging that occurs when kinship and other close relationships are established and strengthened. This point is also made in the narrative that opened this chapter; namely, that the Sisters were first and foremost doing relationship work with the Māori women in their community. The recognition of *whanaungatanga* alongside other cultural imperatives is fundamental to the validity of evaluations of Māori programs and services (Kawakami, Aton, Cram, Lai, & Porima, 2007).

This chapter describes how *Kaupapa Māori* evaluation is appropriate and culturally responsive within this context. We first provide a brief introduction to the colonial context that is Aotearoa New Zealand, before describing principles of *Kaupapa Māori* (literally, a Māori way, and often translated as "by Māori, with Māori, for Māori") and the practices that guide *Kaupapa Māori* evaluation.

AOTEAROA NEW ZEALAND

Māori encounters with others reaching our shores have been both friendly and unfriendly. Dutchman Abel Tasman did not linger long in 1642, but saw enough of the country to name it New Zealand. Then in 1769, English Captain James Cook spent time circumnavigating the country, renaming places, and getting to know the locals. Our ancestors thought of themselves as ordinary, as *tangata maori*, while the newcomers were "other" (Salmond, 1991). Early explorers gave way to whalers and then missionaries and settlers. By the time the British Crown signed the Treaty of Waitangi with Māori in 1840, the land had already been sold by the New Zealand Company to colonists who were on ships, making their way to the "new" land (Orange, 1987). A colonial government was established and the promises of Māori sovereignty and citizenship made in the Treaty were soon eroded by commerce, legislation, and war. A visit by Charles Darwin to the country in 1835 confirmed the supposed superiority of the colonists (Desmond & Moore, 1991). The power and resources of Māori were reallocated to the newcomers, and the political, economic, demographic, and social order of Aotearoa transformed such that Māori became the "other" within this renamed land of New Zealand (Reid & Cram, 2004). The consequences of Māori marginalization within their own territories were widespread and deeply felt.

> The taking of land not only makes people poor; it also makes them more susceptible to diseases that flourish under conditions of poverty, overcrowding, and malnutrition. It destroys or disrupts social networks that provide practical and emotional support in times of need...As well as these immediate effects of land loss, the dispossession of land and other resources propels a group into future socio-economic deprivation as these territories and resources can no longer be used as economic and social equity. (Reid & Cram, 2004, p. 39)

The role of research and evaluation in the colonial agenda should not be underestimated or ignored (Kawakami et al., 2007). The impetus for and maintenance of Māori social exclusion and marginalization have often come from research and evaluation that have placed the blame for Māori "failure" on Māori "deficits," with the solutions being the assimilation or integration of Māori into New Zealand European society (Cram, 2009). In other words social inclusion has until very recently been premised upon Māori changing to be more like Pākehā (White people), a preferred strategy by colonizers worldwide to assimilate minority groups into the dominant society. The impossibility of the social inclusion of Brown folks within an unchanged racist society has been fundamentally ignored by the colonists (Reid & Robson, 2007), and many Māori have done their best to live within New Zealand. Others have kept their feet firmly within Aotearoa and protested the breaches of the Treaty of Waitangi, the theft of Māori land, the punishment of Māori school children for speaking their own language, the imprisonment of dissenters, and many other affronts (Walker, 2004). And then in 1984, at a Māori leaders conference, another stake was put in the ground: that in order for Māori to overcome disadvantage and marginalization, Māori had to be Māori (Public Health Commission, 1994). This opened the window for *Kaupapa Māori*, or a Māori agenda, to be asserted within Māori education and to flow from there into service and program delivery models and research and evaluation across a number of disciplines (Smith L. T., 2012).

KAUPAPA MĀORI

The theory underpinning our evaluation work is *Kaupapa Māori*, which in turn has developed from Māori struggles for sovereignty (Pihama, 2010). If "culture makes us who we are" (Frierson, Hood, & Hughes, 2002, p. 63), then Māori experiences of sovereignty undermined by colonial forces are embedded within our culture and within *Kaupapa Māori*. *Kaupapa Māori* has resonance with other theorizing about interventions to reinclude marginalized peoples and displace oppressive knowledge, for example, worldwide Indigenous theorizing. At a local level, *Kaupapa Māori* is unique, as it addresses the oppression of Māori in our own land and seeks the decolonization of Aotearoa. *Kaupapa Māori* challenges how Māori have been and continue to be constructed within a colonial context that has seen us "othered" by knowledge processes based upon a mix of science, cultural arrogance, and political power (L. T. Smith, 2012).

Kaupapa Māori literally means "a Māori way" and is about the normality of being Māori (Mane, 2009). As Taki (1996, p. 17) explains, the word "*kaupapa* encapsulates . . . ground rules, customs, the right way of doing things." *Kaupapa Māori* therefore embraces Māori philosophies and principles, and privileges Māori knowledge and ways of knowing (G. H. Smith, 1997; L. T. Smith, 2012). Our ancestors existed within a research culture whereby knowledge was updated "as part of ongoing information management practices" (Reid 1999, p. 61). Knowing is positioned within a reflexive cycle of being willing to evolve, grow, and update our knowledge (Henry & Pene, 2001). We are therefore not limited to merely responding to mainstream constructions of us; we can facilitate the revitalization of traditional constructions as well as the formation of new constructions of what it means to be Māori within Aotearoa today. This right is embodied within the Treaty of Waitangi as well as many international declarations of Indigenous rights (Kawakami et al., 2007). For example, the Mataatua Declaration on Cultural and Intellectual Property Rights of Indigenous Peoples (1993, p. 3) calls upon states, national, and international agencies to

> 2.1 Recognise that indigenous peoples are the guardians of their customary knowledge and have the right to protect and control dissemination of that knowledge.
>
> 2.2. Recognise that indigenous peoples also have the right to create new knowledge based on cultural traditions.

This assertion of a Māori space within a colonial society is an act of sovereignty and therefore bound to meet with resistance from those who would question its legitimacy or simply wish to reassert a prejudiced view of Māori founded in scientific colonialism (Nobles, 1991). As well as looking "inwards" to what a Māori world is, *Kaupapa Māori* also looks "outwards" to critique the knowledge and ways of knowing that are part of a colonial agenda (Pihama, Cram, & Walker, 2002). In other words, we are building more space within this country for Māori to be Māori, while also being aware that the reclamation of this space brings with it repercussions from those who do not want to see Māori prosper or do not want to share this land and its resources with the same spirit of generosity that our ancestors had when they signed the Treaty of Waitangi with the British Crown.

There is a growing body of literature regarding *Kaupapa Māori* theories and practices that assert a need for Māori to develop initiatives for change that are located within a distinctly Māori worldview (Cram, Kempton, & Armstrong, 1998; Mane, 2009; Pihama, 2010; Smith & Cram, 1997). To do this, we must borrow strategy from Black American activist W. E. B. Du Bois (1920) and de-center Whiteness in our country as the White settlers do not and should not think they own these lands forever and ever. Smith, Fitzsimons, and Roderick (1998, p. 8) describe *Kaupapa Māori* as an intervention strategy that "encompasses the social change or intervention elements that are common across many different sites of *Māori* cultural struggle, and as the collective set of key intervention elements in the *Māori*-driven, cultural resistance initiatives." There are six key elements or principles of *Kaupapa Māori*, and these are described next.

1. *Tino Rangatiratanga*—**the self-determination principle**. *Tino rangatiratanga* is about having meaningful control over one's own life and cultural well-being. Mead (1985, cited in Jackson, 1993, p. 70) writes, "*te tino rangatiratanga translates*...honestly and sensibly as self-government or as home rule." The acceptance and effectiveness of that

rule is embedded within *mana* (status) (Jackson, 1993). In signing the Treaty of Waitangi in 1840, the sovereign chiefs of Aotearoa New Zealand sought to protect their taken-for-granted, sovereign rights into the future.

2. *Taonga tuku iho*—**the cultural aspirations principle**. *Kaupapa Māori* theory asserts a position that to be Māori is normal and taken for granted. *Te reo Māori* (the Māori language), *matauranga Māori* (Māori knowledge), *tikanga Māori* (Māori custom), and *ahuatanga Māori* (Māori characteristics) are actively legitimated and validated. This principle acknowledges the strong emotional and spiritual factor in *Kaupapa Māori*. *Kaupapa Māori* knowledge has its origins in a metaphysical base that is distinctly Māori. As Nepe (1991) stated, this base influences the way Māori people think, understand, interact, and interpret the world.

3. *Ako*—**the culturally preferred pedagogy principle**. This principle promotes teaching and learning practices that are unique to *tikanga Māori* (custom). There is also an acknowledgment of "borrowed" pedagogies in that Māori are able to choose preferred pedagogies. Rangimarie Rose Pere (1994) writes in some depth regarding *tikanga Māori* concepts and their application to Māori pedagogies.

4. *Kia piki ake i nga raruraru o te kāinga*—**the socioeconomic mediation principle**. This principle addresses the issue of Māori socioeconomic disadvantage and the negative pressures this brings to bear on *whānau* (Māori families) and their children. This principle acknowledges that despite these difficulties, *Kaupapa Māori* mediation practices and values are able to intervene successfully for the well-being of the *whānau*. The collective responsibility of the Māori community and *whānau* comes to the foreground.

5. *Whānau*—**the extended family structure principle**. The *whānau* and the practice of *whanaungatanga* (family connectedness) is an integral part of Māori identity and culture. The cultural values, customs, and practices that organize around the *whānau*, and the collective responsibility of *whānau* members for each other are a necessary part of Māori survival and achievement. There are many examples where the principle of *whānau* and *whanaungatanga* are the foundations of Māori education, Māori health, Māori justice, and Māori prosperity.

6. *Kaupapa*—**the collective philosophy principle**. *Kaupapa Māori* initiatives are held together by a collective vision and commitment. In Māori education, for example, *"Te Aho Matua"* is a formal charter that has collectively been articulated by Māori working in *Kaupapa Māori* initiatives. This vision connects Māori aspirations to political, social, economic, and cultural well-being. Likewise, in Māori

health, a healthy Māori would be healthy politically, culturally, socially, and economically.

These principles are the foundation of *Kaupapa Māori* initiatives—programs, services and projects—that are about enabling Māori to be Māori. Central to *Kaupapa Māori* evaluation is inquiry into whether *Kaupapa Māori* principles are evident in program or service practices. (Refer to Chapter 15 in this volume for a more elaborated discussion on *Kaupapa Māori* evaluation inquiry methods.)

KAUPAPA MĀORI EVALUATION

Askew, Beverly, and Jay (2012, p. 552) define culturally responsive evaluation as "an approach to evaluation in which the recognition of and appreciation for a program's culture, including the cultural backgrounds of program stakeholders, is viewed as fundamental to any assessment of the program's value, merit, and worth." Within culturally responsive evaluation (CRE), this understanding comes from having trained evaluators of color or evaluators with substantial lived experiences in communities of color, with the latter presented as a pragmatic solution to a critical shortage of the former (Hood, 2009). At the very least, this ensures that the evaluation of programs and services will be "with" and "for" communities of color. *Kaupapa Māori* evaluation is an assertion of the right of Māori to conduct evaluations that are "by, with and for" Māori (Jackson, 1996). While non-Māori evaluators cannot undertake *Kaupapa Māori* evaluations, they can conduct evaluations that support a *Māori kaupapa* (i.e., agenda) should they be invited to do so by organizations or communities (L. T. Smith, 2012).

Kaupapa Māori evaluation is about the principled recentering of the Māori world and the legitimation of a Māori reality. It is therefore about the worldview that Māori bring to evaluation. Hart (2010, p. 1) writes that "worldviews are cognitive, perceptual, and affective maps that people continuously use to make sense of the social landscape." In other words, a Māori worldview is a Māori "commonsense." Awareness of this worldview might have been rare when our ancestors considered themselves to be ordinary and normal, but in contemporary society, it has been thrown into conscious view because it is presently an alternative to the dominant worldview that occupies our country.

Guba and Lincoln (1994) adopted Kuhn's terminology of paradigm to describe the different worldviews that researchers bring to their inquiry. The paradigm that researchers ascribe to is the one that best fits their ontological, epistemological, and methodological assumptions (Guba & Lincoln, 1994). Donna Mertens and Amy Wilson (2012) use this terminology to describe the transformative paradigm. They add to the assumptions and also prioritize the axiological assumption that makes explicit the role of values in research and evaluation. Our decision to use this terminology in a discussion of *Kaupapa Māori* evaluation is based upon Linda Smith's (2012) description of terms that may not be strictly traditional, but that serve to unite Māori in movements to decolonize our nation and to decolonize research and evaluation. While the terms that Smith canvases are Māori words, we feel there is value in also exploring the usefulness of the terminology of paradigms to, at the very least, promote discussion and debate about *Kaupapa Māori* evaluation.

A *Kaupapa Māori* evaluation paradigm allows us to acknowledge that the evaluation we undertake as Māori evaluators has different axiological, ontological, and epistemological foundations than Western-oriented evaluation (L. T. Smith, 2012). *Kaupapa Māori* evaluation is prescribed in cultural terms, and makes moral and cultural sense (Durie, 1996; Te Awekotuku, 1991). It is a culturally responsive, by Māori, for Māori, with Māori evaluation response that supports Māori development, societal transformation, and decolonization (L. T. Smith, 2005). The principles or values underpinning *Kaupapa Māori* evaluation are those of *Kaupapa Māori* more generally, as described above, as well as the Community-Up Research Practices described below that inform our day-to-day evaluation practice with stakeholders. We therefore begin with a discussion of ontology to provide insight into Māori reality.

Ontology

The ontological assumption is about the nature of existence or reality, and what can be known about it. As Shawn Wilson (2008, p. 33) states, ontology addresses the question, "What is real?" "Only those questions that relate to matters of 'real' existence and 'real' action are admissible; other questions . . . fall outside the realm of legitimate scientific inquiry" (Guba & Lincoln, 1994, p. 108). For Māori, *whanaungatanga* (kinship relationships) extend into the spirit world and also bind us to our natural environment. We have a *whakapapa* (genealogical) relationship with all things in our world that becomes explicit and localized through the use of *pepehā* (tribal saying). Used orally, the combination of these three cornerstones—*whanaungatanga, whakapapa,* and *pepehā*—locates Māori in a three-dimensional landscape; they are a cultural global positioning system (Paipa, Kennedy, & Pipi 2009). This is highly important to listeners in a gathering who are able to locate the speaker in relation to important landmarks, to their relatives, and to their historical ancestors. Of importance, here is the acknowledgement of those who have passed, and the continual cyclic connection with the past and those in spirit. The language Māori use to describe our links with the past, present, and future reflects a strong connection with the unseen, or spirit. Accordingly, the *Tuakiri* (beyond the skin) *o te Tangata* (a Māori model of health that supports the healing of individuals and *whānau*), for instance, describes that which is beyond the skin, unseen, but often felt (Mataira, 1996). There are few written references to this phenomenon, as this knowledge is still regarded as sacred and therefore not for exploration. However the components of the *Tuakiri* are more widely known, such as *mauri* (life principle), *ngākau* (heart), *wehi* (awe inspiring) and *ihi* (essential force), and underpin all discussions in regard to spirit. (These phenomena are explored more in the chapter on spirit within this volume in Chapter 8.) The acknowledgement of spirit is translated into practices of the current tense that recognize our relationship with the land as sacred, with people and other living things as paramount, and with a journey into the future that holds fast to our past.

Epistemology

Epistemology is the theory of knowledge held by those ascribing to a paradigm or worldview. It is about the relationship between the knower and what is known or knowable (Guba & Lincoln, 1994). Shawn Wilson (2008, p. 33) writes that epistemology addresses the question, "How do I know what is real?" The answer to this question is limited by the inquirer's ontological assumptions (Guba & Lincoln, 1994), as well as his/her axiological assumptions (Mertens & Wilson, 2012). An Indigenous epistemology must therefore encompass the relationships and connections operating among and between the human world, spirit worlds, and the environment (Battiste & Henderson, 2000). For Māori, the relationship between "knower/ researcher" and "knowable/researched" is one of either *whakapapa* (genealogy) or of other relationships that draw these two dimensions together as if they were kin (Greensill, 1999).

Kirimatao Paipa (personal communication, September 2012) talked of the theoretical underpinnings of Māori knowledge, essentially *mōhiotanga, mātauranga, maramatanga*, and their relationship to *Kaupapa Māori*. Being Māori, we are vessels of *mōhiotanga*—knowledge, understanding, awareness, intelligence, insight, perceptions. *Matauranga* Māori or *matauranga* pertains to education, knowledge, wisdom, understanding, and skill of things Māori, whereas imperceptibly, *māramatanga* refers to enlightenment, understanding, insight. *Mōhiotanga* is knowledge; *māramatanga* is understanding; and *mātauranga* is the application according to one's understanding and knowledge. *Kaupapa Māori* is the practical application of the knowledge of things Māori. As Māori evaluators, we apply what we know about *te ao Māori* – the

Māori world – to our evaluation *mahi* (work) with our *whānau,* people and communities, and this relates to our connectivity to our people and our culture. Connectivity also relates to influences such as non-Māori, including Pākehā heritage. Therefore, we ask ourselves "*Ko wai ahau?*"—"Who am I?"; and who and what we know ourselves to be, including all our other parts, is what we bring in terms of *mātauranga, mōhiotanga, māramatanga* to our evaluation *mahi. Kaupapa Māori* is the practical application to our *mahi* of our knowingness and beingness.

Methodology

Methodology is our theory about how to find out things, about how knowledge is gained (Guba & Lincoln, 1994). Shawn Wilson's (2008, p. 34) methodological question is, "How do I find out more about this reality?" The answer is again constrained by the answers given to the ontological and epistemological questions (Guba & Lincoln, 1994). As a broad approach to research and evaluation, *Kaupapa Māori* is a strategy for selecting projects, topics, and themes that can facilitate a positive difference for Māori; developing key evaluation questions; training and mentoring Māori evaluators; and developing more appropriate methods for working with Māori communities. (More is explained in the methodology chapter in this same volume; refer to Chapter 15.) For Māori, knowledge was traditionally used for the good of the people—the tribe (Mead, 2003). This value remains today with *Kaupapa Māori* being about making a positive difference for Māori (L. T. Smith, 2005). *Kaupapa Māori* evaluation is therefore about assessing whether a program or service is operating according to *Kaupapa Māori* principles and achieving what is good for Māori within the wider context of our colonial society and Māori aspirations for decolonization. Within this, the arbitrary distinction often made between qualitative and quantitative research and evaluation methods fall by the wayside as we seek out the method that is right for answering the evaluation questions we are asking.

Axiology

Shawn Wilson (2008, p. 34) asks, "What is it ethical to do in order to gain ... knowledge?" The "Community-Up" Approach describes seven *Kaupapa Māori* ethical knowledge-gathering practices. As Mane (2009, pp. 1–2) writes, *Kaupapa Māori,* and therefore *Kaupapa Māori* evaluation, is "drawn from *tikanga* Māori, from Māori cultural protocols, values, practices and views of the world." The "Community-Up" Approach was first described by Linda Smith (1999) and then expanded upon by Cram and colleagues

(Cram, 2001, 2009; Cram & Phillips, 2012; Pipi et al., 2004), as well as being revisited by Linda Smith (2005). Over this time, the Approach has structured our thinking about how we engage with stakeholders and participants in research and evaluation, as well as how we work together within transdisciplinary teams (Cram & Phillips, 2012). We have also gone from describing the Approach as a guide for how communities should be approached and engaged for purposes of research and evaluation, to more of a catalyst for communities to develop their own protocols and guidelines that answer an axiological question that evaluators may or may not ask them.

Table 14.1 provides an overview of the Approach along with specific evaluation practices in which we have engaged that are reflective of this Approach. Following the table, the cultural values and examples of their implementation within evaluations are described more fully.

Aroha ki te tangata

Kaupapa Māori initiatives are often implemented by people who have a fundamental *aroha* or love for the people they are working with; that is, *aroha ki te tangata*. They are able to connect with those who participate in their programs or services and offer them support and help that addresses their needs and acknowledges their aspirations (Pipi et al., 2003). This is the combination of personal and professional practice that *Kaupapa Māori* evaluators also bring to their work. We take our lead from Māori organizations and from *whānau*. We do not impose our sense of culture on Māori organizations; rather we allow them to lead the way. We understand that Māori are on a continuum of understanding and engagement with *tikanga* (cultural practices). We are ready and capable in all situations. If an organization enacts a full *pōwhiri* (ritual of encounter), we can respond; if they wish to have a cup of tea, we can also respond. This is the same with interviewees; we sense or follow their lead about the level of cultural protocols to be observed and respond accordingly.

He kanohi kitea

The practice of *he kanohi kitea* comes from the traditional saying, *He reo e rangona, engari, he kanohi kitea*—A voice may be heard, but a face needs to be seen. We are recognized and known in our communities, therefore our practice must consider taking a long-term view to our relationships beyond the confines of the project. We also recognize and acknowledge other people and their relationships, and respectfully park personal judgments. This professionalism is also important in long-term evaluation relationships. At

TABLE 14.1 "Community-Up" Approach to Defining Evaluator Conduct

Values	Guidelines	Evaluation Practices
Aroha ki te tangata	*Respect people—allow them to define their own space and meet on their own terms.*	• Being flexible and responsive in our rituals of encounter, taking our lead from the people we are visiting with • Acknowledging relationships and making connections, including *whakapapa, whanaungatanga,* and *kaupapa* linkages • Seeking the support of elders and acknowledging their wisdom and knowledge • Facilitating the coming together of evaluators and stakeholders for the purpose of an evaluation
He kanohi kitea	*Meet people face to face, and also be a face that is known to and seen within a community*	• Being known within our communities • Being respectful in our evaluation relationships with people we may know in other contexts • Ensuring that engagement with indigenous communities has the "willing and able" indigenous team member "up front," guiding and leading, as opposed to White folk leading in indigenous communities • Ensuring there is adequate resources in the budget to engage face-to-face at regular intervals throughout the project
Titiro, whakarongo . . . kōrero	*Look and listen (and then maybe speak)—Develop an understanding in order to find a place from which to speak.*	• Resisting the temptation to be a *whakaputa mōhio* (know-it-all)—look and listen to the situation without feeling compelled to say anything, because they may already know it and may learn more from hearing their own voice, not yours! • Using all our senses to engage with people and to understand what they are telling us—listening from different places—the heart, the head, and the *puku* (gut). Listening and hearing with empathy and care • Using culturally specific mediums of communication (*hui,* talking circle) regularly alongside carefully considered facilitation processes to encourage the engagement of everyone, and particularly those stakeholders who are less confident to talk
Manaaki ki te tangata	*Share, host, and be generous.*	• Being able to reciprocate in many different ways, including building evaluation capacity • Ensuring there is a balance in both evaluator and stakeholder needs being met so that communities feel like they are receiving as well as giving • Ensuring communities and the evaluation team are looked after and their needs are met

(continued)

TABLE 14.1 "Community-Up" Approach to Defining Evaluator Conduct (continued)

Values	Guidelines	Evaluation Practices
Kia tupato	*Be cautious—be politically astute, culturally safe, and reflective about insider/outsider status.*	• Knowing that as evaluators we are not 'insiders' • Seeking guidance and advice from community stakeholders about our potential evaluation approach, timing, and resource implications to ensure an appropriate "fit" for the community or context • Being aware of your limitations—being prepared for the environment you are entering and/or ensure you or your team are suitably equipped and experienced • Ensure *whānau* are safe and are left in a similar or better space then before they were engaged • Being aware of how local people are affected by national policies
Kaua e takahia te mana o te tangata	*Do not trample on the mana or dignity of a person.*	• Choosing and adapting evaluation methods to ensure the experience, practice, and voices of indigenous communities are authentically represented • Be aware of who you are meeting with—what they represent and bring with them • Allowing "time" for stakeholders to share their experiences (particularly where vulnerability exists) • Being fluent and flexible and able to engage • Knowing that relationships are important, as is genuine interest in the people you are representing and engaging with • Maintaining respect and an attitude of care and support during the engagement process as well as throughout the evaluation process, including the recording, collation, analyzing, and dissemination of information
Kia mahaki	*Be humble—do not flaunt your knowledge; find ways of sharing it.*	• Making sure to give back and share information and knowledge • Resist the temptation to be a *whakapata mōhio* (know-it-all)—look and listen to the situation without feeling compelled to say anything, because they may already know it, and may learn more from hearing their own voice, not yours! • Being honest with *whānau*, and if you don't know, find out and get back to *whānau* • Supporting *whānau* to understand and utilize the evaluation findings • Encouraging *whānau* to grow their capabilities

Source: Adapted from L. T. Smith (2006, p. 12, Diagram 1)

the beginning of such a relationship, there may be hesitation about information sharing as relationships of trust are built. After 3–4 years, some organizations are willing so share more information than is strictly warranted for the evaluation. At this time, it is important that evaluators use their professional and ethical guiding principles to distinguish what is known for the purpose of the evaluation from what else the evaluator knows from the relationships she has built and the time she has spent meeting, eating, and being with organizational staff and clients.

Titiro, whakarongo ... kōrero

We listen with many ears: *rongo* is to sense, smell, hear, and feel, and we use all these senses to engage with people. In this way, we look (*titiro*), listen (*whakarongo*), and seek to acquire some knowledge and understanding before we speak (*kōrero*). We also use qualitative and quantitative evaluation methods that put us in the background, so that program participants and other stakeholders can speak about what they know about a program and what they have experienced from being part of it.

Manaaki ki te tangata

We give different kinds of *koha* (offering of thanks) back to organizations and interviewees, including music, *whakapapa* graphics, verbal affirmations and validation, heart conversations as well as the usual reciprocity of cash or vouchers. The building of an ongoing relationship with an organization, tribe, or community where they are able to call upon us for other evaluation or research work, or other support, is also an important way in which we are able to reciprocate.

The best assurance of community reciprocity is to establish an ongoing relationship with the *whānau, hapū,* and *iwi,* which allows a relationship of trust and respect to develop through performance (Cram, Keefe, Ormsby, Ormsby, & Ngāti Kahungunu Iwi Inc., 1997).

Kia tūpato

Kia tūpato is about practicing evaluation with care so that all who are involved are kept safe. Even if we come from or have strong links to a tribal area or community in which we are working, we are never a complete insider when we have our evaluator "hat" on. Merely by staking a claim that we are evaluators, we are connecting ourselves to a body of knowledge or accountabilities that position us to some extent as outsiders. We can use cultural, local, and relationship knowledge, but we are careful not to impose or presume what this knowledge is or means for the people we are working with (L. T. Smith, 2006).

> It's very hard working in your home community...They really hold you to what you say and it's not just that they hold you, you hold yourself because you just have this real sense of responsibility. To do what is right for them, represent them in a way that is fine with them and fine with the institution. It's a lot of work in your mind to get that settled so that you're at peace with it. (Adreanne Ormond, as quoted in Ormond, Cram, & Carter, 2006, p. 185)

Kaupapa Māori evaluation is also about being aware of how national and local policies affect local communities and program providers (Ormond et al., 2006).

Kaua e takahia te mana o te tangata

Kaua e takahia te mana o te tangata is about not trampling on the authority or status of people. It is about maintaining and, where possible, working to build the esteem of people through the acknowledgement of their work and the provision of evaluative feedback to enable them to improve their programs and services. This often means fully exploring the external context within which a program is operating to understand how it is mediating the social and economic circumstances in which people find themselves. An evaluator needs to be both fluent and flexible to "get to the bottom" of what is going on for people in their day-to-day lives. This means having a critical analysis of the world as it currently exists; understanding the determinants of people's behavior, attitudes, and beliefs and actively challenging the status quo that maintains *Māori* disparities.

Kia māhaki

Kia māhaki is about being humble and willing to share knowledge and information; to give back. One of the more obvious ways in which we give back is through building the evaluation capacity of our communities. We can train local people as interviewers and then employ them to work with us on evaluations. This supports local people and also gives back to us, as these people are there to support our next evaluation or research efforts in that community.

These seven practices of the "Community-Up" Approach provide us with a starting point for our evaluation practice within Māori organizations and communities. They can be considered a recipe when that recipe provides guidance that is flexible and adaptive, and open to being co-constructed anew by the people with whom we work. By being culturally responsive, we are also empathetic evaluation practitioners in that the principles of how we engage and practice with Māori communities and organizations are more about them than they are about us.

DISCUSSION

Couched within the intimacies of people's lived realities, culture is fundamental to their needs, wants, and aspirations (Mead, 2003; Sorrenson, 1986). The expression of culture within programs and services signals to people about how they will "fit," whether programs and services will "get" them, and how "real" they can be so as not to jeopardize their access. Culturally responsive evaluation shines a spotlight on the importance of the cultural context within which programs and services operate. Attending "substantively and politically to issues of culture and race in evaluation practice" (Hood, 2001, p. 32) requires a culturally responsive evaluation approach that treats people's cultural worldview as legitimate and valid, while also paying attention to issues of power and privilege in terms of how cultural/ethnic/racial groups are positioned within society. This combination of cultural knowing plus political astuteness enables evaluators to manage expectations about the feasibility and achievement of success that are aligned with cultural principles (Frierson et al., 2002). Our role is also to critique the wider context in which programs and services operate that might limit their potential success through marginalization, colonization, and social injustices meted out to the cultural/ethnic/racial groups that programs and services have been developed to serve (Hopson, 2009; Cram & Mertens, forthcoming).

Māori tribes and communities have experienced the frustration of knowing what their problems are and what possible solutions might be, with these solutions based upon their own values, beliefs, and practices. The funding of *Kaupapa Māori* programs and services over the past 20–25 years has enabled this knowing to be put into practice (Cram, 2005; Pihama et al., 2002). The result has been the growth of *Kaupapa Māori* initiatives in education, health, corrections, and other arenas (Pipi et al., 2003). These initiatives have embodied the *Kaupapa Māori* principles that have been described here: self-determination, cultural aspirations, culturally preferred pedagogy, socioeconomic mediation, extended family structure, and collectivity (G. H. Smith, 1997).

An initial demand in the early 1990s from funders, tribes, and organizations for the culturally responsive evaluation of *Kaupapa Māori* initiatives led to the emergence of *Kaupapa Māori* evaluation. The discourse of paradigms has been used here to explore the ontological, epistemological, methodological, and axiological assumptions of a *Kaupapa Māori* evaluation paradigm. The Māori world is about kinship with other people, with our environment, and with the cosmos. Our evaluation work acknowledges these relationships through the cultural practices, or *tikanga*, that guides the way in which we engage with and work with those involved in evaluations. Our kinship and other relationships are both our evaluation and our personal world.

The *Kaupapa Māori* principles provide guidance about the key elements of a *Kaupapa Māori* program that we might evaluate, for example, the expression of traditional knowledge and *whanaungatanga* (the support of kinship and nonkinship relationships, how these are modeled, strengthened, and extended) (Mauriora ki te Ao, 2009; Penehira & Doherty, 2013). In addition, our inquiry extends into many realms, including the spiritual. (Refer to Chapter 8 in this volume for a more elaborated discussion on spirituality and evaluation in Māori contexts.) The "Community-Up" Approach guides our evaluative journey with Māori organizations and communities so that cultural protocols and practices are acknowledged, valued, and respected. These principles and practices of *Kaupapa Māori* evaluation facilitate culturally responsive evaluation that informs funders about the accountability of Māori programs and services, and informs organizations about how to develop and strengthen their program and service delivery within Māori communities. (The mechanics of this are explored further in Chapter 15 in this volume.) Our experience is that *Kaupapa Māori* evaluation also works well for non-Māori organizations and that we are often evaluating the success of *Kaupapa Māori* organizations' delivery of services and programs that are "by Māori for the whole of their community" (Grennell & Cram, 2008; Smith & Cram, 1997).

Finally, we note that as a Māori evaluator, you know "you're not the boss and you're accountable for the rest of your life" (Ormond et al., 2006, p. 185). Being culturally responsive is more than a one-off moment; cultures morph and transform to maintain their vitality, validity, and sustainability. We are on this journey to the extent that we, as evaluators, also grow and maintain our relevance and ability to undertake authentic work.

Success for a group like the religious order includes justice for those living in impoverishment and the ensuing community change. As this change happens, their theory of what is possible will be revised, and so should our ability and commitment to assess their achievement of their aspirations. To remain culturally relevant as evaluators, we need to continually reassess, learn, live cultural lives, and "up our game" to face the decolonization challenge.

GLOSSARY OF MĀORI TERMS

ahuatanga Māori	Māori characteristics
ako	learn, teach
Aotearoa	New Zealand, often referring in particular to the North Island
aroha ki te tangata	love for the people
he kanohi kitea	a face that is seen
ihi	essential force
kanohi ki te kanohi	to see a person face to face
kaua e takahia te mana o te tāngata	do not trample on the dignity of people
kaupapa	a topic, agenda
Kaupapa Māori	a framework and way of working built on a Māori world view
kia mahaki	be humble
kia tūpato	be careful
koha	offering of thanks
kōrero	speak
mana	status
manaaki ki te tangata	being generous, looking after the person
Māori	Indigenous peoples of Aotearoa New Zealand
māramatanga	enlightenment, understanding, insight
mātauranga	education, knowledge, wisdom, understanding, skill
mātauranga Māori	Māori knowlege
mauri	life principle
mōhiotanga	knowledge, understanding, awareness, intelligence, insight, perceptions
ngākau	the seat of affections, heart, mind
Pākehā	New Zealander of European descent
pepehā	tribal saying
pōwhiri	ritual of encounter
rongo	to hear, sense
tangata	person, people
tangata Maori	ordinary people
te ao Māori	the Māori world
te reo Māori	the Māori language
tikanga Māori	Māori custom
tino rangatiratanga	self-government, sovereignty
titiro	look
wehi	something awesome
whakapapa	genealogy
whakaputa mōhio	know-it-all
whakarongo	listen
whānau	Māori family
whanaungatanga	Kinship, family connection

NOTE

1. The online Māori dictionary (www.maoridictionary.co.nz) gives the expanded definition of *whanaungatanga* as "relationship, kinship, sense of family connection—a relationship through shared experiences and working together which provides people with a sense of belonging. It develops as a result of kinship rights and obligations, which also serve to strengthen each member of the kin group. It also extends to others to whom one develops a close familial, friendship or reciprocal relationship."

REFERENCES

Alkin, M. C., & Christie, C. A. (2004). An evaluation theory tree. In M. Alkin (Ed.), *Evaluation roots: Tracing theorists' views and influences* (pp. 12–65). Thousand Oaks, CA: Sage.

Askew, K., Beverly, M. G., & Jay, M. L. (2012). Aligning collaborative and culturally responsive evaluation approaches. *Evaluation and Program Planning, 35,* 552–557.

Battiste, M., & Henderson, Y. (2000). *Protecting Indigenous knowledge and heritage.* Saskatoon, SK, Canada: Purich.

Cram, F. (2001). Rangahau Māori: Tona tika, tona pono. In M. Tolich (Ed.), *Research ethics in Aotearoa* (pp. 35–52). Auckland, New Zealand: Longman.

Cram, F. (2005). An ode to Pink Floyd: Chasing the magic of Māori and Iwi providers. Earlier version published in Ngā Pae o te Māramatanga, J.S. Te Rito (Series Editor), *Ngā Pae o te Māramatanga–Research and policy seminar series.* Turnball House, Wellington, February 2005. Auckland: Ngā Pae o te Māramatanga.

Cram, F. (2009). Maintaining Indigenous voices. In D. Mertens & P. Ginsberg (Eds.), *Sage handbook of social science research ethics* (pp. 308–322). Thousand Oaks, CA: Sage.

Cram, F., Keefe, V., Ormsby, C., Ormsby, W., & Ngāti Kahungunu Iwi Inc. (1997). Memorywork and Māori health research: Discussion of a qualitative method. *He Pukenga Kōrero, 3* (1), 37–45.

Cram, F., Kempton, M., & Armstrong, S. (1998). *Evaluation report: Te whare tirohanga Māori, Hawkes Bay Regional Prison.* Wellington, New Zealand: Department of Corrections.

Cram, F., & Phillips, H. (2012). Reclaiming a culturally safe place for Māori researchers within multi-cultural, transdisciplinary research groups. *International Journal of Critical Indigenous Studies, 5*(2), 36–49.

Desmond, A., & Moore, J. (1991). *Darwin.* London, UK: Penguin.

DuBois, W E. B. (1920). The souls of whitefolk. In N. Huggins (Ed.), *W.E.B. Du Bois: Writings.* New York, NY: Library of America.

Durie, M. (1996). Characteristics of Māori health research. *Hui whakapiripiri: A hui to discuss strategic direction for Māori health research.* Wellington, New Zealand: Wellington School of Medicine, Te Rōpū Rangahau Hauora a Eru Pomare.

Frierson, H. T., Hood, S., & Hughes, G. B. (2002). Culturally Responsive Evaluation and strategies for addressing it. In J. Frechtling (Ed.), *The 2002 user-friendly evaluation handbook* (pp. 63–73). Arlington, VA: National Science Foundation.

Greensill, A. (1999, October 25–28). Genetic engineering—Māori views and values. *Pacific World.*

Grennell, D., & Cram, F. (2008). Evaluation of Amokura: An Indigenous family violence prevention strategy. *MAI Review, 2,* Article 4.

Guba, E. G., & Lincoln, Y. S. (1994). Competing paradigms in qualitative research. In N. K. Denzin & Y. S. Lincoln (Eds.), *Handbook of qualitative research* (pp. 105–117). London, UK: Sage.

Hart, M. A. (2010). Indigenous worldviews, knowledge, and research: The development of an Indigenous research paradigm. *Journal of Indigenous Voices in Social Work, 1*(1), 1–16.

Henry, E., & Pene, H. (2001). Kaupapa Māori: Locating Indigenous ontology, epistemology and methodology within the academy. *Organisation, 8,* 234–242.

Hood, S. (2001). Nobody knows my name: In praise of African American evaluators who were responsive. *New Directions for Evaluation, 92,* 31–43.

Hood, S. (2009). Evlauation for and by Navajos: A narrative case for the irrelevance of globalization. In K. Ryan & B. Cousins (Eds.), *The Sage handbook of educational evaluation* (pp. 447–464). Thousand Oaks, CA: Sage.

Hopson, R. K. (2009). Reclaiming knowledge at the margins: Culturally responsive evaluation in the current evaluation moment. In K. Ryan & B. Cousins (Eds.), *The Sage handbook of educational evaluation* (pp. 447–464). Thousand Oaks, CA: Sage.

Jackson, M. (1993). Land loss and the Treaty of Waitangi. In W. Ihimaera, H. Williams, I. Ramsden, & D. S. Long (Eds.), *Te Ao Marama: Regaining Aotearoa. Māori writers speak out. Volume 2. He Whakaatanga o te Ao–The reality.* Auckland, New Zealand: Reed.

Jackson, M. (1996). Māori health research and Te Tiriti o Waitangi. *Hui Whakapiripiri: A hui to discuss strategic directions for Māori health research.* Wellington, New Zealand: Te Rōpū Rangahau Hauora a Eru Pomare.

Kawakami, A., Aton, K., Cram, F., Lai, M., & Porima, L. (2007). Improving the practice of evaluation through Indigenous values and methods: Decolonizing evaluation practice—Returning the gaze from Hawai'i and *Aotearoa.* In P. Brandon & P. Smith (Eds.), *Fundamental issues in evaluation* (pp. 219–242). New York, NY: Guilford.

Mane, J. (2009). *Kaupapa Māori:* A community approach. *MAI Review,* (3), Article 1.

Mataatua Declaration on Cultural and Intellectual Property Rights of Indigenous Peoples. (1993, June 12–18). Whakatane: First International Conference on the Cultural & Intellectual Property Rights of Indigenous Peoples.

Mataira, K. (1997). *Te aho matua o ngā kura kaupapa Māori: An interpretation of the Māori language document.* Part of a submission to the Associate Minister of Education by Te Rūnanga Nui o Ngā Kura Kaupapa Māori, 29 September 1997.

Mauriora ki te Ao. (2009). *Te toi hauora-nui: Achieving excellence through innovative Māori health service delivery.* Hamilton, New Zealand: Mauriora ki te Ao/Living Universe.

Mead, H. M. (2003). *Tikanga Māori. Living by Māori values.* Wellington, New Zealand: Huia.

Mertens, D., & Cram, F. (forthcoming). Transformative and Indigenous frameworks for mixed and multi-method research. In S. Hesse-Biber & B. Johnson (Eds.), *The Oxford handbook of mixed and multimethod research.*

Mertens, D. M., & Wilson, A. T. (2012). *Program evaluation theory and practice. A comprehensive guide.* New York, NY: Guilford.

Nepe, T. (1991). *E hao nei e tenei reanga: Te toi huarewa tipuna, kaupapa Maori, an educational intervention.* Unpublished Master of Arts thesis. University of Auckland, New Zealand.

Nobles, W. (1991). Extended self: Rethinking the so-called negro self-concept. In R. L. Jones (Ed.), *Black psychology* (3rd ed., pp. 295–304). Berkeley, CA: Cobb & Henry.

Orange, C. (1987). *The Treaty of Waitangi.* Wellington, New Zealand: Allen and Unwin.

Ormond, A., Cram, F., & Carter, L. (2006). Researching our relations: Reflections on ethics and marginalisation. [*Special supplement*] *Alternative: An international journal of indigenous scholarship,* (Marginalisation), 180–198.

Paipa, K., Kennedy, V., & Pipi, K., (2009). *Lessons learned from working with our own. Pēpēhā—My personal global positioning system.* Workshop presentation to American Evaluation Association Annual General Conference. November 2009. Orlando, Florida.

Penehira, M., & Doherty, L. (2013). Tu mai te oriori, nau mai te hauora! A Kaupapa Māori approach to infant mental health: Adapting Mellow Parenting for Māori mothers in Aotearoa, New Zealand. *Pimatisiwin: A Journal of Aboriginal and Indigenous Community Health, 10*(3), 367–382.

Pere, R. R. (1994). *Ako: Concepts of learning in the Māori tradition.* Wellington, New Zealand: Te Kohanga Reo National Trust Board.

Pihama, L. (2010). Kaupapa Māori theory: Transforming theory. *Aotearoa. He Pukenga Korero, 9*(2), 5–14.

Pihama, L., Cram, F., & Walker, S. (2002). Creating methodological space: A literature review of *Kaupapa Māori* research. *Canadian Journal of Native Education, 26*(1), 30–43.

Pipi, K., Cram, F., Hawke, R., Hawke, S., Huriwai, T. M., Keefe, V., et al. (2003). *Māori and Iwi provider success: A research report of interviews with successful Iwi and Māori providers and government agencies.* Wellington, New Zealand: Te Puni Kōkiri.

Pipi, K., Cram, F., Hawke, R., Hawke, S., Huriwai, T., Mataki, T., et al. (2004, December). A research ethic for studying Māori and Iwi provider success. *Social Policy Journal of New Zealand, 23,* 141–153.

Public Health Commission. (1994). *Our health our future—Hauora pakari, koiora roa. The state of public health in New Zealand.* Wellington, New Zealand: Public Health Commission.

Reid, P. (1999). Te pupuri i te ao o te tangata whenua. In P. Davis, & K. Dew (Eds.), *Health and society: Perspectives from Aotearoa/New Zealand* (pp. 51–62). Auckland: Oxford University Press.

Reid, P., & Cram, F. (2004). Connecting health, people and country in Aotearoa/New Zealand. In K. Dew & P. Davis (Eds.), *Health and society in Aotearoa New*

Zealand (2nd ed., pp. 33–48). Auckland, New Zealand: Oxford University Press.

Reid, P., & Robson, B. (2007). Understanding health inequities. In B. Robson & R. Harris (Eds.), *Hauora: Maori standards of health IV. A study of the years 2000-2005* (pp. 3–10). Wellington, New Zealand: Te Rōpū Rangahau Hauora a Eru Pōmare.

Salmond, A. (1991). *Two worlds: First meeting between Māori and Europeans 1642–1772.* Auckland, New Zealand: Viking.

Smith, G. H. (1997). *The development of Kaupapa Māori: Theory and praxis.* Unpublished PhD thesis. University of Auckland, New Zealand.

Smith, G. H., Fitzsimons, P., & Roderick, M. (1998). *A scoping report: Kaupapa Māori frameworks for labour market programmes. A report to the Māori Employment and Training Commission.* Auckland, New Zealand: International Research Institute for Māori and Indigenous Education.

Smith, L. T. (1999). *Decolonizing methodologies: Research and indigenous peoples.* New York & Dunedin: Zed Books & Otago University Press.

Smith, L. T. (2005). On tricky ground—Researching the native in the age of uncertainty. In N. K. Denzin & Y. S. Lincoln (Eds.), *The Sage handbook of qualitative research* (pp. 1–12). Thousand Oaks, CA: Sage.

Smith, L. T. (2006). Researching in the margins: Issues for Māori researchers—A discussion paper. *Alternative: An International Journal of Indigenous Peoples,* 2(1), 4–27.

Smith, L. T. (2012). *Decolonizing methodologies—Research and Indigenous peoples* (2nd ed.). London, UK/New York, NY: Zed.

Smith, L. T., & Cram, F. (1997). *An evaluation of the Community Panel Diversion Pilot Project. Commissioned by the Crime Prevention Unit, Office of the Prime Minister and Cabinet, Wellington.* Auckland, New Zealand: International Research Institute for Māori and Indigenous Education.

Sorrenson, M. P. K. (Ed.). (1986). *Na To Hoa Aroha, from your dear friend: The correspondence between Sir Apirana Ngata and Sir Peter Buck, 1925–50* (Vol. 1, 1925–29). Auckland, New Zealand: Auckland University Press.

Taki, M. (1996). *Kaupapa Maori and contemporary iwi resistance.* Unpublished MA thesis, Department of Education, University of Auckland, New Zealand.

Te Awekotuku, N. (1991). *He tikanga whakaaro: Research ethics in the Māori community.* Wellington, New Zealand: Manatu Māori.

Walker, R. (2004). *Ka whawhai tonu: Struggle without end* (Rev. ed.). Auckland, New Zealand: Penguin.

Williams, J. (1990). Back to the future: Māori survival in the 1990s. In *Puna wairere: Essays by Māori* (pp. 14–18). Wellington: New Zealand Planning Council.

Wilson, S. (2008). *Research is ceremony. Indigenous research methods.* Black Point, Nova Scotia, Canada: Fernwood.

CHAPTER 15

CULTURALLY RESPONSIVE METHODS FOR FAMILY CENTERED EVALUATION[1]

Kirimatao Paipa, Fiona Cram, Vivienne Kennedy, and Kataraina Pipi

The rito, the centre shoot or heart of the harakeke, or flax, must be cared for to ensure new life and new shoots. It symbolises the need of each person to be nurtured in a whānau-hapū [family-sub-tribe] environment. According to Māori, the whānau-hapū is the heart of life for a person. It is the ground in which kinship and social relationship obligations and duties are learned, and enabled to flourish and flower.

—Henare, (1995)

INTRODUCTION

Whānau (Indigenous families of Aotearoa New Zealand) are described as the building block of Māori (Indigenous New Zealanders) society (Mead, 2003; Ministry of Health, 2002). *Whānau*—the extended family structure—is the fifth principle of *Kaupapa Māori* (by Māori, for Māori) theory (see Chapter 14, this volume). This acknowledges that *whānau* and *whanaungatanga* (family connectedness) are central to Māori (Indigenous

Continuing the Journey to Reposition Culture and Cultural Context in Evaluation Theory and Practice, pages 313–334
Copyright © 2015 by Information Age Publishing

people of Aotearoa New Zealand) culture and Māori identity. Traditionally, a *whānau* or extended family lived under one roof or in adjoining houses in a village and functioned as a social and economic collective (Firth, 1929). The relationships between individuals within a *whānau* were established through *whakapapa* (genealogy), with seniority worked out through both descent lines and generation levels (Carroll, 1970).

The impact of colonization, including the imposition of non-Māori or Western understandings of "family," hindered understandings of traditional Māori family systems (Cram & Pitama, 1998; Durie, 2001). Warfare, education, and Christianity (to name but a few disturbances) also disrupted these family systems, beginning from the early 1800s and continuing to the present day (Simon et al., 2001; Taskforce on Whānau-Centred Initiatives, 2010). Even so, the *whānau* "remains as a persistent way of living and organising the social world" (L.T. Smith, 1996, p. 18).

Understanding how contemporary *whānau* function as a unit, from how *tamariki* (children) are socialized and form their identity through to the role and place of *kaumātua* (elders), is essential if Māori well-being is to be supported (Taskforce on *Whānau*-Centred Initiatives, 2010). The Ministerial foreword to the Ministry of Health's 2002 Māori Health Strategy, *He Korowai Oranga*, places *whānau* at the "centre of public policy," challenging that policy to "create environments that are liberating and enable *whānau* to shape and direct their own lives, to achieve the quality of life Māori are entitled to as *tangata whenua* [Indigenous people of the land] in Aotearoa-New Zealand" (Ministry of Health, 2002, p. iii). It is imperative that our knowledge about *whānau* is sourced from within their day-to-day realities if policies and practices (as well as our knowledge and theory) are to support and facilitate *whānau* health and well-being.

In order for evaluation to be culturally responsive for Māori, evaluators need to understand the important place of *whānau* and *whanaungatanga* within the everyday lives and experiences of Māori. This understanding then needs to be reflected in evaluation designs, including the selection of evaluation methods (Kirkhart, 2005). Even if programs and services are delivered to individual Māori participants, it is imperative that we are able to assess the implications of these services and programs for individuals within the context of their *whānau*. This chapter's approach to culturally responsive evaluation (CRE) is therefore largely as "a system or culmination of practice strategies and frameworks that attend to culture during the various stages and phases of an evaluation, from preparing for the evaluation to disseminating and using the results of study" (Hopson, 2009, p. 431). This is not to dismiss the importance of the *Kaupapa Māori* theory principles that underpin our evaluation work (see Chapter 14 this volume). Rather, it is to situate this chapter's focus on methodology and method, and to acknowledge the importance of decolonizing both if our evaluations are to be responsive to Māori needs and aspirations. Within this we take a principled approach to the identification, development, or adaptation of evaluation methods (Frierson, Hood, Hughes, & Thomas, 2010).

In this chapter, we consider what makes the evaluation methods we use culturally responsive for Māori *whānau*. The *Whānau* Collectives project is briefly described, followed by an overview of the preoccupation with defining *whānau*, mainly so this chapter can move beyond this "red herring." A principled approach to the selection of methods is then explored, with examples provided of the use of these methods within culturally responsive evaluations with Māori.

METHODS AND WHĀNAU COLLECTIVES

The Researching with *Whānau* Collectives[2] (*Whānau* Collectives) project sought research and evaluation methods that would capture the fullness and connectedness of *whānau*. The project recognized that evidence-informed understandings about *whānau* collectives are important for Māori cultural vitality, development, and sustainability. The aim of the *Whānau* Collectives project was therefore to interrogate methods of researching and evaluating with collectives for their appropriateness and usefulness in the study of Māori collectives, in particular *whānau*. Several methods that had the potential to be used in *Kaupapa Māori* (by Māori for Māori) research and evaluation were reviewed, profiled, and pretested with *whānau* collectives.

Defining Whānau

Over the past 30 or so years, research about *whānau* has focused on defining *whānau*. What has emerged is a distinction between *whakapapa whānau*, or those with a shared genealogy, and *kaupapa whānau*, or those who may have a shared genealogy but are mainly together for a common purpose (e.g., sports team, early childhood education) (Metge, 1995). A third type of *whānau* that came largely into being when Māori migrated to urban environments from the 1950s onwards is the household. Walker (2004) describes this unit as a family, while Durie (2003) describes it as a statistical *whānau*. Much of what we know about contemporary *whānau* comes from census data about this third *whānau* unit; that is, aggregated data about individuals living in the same household. This information does not take into account the diversity of *whānau* collectives, which often extend beyond a household; nor does it take into account that something might be happening at the level of the collective that is more than or different from the sum of individual members.

While an interesting exercise, the pursuit of a definition of *whānau* has taken place at a time when society has become more diverse and ways of doing and being "*whānau*" have increased. The "traditional" family unit consisting of a heterosexual, married couple and their children has been challenged by single-parent families, multigeneration families, same-sex couples and children, couples bringing children from previous marriages and unions into a family setting, and many other variations (Families Commission, 2005; Ministry of Social Development, 2004; True, 2005). Family researchers have also argued that the pursuit of a definition of "family" is a red herring that often pulls attention and funding away from research on the facilitators of and barriers to family well-being (Greenstein, 2006). The same critique can be applied to attempts to define *whānau*.

Even so, there is some guidance available for how to define *whānau* in a way that breaks free of the household container (Cram & Pitama, 1998). *Whānau* can be defined as a "collective concept [that] embraces all the descendants of a significant marriage, usually over three or more generations" (G. Smith, 1995). Similarly, the Taskforce on *Whānau*-Centred Initiatives (the Taskforce) (2010, p. 13) defined *whānau* as "a multi-generational collective made up of many households that are supported and strengthened by a wider network of relatives." Within the *Whānau* Collectives project, the decision about the composition of a *whānau* rested with *whānau*; that is, *whānau* members decided who should gather together to talk about the topic or questions being presented by the researcher or evaluator. In this way, the *whānau* that is asked about which model of television they would buy might well be the *whānau* within the household container. The *whānau* that is asked to respond to questions about elder care might well be *whānau* from two or more households who are knowledgeable about the care being provided to their parents or grandparents.

A PRINCIPLED APPROACH TO METHOD SELECTION

Five principles were applied to the identification, screening, and, if needed, revision of methods to use in evaluations that are culturally responsive to Māori lived experiences of *whānau* and *whanaungatanga*. It is difficult to describe the five principles in isolation as they are both processes and methods or, in English, both verbs and nouns. In addition, the principles can be engaged on different levels: personally, within the context of one's own *whānau* or wider *whānau*, collegially with like-minded friends or colleagues, tribally, communally, or nationally. We illustrate some of this complexity under each principle. First, Kirimatao Paipa examines the nature of the principle in terms of her research and evaluation work with *whānau* (see boxed sections). Second, each principle is defined. And third, we provide examples of how each principle can inform the selection of methods for researching and evaluating with *whānau.* We illustrate this with examples related to genograms and ecomaps, PATH (planning alternative tomorrows with hope), and appreciative inquiry.[3]

Whakapapa

I recently used *whakapapa* to grow my knowledge about the context of a research project I was part of. The project was to identify the coping strengths of *whānau* dealing with methamphetamine users in their *whānau.* *Whakapapa* was a natural place to begin my education about methamphetamine. *Whakapapa* allowed me to identify the origins of methamphetamine to a small plant in Asia and to track its movements around the world. *Whakapapa* provided insight into the scientific and medicinal interventions that changed components of a plant into a highly addictive drug. And *whakapapa* helped us understand how the drug became a part of the fabric of New Zealand cities and towns and, in particular, Māori lifestyles. Our team was able to package this information in a bilingual form and then present it back to Māori audiences and *whānau* we were working with to support their understanding of the drug and its movements. These actions resonate with three important principles for Māori—understanding one's origins, reciprocity, and clearing.[4]

For the grandparents, parents, and children who were faced with extreme and bewildering behavior from loved ones who were using the drug and who had no or little knowledge about the drug, *whakapapa* was an important first step in building a relationship with and an understanding of methamphetamine. This meant that *whānau* were able to generate their own criteria, options, and strategies to redefine the boundaries of the drug within their homes and communities. This was an important step in *whānau* taking some kind of control of their environments and giving crucial support to family members who were using.

Whakapapa became a powerful impetus for change, offering a starting point for *whānau* to identify their inner strengths and own pathways to healing. One *whānau* in the project comprised three generations and approximately 23 separate *whānau* belonging to a common ancestor. The grandmother of this *whānau* shared her worries and fears about her *mokopuna* (grandchildren), *tamariki* (children), and *hunaonga* (inlaws) using methamphetamine and how it had affected a large number of her descendants. The relationship this *whānau* had with methamphetamine was intergenerational, complex, and circular. With her permission, *whakapapa* was used to depict the movement of methamphetamine through the three generations of her *whānau.* This identified the users, the buyers, the cooks, and pinpointed the link between psychosis experienced and time in prison. *Whakapapa* identified the strengths in the *whānau,* including nonusers, safe havens, and who was now clean but still vulnerable. In this way, *whakapapa* initiated discussions and prompted actions to take care of the vulnerable.

Definition

Whakapapa means having kinship or familial connections, as indicated above in the term *whakapapa whānau*. If you can visualize the core of an onion and the building of layer upon layer, *whakapapa* would unravel those layers to find the core. Literally, *whakapapa* tracks your connection to *Papatū-ā-nuku* (mother earth), who is at the center of life for Māori. For most Māori, everything we are a part of, take part in, or develop has origins in *whakapapa*. *Whakapapa* can be considered a Māori equivalent of "decision accretion," a term coined by Carol Weiss (1980, p. 382) to describe the "small, uncoordinated steps" of policy decision-making. Used here, it describes the layered, genealogical steps that inform a community or tribe's decision-making, for example, about land tenure, or whether an individual can access knowledge and people. Sometimes you cannot access certain communities or tribal groups without *whakapapa*, or a prior connection to the people, the context, or the area. This is particularly so in rural communities of Aotearoa New Zealand. In the end how, when, and why we connect to people, *kaupapa* (agenda) and places is ultimately very important, and maintaining that connection is even more significant.

It is important to understand the place of *whakapapa* in evaluation; it can be used to track bloodlines as well as history, trends, and influences. Every Māori service or program has a history and *whakapapa* to it, and using *whakapapa* makes the rationale of an intervention explicit. *Whakapapa* can be seen as a way of understanding relationships and making connections. Evaluators also need to be mindful of the historical influences, the effects, and sometimes the emotional pain experienced by Māori tribes and communities. One needs to have a political and a social structural analysis of how events have affected the fabric of Māori society and the relationships we have across communities (Paipa, 2010).

Methods

When selecting evaluation methods, we need to know that a method will enable people to explore and analyze *whakapapa* connections and the relationships within *whānau*. When searching local and international literature for methods that might be useful for research with families as collectives, the genogram stood out as an instrument that depicts *whakapapa* in a diagram similar to that of a family tree. It also provides further information that can depict the connectedness of individuals within *whānau* (Kennedy, 2010b). McGoldrick, Gerson, and Petry's (2008, p. 14) view is that "families are inextricably intertwined . . . and all members of society are ultimately connected." Part of the attraction of the genogram is its ability to display

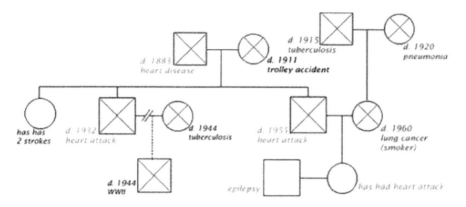

Figure 15.1   Sample genogram depicting health issues across three generations, including year and cause of death where applicable. Legend: □ = male; ○ = female; ✕ = deceased; // = separated. *Source:* McGoldrick et al. (2008). Reproduced with permission.

connections within as well as across generations. It can therefore capture the complexities of *whānau* collectives. The graphic display also provides an effective overview that allows someone who is not familiar with the family to ascertain a lot of information about them in a short time (see Figure 15.1).

Ecomaps can be used in combination with genograms or as a stand-alone tool. They are a useful depiction of relationships and influences between individuals, families, or collectives and their ecological environment (Kennedy, 2010a). Ray and Street (2005) describe ecomaps as a "visual trigger" for discussion about the quality of relationships within and amongst families, the nature of support or care being utilized, and the support still required. This highlights ecomaps as a tool valuable for providing a rich context for the mapping and analysis of the *whakapapa* of *whānau* support networks (see Figure 15.2).

The person-centered planning tool known as PATH (an acronym for Planning Alternative Tomorrows with Hope) provides a useful method that focuses on capacity and strengths while developing a common understanding of a person's past, current situation, and aspirations for the future (Pearpoint, O'Brien, & Forest, 1991). Pipi (2010) writes about how *pakeke* (adults) and *kaumātua* enjoy the dreaming stage as the pictorial presentation of their *moemoeā* (dreams) becomes vivid and reminds them of their past, as often *moemoeā* are based on what *tīpuna* (ancestors) would have wanted and so to look forward is to look back (see Figure 15.3).

Methods that allow participants to talk about the history and future of the organization they work for, including the linkages between people and departments, might also be usefully adapted for evaluations involving *whānau.* Cram (2010) found very little written about the use of appreciative

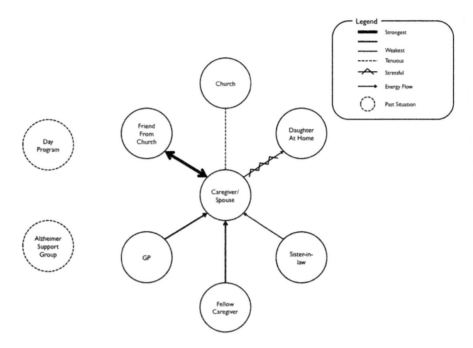

Figure 15.2 Example of an ecomap. *Source:* Adapted from Rempel, Neufeld, and Kushner (2007). Reproduced with permission.

Figure 15.3 Example PATH. *Source:* K. Pipi. Reproduced with permission.

inquiry with families, as it is more popular as an organizational research method. However, appreciative inquiry questions for families (Cooperrider et al., 2008) convinced Cram (2010) that appreciative inquiry might also be used with *whānau* as the questions demonstrated an honoring of *whakapapa* (at least within a nuclear family context).

Whakawhanaungatanga

Whakawhanaungatanga in an evaluation requires me to have some knowledge and awareness of the people I work with. We often work in evaluation teams, with the team acting as a *whānau*. Each team member has strengths and expertise that helps relationships within the team. Acknowledging these strengths among ourselves makes explicit *tuakana* and *tēina* (senior/junior or younger/older sibling or mentor/mentee) relationships. These relationships of *tuakana* and *tēina* are fluid and interchangeable, dependent on where we are in the journey of a project. For example, one or more of the team may have strong contracting and project management experience, another may relish the engagement experience, and yet another may enjoy the solitude of writing. In the context of each other's strengths, we play a combination of leading and supporting roles for each other. I have always found that these relationships foster environments that allow great discussions, debates, and learning.

Alongside this relationship to each other as team members, we also have several relationships to grow within any given project, including relationships with funders, contractors, providers, and the *whānau* and communities we work in. As a Māori evaluator who has the privilege of working among my own relations, there is a responsibility I carry to my own people and overall to all Māori. My lines of accountability are to my people. Whatever work I undertake among or with them is done within relationships of "high trust." They trust me, and others like me, to "do no harm" and, importantly, to add value. This prompts reflective questions about the work I do: What is the value of this work to these people? Does it support, improve, inspire, or attract what is needed for these people to attain the goals that they aspire to?

The relationship we have with the *whānau* and providers we work among is the most important component of what we do. As Māori, this relationship often precedes a project and can often continue past the lifetime of a project. Inevitably, we will meet or take part in other tribal activities together that also require a high trust relationship. The evaluation project is finite; the relationship is enduring.

Definition

Whānau is family. *Whanaunga* is a relative and *whanaungatanga* is the process of establishing and maintaining relationships. *Whakawhanaungatanga* means to make connections or build and maintain relationships. There are different types of relationships, such as blood ties, friendships, collegial, subject-based, funder, or provider based. The process of *whakawhanaungatanga* either utilizes existing networks and/or builds upon them.[5] According to Māoridictionary.co.nz, the definition of *whanaungatanga* is a relationship through shared experiences and working together that provides people with a sense of belonging. It develops as a result of kinship rights and obligations, which serve to strengthen each member of the kin group. It also extends to others to whom one develops a close familial, friendship, or reciprocal relationship.

Methods

Genograms and ecomaps are ideally developed collaboratively with *whānau* and worker(s), as the process encourages engagement and assists in the development of rapport and buy-in. Collaboration also creates an awareness of the fuller picture for *whānau*, the strengths that can be built on, and the weaknesses that can be addressed. The information displayed in both tools is immediately recognizable and easily understood by looking at the graphic display. The value of genograms and ecomaps is that they are tools that assist research to capture the fullness and connectedness of *whānau*, no matter their context. As noted in the *whakapapa* section, a genogram tracks family history and relationships, and comprises a graphic display similar to that of a family tree. Additional to a family tree, a genogram also depicts information about family history as well as different types and qualities of relationships. The familial, emotional, and social relationships that can be depicted across the wider family and across generations, not just a household of individuals, is a strength of this tool.

An ecomap is a tool that depicts an aerial view of relationships and influences on those relationships between individuals, families, and/or collectives and their environment. The ability to map the nature of relationships—who is involved, how they are involved, the benefits of the involvement, whether there is a reciprocated exchange of energy or whether the energy is flowing one way only—gives a clear view of the care and support available and what further support and/or relationship building may be required.

For Pipi (2010), the PATH as a method enables a critical reflection on relationships so that participants are able to reflect on the relationships that serve them well and those that need to be strengthened and maintained in order to achieve their goals. PATH can support *whānau* research that contributes to the discovering, developing, and giving of gifts and investing energy in meaningful activities as one of the five valued experiences of inclusion (O'Brien, Pearpoint, & Kahn, 2010).

One of the reasons Cram (2010) chose appreciative inquiry as a method that could work in evaluation with *whānau* is its potential to help people achieve "dynamic relationships" (Stavros & Torres, 2005), in other words, support *whanaungatanga.* This potential is sourced within Appreciative Inquiry's roots within action research and social constructivist theory, where people are seen as gifted and skilled, human social systems have endless relational capacity, and people's action and attention can be moved to a more positive place through communication (Whitney & Trosten-Bloom, 2003).

Whakawātea

Setting an environment for rich discussion to occur is about ensuring my heart is clear and that my internal biases are known to me. In this way I can act in good faith among others. It may mean having the skills to communicate in the Māori language, or at least offering the option to. While the majority of Māori can now speak and understand English, there are a number of communities in which we work where Māori language is privileged and is the expected mode of communication. There are also elders and young children who express themselves better in Māori. Clearing the way for *whānau* to express themselves means ensuring that team members can easily switch between formal and informal language modes and can interpret and write in both language modes.

A Māori Medium Schools project I worked on required interviews and focus groups to be conducted in Māori. These interactions occurred between *kaumātua* and long-term advocates of total immersion teachings. On one occasion this meant attending a national gathering at a Māori *Whare Wānanga* (University). The reality of this engagement meant meeting a large number of language advocates. While they were not the primary target of the project, it was appropriate (and polite) to meet and extend an invitation to them to input into the project. Being able to interact in both languages allowed a level of sharing to occur that would not have been captured in a monolingual exchange.

Whakawātea is also about responding to other unique ways that people engage. For example, great care needs to be taken to not tax their energy when we work with the elderly from within my own tribal group. This means interviews that are broken up into short blocks and going to the places where they are most comfortable, usually their home. Other age-related conditions come into play such as deafness, so we speak slowly and loudly, repeat questions and write them on white boards, we show pictures to prompt memory, and allow time for absorption, then time for responding, and then time for discussion.

Definition

The term *whakawātea* is used in this context to denote a "clearing" or "cleansing" approach. Sometimes there is a need for conversations to be had or meetings to be held before the "way is clear" for an evaluation to proceed. The word *wā* refers to time and space, so the right time and space is important in considering the steps to be taken in an evaluation. Sometimes the act of *whakawātea* is as simple as conducting prayer, to clear a spiritual path so that one or all may see clearly the pathway ahead. Sometimes the act of having prayer or *karakia* is formally built in to the process, and sometimes it is intuitive on behalf of the evaluator. Sometimes *whakawātea* is about clearing the way so that people can speak from their truth without judgment or fear and with the knowledge that their words are held in a sacred space. *Whānau* are assured that we have their best interests at heart when we take care and time to include them, and often we try to ensure that *whānau* are also present and represented when interpreting, analyzing, or using their words in a written form.

Whakawātea is prevalent in the use of principles for smoothing the way to ensure respectful research, such as self-determination, which includes the right for Indigenous peoples to make decisions about all aspects of their lives; clear benefits to those being researched; and recognition and appreciation for Indigenous culture, values, customs, beliefs, and rights, including an acceptance of a worldview that may not be consistent with Western ideologies (Kennedy & Wehipeihana, 2006).

Methods

The use of genograms and ecomaps with *whānau* would involve ensuring that all of those who wished to contribute were heard. *Whakawātea* is an integral although rarely stated part of the process to ensure smooth passage for the process and the participants. When pretesting ecomaps and genograms, Kennedy (2010a, 2010b) allayed any anxieties and misgivings a *kaumātua* had about needing to recall information. When the *kaumatua* had concerns that he would not be able to relate to the diagrams, it was explained that if this occurred, it would be about the methods not being able to portray the information in an easily understood manner rather than any fault resting with him. In terms of *whakawātea*, had the pretesting been conducted with more *whānau* members, it would have been essential to ensure that all of those who wished to contribute were heard. *Whakawātea* is an integral, although rarely stated, part of the process to ensure smooth passage for the process and the participants.

PATH has the potential to be used as a research and evaluation tool because the process of research involves re-searching for answers and solutions (Cram, 2009). For some participants, there are "mental blocks" that prevent them from looking too far ahead into the future, and despite the notion of hope, they cannot or refuse to see a positive and possible future. Pipi (2010) asserts that in some cases, individuals who tend to "live in the moment" were tested by this idea of looking into the future, particularly when they cannot see past the now. According to O'Brien et al. (2010), sharing ordinary places is another of the five valued experiences of inclusion that acknowledges there is a level of personal preparation required to create the conditions necessary to understand a person's circumstance or situation.

Cram (2010) writes that the emphasis of appreciative inquiry on the positive has been criticized, and she was also skeptical until a very fruitful workshop on appreciative inquiry with Tessie Catsambas prepared the way for her to explore this method further. When she pretested appreciative inquiry with Māori participants in a small rural community, it felt like the positive approach allowed space for a way forward to be found. Although possibly not a "cleansing" as such, it allowed the group to share stories of good gatherings that they then tempered in their own way. There was no push to make them share about the good, bad, or ugly; rather, the sharing about the good times of *whānau* gatherings allowed them to contextualize the role and place of alcohol within those gatherings and how people's drinking was sometimes disruptive.

Whakaae

On a recent project collecting information from gang members and their *whānau*, one of our team provided the initial engagement protocols and warmly welcomed the young men to the process. Once this part of the engagement had occurred, an opportunity to respond was offered. This was then followed by an introduction to the project about why we were there. Questions were then invited, and a back-and-forth dialogue ensued to ensure that there was full understanding amongst us all. Food was shared and conversations of connection occurred. Intuitively gauging a time when everyone was relaxed, I asked the question, "Would you mind me recording you?" Surprisingly for young teenage Māori men, they all answered yes.

Definition

Whakaae relates to agreement, acceptance, consent, and approval—all aspects that must be considered in evaluation. *Whakaae* may relate to participants' willingness to take part in an evaluation or a community's consent for information to be used or approval given to proceed based on agreement. *Whakaae* is the process of coming to an agreement, or not, about a given situation. It can take a considerable length of time dependent on the nature of the topic, particularly where approval is sought, before any information is shared. In order to seek approval or agreement to the process, full disclosure of the project is not only mandatory in an ethical Western approach but is considered essential in a Māori approach in order for *whānau* to make informed decisions. How this message is also conveyed can be considered controversial. Traditionally, a person who could hold people's attention and orally weave and inspire pictures was highly valued. As evaluators, knowing what and why we are doing it is not enough; we must be able to convey this in a way that people understand. Sometimes this takes the form of a dialogue where questions are asked of the evaluators and our knowledge is tested. Silent consent can be assumed if the dialogue continues past the initial information stage. Consent can be checked discretely throughout the evaluation process, as stopping dialogue to introduce a paper-based consent form may be considered rude and out of *tikanga* (protocol).

Methods

It is acknowledged that ethical concerns relate to all evaluation, not solely to the development of genograms and ecomaps. *Whakaae* as a principle was noted in the feedback from stakeholders during the *Whānau* Collectives project; they advocated for ethical considerations about the process of gathering of information from *whānau*. Stakeholders warned of the possible pitfalls in trying to gain consensus from *whānau* regarding decisions about disclosure, sharing of information, ownership of information, and what constitutes informed consent (e.g., full agreement by *whānau* or majority agreement) (Kennedy & Cram, 2010).

Obtaining consent for all those named in genograms and ecomaps may be problematic. The issue may not relate so much to those who consent to provide information, but for others whose names are put forward by participants and for those who may not even realize that they are part of an evaluation (Kennedy, 2010a, 2010b). Other issues that arise relate to maintaining anonymity and confidentiality, reliability and accuracy of information, and the notion that people may not want their networks to be documented (Kadushin, 2005).

Reflections on feedback from participants after pretesting highlighted for Pipi (2010) the value of the PATH as a tool that enables participants to reflect and determine their priority focus for the future. The method requires participants to deliberate on a series of questions that guide their consideration of the future and every aspect of information that is drawn from participants is with their consent.

In the debriefing Cram (2010) did after pretesting appreciative inquiry, participants were very clear that what they would be willing to share within a research space would depend upon who the evaluator was and how he or she was linked through *whakapapa*. Participants were also critical of the language that was used, saying that they would ask differently worded questions. Appreciative inquiry might therefore be used as part of a participatory inquiry where participants get to decide on the questions from the very beginning of the process.

Whakamana

Opportunities to show respect occur regularly throughout interactions with *whānau*, and indigenous evaluators must be able to instigate appropriate formal and informal responses as required, whether this occurs on *marae*, in a mainstream building, or within someone's home. Traditionally knowing how and being able to fluidly reflect and respond to the host peoples' *kawa* or *tikanga* (protocols of engagement) shows respect. Being able to join the two groups together through the reciting of *whakapapa* is another way of respecting the relationships between people and the process of *whanaungatanga* acknowledges evaluators own connections to land and events also shows respect.

The laying of *koha* (gifts) of, for example, food, money, or *tāonga* (gifts of value to the local people) is also valued. Whether I am working with big groups or individuals, the laying of *koha* acknowledges the sharing of information that has occurred. My colleagues and I perform *waiata* (songs that are appropriate to the sharing), and we offer food, money, and petrol vouchers. As stated previously, I have also been able to leave a pictorial form of *whakapapa* with a family, which can be used by them. We have returned people's own stories and photographs to them and have held large gatherings to share evaluation findings. Importantly, where we could, we validated *whānau* journeys by feeding back what we learned from them, highlighting their strengths and sharing our analysis of future possibilities and options open to them. This is our accountability to our people within the contextual reality of our work. In short, it is called giving back, but in my eyes it is about adding value.

Definition

Mana has a number of meanings, including prestige, authority, control, power, influence, status, spiritual powe,r and charisma. *Whakamana* is the enhancement of *mana*. *Mana* enhancement is a conscious process of acknowledgement of individuals, groups, *iwi* (tribes) or communities. In evaluation, this means privileging voices, taking a lead from and being directed by communities with respect to any aspect of their rituals and traditions, acknowledging the importance of their history and context and the *kaupapa* (philosophy and purpose) that drives their services and programs.

"Indigenous peoples want to tell our own stories, write our own versions, in our own ways, for our own purposes... [It is] a very powerful need to give testimony to and restore a spirit, to bring back into existence a world fragmented and dying" (L.T. Smith, 1999, p. 28). *Whakamana* is also about being guided by our ancestors in ways that help us to remember the journey thus far and the road to travel ahead. As stated in 1989 by Sir James Henare, "You have come too far not to go further; you have done too much not to do more" (Te Tai Tokerau Māori Health Strategic Health Alliance and Northland PHOs, 2008, p. ii)

Methods

After pretesting genogram and ecomap methods, *whānau* deemed the process to be beneficial in terms of the input by various members of the *whānau* and the learning about the *whānau* from sharing during the process. *Whānau* appreciated the opportunity to share, learn, and gain an understanding from the contribution of others, while the process provided affirmation that all was well and the outcomes were agreeable. Furthermore, the *whānau* realized the strength and resilience of their *whānau*, while recognizing there were areas that they could contribute to that would provide support for other members of their *whānau* (Kennedy, 2010b).

Pipi (2010) notes that PATH is a quality framework for critical reflection about self and community. Participant feedback indicates that this process of reflection is affirming and validating. It also aligns well with one of the five valued experiences of inclusion of being respected as whole persons whose history, capacities, and future are worthy of attention and whose gifts lead them into valued social roles (O'Brien et al., 2010).

Cram (2010) writes that appreciative inquiry is a strength-based method of inquiry that is compatible with a *Kaupapa Māori* paradigm that emphasizes the importance of being solution-focused, in line with Māori aspirations and Māori development.

> The collaborative approach taken by Appreciative Inquiry is important as it allows whānau to be in the "driver's seat" during the research and therefore able to decide how the research might best serve their aspirations (rather than some preconceived idea that a researcher might have). The researcher's role is to facilitate this process within the bounds of the Appreciative Inquiry method. Whānau will therefore be the key decision-makers with respect to, for example, the Appreciative Inquiry topic(s), the interview questions, the analysis of interview themes, and the Dreaming. (Cram, 2010, p. 8)

The testing of each of these methods within the *Whānau* Collectives project included a *koha* back to those *whānau* and individuals involved as a thank you for the value they added to our understanding of whether or not we had found evaluation methods that would be appropriate and engaging for *whānau*.

DISCUSSION

Selecting appropriate evaluation methods is complex for Indigenous evaluators who carry with them the responsibilities and accountabilities of those who work with their relations (Weber-Pillwax, 2004). For Māori, the challenge is to identify culturally relevant ways of working that make sense to *whānau* and align with *whānau* values with regard to kinship and relational connections. The *Whānau* Collectives project sought to expand our understanding of how Māori collectives, especially *whānau*, might be involved in evaluations and research studies. We wanted methods that would capture the fullness of the relationships and connectedness that exist among *whānau* members that make them so much more than the sum of their component parts/members. These methods can then be used within evaluations that inform *whānau*-related policy to enhance the potential of this policy to support and facilitate *whānau* health and well-being.

When *Kaupapa Māori* is used to inform and guide the choice and use of methods, this often intrinsically and naturally results in the use of Māori ways of knowing and being coming to the fore, sometimes in unplanned and necessary ways. The selection of these methods is therefore guided by Māori principles that acknowledge and embrace the kinship connections and support structures within *whānau*. The principles highlighted here—*whakapapa, whakawhanaungatanga, whakawātea, whakaae,* and *whakamana*—easily translate to a culturally explicit approach to method selection and adaptation. We concluded from the *Whānau* Collectives project that there are evaluation methods that respond to Māori cultural values about *whānau* and family and that can document the lived reality of *whānau* as a collective.

We also noted during the *Whānau* Collectives project that our use of these culturally responsive evaluation methods has the potential to be transformative for *whānau* when they are in the "driver's seat" from the beginning of our engagement with them. We therefore agree that the evaluator is a prime instrument in data collection (Frierson, Hood, & Hughes, 2002); the things that make evaluation methods culturally responsive for Māori *whānau* are often strongly connected to who is undertaking the work. An evaluator's training and expertise is also pivotal to *whānau* being kept safe within an evaluation, especially if sensitive or traumatic experiences are a focus of inquiry (Koller, Raffaelli, & Carlo, 2012). The sensitivity of topics may increase for those who are marginalized or vulnerable within a society, however not all evaluations with vulnerable populations will be on sensitive topics (Lee & Renzetti, 1990). The advice provided by Edwards, McManus, and McCreanor (2005) from their collaborative research with Māori *whānau* about SIDS (Sudden Infant Death Syndrome) is useful in this regard. This includes evaluators keeping themselves safe, accessing *whānau* through guardians (*kaitiaki*), engaging with *whānau* in culturally responsive ways as invited guests, and being attuned to the spiritual practices that may be required (see Chapter 8 in this volume).

We are also exploring with our non-Māori colleagues what culturally responsive evaluation and supporting a Māori *kaupapa* means for them. This involves critical reflection by both Māori and non-Māori evaluators about our roles, responsibilities, accountabilities, and values, lest any of us "proves to be culturally nonresponsive" (Frierson, Hood, & Hughes, 2002, p. 70). At the same time, it is imperative that we all recognize that contemporary *whānau* structures are socially, economically, and culturally (as well as aspirationally) diverse (Ministry of Health, 2002; G. Smith, 1995).

GLOSSARY

Hui	gathering
Hunaonga	inlaws
Iwi	tribe
Kaitiaki	guardian
Karakia	prayer
Kaumātua	elders
Kaupapa	topic
Kaupapa Māori	a Māori way; by Māori, for Māori
Kawa	customs
Koha	gifts
Mana	esteem, status
Māori	Indigenous peoples of Aotearoa New Zealand
Marae	traditional meeting place
Moemoeā	dreams
Mokopuna	grandchildren
Pakeke	adults
Papa-tū-ā-nuku	mother earth
Tamariki	children
Tangata whenua	Indigenous peoples of the land
Tangi	burial rituals
Tēina	younger relative
Tikanga	protocols of engagement
Tīpuna	ancestors
Tuakana	older relative
Waiata	songs
Whakapapa	genealogy
Whakawātea	clearing or cleansing
Whakaae	agreement
Whakamana	enhancement of esteem/status

Whānau	Māori extended family/ies
Whanaunga	relative
Whanaungatanga	family and kinship support networks
Whare Wānanga	university/place of higher learning

NOTES

1. A presentation on this topic was given as part of the "Repositioning Culture and Social Justice in Evaluation" panel at the CREA Inaugural Conference, April 2013, Palmer House, Chicago, IL.
2. This research was supported by Partnership Programme Research grant 08/601 to Fiona Cram and Vivienne Kennedy, from the Health Research Council of New Zealand. Kirimatao Paipa and Kataraina Pipi were contributing authors to this project.
3. Information on the other methods explored in the *Whanau* Collectives project can be found in the 2010 December issue of the *MAI Review* journal (www.review.mai.ac.nz/index.php/MR).
4. Knowing the origin of methamphetamine or its *whakapapa* has been of value for Māori-speaking audiences as this provides a foundation to build an understanding and relationship to the drug. Reciprocity is the idea of returning something of like value back to the participants for the knowledge we have gained as evaluators. Clearing (*whakawatea*) is ensuring that everyone is safe and that the effect of the sharing with evaluators does not leave *whānau* retraumatized or worse off for the engagement.
5. In consultation undertaken by Kennedy and Cram (2010), *Kaumatua* (Elder) Moetatua Turoa discussed our use of the term *whānau* as a verb, stating that what we were talking about was *whanaungatanga*. This is reflected in the aspiration *whānau* have of "reciprocal commitments between and across generations" (Taskforce on *Whānau*-Centred Initiatives, 2010, p. 7).

REFERENCES

Carroll, V. (1970). Introduction: What does adoption mean? In V. Carroll (Ed.), *Adoption in Eastern Oceania. ASAO Monograph No.1* (pp. 3–20). Honolulu: University of Hawaii Press.

Cooperrider Dole, D., Hetzel Silbert, J., Mann, A. J., & Whitney, D. (2008). *Positive family dynamics: Appreciative inquiry questions to bring out the best in families.* Chagrin Falls, OH: Taos Institute Publications.

Cram, F. (2009). Maintaining indigenous voices. In D. Mertens, & P. Ginsberg (Eds.), *SAGE Handbook of social science research ethics* (pp. 308–322). Thousand Oaks, CA: Sage.

Cram, F. (2010). Appreciative inquiry. *MAI Review,* (3), Article 4.

Cram, F., & Pitama, S. (1998). Ko tōku whānau, ko tōku mana. In V. Adair & R. Dixon (Eds.), *The family in Aotearoa New Zealand* (pp. 130–157). Auckland, New Zealand: Addison Wesley Longman.

Durie, M. (2001). *Mauri ora: The dynamics of Māori health.* Melbourne, Australia: Oxford University Press.

Edwards, S., McManus, V., & McCreanor, T. (2005). Collaborative research with Māori on sensitive issues: The application of tikanga and kaupapa in research on Māori sudden infant death syndrome. *Social Policy Journal of New Zealand,* (25), 88–104.

Families Commission. (2005). *Focus on families.* Wellington, New Zealand: Famiies Commission.

Firth, R. (1929). *Primitive economics of the New Zealand Maori.* London, UK: Routledge.

Frierson, H. T., Hood, S., & Hughes, G. B. (2002). Culturally Responsive Evaluation and strategies for addressing it. In J. Frechtling (Ed.), *The2002 user-friendly evaluation handbook* (pp. 63–73). Arlington, VA: National Science Foundation.

Frierson, H. T., Hood, S., Hughes, G. B., & Thomas, V. G. (2010). A guide to conducting culturally responsive evaluations. In J. Frechtling (Ed.), *The 2010 user-friendly handbook for project evaluation* (pp. 75–96). Arlington, VA: National Science Foundation.

Greenstein, T. N. (2006). *Methods of family research* (2nd ed.). Thousand Oaks, CA: Sage.

Henare, M. (1995). *Te Tiriti, te tangata, te whānau: The Treaty, the human person, the family. In Rights and responsibilities. Papers from the International Year of the Family Symposium on Rights and Responsibilities of the Family held in Wellington, 14 to 16 October 1994.* Wellington, New Zealand: International Year of the Family Committee in association with the Office of the Commissioner for Children.

Hopson, R. K. (2009). Reclaiming knowledge at the margins: Culturally responsive evaluation in the current evaluation moment. In K. Ryan & B. Cousins (Eds.), *International handbook of educational evaluation.* Thousand Oaks, CA: Sage.

Kadushin, C. (2005). Who benefits from network analysis: Ethics of social network research. *Social Networks, 27*(2), 139–153.

Kennedy, V. (2010a). Ecomaps. *MAI Review,* (3), Article 4.

Kennedy, V. (2010b). Genograms. *MAI Review,* (3), Article 5.

Kennedy, V., & Cram, F. (2010). Ethics of researching with whānau collectives. *MAI Review,* (3), Article 2.

Kennedy, V., & Wehipeihana, N. (2006). *A stock take of national and international ethical guidelines on health and disability research in relation to Indigenous People.* Wellington, New Zealand: National Ethics Advisory Committee Te Kahui Matatika o te Motu.

Kirkhart, K. L. (2005). Through a cultural lens: Reflections on validity and theory in evaluation. In S. Hood, R. K. Hopson, & H. T. Frierson (Eds.), *The role of culture and cultural context: A mandate for inclusion, the discovery of truth, and understanding in evaluative theory and practice* (pp. 21–39). Greenwich, CT: Information Age.

Koller, S. H., Raffaelli, M., & Carlo, G. (2012). Conducting research about sensitive subjects: The case of homeless youth. *Universitas Psychologica, 11*(1), 55–65.

Lee, R. M., & Renzetti, C. M. (1993). The problems of researching sensitive topics: An overview and introduction. In C. M. Renzetti, & R. M. Lee (Eds.), *Researching sensitive topics.* Newbury Park, CA: Sage Publications.

McGoldrick, M., Gerson, R., & Petry, S. S. (2008). *Genograms: Assessment and intervention* (3rd ed.). New York, NY: Norton.

Mead, H. M. (2003). *Tikanga Māori. Living by Māori values.* Wellington, New Zealand: Huia.

Metge, J. (1995). *New growth from old: The whānau in the modern world.* Wellington, New Zealand: G.P.

Ministry of Health. (2002). *He Korowai Oranga—Maori health strategy.* Wellington, New Zealand: Ministry of Health.

Ministry of Social Development. (2004). *New Zealand families today.* Wellington, New Zealand: Ministry of Social Development.

O'Brien, J., Pearpoint, J., & Kahn, L. (2010). *The PATH and MAPS handbook: Person-centered ways to build community.* Toronto, ON, Canada: Inclusion.

Paipa, K. (2010, June 25–26). *An approach to learning second languages.* Te Ataarangi. Stabilising Indigenous Languages Conference, University of Oregon.

Pearpoint, J., O'Brien, J., & Forest, M. (1991). *Planning positive possible futures, planning alternative tomorrows with hope (PATH).* Toronto, ON, Canada: Inclusion.

Pipi, K. (2010). The PATH planning tool and its potential for whānau research. *MAI Review, 3.*

Ray, R. A., & Street, A. F. (2005). Ecomapping: An innovative resesarch tool for nurses. *Journal of Advanced Nursing, 50*(5), 545–552.

Rempel, G. R., Neufeld, A., & Kushner, K. E. (2007). Interactive use of genograms and ecomaps in family caregiving research. *Journal of Family Nursing, 13*(4), 403–419.

Simon, J., Smith, L., Cram, F., Hohepa, M., McNaughton, S., & Stephenson, M. (2001). *A civilising mission? Perceptions and representations of the Native schools systems.* Auckland, New Zealand: Auckland University Press.

Smith, G. (1995). Whakaoho whānau ohangā: The economics of whānau as an innovative intervention into Māori cultural and educational crises. *He Pukenga Kōrero, 1,* 18–36.

Smith, L. T. (1996). Kaupapa Māori health research. In *Hui Whakapiripiri: A hui to discuss strategic directions for Māori health research* (pp. 14–30). Wellington, New Zealand: Te Rōpū Rangahau Hauora a Eru Pōmare.

Smith, L. T. (1999). *Decolonizing methodologies: Research and indigenous peoples.* New York, NY: Dunedin, New Zealand: Zed/Otago University Press.

Stavros, J. M., & Torres, C. B. (2005). *Dynamic relationships: Unleashing the power of Appreciative Inquiry in daily living.* Chagrin Falls, OH: Taos Institute Publications.

Taskforce on Whānau-Centred Initiatives. (2010). *Whānau Ora: Report of the Taskforce on Whānau-Centred Initiatives, to Hon. Tariana Turia, Minister for the Community and Voluntary Sector.* Wellington, New Zealand: Taskforce on Whānau-Centred Initiatives.

Te Tai Tokerau Māori Health Strategic Health Alliance and Northland PHOs. (2008). *Te Tai Tokerau Māori health strategic plan 2008-2013.* Whangarei, New Zealand: Te Tai Tokerau Māori Health Strategic Health Alliance and Northland PHOs.

True, J. (2005). *Methodologies for analysing the impact of public policy on families.* Wellington, New Zealand: Families Commission.

Walker, R. (2004). *Ka whawhai tonu: Struggle without end* (Rev. ed.). Auckland, New Zealand: Penguin.

Weber-Pillwax, C. (2004). Indigenous researchers and Indigenous reseach methods: Cultural influences or cultural determinants of research methods. *Pimatisiwin: A Journal of Aboriginal and Indigenous Community Health, 2*(1), 77–90.

Weiss, C. H. (1980). Knowledge creep and decision accretion. *Science Communication, 1*(3), 381–404.

Whitney, D., & Trosten-Bloom, A. (2003). *The power of Appreciative Inquiry.* San Francisco, CA: Berrett-Koehler.

CHAPTER 16

CULTURALLY RESPONSIVE INDIGENOUS EVALUATION

A Practical Approach for Evaluating Indigenous Projects in Tribal Reservation Contexts

Nicole R. Bowman (Mohican/Munsee)
Bowman Performance Consulting
and University of Wisconsin–Madison

Carolee Dodge Francis (Oneida)
University of Nevada, Las Vegas

Monique Tyndall (Mohican/Munsee/Omaha)
Goucher College

ABSTRACT

Culturally responsive evaluations in Indigenous or Tribal government reservation geographic contexts are complex and multifaceted studies. These contexts include the intersection of multiple legal jurisdictions across federal, state, and Tribal governments based on funding source(s) and implemen-

Continuing the Journey to Reposition Culture and Cultural Context
in Evaluation Theory and Practice, pages 335–359
Copyright © 2015 by Information Age Publishing
335

tation site(s). Additionally, the cultural and linguistic components of Indigenous contexts vary greatly across communities where program evaluations are being conducted. Through a contemporary case example, the authors provide a framework for co-constructing a culturally responsive evaluation design and describe practical strategies for evaluating a federally funded program implemented within a Tribal government reservation context. Implications for replicating future culturally responsive evaluations are shared to move toward building a larger body of empirical studies guided by Indigenous evaluation frameworks, theories, and formal policies (i.e., the United Nations Declaration of Indigenous Rights).

Understanding Indigenous[1] culture and contexts is critically important in developing an effective Indigenous evaluation or research design. Awareness of diversity within and across Indigenous communities, understanding of the unique cultural and traditional norms, and ability to navigate the various contexts in which an Indigenous evaluation is carried out all contribute to successful research and evaluation. These contexts include the intersection of multiple legal jurisdictions across federal, state, and Tribal governments based on funding source(s) and implementation site(s). Too often, the absence and exclusion of Indigenous epistemologies, frameworks, methodologies, communities, and other resources from Western or mainstream academic research significantly contributes to gaps in policy, programming, and intended outcomes for Indigenous people.

Indigenous research conducted by Indigenous or non-Indigenous scholars must be ethical, culturally sensitive (Tillman, 2002) and appropriate for the communities where the research is conducted (Grande, 2004; Hood, Hopson, & Frierson, 2005; Kovach, 2010; LaFrance & Nichols, 2009; LaFrance, Nichols, & Kirkhart, 2012; Oakes, Riewe, Edmunds, Dubois, & Wilde, 2003; Smith, 2012). By including culture and context in a study's design, researchers and evaluators create a rigorous and responsive method (Hood et al., 2005), which increases opportunities for documenting the truth, allows for authentic participation of a wide variety of stakeholders, and increases the multicultural validity of a study (Kirkhart 1995a, 1995b, 2005; LaFrance et al., 2012).

Understanding historical context in this field is essential: researchers must acknowledge and address the dynamics of power (Gitlin, 1994) and disempowerment when creating research or evaluation studies conducted with Indigenous people. Prior to European contact, Indigenous people inhabiting North America used their own systems of self-governance to sustain high levels of health, education, social, and community welfare of Tribal people. Each tribe was unique in its culture; customs, worldview, traditions, and other teachings were grounded in a way of life that was distinct to each particular tribe. From Tribal histories, documents, and other Indigenous artifacts, we understand that life was not merely maintained, but Indian people thrived prior to European contact. Tribes met the needs of their people through a blend of self-governance and cultural traditions in which the community members participated and provided accountability.

European contact forced North American tribes from their ancestral homelands, destroyed their communities (culturally and literally), and forced assimilation to a European way of life that is now considered mainstream North American culture. As centuries passed, tribes made treaty agreements with the federal government in which they gave up lands and other resources; in return, the federal government was to provide for their health, education, and general welfare. Eventually, under sovereignty and self-determination laws, tribes established Federal Indian Policy with the U.S. government.

Given this historical context, it is understandable that sovereignty and self-determination are paramount concerns in evaluations in Indigenous contexts. Tribal sovereignty and self-determination are not merely federal-level legal distinctions, but also have implications in terms of documenting, monitoring, improving, and supporting nation-building efforts carried out by Tribal governments and Tribal programs (Harvard Project on American Indian Economic Development, 2008; Jorgensen, 2007). Tribal identity, culture, health, education, and long-term socioeconomic success depend on nation-building efforts in which evaluation can be a key factor. Truly effective evaluation requires respect for and ability to navigate within this multijurisdictional (federal, state, local, and Tribal) environment.

In this chapter, we discuss what constitutes culturally responsive evaluation in the Indigenous context, focusing on theory, research, and policy that inform construction of culturally responsive Indigenous evaluation frameworks, political/legal considerations in Indigenous evaluation, and cultural/traditional concerns. We also describe the current state of culturally responsive evaluation in the Indigenous context, explain barriers to culturally responsive evaluation, and explore how those barriers are being addressed. We then use a case example to illustrate how principles of culturally responsive evaluation can be employed in a real-world Indigenous context in order to "see the world through the eyes of our ancestors and translate the best knowledge of the world into acceptable modern scientific terminology" (Deloria & Wildcat, 2001, p. 28). In conclusion, we discuss progress toward culturally responsive evaluation in Indigenous contexts and steps for future growth.

CULTURALLY RESPONSIVE EVALUATION IN THE INDIGENOUS CONTEXT

Overview

Evaluators and researchers must understand that Indigenous people, programs, and communities exist within various geographic contexts: rural, urban, and Tribal reservation lands. Tribal reservations are part of the 565 federally recognized tribes acknowledged by the U.S. government. Each of these Tribal governments has their own set of elected officials, their own Tribal governance operational structure, and their own laws, policies, and procedures. Beyond Tribal governments, the focus of the case example in this chapter, there are also urban Indian communities. Urban Indian communities are found in large cities across the United States (e.g., New York, NY; San Francisco Bay Area, CA; Minneapolis, MN, Chicago, IL). Urban Indian communities normally have a community center, health center, and other urban Indian programming offices where services and resources are available to Indigenous people living off the reservation. Off-reservation Indians also reside in rural and suburban areas; generally, these people either go to Tribal reservations or urban Indian centers to receive services and programming. All these communities have varying legal jurisdictions, implement policy and programs differently, and have unique cultural norms set by the community members living in the geographic space.

Theory, Research, and Policy Informing Culturally Responsive Indigenous Evaluation

Because the academic base of Indigenous evaluation theory is not as robust or long-standing as work in other fields, we look to Indigenous guidelines from the research, education, and policy fields to anchor our evaluation work. Our chapter, like many of our Indigenous evaluation colleagues' presentations and published works, humbly offers our perspectives to further contribute to this knowledge base.

Tribal Critical Theory is a theoretical framework and method used to examine Indigenous people throughout the world for personal and Tribal empowerment and liberation (Brayboy, 2005; Pulitano, 2003). Unlike Critical Race Theory (CRT), which asserts that racism is endemic to society, TCT holds that colonization[2] is endemic to society (Brayboy, 2005). Brayboy's (2005) summary of TCT explains that this theory recognizes that Indigenous peoples strive toward Tribal sovereignty, Tribal autonomy, self-determination, and self-identification; this can conflict with governmental policies that are tied to the problematic goal of assimilation. TCT emphasizes the importance of Tribal beliefs, philosophies, and customs for understanding the lived reality of Indigenous people as well as the differences among individuals and groups. It also recognizes the importance of story as a legitimate data source and building block of theory, and insists that the interconnected nature of theory and practice demands that researchers work toward social change.

Evaluation designs influenced by TCT have the potential to employ Indigenous strategies that are authentic and alternative ways of knowing (Jacobs, 2008; Mertens & Cram, 2013; Mertens & Wilson, 2012) as well as contextually responsive, culturally relevant, and educationally empowering now and for the next seven generations[3] (Bergstrom, Cleary, & Peacock, 2003; LaFrance & Nichols, 2009).

Indigenous Evaluation Frameworks (IEF) situates an evaluation in context and relationship to the place, setting, and community in which the evaluation is carried out (LaFrance et al., 2012). In their work, LaFrance and Nichols (2010) identify four key values that must be included in creating IEF: being a people of a place, recognizing gifts, honoring family and community, and respecting sovereignty. IEF is a holistic framework that is conceptualized, designed, and carried out in a nonlinear way, with relationships and subrelationships concurrently informing one another and the evaluation as a whole. As Indigenous evaluators and authors, we often say, "We work with you, not on you" when serving an Indigenous community or client with an evaluation study. An analogy used by elders to describe this process is to envision sitting in a circle around the lodge or campfire and talking equally about perspectives, strategies, decisions, and usefulness of information for now and the next seven future generations. This philosophy differs from many Western theories and methods where evaluation and research is deemed an objective, disconnected, "study" of a program, project, community, or people.

The principles of TCT and IEF align with a larger, national, "Tribally driven" Indian research agenda (National Congress of American Indians Policy Research Center [NCAI PRC], 2013) that incorporates the following Indigenous guidelines (Strang & von Glatz, 2001):

- embracing the spirit of Indigenous sovereignty and self-determination within [an evaluation] context;
- providing educational research [and evaluation] for Tribal student, family, and community empowerment;
- legitimizing and liberating the Indigenous voice and perspective while deconstructing majority educational paradigms; and
- purposefully instructing and disseminating scholarly discourse within Native and non-Native publications, research and policy forums, public debates, educational or academic [and evaluation] communities and contexts.

As Indigenous evaluators, we consider these principles of Tribal control of a research agenda and evaluation central to our professional and academic evaluation work.

The Political/Legal Context of Indigenous Evaluation

Sovereignty and self-determination.

The late Daniel K. Inouye, U.S. Senator from Hawaii, testified many times that, "the sovereign status of Indian Nations predates the formation of the United States" (Wilkinson, 2004, p. xi). As a lifetime advocate for the political and legal rights of Indigenous people in the United States (Native Hawaiian, Alaska Native, and Native Americans), Senator Inouye understood the fundamental right of Tribal nations and Indian people to self-governance. Sovereignty (broadly), under federal law, recognizes that Indian nations are sovereign governments separate from the federal and state government, with their own inherent and unique rights to govern (Cohen, 1942; Pevar, 2012; U.S. Department of the Interior [DOI], 2013a; Wilkins & Lomawaima, 2001). Internationally, these distinct and legal protections extend to Indigenous people to safeguard their economic, social, cultural, linguistic, and political freedoms through the United Nations Declaration of Rights for Indigenous People (UN, 2008), including tribes or Indigenous governments in the United States, Australia, Canada, and New Zealand.

Researchers and evaluators must understand that when they conduct research within Tribal contexts, they are no longer under the jurisdiction of the state or federal government but rather that of the Tribal government. Thus, recognizing the tenets of Tribal sovereignty, self-governance, and self-determination, how these tenets intersect with state and federal laws and programs and their practical and logistical implications is critical to conducting culturally responsive, competent, and practical evaluations in Indian Country.

Multijurisdictional approaches to Indigenous evaluation.

Tribal governments follow their unique Tribal constitutions and are responsible for upholding Tribal law as well as protecting Tribal members' safety, rights, and well-being from non-Indian governments, organizations, and people. However, there is uneven capacity for evaluation across the 565 Tribal governments in the United States (DOI, 2013b). Tribal Institutional Review Boards (IRBs) and other human subject protocols are not consistent across Tribal governments or other Tribal organizations, and the comprehensiveness and formality of these ordinances, policies, and procedures vary widely. For example, fewer than 10% (Bowman, 2006a) of 565 recognized Tribal governments (Norris, Vines, & Hoeffel, 2012) have IRBs. Furthermore, of the 35 Tribal colleges operating in the United States, only 25% of them have their own IRB (Bowman, 2006a). Fewer than 1% of the Tribal governments have Tribal policies or Tribal IRBs for research, evaluation, and policy studies (Bowman, 2006a), and roughly 1% had ordinances, policies, and procedures formally developed for their Tribal IRB to work in conjunction with non-Tribal partners (DOI, 2013b). This is problematic because when Tribal governments or Indigenous organizations (Tribal colleges, Tribal nonprofits, etc.) do not establish their own IRBs and other evaluation policies, they are more susceptible to designs, data, and programs that are not valid or effective for Indian populations in the long term (Bowman, 2006a; Deloria, 2002; NCAI PRC, 2013). The current lack of capacity and infrastructure to support culturally responsive evaluation that is led or overseen by Indigenous organizations or Tribal governments contributes to confusion and misunderstanding in the political/legal context of evaluation.

This confusion around the political/legal context is compounded by the current disconnect and lack of clarity between Indian and non-Indian people in terms of how policies are carried out through programming, documenting best practices, conducting appropriate evaluations, and human subject protection in Indigenous contexts at the institutional and systemic level. Often, federal and state governments do not recognize or understand the collective responsibilities and power of Tribal government IRBs (National Institute of Justice, 2013). In terms of education, the jurisdiction and authority for the education of Indian students who do not reside on a reservation has not been clearly established by case law (Native American Rights Fund, 2000), leaving it unclear as to who is responsible for ethical and culturally appropriate research on and off the reservation—external funding agencies or tribes? This lack of clarity leaves legal gaps and little leverage for Tribal governments or Indigenous organizations to negotiate or protect their human subjects and Tribal intellectual property, or keep cultural protection safeguards in place when working on programs funded by non-Indian governments, universities, and other nonprofit or for profit organizations.

We can look to work done in the justice and health fields for practical guidance in this regard when creating evaluations in Indigenous legal/political contexts. *Multijurisdictionality* is a legal term applied most often in justice contexts (Bureau of Justice Assistance, 2012). The federal government, usually through the justice and health departments, uses a multijurisdictional approach with state, municipal, and Tribal governments. This multijurisdictional approach links all forms of government into an interconnected system that helps agencies form policy task forces and working groups; develop information and resource sharing practices; form political alliances, create memos of understanding and legal ordinances or structures; and carry out research and evaluation studies to properly document evidence-based programs and practices carried out in municipal, state, federal, and Tribal contexts.

The evaluation community could benefit from a multijurisdictional framework when working in Indian Country, and much work has been done to identify and establish the foundations of a multijurisdictional approach to evaluation in the Indigenous context (Bowman, 2005, 2006a, 2006b, 2007a, 2007b, 2008, 2011; Bowman & Dodge Francis, 2014; Bowman & Tyndall, 2014). From multijurisdictional work in other fields, we have determined that good evaluation design and implementation in the Indigenous context

- considers Tribal, state, federal, and international laws and policies for human subject protection, research or evaluation, intellectual and cultural property rights, data sharing agreements, and/or ownership, publication, and dissemination agreements that already exist;
- identifies connections and differences between Tribal grantee and non-Tribal funding agency policies and procedures;
- acknowledges current infrastructure and builds on commonalities and strengths in policies, reporting formats, and expectations;
- identifies and articulates policy and procedure gaps or differences in order to bridge gaps to achieve consensus;
- provides visual examples of forms, instruments, or other databases to demonstrate the grantee's potential evaluation methodology;
- uses or modifies existing Tribal instruments, databases, or processes;
- considers from the Tribal perspective how evaluation may enhance the development of current or new capacities, policies, or protocols for sustaining programming after the grant has ended;
- shares successes and best practices with other Tribal governments and Indigenous organizations, with the knowledge, consent, and participation of Tribal constituents;
- obtains permission to share, present on, or publish information outside of the Indigenous context in order to protect human subjects, cultural protections, and intellectual property rights.

By incorporating these best practices, the formal component of Indigenous evaluation recognizes existing Tribal capacity, considers local evaluation needs, and addresses what the funder requires. Both the funder's requirements and the needs of the governing local agency (Tribal government, Tribal nonprofit board, Tribal school board, etc.) are considered and included in the evaluation design.

The Cultural/Traditional Context of Indigenous Evaluation

In this section, we explore the cultural/traditional context of indigenous evaluation. The cultural/traditional context takes into account the community's shared collection of learned and socially transmitted behaviors, beliefs, and institutions that act as a template to shape behavior and consciousness from generation to generation.

Evaluation and evaluators in the cultural/traditional context.

Evaluation completes the circle of research, development, and practice. However, an evaluator must possess the skills, knowledge, and competencies to design and carry out a culturally responsive evaluation that uniquely addresses an Indigenous context and project. An evaluator must be prepared to include multicultural validity (Kirkhart, 2005) because it is central to creating an evaluation design that produces valid, reliable, culturally responsive, and contextually appropriate findings. Cultural incompetency or lack of a multicultural and contextual lens in evaluation leads to nonresponsive evaluation designs and methods that can generate inaccurate, inappropriate, or even harmful findings.

Tribal governments and Indigenous organizations must often rely upon outsiders and/or a non-Indian person, public agency, or other organization to conduct evaluation work. Currently, there are few Indigenous evaluation scholars trained to participate in evaluation-related activities. Of course, their near absence in the community of evaluation scholars is due in part to their near absence on the faculties of our colleges and universities (Turner, 2002) and in graduate programs that serve as a pipeline for evaluation practitioners and/or scholars. Native Americans are by far the least represented of all racial/ethnic groups in U.S. graduate programs (U.S. Census Bureau, 2012), which helps explain why we lack a sufficient pool of technically and culturally responsive evaluators[4] for and from Indian Country.

Therefore, in these situations, the evaluator for an Indigenous project in an Indigenous context becomes responsible not only for designing the evaluation, but for being a trusted teacher who can help facilitate capacity building with the community being evaluated and the project members carrying out the grant or program being evaluated. A culturally responsive evaluator has the knowledge, skills, and abilities for evaluation but also is intentional and inclusive when selecting and implementing evaluation design and methods based on the cultural and contextual needs of the project, context, participants, and stakeholders.

Defining the cultural/traditional context.

Cajete (1994) reminds Indigenous people to look to the mountain for guidance, where the mountain represents traditional Indigenous knowledge. This knowledge is located within the cultural/traditional context, which is equally as important as the political/legal (or formal Tribal government) context. This context includes beliefs, behaviors, and institutions, and is governed by core values and protocols carried out by the community's traditional leaders, elders, and students. It has elements that predate the influence of European cultures and the assimilation policies administered by colonial and modern America. Despite efforts to colonize Indigenous peoples, their epistemologies in one form or another continue to exist today.

The cultural/traditional context includes formal and informal but traditional teachings and leadership most often held by elders, medicine men or women, linguists, and other knowledge keepers of Tribal history and culture. These are not elected officials; rather, they are leaders dictated by cultural protocols, oral histories, and familial lines. The cultural/traditional context for an Indigenous evaluation design also includes members living on or off the reservation who are not traditional or cultural leaders or elected officials of the Tribal government. Most often these are the members of the Tribal population who coexist daily with others who are engaged in regular community (sociocultural) activities, are the participants in or recipients of Tribal programming and resources, and are responsible for holding accountable the elected and employed members of the Tribal government.

The Indigenous epistemic culture distinguishes between various settings of knowledge production and emphasizes their contextual aspects (Knorr Cetina, 1999); this differs from the Western epistemic culture. The Indigenous protocols around how knowledge is gained, used, shared, protected, and respected must be acknowledged and upheld above all other epistemic cultural protocols. Indigenous epistemic culture is not monolithic; each Indigenous community has a unique way of learning, thinking, and doing; influenced by language, culture, and beliefs, that must be taken into account.

For Indigenous communities, simply measuring outcomes and evaluating what needs improvement is not considered a comprehensive design. Inclusion of process data, documentation of what is working, and including measurements for sustainability after the grant monies are gone or the evaluation study has concluded is considered a balanced approach to evaluation in Indigenous contexts. Therefore, the process of carrying out an evaluation is just as important—if not more so—than the final evaluation products (reports, instruments, presentations, publications, etc.); in other words, the journey is as important as the destination. Both the process and the products of an evaluation study must be sustainable and useful to the Tribal government and community it serves long after the evaluation or research project has been completed.

Components of the cultural/traditional context.

Components of the cultural/traditional context include geographic location; cultural and language protocols; heritage, lineage, and familial relationships; access rights to knowledge and to disseminate that knowledge; and review and endorsement from community cultural/traditional practitioners. All these components inform what cultural information can or cannot be collected and how, in order to produce a version of the community cultural/

traditional knowledge that is valid and appropriate for a broader audience outside of the local Indigenous community. The discussion that follows is not comprehensive, but provides an overview of several of the cultural considerations that must be addressed in the cultural/traditional context.

Access rights to knowledge.

In addition to working with elected Tribal officials or Tribal employees, it is important to also seek out those community leaders, elders, and traditional teachers who uphold informal but powerful cultural protocols. Culturally responsive evaluation in the Indigenous context goes beyond the legal and academic structures of an evaluation by including cultural, linguistic, and other community safeguards that protect Indigenous communities knowledge and data. Providing a traditional gift (which may be tobacco, venison, cloth, or something else, depending on the cultural practices of the Tribal community) as permission or a thank you for considering the evaluation design and participating in the study is an example of a community safeguard. Discussing in advance the proposed study and methods and asking what the community would like in return for participating in and supporting the study are examples of respecting the safety of the community.

In terms of data collection, evaluators must be aware that knowledge is shared in negotiated spaces; for example, information gleaned in a sacred space like a sweat lodge or teaching circle may not be available to or shared with outside investigators and the wider world in the way that information from more public ceremonies or discussions might be. It is worth noting that the protection of Indigenous knowledge has taken on even more significance as the number of industries or commercialized businesses seeking to use biodiversity and the Indigenous knowledge related to it have grown. Given the historical treatment of Indigenous people, incorporating this component into Indigenous evaluation design is critical to building trust with communities who have been and continue to be disempowered, disenfranchised, and decimated by non-Indian policies, organizations, and governments.

Oral versus written knowledge transmission.

Traditionally, for Indigenous people, knowledge development, collection, and transfer are primarily oral processes. Western or European processes for data collection and evaluation privileges statistics and the written word as the principal ways of documenting data, transferring knowledge, or citing evidence in research or evaluation studies. Not only is this a cultural and methodological disconnect, but it also creates capacity, infrastructure, and resource issues for improving the policy process or program impact through evaluation and raises methodological questions. For instance, are oral history methods better suited for assessment and evaluation versus an online survey? How do linguistic translations from the Native language differ among participants and how does this interpretation impact the evaluation data being collected?

Culturally responsive evaluation in this context does not privilege the written word but understands that oral traditions in Indigenous contexts are often more sacred, respected, and protected than the written protocols. Safeguards can be orally transmitted (Indigenous Peoples Council on Biocolonialism, 2004; Mihesuah & Wilson, 2004; Smith, 2012) but can also be created in writing with shared memorandums of understanding, formally approved IRB or Tribal government protocols, and other human subject protection processes agreed upon by the Indigenous and non-Indigenous participants and organizations. Samples of such protocols and formal agreements can be found by contacting Tribal government agencies and Indigenous scholars, or through checking Indigenous websites from Tribal colleges, Tribal nonprofits, and other Tribal for-profit organizations that conduct regular research in Indian Country.

Social and political status.

Evaluators must remember that context matters and that safeguards vary because Tribal communities, organizations, and governments are not monolithic. The cultural and linguistic practices of each Tribal community (and within families or clans of a Tribal community) dictate political status, social responsibilities through family and clans, and leadership based on matrilineal or patrilineal grounds. Evaluators must understand and address the fact that their own personal characteristics (male or female, insider or outsider, traditional or nontraditional, Native or non-Native, elder or adult, etc.) can all affect the safeguards needed by the Tribal community in a research context as well as the level of access a researcher has within the Indigenous context.

To summarize, cultural context must inform the evaluation design, processes, and methods. Without these knowledge, skills, and competencies, an evaluator will potentially create evaluation studies, use approaches, and generate findings that are inconsistent, incongruent, and/or are invalid with the Indian people and community that the program is supposed to serve.

Benefits of incorporating the cultural/traditional context.

The incorporation of the cultural/traditional context in the evaluation process is essential to Tribal communities, due to the shared belief or truth that by maintaining, respecting, and continually incorporating the beliefs, protocols, and practices of our traditional Tribal ways we can, "see the world through the eyes of our ancestors and translate the best knowledge of the world into acceptable modern scientific terminology" (Deloria & Wildcat, 2001, p. 28).

This cultural knowledge may inform evaluators of goals, measurable outcomes, and impact indicators that otherwise would not have been foreseen. Using resources available to a culturally responsive evaluator from the cultural/traditional context (in conjunction with the political/legal context and funder requirements) helps to build a comprehensive evaluation design, one that truly reveals and captures the underlying cultural knowledge, challenges, and experiences that influence the lives of Indigenous peoples living in the local and broad community from the Tribal participants who are part of the evaluation.

Recognizing and using elements from a cultural/traditional context is a process for decolonizing (Wilson & Yellowbird, 2005) an evaluation in an authentic attempt to re-write and re-right (Smith, 2012) history and create capacity for better decision-making in the future to benefit Indigenous communities and participants. Responsive evaluation approaches will generate useful program information, authentically engage all participants, and will help to shape future policy and practice that will positively affect the next seven generations.

CULTURALLY RESPONSIVE EVALUATION: A CASE EXAMPLE

In this section of the chapter, we use a case example from our work to illustrate how the culturally responsive Indigenous evaluation strategies, frameworks, and competencies discussed earlier in the chapter can be applied in real-world Indigenous contexts.

Background

In 2005, the Centers for Disease Control and Prevention (CDC) released a funding opportunity, entitled *Health Promotion and Diabetes Prevention Projects for AI/AN Communities: Adaptations of Practical Community Environmental Indicators* (CDC, 2005), NDWP/DDT/NCCDPHP. The funding opportunity was to establish 3-year cooperative agreements within Tribal communities. The program purpose of the CDC grant was to "strengthen local capacity of AI/AN communities in implementing limited, practical community environmental interventions for health promotion and diabetes prevention" (CDC, 2005, p. 29761). It should be noted that this grant did not constitute a research methodology but reflected a public health perspective (CDC, 2008). The Indigenous community in which our work was conducted was one of eight CDC grantees.

Given the unique political/legal and cultural/traditional distinctions of Indigenous people and communities, our evaluations most often use a responsive Indigenous case study design. Case studies address why decisions or strategies were used, how they were implemented, and describes what type of results there were (Schramm, 1971). Research or evaluation in Western contexts is usually experiential, prioritizing the impressions of the observer, standardized measures, and statistical aggregation (Stake, 1986). In contrast, in this instance, the Indigenous project evaluation model incorporated distinct Tribal voices from the breadth of community and the health promotion and prevention project. The evaluation focused on assets, barriers, and the incorporation of traditional teachings into programming, and employed a mixed and multimethod evaluation to the design. Our study design used data collection instruments to collect and confirm data throughout the project. Evaluation findings helped shape data-driven discussions, were used to modify program implementation efforts, and also annually revealed best practices associated with the most effective program activities. This design allowed continuous program evaluation and built upon the human and infrastructure capacities for future evaluations. A constant and comparative process for analysis was used throughout the evaluation, and continual community member-checking for formative and summative evaluation findings was employed throughout the evaluation process.

Evaluation Participants

The Indigenous community is a federally recognized Indian tribe occupying a reservation that was established by treaty agreements between the Tribal government and U.S. federal government. The Tribal government operates pursuant to a constitution promulgated under the Indian Reorganization Act, 1934. The tribe's land base exists within the Midwest. The reservation boundaries encompass two townships where approximately 21,000 acres are either held in trust or owned by the tribe. The villages closest to the reservation have a population no greater than 600 residents. Moderate-to-large urban Indian communities that have impact on social and economic conditions of the tribe are located 60–170 miles away. Like many tribes, this Indigenous community was displaced from the ancestral territory, which they inhabited for millennia, by colonial forces. Losing Tribal lands and ways of life that depended on them resulted in a culture shift away from a long-established economy and system of governance that was elaborate and complex.

Fewer than 3,000 people live within the reservation boundaries. Demographics from the 2010 Census noted an unemployment rate of 14.6% on the tribe's reservation. The median household income level in 2009 was

$36,908. For female full-time year-round workers, the median earning level was $23,917; for male full-time year-round workers, the median earning level was $28,365. The average per capita income was $15,272. According to the 2010 U.S. Census, 15.1% of Tribal families living on the reservation lived in poverty in 2009; all of these families had children under age 18.

Case Study Evaluation Design

The four project goals of the CDC grant for this particular grantee were to assist the community in identifying, implementing, and evaluating environmental health interventions for youth; assist youth in establishing life-long healthy nutrition and physical activity behaviors; involve parents in all aspects of the proposed program; and impact and positively influence the community for establishing lifelong healthy eating and physical activity behaviors through programs, activities, and environmental changes (policies). In order to evaluate this project, we used the following culturally responsive Indigenous evaluation methods.

Community collaborations.
Self-determination respects, recognizes, and values the inherent worth of Indian culture; is responsive to the community's needs as voiced by all members of society; builds programs around Indian assets and resources; and employs Indians in every part of the process including, program, policy, implementation, and evaluation. Based upon this foundation, we moved forward with co-planning our evaluation with the key assumption that everyone shares responsibility for achieving positive community wellness. Our evaluation process honored and incorporated the value of self-determination in several ways.

Before the evaluation research began, evaluators and participants worked together to create a culturally relevant evaluation plan in a dialogue and brainstorming process that honored the "seven-generations" teachings of including elders', community members', and youth perspectives as we consider how current actions and behaviors impact future generations. Rather than imposing outside data collection methods upon the community, we asked community members to help identify existing data sources (e.g., agendas, media releases, community center sign-in sheets, etc.) to use in our evaluation as a community collaboration and means to consensus-based decision making. Monthly work and advisory meetings with project participants continually revisited how program implementation was meeting or not meeting the self-identified needs of the community resulting in a flexible evaluation design that continued to address real-life issues through realistic and locally viable solutions.

The evaluator and project stakeholders worked together to jointly communicate successes and involve local schools, community organizations, and other Tribal governmental offices and programs. Communicating successful outcomes with Tribal and community partners leveraged more growth, secured shared resources, and strengthened sustainable program efforts for continuing positive changes and programming long after the grant ended. For example, grant work done to upgrade ballfields inspired local government spending on upgraded fencing around the fields as well as new uniforms for ballplayers. When new playground equipment was installed at the at pow wow grounds, the Tribal Roads and Planning Department contributed extra funds for wood chips for the playground area.

Cultural relevance.

Ensuring that evaluations are culturally relevant allows communities to heal, strengthen, and preserve Indigenous societies now and for the next seven generations. Our evaluation process honored the unique culture and traditions of this community in many ways. We began the evaluation process by approaching elders and community leaders with appropriate gifts (in this case, tobacco and traditional foods like venison and berries) as we asked their permission to begin and for their help in this project.

In particular, we ensured that our evaluation used culturally appropriate data collection methods and instruments. As discussed above, we worked with the program participants to identify existing data sources that meet evaluation needs rather than imposing our own measurement methodology. Where we did identify data collection gaps, we worked together with community members to find new, culturally relevant ways to collect data. For example, students in the community who participated in the collaborative process identified themselves as "data warriors" (a culturally resonant term) and brainstormed ways to gather needed data, including collecting local restaurant menus and taking pictures of vending machines used in the community to document their contents. "Pow wow pedometers" measured the number of steps taken and calories burned by fancy dancers versus traditional dancers at ceremonies. These data collection methods and instruments quantified healthy behavioral changes and involved participants in a way that honored the principal of "working with" rather than "working on." These data collection methods were unique to the grantee but also became an opportunity to expand Indigenous knowledge and understanding from the funders' perspective.

As the grant program continued, evaluators worked with participants to identify ways that program elements could be culturally relevant and meet program goals. New policies were created around traditional food use and access. Participants worked to acquire ancestral food knowledge and incorporate traditional healthy food into daily menus as well as special social-cultural events like pow wows, field trips, and ceremonies. Student data collectors, their families, and actively engaged project participants influenced policy around healthy choices in community center vending machines and food provided at community center events. The goal of all program elements was to incorporate healthy lifestyle choices in ways that were culturally relevant and sustainable after the CDC program concluded.

Dissemination.

Sharing knowledge and respect for Indigenous knowledge rights is another key component of culturally responsive evaluation. At each stage of the project implementation and evaluation process, evaluators worked to communicate program status to participants and to listen and respond to participants' ideas and concerns. Monthly work and advisory meetings ensured that information was shared for decision making, assessing impacts, and for making project or program modifications in an ongoing process. Our evaluation team worked to share project data with the wider community in multiple formats. We were sure to encompass the oral dimension of Indigenous knowledge sharing in meetings, presentations, traditional talking circles, and participation in community events. Project staff prepared reports for the local Tribal government, school district boards of education, in the Tribal newspaper, on the Tribal website, and the national funding agency on a quarterly to semiannual basis. One program element was monthly demonstrations showing how to make Indigenous and traditional food in healthier ways; another was a cookbook that highlighted new knowledge about healthy traditional foods. Visual formats, such GIS mapping related to the project, as well as project photographs, helped tell the story of this project to the community. We also used more traditional Western practices, such as sharing information through non-Tribal newsletters, press releases, and written reports to communicate with the project participants and the wider community. Open communication within the Tribal community helped shape new choices in Tribal programming, Tribal recreation center menus, and through the local school's health curriculum and cafeteria menus.

With careful and respectful consideration of the appropriate use and sharing of knowledge in this context, we worked with participants to share our findings with the wider public. Co-authored reports and presentations by Tribal and non-Tribal organizations and staff members increased trust, built relationships, built capacities for technical reports and presentations, and gave credibility to and shared responsibility for the evaluation study findings. The data was used in further grants, collaborative programming, and leveraging additional resources to carry out health initiatives extending to Tribal and non-Tribal schools, restaurants, parks, and other communal spaces or contexts.

This example of a culturally responsive evaluation demonstrates how evaluators can empower Indigenous communities and individuals through evaluation by honoring traditional knowledge, making evaluation useful to community needs, and by respecting Indigenous ownership of evaluation data.

DISCUSSION

"Indiginizing" Evaluation

As illustrated by the case study above, culturally responsive evaluation can help build capacity throughout the evaluation process if empowerment (Fetterman, Kaftarian, & Wandersman, 1996), Indigenous, (Bowman, 2006a; Denzin, Lincoln, & Smith, 2008; Kovach, 2010; LaFrance & Nichols, 2009; LaFrance et al., 2012; Mertens & Cram, 2013; Smith, 2012), and utilization focused (Patton, 2012) approaches are used.

Table 16.1 demonstrates how we transform the seven steps of colonialism as defined by Frideres and Gadacz (2000) to create a more culturally responsive case design and process for conducting Indigenous evaluations.

Progress Toward Culturally Responsive Evaluation in the Indigenous Context

Currently, few Tribal governments or Indigenous organizations use evaluation data as an effective tool for shaping Tribal or multijurisdictional public policy, making budgetary decisions, and/or to drive programmatic decision making. In any work toward this goal, the tenets of trust, data ownership, and sovereign rights of Tribal people on or off the reservation need to be part of a concerted dialogue by all parties (Tsosie, 2007). Building this capacity will require a significant investment in time and money for restructuring, building infrastructures (technology, data collection systems, creating ordinances, policies, etc.), providing staff development, and supporting organizational development to carry out new ordinances, policies, and procedures across Tribal government or Indigenous organizations and systems. The scope of training, technical assistance, and interfacing of Indian and non-Indian governments, systems, and programs needed to develop common evaluation policy, culturally responsive evaluation designs, and data collection or sharing systems is staggering. But without evaluation capacity building within, across, and outside of Indian Country, the pattern of long-term educational, economic, health, and other disparities that Indian people have endured will likely continue.

TABLE 16.1 Indigenizing Evaluation

Seven Steps of Colonialism (Frideres & Gadacz, 2000)	Seven Steps to Decolonialize and Indigenize (Bowman, 2007a)
1. Uninvited arrival of colonizers into territory	1. Utilization of a traditional knowledge council and community elders work together in the community
2. Destruction of Indigenous social and cultural institutions	2. Use of traditional knowledge (oral and written), Indigenous institutions, and non-Indian organizations if endorsed by Tribal community as a process to add to local Indigenous knowledge base
3. Creation of economic dependency of Indigenous people on colonizers	3. Providing traditional gifts as part of the evaluation process for allowing me to work in the community and for their participation in the research
4. Establishment of external political control	4. Indigenous intellectual knowledge, approval of evaluation, and ownership of data by Tribal community is controlled by Indigenous community and is formalized through memos of understanding with researcher and research organization
5. Provision of low level social services	5. Evaluation data provides information to inform and improve local services being provided by Tribal and non-Tribal governments for Indigenous community members
6. Use of a color line; i.e., racism, to justify the above	6. Critical examination by an external traditional knowledge council and participants to prohibit racism, end colonist practices in evaluation, and promote the value and use of Indigenous knowledge and processes
7. Weaken the resistance of the Indigenous people	7. Empower Indigenous communities and individuals through evaluation by honoring traditional knowledge, making evaluation useful to community needs, and through Indigenous control/ownership of evaluation data

Despite challenges, we see hopeful progress toward more culturally responsive evaluation practices. Tribes, along with many professional and political support organizations like the National Congress of American Indians (NCAI), Native American Rights Fund (NARF), and Tribal Education Departments National Assembly (TEDNA), have politically engaged state and federal government systems and non-Indian organizations to help address capacity issues. For instance, NCAI, NARF, and TEDNA have worked with non-Indian governments and organizations to help develop Tribal policy, facilitated Tribal consultation sessions with non-Tribal governments, and have convened training and technical assistance sessions. An increasing number of tribes are moving proactively to create their own IRBs under the Department of Health and Human Services, Code of Federal Regulations, Title 45 Public Welfare, Part 46 Protection of Human Subjects, which was first issued in 1974 (Department of Health and Human Services, 2009). These federal, tribal, and other international (UN, 2008) ordinances, policies, and guidelines in promoting and designing culturally responsive evaluation approaches can be used to move us toward addressing current low capacity and resource issues as well as building a stronger empirical literature base for academia.

To broaden the pool of culturally responsive Indigenous evaluators, varying levels of collaboration are essential to ensure current and future programming growth for the inclusion of Indigenous evaluators and to fill the publication gaps in evaluation literature and academic studies. There are long- and short-term impacts to be considered: creating a formal plan, task force, or coalition of like-minded colleagues in combination with Tribal colleges, Tribal governments, and other Tribal organizations (nonprofit or corporate) would be a good way to begin this journey.

For Tribal communities, culturally responsive evaluation models and practices have heightened the awareness of bridging cultural context issues of Native/non-Native, federal/self-governance, Western/Indigenous epistemology and consideration of the evaluators' own world perspective. It is critically important that Tribal governments and Indigenous organizations have the right, ability, and responsibility to adapt and use their cultural knowledge; the power to create ordinances, policies, and protocols for intellectual and cultural protection, preservation, and monitoring of evaluation projects; and the authority to establish, implement, and hold accountable the use of standardized measures for program effectiveness and services to create political and cultural norms that are reflective of their people on and off the reservation.

As Tribal communities move forward into the world of program evaluation, a hybrid model of Westernized institutional structures and an authentic culturally responsive system should be the goal. As in many transformations, the question that usually surfaces is "How does the angst of acculturation stay balanced and true to American Indian ideologies?" (Dodge Francis, 2009, p. 87). The impact of academia, evaluators, and community partnerships outside of Tribal communities will play a significant role in defining, shaping, and supporting the contextual framework of evaluation methodology, implementation, and outcomes of an evaluation approach selected within a Tribal setting. Tribal communities must not lose sight of the quest to create or attain a culturally responsive evaluation system that embraces their hegemonic ability to dictate the mission, infrastructure, or organizational framework. This does not always come easily or overnight given the challenges noted earlier in the chapter.

In conclusion, this chapter synthesizes available Indigenous evaluation theories, knowledge, and frameworks in combination with evaluation resources provided to us from other disciplines and non-Indigenous sources. We do this with the hopeful vision of "continuing the journey." Our work and that of others, both named and unnamed in our chapter, inspires us to be part of the work of building the theoretical and empirical basis of

Indigenous evaluation. We will continue to "position" ourselves as professionals working toward a deeper academic base for Indigenous evaluation with the help of our evaluation community, colleagues, and friends. In the natural time and process, we look forward to how we may eventually "reposition" ourselves as we continue on the journey to construct, deconstruct, practice, and learn more deeply about the Indigenous footprint for evaluation theory and practice. It is our prayer that together we may continue walking this good path. *Anushiik.*

AUTHOR NOTE

Correspondence concerning this manuscript should be addressed to Nicole Bowman (Mohican/Munsee), President/Founder, Bowman Performance Consulting, 271 River Pine Drive, Shawano, Wisconsin 54166. E-mail: nicky@bpcwi.com

NOTES

1. We use multiple terms in this chapter for describing Native Americans or Native American communities. Indigenous is used as a general term; it is also used interchangeably with Indian, Native American, American Indian, First Nation, by naming a specific tribal affiliation or languages, and/or via other Indigenous phrases as we deemed appropriate or as noted within cited source materials.

2. Colonization is when an alien people invade the territory inhabited by people of a different race and culture and establish political, social, spiritual, intellectual, and economic domination over that territory (Yellow Bird, 1999). Colonization is a political act that marginalizes Indigenous people (Adams, 1997).

3. The expression "seven generations" is a widely accepted Indigenous cultural understanding. This metaphor refers to a sustainability theory based upon ancient epistemology shared among multiple Woodland and Indigenous Nations (Benton-Banai, 1988; Bergstrom et al., 2003). The seven generation model argues that leadership, communities, and individuals need to be mindful that decisions they make affect the livelihood of all future generations (Dumont, 1996), including humans, animals, and plants. (LaDuke & Alexander, 2004). The model also advocates for leadership to take actions that sustain best practices in governance (Williams & Works, 2007) in order to ensure wellness for all in creation.

4. We deliberately chose the term "culturally responsive evaluator" versus "culturally competent evaluator." An evaluator may be culturally competent but may not always choose to be responsive when conducting Indigenous evaluations.

REFERENCES

Adams, H. (1997). *A tortured people: The politics of colonization*. Penticton, BC, Canada: Theytus.

Benton-Banai, E. (1988). *The Mishomis book: The voice of the Ojibway*. Hayward, WI: Indian Country Communications.

Bergstrom, A., Cleary, L. M., & Peacock, T. D. (2003). *The seventh generation: Native students speak about finding the good path*. Charleston, WV: ERIC Clearinghouse on Rural Education and Small Schools.

Bowman, N. (2005, October). *Government to government evaluation: Issues and strategies for conducting evaluation with Tribal governments*. Paper presented at the annual conference of the American Evaluation Association, Toronto, Ontario, Canada.

Bowman, N. (2006a, June). *Tribal sovereignty and self-determination through evaluation*. Paper presented at the Tribal Leader/Scholar Forum of the National Congress of American Indians-Policy Research Institute, Sault St. Marie, MI.

Bowman, N. (2006b, November). *Indigenizing evaluation: New tools and techniques grounded in time honored traditions*. Paper presented at the annual conference of the American Evaluation Association, Portland, OR.

Bowman, N. (2007a, Spring). Cultural validity creates sovereignty and self-determination. *Winds of Change, 22*(2), 52–55.

Bowman, N. (2007b, April). *Mapping 'common ground' through interactive dialogue: Fostering cross-cultural research collaborations between Native educational research and research in the larger field of education*. Paper presented at the annual meeting of the American Educational Research Association, Chicago, IL.

Bowman, N. (2008, November). *Measuring cultural issues in multiethnic evaluation*. Paper presented at the annual conference of the American Evaluation Association, Denver, CO.

Bowman, N. (2011, November). *Valuing Indigenous rights: Implications of the UN Declaration on the rights of Indigenous peoples for evaluation*. Paper presented at the annual conference of the American Evaluation Association, Anaheim, CA.

Bowman, N. R., & Dodge Francis, C. (2014, October). *Responsive Indigenous evaluation: A cultural & contextual framework to use in Indian country*. Paper presented at the annual conference of the American Evaluation Association, Denver, CO.

Bowman, N. R., & Tyndall, M. (2014, September). *Responsive Indigenous evaluation: A cultural & contextual framework for Indian country*. Paper presented at the annual conference of the Center for Culturally Responsive Evaluation and Assessment, Chicago, IL.

Brayboy, B. (2005). Toward a tribal critical race theory in education. *The Urban Review, 37*(5), 425–446. doi:10.1007/s11256-005-0018-y

Bureau of Justice Assistance. (2012). *What are multijurisdictional task forces*. Retrieved from https://www.bja.gov/evaluation/program-law-enforcement/forces1.htm

Cajete, G. (1994). *Look to the mountain: An ecology of Indigenous education*. Skyland, NC: Kivaki.

Centers for Disease Control and Prevention (CDC). (2005). Health promotion and diabetes prevention projects for American Indian/Alaska Native (AI/AN)

communities: Adaptations of practical community environmental indicators. *Federal Register, 70*(99), 29760–29765.

Centers for Disease Control and Prevention (CDC). (2008). *CDC: FY 2008 annual tribal budget and consultation report.* Retrieved from http://www.cdc.gov/minorityhealth/reports/08/TBC_FY08_Report.pdf

Cohen, F. S. (1942). *Handbook of federal Indian law.* Washington, DC: Government Printing Office.

Deloria, V., Jr. (2002). *Evolution, creationism, and other modern myths: A critical inquiry.* Golden, CO: Fulcrum.

Deloria, V., Jr., & Wildcat, D. R. (2001). *Power and place: Indian education in America.* Golden, CO: Fulcrum.

Denzin, N. K., Lincoln, Y. S., & Smith, L. T. (Eds.). (2008). *Handbook of critical and Indigenous methodologies.* Thousand Oaks, CA: Sage

Department of Health and Human Services. (2009). *Code of federal regulations, title 45 public welfare, part 46 protection of human subjects.* Retrieved from http://www.hhs.gov/ohrp/policy/ohrpregulations.pdf

Dodge Francis, C. (2009). *The art of looping linear: Perspectives from tribal college students and faculty.* Saarbrücken, Germany: VDM.

Dumont, J. (1996). What was given in the beginning is still there: An interview with Jim Dumont. In D. Thorpe (Ed.), *People of the seventh fire: Returning lifeways of Native America* (pp. 76–81). Ithaca, NY: Akwe:kon Press, Cornell University American Indian Program.

Fetterman, D. M., Kaftarian, S. J., & Wandersman, A. H. (Eds.). (1996). *Empowerment evaluation: Knowledge and tools for self-assessment & accountability.* Thousand Oaks, CA: Sage.

Frideres, J. S., & Gadacz, R. R. (2000). *Aboriginal peoples in Canada: Contemporary conflicts* (6th ed.). Toronto, ON, Canada: Prentice Hall.

Gitlin, A. (Ed.). (1994). *Power and method: Political activism and educational research.* New York, NY: Routledge.

Grande, S. (2004). *Red pedagogy: Native American social and political thought.* Lanham, MD: Rowman & Littlefield.

Harvard Project on American Indian Economic Development. (2008). *The state of native nations: Conditions under U.S. policies of self-determination.* New York, NY: Oxford University Press.

Hood, S., Hopson, R., & Frierson, H. (Eds.). (2005). *The role of culture and cultural context.* Greenwich, CT: Information Age.

Indigenous Peoples Council on Biocolonialism. (2004). *Collective statement on Indigenous peoples on the protection of Indigenous knowledge agenda item 4(e): Culture.* Retrieved from http://www.ipcb.org/resolutions/htmls/pf2004.html

Jacobs, D. T. (2008). *The authentic dissertation: Alternative ways of knowing, research, and representation.* New York, NY: Taylor & Francis.

Jorgensen, M. (2007). *Rebuilding native nations: Strategies for governance and development.* Tucson: University of Arizona Press.

Kirkhart, K. E. (1995a). Multiculturalism, validity and evaluation theory. *Evaluation Theories, 2*(2), 1–3, 5–6.

Kirkhart, K. E. (1995b). Seeking multicultural validity: A postcard from the road. *Evaluation Practice, 16*(1), 1–12.

Kirkhart, K. E. (2005). Through a cultural lens: Reflection on validity and theory in evaluation. In S. Hood, R. Hopson, & H. Frierson, (Eds.), *The role of culture and cultural context* (pp. 21–39). Greenwich, CT: Information Age.

Knorr Cetina, K. (1999). *Epistemic cultures: How the sciences make knowledge.* Cambridge, MA: Harvard University Press.

Kovach, M. (2010). *Indigenous methodologies: Characteristics, conversations, and contexts.* Toronto, ON, Canada: University of Toronto Press.

LaDuke, W., & Alexander, S. (2004). *Food is medicine: Recovering traditional foods to heal the people.* Minneapolis, MN: Honor the Earth.

LaFrance, J., & Nichols, R. (2009). *Indigenous evaluation framework: Telling our story in our place and time.* Alexandria, VA: American Indian Higher Education Consortium.

LaFrance, J., & Nichols, R. (2010). Reframing evaluation: Defining an Indigenous evaluation framework. *The Canadian Journal of Program Evaluation, 23*(2), 13–31. Retrieved from http://www.aihec.org/programs/documents/ NSF-TCUP/DefiningIndigenousEvaluationFramework_LaFrance-Nichols Nov2010.pdf

LaFrance, J., Nichols, R., & Kirkhart, K. E. (2012). Culture writes the script: On the centrality of context in Indigenous evaluation. *New Directions for Evaluation, 2012,* 59–74. doi:10.1002/ev.20027

Mertens, D., & Cram, F. (2013, May). *Transformative and Indigenous frameworks for mixed and multi-method research.* Manuscript submitted for publication.

Mertens, D. M., & Wilson, A. T. (2012). *Program evaluation theory and practice: A comprehensive guide.* New York, NY: Guilford.

Mihesuah, D. A., & Wilson, A. C. (Eds.). (2004). *Indigenizing the academy: Transforming scholarship and empowering communities.* Lincoln: University of Nebraska Press.

National Congress of American Indians Policy Research Center (NCAI PRC). (2013). *Policy Research Center tribal research regulation toolkit.* Retrieved from http://www.ncaiprc.org/research-regulation

National Institute of Justice. (2013). *Conducting research in tribal communities.* Retrieved from http://www.nij.gov/topics/tribal-justice/research/conducting. htm

Native American Rights Fund. (2000). *Tribal-state partnerships: Cooperating to improve Indian education.* Retrieved from http://www.narf.org/nill/documents/ NARF_tribal_state_partnerships.pdf

Norris, T., Vines, P. L., & Hoeffel, E. M. (2012). The American Indian and Alaska Native population: 2010. *2010 Census Briefs* (C2010BR-10). Retrieved from http://www.census.gov/prod/cen2010/briefs/c2010br-10.pdf

Oakes, J., Riewe, R., Edmunds, A., Dubois, A., & Wilde, K. (Eds.). (2003). *Native voices in research.* University of Manitoba, Canada: Aboriginal Issues Press.

Patton, M. Q. (2012). *Essentials of utilization-focused evaluation.* Thousand Oaks, CA: Sage.

Pevar, S. L. (2012). *The rights of Indians and tribes* (4th ed.). New York, NY: Oxford University Press.

Pulitano, E. (2003). *Toward a Native American critical theory.* Lincoln: University of Nebraska Press.

Schramm, W. (1971, December). *Notes on case studies of instructional media projects.* Working paper for the Academy for Educational Development, Washington, DC.

Smith, L. T. (2012). *Decolonizing methodologies: Research and Indigenous peoples* (2nd ed.). New York, NY: Zed.

Stake, R. E. (1986). *Quieting reform: Social science and social action in an urban youth program.* Urbana: University of Illinois Press.

Strang, W., & von Glatz, A. (2001). *American Indian and Alaska Native education research agenda: Research agenda working group.* Washington, DC: U.S. Department of Education.

Tillman, L. C. (2002). Culturally sensitive research approaches: An African-American perspective. *Educational Researcher, 31,* 3–12. doi:10.3102/0013189X031009003

Tsosie, R. (2007). Cultural challenges to biotechnology: Native American genetic resources and the concept of cultural harm. *The Journal of Law, Medicine & Ethics, 35,* 396–411. doi:10.1111/j.1748-720X.2007.00163.x

Turner, C. S. V. (2002). *Diversifying the faculty: A guidebook for search committees.* Washington, DC: Association of American Colleges and Universities.

United Nations (UN). (2008). *United Nations declaration on the rights of Indigenous peoples.* Retrieved from http://www.un.org/esa/socdev/unpfii/documents/DRIPS_en.pdf

U.S. Census Bureau. (2012). *Higher education—Institutions and enrollment 1980 to 2009.* Retrieved from http://www.census.gov/compendia/statab/2012/tables/12s0278.pdf

U.S. Department of the Interior (DOI). (2013a). *What we do.* Retrieved from http://www.doi.gov/whatwedo/firstamericans/index.cfm

U.S. Department of the Interior (DOI). (2013b). *Tribes.* Retrieved from http://www.doi.gov/tribes/index.cfm

Wilkins, D. E., & Lomawaima, K. T. (2001). *Uneven ground: American Indian sovereignty and federal law.* Norman: University of Oklahoma Press.

Wilkinson, C. (2004). *Indian tribes and sovereign governments.* Oakland, CA: American Indian Resources Institute.

Williams, S. M., & Works, S. S. (2007). Preservation of life: Guiding principles of Indian tribal governments. In Harvard Project on American Indian Economic Development, *The state of the native nations: Conditions under U.S. policies of self-determination* (p. 188). New York, NY: Oxford University Press.

Wilson, A., & Yellow Bird, M. (2005). *For Indigenous eyes only: A decolonization handbook.* Santa Fe, NM: School of American Research Press.

Yellow Bird, M. (1999). Indian, American Indian, and Native Americas: Counterfeit identities. *Winds of Change: A Magazine for American Indian Education and Opportunity, 14*(1).

CHAPTER 17

PARTNERING WITH PACIFIC COMMUNITIES TO GROUND EVALUATION IN LOCAL CULTURE AND CONTEXT

Promises and Challenges

Joan LaFrance
Sharon Nelson-Barber
Elizabeth D. Rechebei
Janet Gordon

INTRODUCTION

Over the last several years, research and evaluation scholars have become more aware of and concerned with the need to conduct their efforts in ways that are mindful of indigenous peoples' rights and concerns (LaFrance & Crazy Bull, 2009). This has led to national policies at the government level. For example, in Canada, researchers must submit their proposals to Research Ethics Boards that follow the Tri-Council Policy Statement (TCPS) for research. Section 6 of the TCPS directs researchers to a number of

Continuing the Journey to Reposition Culture and Cultural Context
in Evaluation Theory and Practice, pages 361–378
Copyright © 2015 by Information Age Publishing

documents that outline ethical guidelines for working with First Nations and Aboriginal communities. Noting that in Canada and elsewhere, indigenous peoples have "distinctive perspectives and understandings embodied in their cultures and histories," the policy statement "recognizes the international consensus that has developed over recent decades that Aboriginal Peoples have a unique interest in ensuring accurate and informed research concerning their heritage, customs, and community," (Canadian Institutes of Health Research, Natural Sciences and Engineering Research Council of Canada, Social Sciences and Humanities Research Council of Canada, 2005, p. 6.2).

The Health Research Council of New Zealand issued *Guidelines for Researchers on Health Research Involving Maori*. The guidelines are intended to inform researchers about when consultation is necessary and the processes to use when initiating consultations with Maori. The document notes that one of the purposes of the guidelines is to "ensure that the research outcomes contribute as much as possible to Maori health and well-being, while the research process maintains or enhances mana Maori (Maori authority or power)" (Health Research Council of New Zealand, 1998, p. 3).

All researchers in the United States are bound not only by governmental and academic institutions' Internal Review Boards (IRBs), but more importantly by a growing number of tribal IRBs and regulations regarding the research about and evaluation of peoples and programs (Bowman, 2006). Organizations such as the American Evaluation Association (AEA) have adopted a formal statement on cultural competence in evaluation (AEA, 2011).

Even more striking are the growing movements to take control of evaluation and research processes, and define what qualifies as indigenous research and evaluation. Linda Tuhiwai Smith (2012) draws on the definitions of Graham Smith in defining *Kaupapa Maori* research as that which is related to being Maori. According to Smith (p. 187), *Kaupapa Māori*

- Is related to "being Māori,"
- Is connected to Māori philosophy and principles,
- Takes for granted the validity and legitimacy of Māori,
- Takes for granted the importance of Māori language and culture, and
- Is concerned with the "struggle for autonomy over our own cultural well-being."

Māori evaluators frequently refer to *Kaupapa Māori* when describing culturally appropriate evaluation practice. (See for example Cram, McCreanor, Smith, Nairn, & Johnstone, 2006; Kawakami, Aton, Cram, Lai, & Porima, 2008; Mertens, Cram, & Chilisa, 2013).

Beginning in 2004, the American Indian Higher Education Consortium of tribal colleges and universities began to formalize an *Indigenous*

Evaluation Framework (LaFrance & Nichols, 2009, 2010) intended to pre-pare personnel in tribal colleges to take ownership of their own evalua-tion processes. The Framework grew out of an extensive consultation with American Indian evaluators, educators, and cultural experts. Although it does not reject Western evaluation practice, the Framework places evalu-ation within American Indian epistemology and core values. This episte-mology, or ways of knowing, is founded on the traditions of a people, their creation stories, clan origins, and their oral record of encounters with the world. It also includes empirical knowledge and that which is acquired through dreams, visions, and ceremonies. Core values acknowledge that tribal peoples are located in a specific place, that community and family are paramount, and that there is a deep respect for the gifts of each mem-ber of the community. A value central to indigenous peoples is sovereignty, which is expressed politically and through preservations of language and culture. The Framework suggests a process by which tribal communities can use their own ways of knowing and core values to guide their evaluation practices. It recognizes that American Indian tribes assess merit based on their traditional values and that by defining the meaning of evaluation and practice in their own terms, American Indians take ownership rather than respond to Western practices. The Framework stresses the importance of ensuring that evaluation supports tribal sovereignty and self-determination.

Around the same time that this effort was taking place, Pacific leaders from across Micronesia assembled in the Republic of the Marshall Islands to "re-think education in the Pacific" as a route to survival, transforma-tion, and the sustainability of its peoples (Sanga, Niroa, Matai, & Crowl, 2004). The formation of a Commission on Education in Micronesia came about for the purposes of advocating for inclusion of indigenous knowl-edge, philosophies, and practices in the education of Micronesian chil-dren; and offering guidance and support to individuals, groups, and agen-cies in promoting and enhancing the integration of indigenous knowledge, philosophies, and practices in the education of indigenous Micronesians (Rechebei, 2004). This notion of attending to the inclusion of indigenous perspectives extended to the desire for research to be responsive to the needs of Pacific island peoples both at universities and in the policy arena. More recently, the Commonwealth of Northern Mariana Islands (CNMI) and the Republic of Palau are seeking to create research review boards, indicating a growing awareness, as well as unease, about research and how it impacts local populations (E. Rechebei, personal communication, March 2014; Senase, 2011).

Mekinak Consulting, an American Indian evaluation firm owned by one of the authors of the *Indigenous Evaluation Framework*, now joins forces with Pacific Resources for Education and Learning (PREL), the lead organization administering two National Science Foundation (NSF) projects, in an effort to increase indigenous evaluation capacity in island nations across the north Pacific. This chapter describes the promises and the challenges faced by a small group of external evaluators as they study the work of the projects while shaping their evaluation processes in ways that are respectful of Pacific indigenous contexts, protocols, and practices. In these settings, working toward an "indigenized" evaluation process means attending to the immense geography and numerous diverse groups of indigenous languages and cultures. A brief description of the uniqueness of these contexts follows, along with information about the nature of the projects being evaluated. The remaining discussion is devoted to many of the situational challenges that arose in these circumstances and the strategies devised to address them.

THE PACIFIC CONTEXT

The Pacific islands of interest in this chapter include the state of Hawai'i; the U.S. territories of American Samoa, Guam, the CNMI under a Covenant Agreement with the United States of America; and three independent nations freely associated with the United States under the Compact of Free Association. These include the Federated States of Micronesia (FSM), the Republic of the Marshall Islands (RMI), and the Republic of Palau. Descended from various cultural groups who navigated and established societies throughout Oceania thousands of years ago, the populations are linguistically and culturally diverse. The region encompasses roughly 17 dominant ethnic and cultural groups that speak at least 20 languages and numerous dialects. The population of nearly 2 million people inhabit islands and atolls spread across almost 5 million square miles of the Pacific Ocean. This vast area (noted within the triangle in Figure 17.1) is almost 50% larger than the continental United States.

As many of these islands are now independent nations associated with the United States or members of the U.S. territorial commonwealth, they look to Western traditions of schooling, curriculum, teacher training, and program evaluation. Many schools conduct classes in the heritage language through grade 3 and begin English instruction by grade 4. Also, many islanders, including teachers, are English-language learners. Still, despite a long history of outside influence, traditional leadership remains strong, operating alongside elected leadership for both state and national governments. For example, some Pacific Islanders honor long-established beliefs that certain knowledge is private and owned by the family, and they follow traditional protocols for passing on knowledge to younger generations. Other Islanders are open to considering Western perspectives and strategies.

Above all, in these places of diverse history, language, culture and more, trust-building and collaboration are essential for capacity-building (Heine

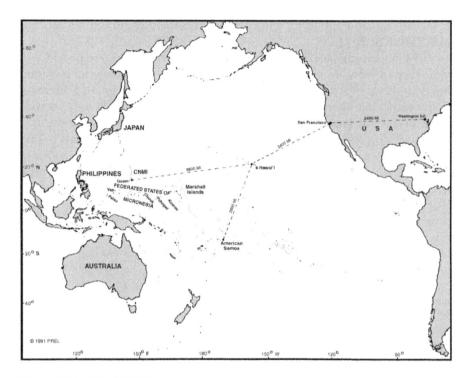

Figure 17.1 The USAPI.

& Chutaro, 2003; Hezel, 2001). With over 20 years delivering technical assistance in the region, PREL understands comprehensive, inclusive, and iterative processes that draw on broad perspectives and expertise grounded in local practice, and contextualized to specific locales. This way of operating is enhanced by PREL's embedded staff, many of whom are indigenous members of their communities and who have nuanced understandings and deep knowledge of ways to effectively collaborate with regional education stakeholders, infrastructures, and capacities. PREL's mission, experience, and capacity in the region provide optimal circumstances for partnering to conduct responsive evaluation.

TWO FOCAL PROGRAMS

Two projects are being carried out across the region: the Pacific Islands Climate Change Education Partnership (PCEP) and Mathematics and Culture in Micronesia: Integrating Societal Experiences (MACIMISE). These projects began in 2010 and 2009, respectively. Mekinak Consulting has been the external evaluator for PCEP since its inception and assumed this role for MACIMISE in 2012.

PCEP is a multifaceted effort to enhance regional capacity to provide climate change education in schools and communities. The current program has a number of strands. It is working to formulate a Climate Education Framework that aligns the new Next Generation Science Standards with the educational standards of the independent nations in the region. It is implementing several different professional development programs to prepare teachers to discuss climate change. It works with local organizations to develop curriculum materials and fosters community and school partnerships to engage classroom teachers with local environmental agencies so that they can create opportunities for field-based climate change education activities. Throughout all of these activities, PCEP strives to incorporate indigenous knowledge about climate and align the work closely to the traditional beliefs and experiences of the local populations. Figure 17.2 illustrates PCEP's model for change.

MACIMISE supports the development of community-based elementary mathematics units associated with local heritage practices (Dawson, 2013). It also positions its participants to earn a master's or doctoral degree from the University of Hawai'i, Mānoa (UHM). From its inception, MACIMISE made clear efforts to "indigenize" the program, given some of

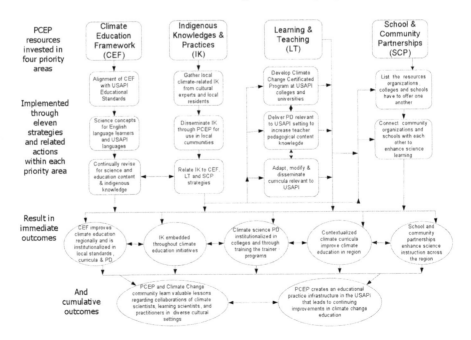

Figure 17.2 Pacific Islands Climate Change Education Theory of Action.

the evaluative findings of precursor projects.[1] The comment below captures one of the key frustrations of previous work:

> For 8 years we've studied western mathematics, mainland mathematics, and teaching approaches that are suited to mainland children. Why don't we ever look at Yapese cultural practices and languages, examine them for the embedded mathematical knowledge, and then create lessons and units of work for our children that are based on things they've experienced? Not many Micronesian children have ever experienced snow, but they sure know about fishing in the vast Pacific Ocean. (Fagolimul, Personal Communication, 2008)

Mekinak Consulting was contracted to serve as the external evaluator in year 3 of the project, inheriting the plan devised by the original evaluators, whose approach will be described later in the chapter. Because it entered the project some time into the project, Mekinak was not involved in the initial work with the communities to define goals and practices for the evaluation. Subsequently, however, efforts have remained continuous in finding opportunities to ensure culturally responsive practice.

Mekinak first developed a MACIMISE program model, which is illustrated in Figure 17.3. The program includes building locally based research capacity to enable the development of place-based curriculum, which can then be rigorously tested. The MACMISE theory of change makes a number of important assumptions that are explored through the evaluation and relate to the flow of activities. There is an assumption that a successful distance graduate education (e.g., a cohort model, a combination of synchronous online and face-to-face courses, etc.) can be delivered across the Pacific islands. There are also assumptions that local educators can become researchers of culture-based mathematics and that they can develop curriculum using the knowledge base from instruction offered through a graduate program. Indigenous elders and cultural experts are assumed to be willing to share traditional knowledge related to mathematical conceptual reasoning and skill building. Thus far, all of the above assumptions have been shown to be true. Future evaluations will assess whether the following will hold true: the assumption that culture-based mathematics units will increase student interest in and mastery of mathematics.

PARTNERING WITH COMMUNITIES TO GROUND EVALUATION WITHIN LOCAL TRADITIONS

For both PCEP and MACIMISE, the external evaluators' experiences working alongside the PREL network of employees who are embedded in and/or are from the participating island localities proved invaluable for gaining

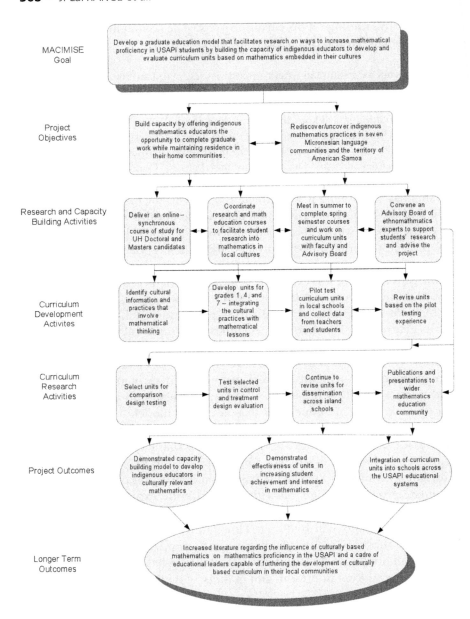

Figure 17.3 Macimise Program Model.

the kinds of foundational understandings that lead to local capacity building and exploring ways to capture indigenous values and knowledge.

Evaluation Planning for PCEP

During the planning phases of PCEP, Mekinak Consulting collected educational needs-assessment information related to climate change from principals and leadership in the Ministries and Departments of Education throughout the region. We found that resources that are often taken for granted in the continental United States are not necessarily accessible in the Pacific. For example, online surveying is of limited use, given issues of Internet access in many of the island communities. Random sampling of schools is problematic. On the one hand, the distribution of schools across a number of islands within island networks is prohibitive. In some locations, such as in the state of Yap in the FSM, travel to the outer islands can take weeks, given the limited availability of boats that routinely make the trip. Mail service is also challenging, as sometimes it takes weeks or months to deliver letters and packages. On the other hand, and more saliently, random sampling is not a "Pacific way." With communities of the Pacific more communal and collaborative, the preference would be to be inclusive. Also, societal hierarchies and filial relationships can dictate decisions about who participates in a given activity and who might not. Convenience sampling can yield representative findings and, in this case, can be very appropriate. Due to the small size of island communities and the fact that they are much more homogeneous than communities outside of the Pacific, one can get a picture of the situation through a smaller, nonrandomized sampling.

In these situations, PREL staff located on the main islands of the RMI, Palau, and the four states of the FSM stepped in to distribute hard copies of the needs assessment to school principals using a convenience sample based on schools that were locally accessible. Principals in 37 schools completed the survey. PREL staff members then collected, scanned, and emailed the data to the evaluators in their home location.

Supporting concerns about the limitations of technology, with the exception of Guam, where 54% of principals reported that teachers in their schools have access to computers, none of the other schools have computers for teachers. Similarly, computer use by students is limited, and only in Kosrae and Palau did principals report having schools that house computer labs. CNMI teachers have access to computers and the Internet; however, not all schools have connections to the Internet; for those that do, connections are slow or unreliable.[2] It is not surprising that most school principals characterized students' ability to use the Internet to download files and media as "very poor" to "poor."

Results of the needs assessment showed clear variation across the islands regarding the need for better curriculum, teacher training, and resources to address climate change. In general, the principals reported that they were "not satisfied" or "somewhat satisfied" with the inclusion of island-based environments in their curriculum materials. Most of them rated their curricula for climate change education "very poor" or "poor" and expressed a "very important" need for teachers and other educators to have opportunities for professional growth in the science of climate change, its impacts, and adaptation strategies. Specifically, principals suggested staff development in the following areas: teaching science using inquiry, incorporating indigenous knowledge into science, teaching science literacy, and developing school-community partnerships for science projects. Accordingly, the needs assessment identified local preferences that reinforce PCEP's strategies of focusing on face-to-face professional development and train-the-trainer models to create cadres of community teachers who can support the learning of other teachers. PCEP is also working with local partners to develop curriculum materials featuring island environments.

Although we are finding use of hard-copy surveys (rather than online versions) to be more appropriate in the region, we must acknowledge that the surveys are themselves Western in orientation. With orality highly valued among Pacific cultures, it is most desirable to tap these skills for evaluation purposes. Focus groups can be very effective in these cases, particularly if conducted in the heritage language. Other strategies should be honored, such as separating men from women in the discussions to avoid protocols that expect men to speak and women to remain silent. Most importantly, it would be inappropriate to force a Western research standard such as randomization in situations that do not have the infrastructure or, one could argue, the need to meet such a standard.

Acknowledging Mekinak's need to use several Western approaches to information gathering, we are paying particular attention to indigenous views of evaluation that will emerge as communities engage in their own evaluation planning. This strategy builds local capacity by creating opportunities to embed evaluative thinking into activities while also providing opportunities to learn how Pacific islanders define their own sense of success.

As we entered the second year of PCEP, we saw opportunities to directly engage participants in doing their own evaluations of their activities. For example, in Kosrae, a community of elders, educators and environmental organizations are developing videos based on elders' stories and observations of the natural mangrove environments. The elders are using the heritage language to share their observations and stories. The local committee is working on ways to translate the information using voiceover explanations rather than direct translations. Local educators are developing lesson plans based on the videos for use in schools. Rather than impose an outsiders' set of evaluation questions to be explored through this project, our approach is to focus the committee on their own definitions of what they believe success would look like in this project and to describe the ways in which they will know if this success was realized. Once they have defined their criteria for success and the evidence they seek, PREL and Mekinak Consulting will be responsive to their plan and support the evaluation in ways they request.

A second opportunity to respond to local evaluation planning is the evaluation of the Local Professional Learning Communities (LPLC). These groups are composed of educators (administrators and teachers), representatives from environmental organizations, and community members. Their role is to oversee and coordinate the various PCEP activities in their entity. Our interest is in tracking the degree to which PCEP has established working partnerships across different community sectors to address climate change education. However, we believe that the LPLC will need to explore the collaboration through their own evaluation of their work rather than relying on predefined definitions of collaboration. Our plan is to facilitate a series of discussions among the LPLCs in a few of the entities that will elicit their views regarding collaboration and how they see it occurring or not occurring within their LPLC.

There are a number of professional development projects for teachers within PCEP. Culturally responsive evaluation will necessitate addressing the needs of teachers, many of whom are English-language learners, in the process of coordinating evaluation activities with the providers of the professional development. One avenue is to encourage the use of concept mapping in pre- and postassessments of teachers' understanding and knowledge of climate-change science they learned during the professional development. We face a challenge in evaluating teacher change in science self-efficacy and attitudes regarding climate change (two areas of interest in the PCEP overall evaluation). We have surfaced a number of surveys with a history of good reliability. However, they present challenges in the area of validity to our context as well as in their assumptions regarding English-language competency. We have greatly altered the surveys to make them shorter, use concise and clear language, and include context-appropriate references.

There are multiple audiences for the PCEP evaluation, including PREL and its partners, the educators and community members living on the islands, and the NSF. We hope to meet the expectations of these groups by incorporating a storytelling approach in evaluation reporting. The multiple activities (capturing the indigenous knowledge of local experts in Kosrae, learning about collaboration from an islander point of view, assessing change in teachers participating in professional development) are all different stories, each of which will reveal lessons learned as well as insights into culturally appropriate ways to do evaluation in the Pacific. This approach supports local ownership of the evaluation and will likely lead to more engagement in the use of lessons learned. These same lessons will also be important to PREL and the NSF as we seek insights about how to mobilize local communities in climate change education.

MACIMISE Evaluation

As mentioned earlier, Mekinak Consulting inherited an evaluation plan developed early in the program. The first major opportunity to be more responsive to the communities came in redesigning the evaluation to fit more closely with the realities of working in the Pacific region. The initial evaluation proposed a mixed-methods design, with formative evaluation involving interviews and focus groups to address questions such as

- How and what kinds of support and assistance are the MACIMIS-Eers receiving from the instructors of the graduate courses as well as from village elders who are the keepers of traditional knowledge?
- How adequately is the MACIMISE project preparing the students as sociocultural researchers?
- To what extent do the courses and activities students engage in enable them to discover/recover the indigenous mathematics of their islands?

Mekinak concurred that the qualitative methods to address these questions were appropriate for the project and important for our evaluation. However, we were concerned with the quasi-experimental design proposed for the following question: "Does knowledge of recovered culturally based mathematics significantly improve indigenous student scores on standardized mathematics tests at grade 1, 4, and 7–8?"

The proposed design used a process that would match teachers of experimental classes (the new mathematics units) and teachers of control classes (standard units) with teachers randomly assigned to either an experimental or control group. The design was based on the assumption that the 24 MACIMISEers would each develop one unit to be tested through the evaluation. Thus, each entity would have three units to test (a first-, fourth-, and seventh-grade unit). However, "standardized" tests are not administered to first graders. In addition, the developed units are only one week in duration and cover a limited corpus of math skills, such that only a few items on the national exams used in the region actually align with any lesson in a unit. Finally, these exams are not calibrated for culture-related mathematics.

As discussed in the previous section, the considerable geographic distance across which some of the island states are dispersed, combined with island entities' small size and few schools or only one school on an island, again presented a challenge. Returning to the State of Yap, which is spread across 23 inhabited islands, with some outer islands situated 500 miles from the main island, finding a matching classroom in schools on smaller islands is not only logistically difficult but also, in some cases, linguistically difficult, as languages can differ even within island nations. Such major geographical and educational realities made the integrity of the original plan precarious at best.

Though Mekinak recognized many of the shortcomings of using well-known evaluation practices in diverse communities, we are not yet equipped to align our work specifically with local ways and processes, as we are still learning. Our approach has been formative as we make adjustments along the way to accommodate the borders of Western and indigenous perspectives. Along these lines, we also need to make an important point.

When the MACIMISE evaluation was initially devised, a quasi-experimental design was considered important. Essentially, the evaluators proposed it because they believed it was what the funders wanted to see. At the time, in order to be competitive, this was the preferred evaluation standard to assess the effectiveness of a new curriculum (see Public Law 107–110, No Child Left Behind Act, January 8, 2002). It is significant that this "evidence-based" element was viewed as critical to a competitive grant application, suggesting that the assumption of the "gold standard" (research using randomized designs) has the power to drive the design of research and evaluation, more so than the context in which the inquiry is based (Walters, Lareau, & Ranis, 2009).

Mekinak Consulting recognized the importance of redesigning the evaluation to be responsive to the context while also testing the new curriculum units and encouraging participant engagement. We established a pilot testing process for each of the units. With guidance from the Mekinak team, each of the participants took responsibility for conducting the pilot test of his/her unit, and in so doing, led this phase of the evaluation. They assessed their units using a three-point scaled rubric that rated the lessons on 15 items related to (a) clarity of goals and alignment with local educational standards and ethnomathematics, (b) teacher preparation and instruction, (c) instructional strategies and pacing, (d) use of local language, and (e) assessment. In addition to assessing the pilot with the rubric, participants conducted their own interviews with the pilot test teachers using a question guide developed by Mekinak.

To keep data collection grounded within the region, Mekinak is following up on the MACIMISEers' own teacher reviews by conducting focus groups with some of the pilot teachers. Local PREL staff, who are known to the teachers, are familiar with the units, and can carry out focus groups in the local languages, will conduct these groups.

We have also posed a question to revise the initial query that assumed a quasi-experimental design and use of standardized tests. We intend to answer the question, "Is there evidence that the curriculum units incorporated indigenous mathematics and contributed to student interest in and mastery of mathematical concepts/skills of the units?"

The pilot phase identified units that appear ready for further testing. These units will be more closely assessed using a case-study design. Each case will include a rich description of the local community context, including interviews with participants, local PREL staff, principals, and teachers in the schools and classrooms who will test the units. We will use a pre- and postassessment of student learning based on the content of units and a pre- and postassessment of student interest in mathematics. We intend to administer the pre- and postmathematics assessment and postinterest in mathematics in a control classroom. However, we are including the MACIMISEers and pilot teachers in the planning and execution of the treatment/control design. MACIMISEers are identifying the treatment classrooms and control classrooms and arranging for the administration of the unit test. The control classrooms are in the same schools where the unit is being tested. We will be able to collect student scores on the nation's standardized assessments to analyze how well the students are matched.

Together, the MACIMISEers and the teachers who piloted the unit are working with UHM faculty to revise the lessons based on learnings during the piloting phase. The MACIMISEers are working with local school administrators to recruit control teachers. The units will be taught again, and measures of content learning as well as interest in mathematics are being conducted in the treatment and control classroom. We envision this test

Figure 17.4 MACIMISEers, UH Faculty and Advisory Board in Palau, 2012.

of the use of the curriculum as one aspect of the case studies and not as a wide-scale evidence-based test of the curriculum units.

Local PREL staff is facilitating the work on the ground and will conduct formal observations in treatment classrooms and assist with follow-up teacher interviews. We anticipate that Mekinak staff will travel to two or more island entities during this phase to engage MACIMISEers, administrators, teachers, and cultural experts who contributed to the units in discussions about their learnings and ways to capitalize on these understandings to create more opportunities for the development of culturally congruent mathematics curriculum and instruction in the region.

CONCLUSION

This chapter briefly introduces current program evaluation work in the Pacific region that is attentive to local culture. Given the scarcity of efforts to "indigenize" evaluation practices in these localities, there is much to learn about ways to infuse cultural understandings in such a process. Still, the PCEP and MACIMISE program evaluations demonstrate that carefully constructed evaluation activities can offer opportunities to be responsive to the local context and diverse groups of indigenous languages and cultures in the Pacific, as called for by groups such as the Commission on Education in Micronesia.

Ultimately, it is important that islanders explore their own ways of knowing and the cultural values and practices that they consider fundamental to responsive evaluation. To some degree, this is happening within MACI-MISE, as some of the participants have explored the evaluation of the mathematics units they developed as part of their doctoral work. The promise such understandings offer for capturing diverse experience is evident in many of the testimonials from MACIMISEers who have commented on their realization that cultural elements can provide a meaningful foundation for teaching mathematics. The following teaching observation exemplifies students' increased engagement:

> Whenever I teach a course that is straight from the book, whenever I ask questions, [the students] never answer the questions. It's kind of like a tradition here that when you ask questions, everybody just looks at you. I don't know why; maybe they just...don't want to show off. But when I asked them questions regarding the counting system in our culture, I was really surprised. When I talked about the counting system, they were all, like, sharing information, like, yeah I used this to count these items. I was surprised because they understood what I was talking about. So I have to go back and think about the way I present my lessons. At first, I thought they were very slow because they cannot follow along when I'm teaching them, but I realized that when they

know the concept [from their own culture, they want to talk], but they are not really engaged with the discussion of that particular lesson [when it is from the book]. (MACIMISEcr interview, 2012)

In keeping with the recommendations of the Commission on Education in Micronesia, we encourage local efforts to define indigenous evaluation in the region and support local ownership of evaluation practices. We believe that by working through partnerships with governmental and non-governmental organizations, schools, teachers, and community members, evaluation teams can find opportunities to identify key cultural elements that aid the development of appropriate evaluation design, assessment of program assumptions, and data-to-measure outcomes. We are eager to share our evolving successes and the many challenges we will likely face over the next few years as we work across islands to implement evaluation case studies that employ multimethod and multicultural designs to assess partnerships, teacher pedagogical content knowledge, and student learning and engagement. We acknowledge that there remains much to learn as we continue to support evaluation practices grounded in local traditions, and we look forward to learning from Pacific islanders as they define, elucidate, and write about their practices.

ACKNOWLEDGMENTS

The preparation of this chapter was supported in part by grants from the National Science Foundation to Pacific Resources for Education and Learning (DRL-0918309 and DUE-1239733). The findings and opinions expressed here are those of the authors and do not necessarily reflect the views of the funding agency.

The authors also acknowledge the thoughtful critique of earlier versions of this chapter by Marylin Low (PCEP Principal Investigator) and Sandy Dawson (MACIMISE Principal Investigator).

NOTES

1. ESI: 9819630 and ESI: 0138916 centered on developing a cadre of teacher leaders.
2. CNMI administrators did not participate in the initial survey. Information regarding computers and Internet access was shared by a co-author.

REFERENCES

American Evaluation Association (AEA). (2011, April 22). *American Evaluation Association statement on cultural competence in evaluation.* Washington, DC: American Evaluation Association. Retrieved from http://www.eval.org/p/cm/ld/fid=92

Bowman, N. (2006, June). *Tribal sovereignty and self-determination through evaluation.* Paper presented at the annual meeting of the National Congress of American Indians, Sault Ste. Marie, MI.

Canadian Institutes of Health Research, Natural Sciences and Engineering Research Council of Canada, Social Sciences and Humanities Research Council of Canada. (2005). *Tri-council policy statement: Ethical conduct for research involving humans.* Retrieved March 31, 2014, from http://www.pre.ethics.gc.ca/eng/policy-politique/initiatives/tcps2-eptc2/Default/.

Cram, C., McCreanor, T., Smith, L., Nairn, R., & Johnstone, W. (2006). Kaupapa Māori research and Pākehā social science: Epistemological tensions in a study of Māori health, *Hūlili, 3,* 41–68.

Dawson, A. (2013). Mathematics and culture in Micronesia: The structure and function of a capacity building project. *Mathematics education research journal, 25*(1), 43–56.

Fagolimul, J. (2008). Personal communication.

Health Research Council of New Zealand. (1998). *Guidelines for researchers on health research involving Maori 1998.* Auckland: Health Research Council of New Zealand.

Heine, H., & Chutaro, E. (2003, October). *A double-edged sword: A study of the impacts of external educational aid to the Republic of the Marshall Islands.* Paper presented at the Rethinking Educational Aid in the Pacific Conference, Nadi, Fiji.

Hezel, F. X. (2001, March). The myth of education: A second look. *Micronesian Counselor, 33.* Kolonia, Pohnpei, Federated States of Micronesia: Micronesian Seminar.

Kawakami, A., Aton, K., Cram, F., Lai, M., & Porima, L. (2008). Improving the practice of evaluation through indigenous values and methods: Decolonizing evaluation practice: Returning the gaze from Hawai'i and Aotearoa. In N. Smith & P. Brandon (Eds.), *Fundamental issues in evaluation.* New York, NY: Guilford.

LaFrance, J., & Crazy Bull, C. (2009). Researching ourselves back to life: Taking control of the research agenda in Indian country. In D. Mertens & P. Ginsberg (Eds.). *Sage handbook of social science research ethics.* Thousand Oaks, CA: Sage.

LaFrance, J., & Nichols, R. (2009). *Indigenous evaluation framework: Telling our story in our place and time.* Alexandia, VA: American Indian Higher Education Consortium.

LaFrance, J., & Nichols, R. (2010). Reframing evaluation: Defining an indigenous evaluation framework. *The Canadian Journal of Program Evaluation, 23*(2), 13–31.

Mertens, D., Cram, F., & Chilisa, B. (Eds.). (2013). *Indigenous pathways into social research.* Walnut Creek, CA: Left Coast.

Rechebei, E. (2004, October 27–29). *Rethinking education in Micronesia: Education policies and realities in Micronesia.* Paper presented at the 1st Rethinking

Education in Micronesia Conference: Honoring our Indigenous Voices and Visions, Republic of the Marshall Islands.

Sanga, K., Niroa, J., Matai, K., & Crowl, L. (Eds.). (2004). *Re-Thinking Vanuatu education together.* Suva, Fiji: Ministry of Education, Port Vila/University of the South Pacific, Institute of Pacific Studies.

Senase, J. (2011, February 9). Palau senator proposes creation of research review board. *Marianas Variety.* Retrieved July 31, 2013, from http://www.mvariety .com/regional-news/palaupacific-news/34104-palau-senator-proposes-creation-of-research-review-board?tmpl=component&print=1&layout=default&page=

Smith, L. T. (2012). *Decolonizing Methodologies.* London, UK: Zed.

Walters, P. B., Lareau, A., & Ranis, S. H. (2009). *Education research on trial: Policy reform and the call for scientific rigor.* New York, NY: Routledge.

TOWARD THE NEXT GENERATION AND NEW POSSIBILITIES OF CULTURALLY RESPONSIVE EVALUATION

Stafford Hood
University of Illinois, Urbana Champaign

Rodney Hopson
George Mason University

Henry Frierson
University of Florida

We finish the book understanding that the work of CRE is hardly done. How could it be when the idea of what it means to be responsive and what it means to incorporate culture in evaluation represent two histories with distinct traditions in the field? What we attempt to do in blending these ideas is to call for a more nuanced and responsible approach or method to evaluation. While the last thing we need in the field is yet another approach, model, or method, we believe that the time for CRE is an ines-

*Continuing the Journey to Reposition Culture and Cultural Context
in Evaluation Theory and Practice*, pages 379–385
Copyright © 2015 by Information Age Publishing
All rights of reproduction in any form reserved.

capable reality. We as the editors and authors of the book as well as our broader community devoted to this work, are ready and in fact compelled to build subsequent generations of this CRE community. It's a task that we are prepared to undertake because this is the time to do so. This epilogue is provided as an ending to this volume but more importantly a next step in generating new ideas for the possibilities of CRE. What follows are the final pages in an attempt to explore the key elements of the book while signaling directions for the future.

The chapters in the initial section, "CRE Theoretical and Historical Legacies and Extensions," explore and extend theoretical and historical legacies of CRE, marrying familiar theoretical concepts in evaluation with CRE. Beginning with the chapter by Bledsoe and Donaldson, the authors provide one of two initial chapters that integrate CRE with evaluation theory. Bledsoe and Donaldson's proposal of a culturally responsive theory driven evaluation (TDE) is long overdue. In integrating TDE and CRE, the authors do more than bring these frameworks together; they explore opportunities and challenges for conducting TDE in a culturally responsive way. The following chapter by Casillas and Trochim also recognizes flexibility in how evaluators implement CRE by integrating how systems thinking in evaluation fits with CRE theory. As such, in proposing marriage between systems and CRE, the authors illustrate the potential for developing and aligning methodological approaches for moving the field forward. By using a systems approach, the authors provide a much needed framework for thinking about and implementing CRE.

The following chapter by LaFrance, Kirkhart, and Nichols is a conversation on and reflection of culture and Western evaluation notions of validity. Their chapter expands the construct of validity by exploring how it is viewed and operationalized within Indigenous epistemology while engaging in a critical discussion on the centrality of culture in the work of evaluators. Inherent in their work is the need to probe further into cultural expressions of how trustworthiness or correctness is understood in tribal and cultural contexts. Their reflexive conversations ultimately raise questions on the *validity of validity* and the relevance of such discussions in evaluation practice.

The final chapter in this section, by Frazier-Anderson and Bertrand-Jones, continues the historical narrative of a Rose Butler Browne as a pioneer in culturally responsive evaluation approaches. The authors capture the relevance of her life through her biographical work as the chapter suggests how the history of CRE continued with Dr. Butler Browne. In addition to her deep commitment to equality and justice for African Americans, the authors provide examples and illustrations of Dr. Butler Browne's life indicative of acting on her "responsibility" as an African American woman to give voice to the traditionally disenfranchised intended to be served by the programs and therefore congruent with an important tenet in CRE.

The volume's second section, "Evaluators' Journeys of Introspection and Self-Exploration," is intentionally reflexive and illustrates the CRE journey by evaluators in practice contexts. Greene's chapter reflects on lessons and insights from a traveling study leave in Aotearoa New Zealand in 2012. Based on rich and valuable experiences and insights from colleagues, Greene recognizes the inevitable political work of culturally responsive evaluators and calls for vigilance and regard for cultural self-determination. Her notions of CRE aspire to more explicitly and officially include notions of responsibility and relationships as being foundational with clear statements of values and declarations of cultural respect are essential for "understanding."

The chapter by Symonette introduces the *Integral Evaluator* model as a holistic framework for assessing and exploring our work as evaluators. She prioritizes evaluation in service of enacting socially just interventions through the use of diversity-grounded, equity-minded assessment and evaluation processes. In describing the quadrants of the Integral Evaluator model, Symonette raises critical questions of the evaluator to focus on reflective practice, clear identification of constituencies, and inward focus on self as instrument,

The Torrie et al. chapter describes the journey of five self-identified Pākehā (White, in the context of Aoteaora New Zealand) evaluators who use their chapter to engage in a dialogue about the roles of culture and cultural context in evaluation. In their chapter, they address four core questions related to what it means to be a Pākehā evaluator within Māori space in the historical and contemporary context of Aotearoa New Zealand. Their chapter develops an octopus heuristic framework through which to decode multiple starting points of engagement and discourse for them as Pākehā evaluators. Ultimately, the authors use their conversations and journey to develop new ways of defining terms appropriate to the cultural evaluation mission, building shared understandings and common vocabularies of experiences.

Like the previous chapter, the Kennedy et al. chapter is a conversation. Kennedy et al.'s chapter contemplates the importance of spirituality in the everyday lives of Māori and Pasifika peoples and how Māori and Pasifika evaluators acknowledge, value, and represent spirituality in their evaluation work. By exploring the connections between spirituality and evaluation through their own *wananga* (forum for discussion and learning), a number of themes emerge related to the core work in the research and evaluation space. Their task was not to make spiritual elements of the program more rational but to weave their own assessments of program value and merit into their subjective understandings of how spirituality is an aspect of a program's vision, design, implementation, and success. Their hope and challenge for future directions is to infuse their evaluation work with concepts of Māori spirituality and cosmology.

The McBride chapter closes the second section of the book. By drawing from psychology and cultural neuroscience, the author intends for the chapter to help hone evaluation practice and impact that address cultural reactivity. By presenting two core dimensions of CRE in the current literature, McBride suggests a third dimension that focuses on intrapersonal and interpersonal dynamics for the purpose of advancing the application of CRE. This third dimension incorporates particular cognitive, social, and emotional skillsets that address stereotypes, empathy, and attribution/interpretation. Her chapter suggests that culturally responsive evaluators pay attention to further develop their cognitive development as well as social and emotional intelligence to enhance evaluation practice.

The chapters in the third section "Applications of CRE in Global and Indigenous School Contexts," have provided us with a look at the work of evaluators/researchers who are "committed outsiders" working to improve the educational experiences of racial minorities. O'Hara et al. contend that the long-standing culture of assessment, as manifested by its Irish Leaving Certificate test, is far too rigid, punitive, and counterproductive to effectively meet the educational needs as well as those for equitable existence of its immigrants and "Travellers" (Roma) in Ireland. They provide compelling evidence to support that meaningful involvement of students in the assessment and decision-making process can result in a richer, culturally responsive, and inclusive learning and living environment. The authors loudly call for Ireland's traditional standardized assessment system to be reformed so that it is more culturally responsive, open, and committed to more "sensitive" forms of assessment. Without such reform, they believe it is highly likely that Ireland's new immigrants will experience the same level of suffering that has been historically experienced by its Traveller community.

The Mitakidou et al. chapter resonates with the Irish focus on the impact of the Greek assessment system on the educational experiences of the Roma in Greece. However, this look at the Greek assessment system focuses on the potential of assessment to improve the typical dismal learning experiences of Roma children in Greek schools. The authors argue that an assessment system could potentially provide a continuous flow of student performance evidence to teachers that they could in turn use as a source for student motivation while also informing their teaching. In order for this to be accomplished, Mitakidou et al. similarly call for assessment to be more culturally relevant and utilize "contextualized assessment material" that engages both students and parents so that they better understand student performance information and expected educational goals.

The White and Senese chapter tells an uncomfortable story of a federally funded project to increase the number of Native America (Diné/Navajo) elementary and secondary teachers for Navajo Nation schools and its subsequent evaluation. The subsequent external evaluation (by a nonindigenous evaluator) of the project was highly critical of the project and its implementation. The evaluation reported that the project provided an inadequate level of cultural responsiveness and the potential for "transcendent change" of the participants minimal since the program operated "within systems led and defined by predominantly white institutions." The authors also reported their reasonable concern about the evaluator publishing the report without the appropriate permissions or their having the opportunity to respond to program's deficiencies reported in the evaluation report such as their failure to address "the assimilationist and colonists approaches" of the program. The authors appropriately raise several uncomfortable (but needed) introspective questions that are evident in other chapters in this volume: when does nonmembership in a cultural group disqualify one for the purposes of being culturally responsive, even when the researcher/investigator as nonmembers "work[s] toward solidarity" with the cultural group they are attempting to serve?

The chapters included in the final section, "Claiming New Territories of CRE: Culturally Specific Methods, Approaches, and Ecologies," provide insights and illumination about what CRE looks like in its application across culturally diverse international contexts and particularly indigenous settings. The Mertens and Zimmerman chapter articulates a clear and appropriate linkage between the transformative paradigm and CRE. However, it also takes a useful and critically important step to ground this linkage within the context of evaluations in the deaf and international development communities. The chapter calls our attention to the fact that while CRE has been primarily connected to race/ethnicity and indigenous communities, its kindred relationship with the transformative paradigm "enriches thinking about how to address cultural complexity." The authors view "transformative culturally responsive evaluation" as pushing us beyond typical CRE theoretical and practical orientations and also "seeks to deconstruct the asymmetrical hegemony" that has been the obstruction for the traditionally disenfranchised in our global society.

Fiona Cram and her fellow Māori co-authors provide us with the unique insight of the interconnectedness of CRE with the culturally specific evaluation approach of *Kaupapa Māori* (i.e., a Māori way). The foundation of *Kaupapa Māori* evaluation is one of simplicity as it is first grounded in the discovery of the true (*tika*) *kaupapa* agenda in order for evaluators to determine what are not only the right methods but also the right people to undertake the evaluation. The authors note that the principles of supporting relationships (kinship and nonkinship) and spirituality are key principles in *Kaupapa Māori* that facilitate the utilization of cultural protocols and practices that are "acknowledged, valued and respected . . . [that] facilitate culturally responsive evaluation."

These same Māori authors return to this conversation in another chapter with Kirimatao Paipa as the lead author. In this chapter, they illustrate the application of *Kaupapa Māori* utilizing culturally responsive methods with a "family-centered evaluation" approach for the *Whanau* (Family) Collectives project. The authors note the responsibility of Indigenous evaluators and their accountability to the communities they serve with the particular challenge "to identify culturally relevant ways of working that make sense to *whanau* [family] and align with *whanau* values with regard to kinship and relational connections." This evaluation approach is not only congruent with a CRE approach but also stretches previously identified examples by exploring how Māori collectives (especially families) can be substantively involved in evaluation and research studies. Such an approach could reasonably be applied beyond a Māori or indigenous context as the authors argue there are indeed evaluation methods more responsive to Māori cultural values about family while also documenting the "lived reality of *whanau.*"

Bowman et al. and her fellow North American indigenous co-authors speak to the challenge of conducting evaluation in indigenous communities when it is not an accepted and respected approach as is found in the case of the Māori in New Zealand. The experience of Indigenous and Tribal communities in the United States also requires culturally responsive evaluation approaches, but the battle must be waged on multiple fronts. The authors use a case example to provide a framework for how a culturally response evaluation design might be "co-constructed" and the strategies that could be used when evaluating a program within a Tribal government reservation context. While they assert the critical importance of evaluation in this context they argue that first "the tenets of trust, data ownership, and sovereign rights of Tribal people on or off the reservation need to be part of a concerted dialogue by all parties." They assert that CRE "models and practices have heightened the awareness of bridging cultural context issues of Native/non-Native, federal/self-governance, Western/Indigenous epistemology, and consideration of the evaluators' own world perspective."

The LaFrance et al. chapter provides a unique look at an evaluation in the indigenous communities of island nations across the Pacific Ocean by indigenous evaluators. Such a look or insight is limited to, and possibly non-existent in, the evaluation literature. The authors share their experiences and challenges to implement culturally responsive evaluation strategies in the evaluation of two federally funded projects that include the State of Hawaii, U.S. territories "American Samoa, Guam, the CNMI under a Covenant Agreement with the United States of America, and three independent nations freely associated with the United States under the Compact of Free Association. These include the Federated States of Micronesia (FSM), the Republic of the Marshall Islands (RMI), and the Republic of Palau." The evaluators illustrate their efforts to design and implement evaluations in this Pacific region that are "attentive to local culture" and could possibly build a foundation for indigenizing evaluation practices in these communities. These evaluators reconfirm one of the core principles of CRE as being an "ultimate" priority of this work that "islanders explore their own ways of knowing and the cultural values and practices that they consider fundamental to responsive evaluation." In this regard, it is critically important that these communities define what "indigenous evaluation" should look like for them and take "ownership of evaluation practices."

We are pleased at what we have accomplished in this volume that has allowed us to reflect on what has transpired with the field and our evaluation community within the context of culturally responsive evaluation. This collection of chapters reflects our collective growth as a community in our thinking, practice, and younger cadre in our journeys as aspiring culturally responsive evaluators. While this book provides partial insights to our growth as a community, it also provides a glimpse of the introspective growth that is occurring individually as we resonate with the challenges in this work reported by our sisters and brothers on this journey. Once again we find ourselves at a place where we have partially answered some of what we considered to be better and possibly more refined questions only to recognize the partial answers to these questions have resulted in more questions. Once again, much has been learned on this journey from our initial conceptualization of this second installment exploring culture and cultural context in evaluation. We continue to be challenged by what still lies ahead for us in this journey. However, we remain undaunted about taking the next step wherever it leads us. As we conclude this second installment, we will take a moment to reflect and breathe. Then once again we will take yet another step or to generate new or at least refined ideas about the possibilities of CRE.